MW00813310

Making Christianity Manly Again

Making Christianity Manly Again

Mark Driscoll, Mars Hill Church, and American Evangelicalism

JENNIFER McKINNEY

OXFORD
UNIVERSITY PRESS

OXFORD
UNIVERSITY PRESS

Oxford University Press is a department of the University of Oxford. It furthers
the University's objective of excellence in research, scholarship, and education
by publishing worldwide. Oxford is a registered trade mark of Oxford University
Press in the UK and certain other countries.

Published in the United States of America by Oxford University Press
198 Madison Avenue, New York, NY 10016, United States of America.

Library of Congress Cataloging-in-Publication Data
Names: McKinney, Jennifer, author.
Title: Making Christianity manly again : Mark Driscoll, Mars Hill Church,
and American evangelicalism / Jennifer McKinney.
Description: New York, NY, United States of America : Oxford University Press, [2023] |
Includes bibliographical references and index.
Identifiers: LCCN 2022040668 (print) | LCCN 2022040669 (ebook) |
ISBN 9780197655795 (c/p) | ISBN 9780197655818 (epub)
Subjects: LCSH: Christianity and politics—United States—History—21st century. |
Evangelicalism—Political aspects—United States—History—21st century. |
Trump, Donald, 1946– |
Presidents—United States—Election—2016.
Classification: LCC BR115 .P7 M3535 2023 (print) | LCC BR115 .P7 (ebook) |
DDC 261.7—dc23/eng/20221115
LC record available at https://lccn.loc.gov/2022040668
LC ebook record available at https://lccn.loc.gov/2022040669

DOI: 10.1093/oso/9780197655795.001.0001

1 3 5 7 9 8 6 4 2

Printed by Sheridan Books, Inc., United States of America

For my students

Contents

Preface and Acknowledgments

As a young academic I felt I had a handle on the intricacies of American evangelicalism. My dissertation addressed the impact of evangelical renewal movements (ERMs) in mainline denominations. Yet I was unaware of Mark Driscoll and Mars Hill Church when I moved to Seattle in the fall of 2001. Soon after I began teaching at Seattle Pacific University (SPU), I was alerted to Driscoll and his church when the student newspaper published a story about a Bible study Driscoll was leading on campus. The article quoted a student from the Bible study who complained that Driscoll regularly disparaged women and described a godly man as having "a 40-ounce beer in one hand, a slab of meat in the other, and a naked woman (his wife) in front of him." The article solidified concerns from faculty, administrators, and some students about Driscoll and his teaching. Subsequently, Driscoll was asked to stop leading the weekly group. The reasons given by the school's administration for Driscoll's ouster were vague. The Dean of the Chapel said university policy wasn't followed, while the Dean of Students reported that university policy wasn't clear. Students who attended Mars Hill Church objected to the decision to stop the Bible study, complaining that SPU administrators and faculty simply didn't like Driscoll's style and his teaching on the roles of women. Regardless of the reason, Driscoll's being asked to leave campus was controversial and polarized much of the student body, a significant number of whom attended Mars Hill Church.

As the controversy over Driscoll's presence and teaching on campus escalated, Tim Dearborn, SPU's Dean of the Chapel, moderated a campus debate between professor of Christian Scriptures Rob Wall and Driscoll. Attending that debate changed my research and teaching interests. Listening to the debate on the role of women in the church impacted me as a woman, as an evangelical Christian, and as a sociologist. I was deeply disturbed at Driscoll's assumptions regarding gender. While I continued presenting conference papers for the Society for the Scientific Study of Religion (SSSR) and the Religious Research Association (RRA) on the role of ERMs in mainline denominations, I found myself contemplating evangelicalism and gender.

In November 2006 Driscoll made national headlines when he blamed Ted Haggard's wife (specifically) and wives of pastors (generally) for "letting themselves go" and not being "sexually available" for their husbands. Driscoll's comments were met with a public outcry, and I was met with a personal revelation. While I had initially struggled with Driscoll's rhetoric as a Christian woman, I realized that I could employ the tools of sociology to understand the broader patterns of his rhetoric. I began reading broadly in the sociology of gender, audited a graduate course on gender at the University of Washington taught by Julie Brines, and volunteered to serve as convener for gender and religion panels at the annual SSSR/RRA meetings.

Sociologists critique social patterns and structures asking why they look the way they do, how they are sustained, and who benefits from them. Social structures pattern our behavior and beliefs into routines of activities, absorbing the rules and cues from other social influences, legitimating the necessity of how and why these arrangements, practices, and relationships function. Like other social institutions, American Protestantism is structured to reflect and absorb the values and practices of the larger culture. When shifts in the larger culture occur, social institutions adapt, responding to new needs and demands. Americans in general, and American Protestants in particular, have trouble seeing the impact of larger social structures and forces in our lives. This leaves us vulnerable to adapting to an American status quo without recognizing that American beliefs and practices necessarily shape Protestant ones. As Christian sociologist Richard Perkins wrote in *Looking Both Ways: Exploring the Interface between Christianity and Sociology*, American Protestantism "has become imbued with a number of cultural traits that aren't the least bit biblical but are solidly middle-American."[1]

The goal of sociology is to unmask taken-for-granted assumptions to examine which assumptions transform people. Using the sociological imagination to critically assess the worldviews we take for granted allows individuals to better control the effects of unconscious assumptions, rather than allowing assumptions to control individuals. Like the gender ideals in the wider culture, religious ideals of gender change over time. American evangelicals, however, are more likely than other Americans (and other American Christians) to prescribe social roles by gender, which today is marked by an emphasis on masculinity.

Mark Driscoll and Mars Hill Church represent American evangelicalism's penchant for relying on a highly gendered theology. Located just across the ship canal from SPU, Mars Hill Church's and Driscoll's influence on the

SPU community was substantial. I had many conversations with students second-guessing their calls to ministry, their career plans, and their place in the church because of the influence of Mars Hill Church and Driscoll's theology. I was also consulted by a department chair who asked what to do when a promising young STEM major had been told by her resident assistant and peers that getting a STEM degree was opposed to the plan God had for women; God's plan involved women marrying and having children, not utilizing STEM degrees (subsequently the student changed her major).

Using the tools of sociology allowed me to more objectively examine Driscoll's rhetoric, by locating his theology and teaching in historical and sociological context. Sociology helped me explain and predict why (and when) a church like Mars Hill, with teaching like Driscoll's, becomes so popular. I hope putting the discipline to work on these issues helps those who struggle with what these teachings mean for them individually, for the church, and for the American religious landscape.

I would like to acknowledge my indebtedness to several colleagues, friends, and family for their support throughout the process of researching and writing this book. Sara Koenig and Karen Snedker provided me with valuable feedback and encouragement in our weekly research group meetings. I am humbled by their commitment to my professional and personal development. Kevin Neuhouser was also generous with his insights and feedback on my work. I am thankful for the support of SPU colleagues Bob Drovdahl, David Diekema, Raphael Mondesir, Joshua Tom, Rob Wall, Doug and Cindy Strong, and Becky Hughes, as well as Bruce Congdon, former dean of the College of Arts and Sciences and Margaret Diddams, former director of the Center of Scholarship and Faculty Development for financial support through a variety of faculty research and SERVE grants. Colleagues at the University of Washington, Steve Pfaff and Jim Wellman, have also offered valuable feedback and encouragement for this project.

I thank mentors, friends, former students, and family who have helped steward my sociological imagination and have supported this work directly and indirectly: Mike Bailey, Joe and Margaret Britton, Jim Davidson, Alysun Deckert, Roger Finke, Laura Fitzwater, Andria Fredricks, Susan Haldeman, Courtney Irby, Heather Juul, Jess Miller, Paula Mitchell, Renee and James B. Notkin, Mariel Rieland, Lorraine Shaman, Megan Simmons, Cathy Thwing, Linda Wagner, Nicole Warnemuende, and Robi Wrigley. I also thank Theo Calderara, Cynthia Read, and Rachel Ruisard at Oxford

University Press, as well as the anonymous reviewers who offered constructive feedback on the manuscript. Finally, I thank my family, Bill, Joyce, Jon, and Katie McKinney, and Cyndi Isbell. While I appreciate the support and encouragement of my colleagues, friends, and family, this book and any shortcomings herein reflect my own work and conclusions.

Introduction

Pussified Nation

Bewildered by the 81 percent of white evangelicals voting for Donald Trump in the 2016 presidential election, postelection commentators asked, "How could 'family values' conservatives vote for a man flouting every value they espoused?" or more colorfully, "How could so many conservative evangelicals have voted for a thrice-married casino mogul who has bragged about assaulting women and rarely goes to church?"[1] These questions were valid, because evangelical support for political candidates had traditionally hinged on a candidate's moral behavior. In a 2011 Public Religion Research Institute (PRRI) survey, for example, 30 percent of white evangelical Protestants agreed with the statement, "Because things have gotten so far off track in this country, we need a leader who is willing to break some rules if that's what it takes to set things right."[2] By 2016, the percentage of white evangelical Protestants agreeing with that statement had more than doubled, increasing to 72 percent.[3] In fact, breaking the rules seemed to galvanize Trump's appeal. The more raucous Trump and his campaign became, the more white evangelicals rallied to him, ultimately delivering him a victory.[4]

What seemed counterintuitive to outsiders was a result of a confluence of factors dating back to the cultural revolutions of the 1960s.[5] By the 2016 election, white evangelicals were not looking for a candidate who was gentle or moral. They were looking for a candidate—a man—who would fight for them. They simply "needed the right warrior to lead the charge."[6] Former Liberty University president, Jerry Falwell Jr. told CNN's Anderson Cooper that Donald Trump was "the man for this point in history"; after all, "We're not electing a Pastor-in-Chief. We're electing a Commander-in-Chief."[7] Another high-profile evangelical Trump supporter, the Reverend Robert Jeffress of Dallas's First Baptist Church, said he was looking for "the meanest, toughest, son-of-a-you-know-what I can find in that role."[8] After evangelicals had propelled Trump to victory, Franklin Graham told *The Atlantic*'s Emma Green that God had put Trump in office, saying Trump had "offended gays.

Making Christianity Manly Again. Jennifer McKinney, Oxford University Press. © Oxford University Press 2023.
DOI: 10.1093/oso/9780197655795.003.0001

He offended women. He offended the military. He offended black people. He offended the Hispanic people. He offended everybody! And he became president of the United States. Only God could do that."[9] Graham was not alone. Many evangelicals believe Trump was chosen by God to lead the nation. Peter Wehner, senior fellow at the Ethics and Public Policy Center, writes, "The enthusiastic, uncritical embrace of President Trump by white evangelicals is among the most mind-blowing developments of the Trump era," especially for a group who insisted on personal integrity and character during the Clinton presidency.[10] By the 2018 midterm elections, Jerry Falwell Jr. encouraged evangelicals to stop electing "nice guys" and "wimps" in favor of electing "street fighters" like Trump.[11] By 2019, white evangelical support for Trump was twenty-five percentage points higher than the national average.[12] Evangelical support for Trump was not an aberration, but the result of an infatuation with patriarchal authority: "Evangelicals hadn't betrayed their values. Donald Trump was the culmination of their half-century-long pursuit of a militant Christian masculinity."[13]

Trump resonated with evangelicals because he promised them a return to a conservative Christian-friendly nation.[14] Evangelicals champion a "family values" platform, which Trump's campaign latched onto, promising to appoint Supreme Court candidates who were antiabortion and to draft policies that would limit LGBTQ+ rights, two of their key issues.[15] Trump claimed to be a defender of Christianity, which he and his campaign characterized as "under siege," with "very bad things" happening.[16] Sociologist Gerardo Marti describes a rally at Oral Roberts University, where Trump said, "There is an assault on Christianity . . . on everything we stand for, and we're going to stop the assault."[17] Evangelicals believe they are "engaged in an existential struggle against a wicked enemy"—American liberals.[18] Trump not only represented a majority of white evangelicals' desire to restore an evangelical-friendly nation, but a Christian nationalist goal of defending "the power and values they perceive are threatened."[19] A significant "liberal" threat to the nation and the nation's families, bedeviling white evangelicals and Christian nationalists was feminism, the natural enemy of patriarchal authority.

Political and evangelical opposition to feminism resulted from the cultural revolutions of the 1960s. Seeing themselves as "custodians of morality," evangelicals worried that the civil rights movement, sexual revolution, second-wave feminism, and the gay rights movement signaled the collapse of

American society, primarily by invalidating gender differences (traditional roles) and leading to failing families and a failing nation.[20] In her work on evangelicalism and militant masculinity, historian Kristin Kobes Du Mez describes how the evangelical "family values" platform championed patriarchal authority, believing God had empowered men to exercise their authority in the home, as well as in society. Du Mez writes that evangelicals "elevated and revered men" exhibiting "the same traits of rugged and even ruthless leadership that President Trump now paraded on the national stage."[21] White evangelicals and Christian nationalists lionize "hierarchies between men and women" and seek to restore traditional gender roles.[22] Trump promised to restore these ideals.

Not all white evangelicals supported Trump. Former president of the Southern Baptist Convention's Ethics and Religious Liberty Commission, Russell Moore, for example, said, "Trump's vitriolic—and often racist and sexist—language about immigrants, women, the disabled, and others ought to concern anyone who believes that all persons, not just the 'winners' of the moment, are created in God's image."[23] But while many evangelicals abhorred Trump's vitriol and language, many more appreciated his standing up to the media and his making no apologies for his politically incorrect statements, even if those statements may have included profanity or misogyny:[24] "I did try to fuck her. She was married." "I moved on her like a bitch." "Grab 'em by the pussy. You can do anything." "You could see there was blood coming out of her eyes, blood coming out of her wherever."[25] Investigative journalist and Christian radio host Julie Roys said, "I honestly don't know what makes me more sick. Listening to Trump brag about groping women or listening to my fellow evangelicals defend him."[26]

Yet for many white evangelicals Trump embodied a traditional masculine ideal of power and status. Trump was verbally tough and aggressive, dominating his opponents during the primary debates and exuding an alpha male presence. Trump's exaggeration of stereotypically masculine traits—bragging about his high levels of testosterone and the size of his penis, illustrating callous attitudes toward women, inciting violence toward journalists at his rallies, and rejecting any hint of weakness or fear—epitomized a hypermasculinity.[27] For most white evangelicals, Trump represented a return to a "Christian America," where (white) patriarchal authority would be reasserted after eight years of America's first African American president, who advocated policies—supporting abortion rights, enshrining marriage equality—at odds with the family values platform.[28]

This hypermasculine Trump appealed to white evangelicals, who embraced an increasingly hierarchical and masculinity-infused Christianity that champions male-dominated power in family relationships, as well as politics.[29]

Evangelicals were primed to vote for a candidate like Trump by hypermasculine pastors like Mark Driscoll of Seattle's Mars Hill Church. As conservative evangelical megachurch pastor John MacArthur stated, "The evangelical interest in Donald Trump—in his crassness, rudeness, brashness and profanity" was "prepared by Mark Driscoll."[30] The similarities between Driscoll and Trump are striking. Both men understand how to tap into the zeitgeist of the moment, both instinctively know how to whip up a crowd, both are well known for their non–politically correct (non-PC) styles and ribald speech. Both men have been described as bullies, both exude a hypermasculine persona, and both have built powerful brands based on authoritarian leadership. Both men promised a return to a nostalgic 1950s America; Trump by "Making America Great Again," and Driscoll by "Making Evangelicalism Manly Again."

Men like Donald Trump and Mark Driscoll are talented communicators who draw people into their ventures. Their rhetorical gifts and ability to connect deeply with others imbue them with an authority that invites implicit trust in their leadership.[31] Donald Trump's perceived success as a real estate magnate along with his hypermasculine persona defined him as an appropriate leader for those hoping to return to a nostalgic America. Similarly, Mark Driscoll's megachurch empire signaled his entrepreneurial acumen to propel his mission of planting churches across the globe to teach men to take the church and make Christian America manly again.[32]

In their work on American megachurches, James K. Wellman, Katie E. Corcoran, and Kate J. Stockly describe megachurch pastors like Driscoll as "energy stars." These inevitably charismatic pastors generate the emotional energy necessary to connect to thousands of people as they empathize and elevate their adherents' problems and dilemmas.[33] Not only are megachurch pastors beloved, the relationship and trust they develop with their members connect them to "the ultimate truth."[34] As Wellman, Corcoran, and Stockly state, "There is really no way to overestimate the megachurch pastor's impact on the vitality of these churches."[35] Mark Driscoll was the right man at the right moment to build an evangelical empire that encompassed multiple church campuses, built theologically aligned congregations across continents, and created its own music label, training resources, and publication arm. Driscoll's Mars Hill Church became a touchpoint, and a flashpoint, for a hypermasculine Christian movement.

Mark Driscoll and Mars Hill Church

Most American megachurches hold a conservative theology[36] and Mars Hill Church was no different. At Mars Hill, Mark Driscoll capitalized on conservative Protestant theology to build his megachurch empire on a hypermasculine doctrine. Driscoll's theology was not completely new, he was "indebted" to previous Protestant masculinity movements and a growing number of evangelical writers focused on masculinity, however, Driscoll's "ideas and rhetoric went far beyond theirs."[37] Though his trendy packaging could sometimes mask his militant "culture-warrior mentality," Driscoll was just as belligerent as his predecessors, if not more so.[38]

At its height, Seattle's Mars Hill Church (1996–2014) regularly made the *Church Report* and *Outreach Magazine*'s lists of the most innovative and fastest-growing churches in the nation. According to their 2013 *Annual Church Report*, Mars Hill Church averaged more than 12,000 weekly attendees at their fourteen campuses across four states.[39] More than 21,000 people attended the church's Easter service that year, with an additional 50,000 people, representing 135 nations, tuning into the online broadcast. Mars Hill hosted 584 community groups with approximately 7,000 participants. The church's app had more than a half a million downloads, and 2.7 million people visited the Mars Hill website. The popularity of founder and teaching pastor Mark Driscoll made Mars Hill sermons a top ten Religion & Spirituality podcast in the United States, the United Kingdom, Canada, Australia, and New Zealand. The church collected almost $25 million in tithes and offerings, with total assets listed at nearly $35 million.[40] As the largest church in Seattle and Washington State, Mars Hill Church's growth was attributed to the colorful, charismatic, and controversial Driscoll.

Throughout his tenure at Mars Hill Church, Driscoll earned several monikers, including the "the cussing pastor," the "Rush Limbaugh of Christianity," and the "penis homes" pastor.[41] Driscoll made headlines for quips taken from his sermons (referring to the movie *Avatar* as "the most demonic, satanic movie I've ever seen"), interviews ("If you just sign up for a little yoga class, you're signing up for a little demon class"), Facebook posts ("[name] the most effeminate, anatomically male worship leader you've ever personally witnessed"), and Tweets ("If you are not a Christian, you are going to Hell. It's not unloving to say that. It's unloving not to say that").[42] Famous for his non-PC jibes, Driscoll inspired his own insult generator, "The Driscollizer," which randomly selected insults from his sermons, interviews, and conference talks (e.g., "If you drive a minivan, you're a mini man" from the 2013 Catalyst Conference).[43] Driscoll was well aware of his reputation and described his speaking style to progressive magazine *Mother Jones* saying, "I'm very confrontational, not some pansy-ass therapist."[44]

Driscoll's over-the-top, hypermasculine rhetoric became well known in evangelical circles (and Seattle, generally). In 2008, *The Wittenburg Door* website ran a satirical article on Driscoll titled, "Mark Driscoll Kicks His Own Ass." The article focused on Driscoll's "need for pastors to be more alpha," by mimicking well-known Driscoll-isms, like his "riff" on effeminate pastors: "The problem with our churches today is that the lead pastor is some sissy boy who wears cardigan sweaters, has The Carpenters dialed in on his iPod . . . and generally swishes around like Jack from *Three's Company* whenever Mr. Roper was around." The article also fabricated a story of Driscoll asking five conference participants to take the stage with him and punch him, with Driscoll saying, "Hit me with your best shot. Go on. I won't hit you back." "When none of the five took a swing," the article says, "Driscoll had them escorted from the building and proceeded to hit himself five times."[45] The satire was so on point that quotes from the article regularly appear on lists of inspiring things Driscoll has said. In my interviews, two people referred to a story "making the rounds" that Driscoll had invited people on-stage to punch him, so that he could claim he was "taking hits for the gospel."

Seattle seemed an unlikely place to build a conservative evangelical empire. As one of the most highly educated, politically and socially progressive cities in the nation, the success of Driscoll's conservative theology appears contradictory. Yet, Driscoll's success is indelibly connected to the perception of Seattle as a liberal city.[46] Driscoll's conservative theology, contrasted to the city, made Mars Hill Church members feel they were building a counterculture in the heart of Seattle.[47] Driscoll's singular style and claims to exclusive Christian truth built the thriving multisite megachurch partially by creating an us-versus-them mentality: members of Mars Hill versus the liberal Seattle culture, members of Mars Hill versus other Christian churches and denominations, and sometimes even members of Mars Hill versus other members of Mars Hill. Driscoll's description of his life before Mars Hill offers some insight into the man behind the rise and fall of Mars Hill Church.

The Road to Mars Hill

Expanding on his biography in the 2012 book *Real Marriage: The Truth about Sex, Friendship & Life Together*, Driscoll partially attributed his family's relocation from North Dakota to Seattle to his father's family, which he described as "uneducated alcoholics, mental patients, and women beaters."[48] Driscoll described his south-Seattle neighborhood as "rough" with strip clubs, "seedy" massage parlors, and hourly rate motels just down the street.[49] Driscoll says he considered himself moral and religious, which kept him out of trouble, however, he also writes that he had "a short wick, a foul mouth, and bad temper that resulted in doling out more than a few beatings to various guys."[50]

While he describes his growing up Catholic, Driscoll dates his conversion to Christianity to his freshman year at Washington State University.[51] Reading from the Bible his girlfriend Grace—an evangelical pastor's daughter—had given him, Driscoll was convicted one night in his dorm room by a verse from the New Testament book of Romans that his life "belonged to Jesus Christ."[52] Later, at a church men's retreat, Driscoll heard God instruct him to marry Grace, preach the Bible, train men, and plant churches, which Driscoll followed to the letter. The couple graduated from college and moved to Seattle, where Driscoll worked a variety of jobs. After volunteering for a suburban megachurch's college ministry, Driscoll felt it was time to start his own church.[53]

Together, Mike Gunn, Lief Moi, and Mark Driscoll founded Seattle's Mars Hill Church in 1996. The church initially met as a small-group Bible study in the living room of Driscoll's rented home. The Bible study soon outgrew the living room, however, and moved into multiple venues throughout Seattle. As the church grew, it was not uncommon for Driscoll to shuttle between three locations to deliver his Sunday sermons, sometimes preaching up to seven services. Mars Hill found permanent meeting space in Seattle's Ballard neighborhood in 2003, purchasing a 40,000 square-foot former auto-parts warehouse. The following year, averaging more than 1,200 weekly attenders, the church had already outgrown its new space. To accommodate this growth Mars Hill offered five Sunday services and quickly became known as a place where "twentysomething girls in glittering half-sweaters, sloppy emo boys with tattooed arms and disheveled hair" could find a church home.[54]

By their tenth anniversary in 2006, Mars Hill Church averaged 4,000 weekly attenders and boasted six paid elders on staff, after having roughly doubled the number of members each year, becoming the largest church in Washington State and one of the fastest growing churches in the nation.[55] Additional milestones for the church included being listed by the *Church Report* as the twenty-third most influential church in the country and their sermons becoming iTunes's fourth-most downloaded spiritual podcast. To accommodate its rapid growth, Mars Hill moved to a multisite campus model, eventually encompassing fifteen campuses in four states. Mars Hill also partnered with the Acts 29 Church Planting Network, cofounded by Driscoll in 1998, to build churches that were theologically aligned with Reformed doctrines.[56] Ever the consummate entrepreneur, Driscoll created The Resurgence in 2009, an online clearinghouse of ministry materials used to train thousands of (mostly male) Christian leaders, supplying them with articles written by prominent evangelicals, books published by Mars Hill's literary arm (Re:Lit), and access to leadership training events. Driscoll also served as a member of The Gospel Coalition, a broad network of evangelical churches in the Reformed tradition seeking to communicate the "costly call" and "comforting consolation of Jesus Christ" in an "unsteady" and "sin-sick world."[57] Driscoll's entrepreneurial successes, broad networks, outrageous style, and online visibility helped him garner half a million Twitter followers and made Mars Hill Church a Seattle destination.

Preaching from an elevated stage flanked by security guards, at the flagship Ballard campus, Driscoll delivered his sixty-plus minute sermons each week. The long, dark auditorium was punctuated with multiple big-screens projecting Driscoll throughout the space, where churchgoers soaked in his message. He was riveting. An estimated 250,000 people from around the world listened to Driscoll's weekly sermons, with 15 million sermons accessed each year.[58] Drawing larger and larger crowds with his always colorful and often controversial teachings (on masturbation: "if you are single you must remember that your penis is homeless and needs a home. But, though you may believe your hand is shaped like a home, it is not"; on men's authority: "Every single book in your Bible is written by a man"; on Old Testament queen, Esther: "Her behavior is sinful and she spends around a year in the spa getting dolled up to lose her virginity with the pagan king like hundreds of other women"), Driscoll solidified his, and Mars Hill Church's, place within Seattle and within American evangelicalism, polarizing both.[59]

An Offensive Gospel

In the words of Collin Hansen, author and former *Christianity Today* editor, "If [Driscoll] hasn't offended you, you've never read his books or listened to his sermons."[60] Driscoll's provocative, confrontational, and graphic speaking style (preaching on "Godly" versus "un-Godly" masturbation and "biblical" oral sex, for example) alienated mainline and liberal Protestants, the unchurched (among others), and many conservative evangelicals otherwise aligned with his theology. The Southern Baptist Convention (SBC), though sympathetic to Driscoll's theology, deplored his style. In 2009, the SBC targeted Driscoll in five separate motions, exhorting SBC entities to refrain from inviting event speakers who "are known for publicly exhibiting unregenerate behavior . . . such as cursing and sexual vulgarity [and] immorality."[61]

In his book *Young, Restless, Reformed: A Journalist's Journey with the New Calvinists*, Collin Hansen describes Driscoll's theology as "unflinching Calvinism" with a focus on biblical inerrancy, penal substitutionary atonement, heaven and hell, and (anti)homosexuality; or in Driscoll's words, "people suck and God saves us from ourselves."[62] Driscoll and Mars Hill were at the center of the Young Restless and Reformed Movement (YRRM), or New Calvinist movement. New Calvinism sought to revitalize evangelicalism by embracing classic Calvinist doctrines but with an injection of masculinity.[63] New Calvinism's masculine-centered theology emphasized God's wrath using "the story of a vengeful Father-God taking out his rage on his own Son."[64] This Calvinist resurgence had a strict gender complementarianism at its heart, and New Calvinist pastors emphasized "patriarchal power" at the core of its gospel and hinting at the seeds of authoritarianism embedded in the tradition.[65]

New Calvinism's elder statesman John Piper described the movement as holding to biblical inerrancy (literalism), complementarian theology, and a "culturally affirming" theology that held "culturally alien" positions on issues like (anti)abortion and (anti)homosexuality.[66] In 2009, *Time Magazine* named New Calvinism/YRRM one of the "Ten Ideas Changing the World Now," with the "pugnacious" Driscoll listed as a movement leader.[67] On his blog, Driscoll responded to the article and reflected on the New Calvinist doctrines he believed were simply nonnegotiable for the Christian faith,[68] which were reflected at Mars Hill Church, where four theological distinctives were highlighted: Reformed theology, complementarian relationships, spirit-filled lives, and missional churches. Driscoll's and Mars Hill Church's hypermasculine complementarian theology became one of its most notorious elements.

Men and Women Are Different

Attributed to Genesis 2, complementarian theology holds a "separate but equal" relationship between men and women, where men and women have separate roles but are created equally in worth. The theology paradoxically ascribes equality between men and women, but also subscribes leadership and authority to men and submission to women. Complementarian theology's language of hierarchy may be augmented with the language of equality to defuse concerns that subordination devalues women, while still reinforcing men's power.[69] In *Confessions of a Reformission Rev.*, Driscoll attributes complementarianism to biblical inerrancy, describing himself as an "intense biblical literalist who believes that the man is the head of the home, that the man should provide for his family, that children are a blessing, and that we would not have so many deceived feminists running around if men were better husbands and fathers because the natural reaction of godly women to godly men is trust and respect."[70] Acknowledging critics of his complementarian doctrine, Driscoll added, "For some, this theological instruction was as popular as a fart in an elevator."[71]

Mars Hill's complementarian theology was twofold. In regard to leadership, the church cited the New Testament book of 1 Timothy (2:11–3:5) as prohibiting women from teaching or having authority over men in the church, barring them from becoming elders or pastors at the church.[72] Mars Hill affirmed that women could learn theology but required them to learn in "quietness and submission," which Driscoll described as women learning with "a peaceable demeanor."[73] Women submitted to the authority of their husbands, softening "the rough edges of independence and rebellion" to which they were purportedly prone.[74] Second, Driscoll's complementarianism boldly put men at the forefront of Protestant Christianity, saying, "A complementarian church must focus on raising up men, particularly young men, to be responsible, loving leaders in their families and churches, like Jesus."[75] Driscoll's was a strict, hypermasculine complementarianism seeking to save men from a Christian culture that had driven men away from the church by emasculating Christ, when the real Jesus was "a prizefighter with a tattoo down his leg, a sword in his hand, and the commitment to make someone bleed."[76]

Driscoll focused on reaching and teaching men, often at the expense of women, LGBTQ+ people, and men who did not meet his standard of masculinity. The late Christian author and blogger Rachel Held Evans wrote that Driscoll had "consistently used offensive and hateful language to speak about gay and lesbian people, spoken crassly and condescendingly about women, and exhibited scary, bullying behavior toward men who [failed] to conform to his rigid vision of masculinity."[77] Driscoll's strict complementarianism left no alternatives, as he asserted, "anything but one man, one woman, one God, one life" was "sexually immoral."[78] Driscoll stated that acceptance of homosexual relationships was a result of walking away from the scripture and likened homosexuality to "letting cancer come into a body."[79]

Critics pointed out Driscoll's antifeminist and antihomosexual rhetoric, yet often missed the root of his theology: hypermasculinity. Driscoll took men to task for being "neutered" by a feminized culture and church. Driscoll's antipathy for anything feminized was made clear in "Midrash," an online forum created by Driscoll in December 2000. Posting under the pseudonym William Wallace II, a nod to Mel Gibson's character in the movie *Braveheart*, Driscoll generated the "Pussified Nation" thread. The thread's opening salvo illustrates Driscoll's contempt for feminism and "pussified" men, the culture, and the church:

We live in a completely pussified nation. We could get every man, real man, as opposed to pussified James Dobson knock-off crying Promise Keeping homoerotic worship loving mama's boy sensitive emasculated neutered exact male replica evangellyfish, and have a conference in a phone booth. It all began with Adam, the first of the pussified nation, who kept his mouth shut and watched everything fall headlong down the slippery slide of hell/ feminism when he shut his mouth and listened to his wife who thought Satan was a good theologian when he should have lead [*sic*] her and exercised his delegated authority as king of the planet. As a result, he was cursed for listening to his wife and every man since has been his pussified sit quietly by and watch a nation of men be raised by bitter penis envying burned feministed [*sic*] single mothers who make sure that Johnny grows up to be a very nice woman who sits down to pee.[80]

Driscoll's graphic language and disdain for expressions of masculinity not meeting his ideal—as well as his derision for feminism—were alarming. The publication of the Pussified Nation thread exposed Driscoll's earliest antifeminist and antihomosexuality rants. Driscoll apologized for the thread and pointed critics to *Confessions of a Reformission Rev.*, where he had explained the thread's creation served to counter "emerging church-type feminists and liberals" "infiltrating" the forum.[81] While Driscoll's views seemed anachronistic to Seattle's culture, his hypermasculine theology struck a chord and spurred the church's rapid growth. Attendance at Mars Hill skyrocketed *because* of Driscoll's theology and no-holds-barred rhetoric. Driscoll's goal of reaching young, single men bore fruit, with his claiming Mars Hill was "over half male, single, in their twenties."[82]

While national Christian magazines took note of the upstart pastor and the fast-growing Mars Hill Church, Driscoll and his hypermasculine complementarianism fully entered the national stage in November 2006, when he responded to the plight of Ted Haggard. Accused of illicit drug use and solicitation of male prostitutes, Haggard, then president of the National Association of Evangelicals (NAE), was forced to step down from his position with the NAE and from the pastorate of his 14,000-member Colorado church. Weighing in on the controversy, Driscoll incited local and national outcry:

> Most pastors I know do not have satisfying, free, sexual conversations and liberties with their wives. . . . It is not uncommon to meet pastors' wives who really let themselves go; they sometimes feel that because their husband is a pastor, he is therefore trapped into fidelity, which gives them cause for laziness. A wife who lets herself go and is not sexually available to her husband . . . is not responsible for her husband's sin, but she may not be helping him either.[83]

Intending to encourage young men in the ministry by highlighting struggles pastors may face, the outrage for Driscoll's comments centered on his blaming wives for husbands' sins. In Seattle, where Driscoll's reputation for misogyny had long preceded the blog post, a local movement called People Against Fundamentalism (PAF) mobilized. PAF organized a protest at Mars Hill citing Driscoll's persistence "in making demeaning and degrading comments about women from his pulpit, on his blog, and at numerous national conferences."[84] PAF demanded Driscoll publicly apologize for his comments and be fired from his position as a religion columnist for the *Seattle Times*. The protest was averted when Driscoll met with PAF leaders and agreed to apologize for his remarks.[85] While the kerfuffle over the blog post subsided, Driscoll's brash style and hypermasculine rhetoric continued to garner adherents to Mars Hill, locally, nationally, and internationally. Driscoll's fame and the church's reach grew, and by 2008 Driscoll's sermons had been accessed from the church's website more than 10 million times. Prominent features of these sermons included frank discussions of sex and the "biblical" mandate of male authority and female submission. Always colorful, Driscoll's charisma and non-PC rhetoric remade complementarianism a hip alternative to egalitarianism.

Combatting a Chickified Church

Driscoll blamed a deficient and feminized view of Jesus for creating a "Richard Simmons, hippie, queer Christ" and "neutered, limp-wristed, popular Sky Fairy."[86] According to Driscoll, this view emasculated men and created a vacuum of male leadership in churches: "Statistically most men are not impressed by Jesus. Statistically most men are not fearful of Jesus. Statistically most people who worship Jesus are female."[87] Feminism and a lack of male leadership had damaged the church, from Driscoll's perspective, which he described in a promotional video for John Piper's Desiring God Conference in 2006. The "problem in the church today," Driscoll said, is because "it's just a bunch of nice, soft, tender chickified church boys," which is "just sad, you know?" The architecture of churches and the "whole aesthetic," Driscoll said, "is real feminine. The preacher's kind of feminine, and the music's kind of emotional and feminine." If anyone wonders why the contemporary church isn't "innovative," Driscoll says, it's because, "all the innovative dudes are home watching football, or they're out making money, or climbing a mountain, or shooting a gun, or working on their truck. They look at the church like that's a nice thing for women and children."[88]

Driscoll's antidote to the "chickification" of "church boys" was to train men, teaching them to reclaim leadership and authority, and retake the church. Mars Hill sponsored "boot camps" and Fight Clubs to teach men "how to get a wife, have sex with that wife, get a job, budget money, buy a house, father a child, study the Bible, stop looking at porn, and brew decent beer."[89] Mars Hill Church held men's "advances" instead of "retreats" to reinforce men's power.

Embedded within his masculine ideal was a Jesus more Rambo than "Prince of Peace," more "warrior" than "hippie, diaper, halo Christ."[90] Driscoll later broadened his rhetoric to describe Jesus as both "tough" and "tender," however, his theology tacitly required a tough, rather than tender, Jesus.

A Neo–Muscular Christianity

Driscoll built on a decidedly gendered theology to become the quintessential voice of an innovative hypermasculine Christianity, influencing evangelicals to adopt strict hierarchical gender ideals and practices. His gender rhetoric and theology, coupled with Mars Hill's prolific online presence, made Driscoll someone to emulate. Driscoll's focus on men and masculinity moved evangelicals away from a Jesus portrayed as "a wuss who took a beating and spent a lot of time putting product in his long hair" toward a Jesus who was victor, warrior, and king.[91]

Masculinity does not exist in a vacuum; it has implications for men and women. Driscoll drew strict lines between the roles of men and women, saying, "Chicks should be chicks, dudes should be dudes," because "gender roles are not subject to cultural change and preference."[92] This biologically essentialist gender differentiation was self-evident to evangelicals, including Driscoll, who explained, "I have three sons, two daughters, and I can assure you," that men and women are different: "My sons pee in the yard and my daughters like to go shoe shopping. . . . That's how God intended it."[93]

While Driscoll regularly stated that men and women were created equally in God's image, his complementarian theology placed women in a subordinate position to men, following the authority of God (Father) and Jesus (Son). Driscoll stated that "the man is the head" and woman "his helper," claiming the Bible, "lays out authority and respect for authority and submission to authority." Driscoll clarifies the line of authority, saying it starts with "God the Father, and then who? Jesus Christ, and then who? The husband or the man, and then what? The woman or the wife." In an aside, Driscoll addressed women saying, "A lot of you women will say, 'I don't need to submit to any authority.' Well, you're not any better than Jesus, and if it was good for him, it's good for you."[94] In this complementarian theology men were subject to the authority of God and women subject to the authority of their husbands. The hierarchical structure constructed by Driscoll contradicted his contention that men and women were equal, if different.

Initial criticism of Driscoll's complementarian theology addressed his ideals of women. Within this theology, however, most men were also subordinate to Mark Driscoll. By the end of the 2000s, criticism of Driscoll shifted to the implications of his hypermasculine theology on men. Local Presbyterian pastor Katie Ladd stated that in "declaring Jesus a 'masculine dude,' " the transformative message of the gospel was subverted.[95] Brandon O'Brien, associate editor of *Leadership* magazine, stated that Driscoll's imagining of Jesus as a model of masculinity missed the mark by offering "an extremely narrow view of masculinity," excluded women from "real discipleship," and blamed them for "neutering the gospel."[96] Others were offended by Driscoll's devaluing women's contributions to the church and society. Regardless of the criticism, Driscoll was not apologetic about his hypermasculine doctrine, stating, "We see Mars Hill as a man factory. Boys come in. Men go out. Period. That's what we're about."[97]

The Man, the Message, and the Mission

Driscoll's revamping of evangelicalism was on the cutting edge of pop culture, but his strict message seemed "radically unfashionable, even un-American."[98] Driscoll's aggressive style drew considerable critique, but "a significant number of young people in Seattle—and nationwide" reported that this was "exactly what they [wanted] to hear."[99] Regardless of the criticism, or perhaps due to the criticism, Driscoll's hypermasculine rhetoric and complementarian theology grew Mars Hill Church.

Driscoll's hypermasculine doctrine was not completely new within American Protestantism. Similar gender theologies had appeared with the Muscular Christianity movement at the turn of the twentieth century, as well as during the iconic "long decade" of the 1950s. Driscoll's theology provided the most visible portrait of the re-emergence of masculine-centered theology within American evangelical Protestantism. Driscoll's teaching attached men to a primary relationship with God, and connected women to God through their husbands, or in the case of single women, their fathers. In an April 2006 sermon, Driscoll stated that, "God made the man and put him in charge and gave him a job description . . . and the woman was made to help him. . . . Women will be saved by going back to that role that God has chosen for them."[100] In the same sermon, underscoring his primary thesis that men lead and women follow, Driscoll also stated, "There is no occasion where women led a society and were its heads and the men complied and followed. . . . It's a matter of biblical creation."[101] Although historically false (i.e., "fake news"), Driscoll's assertion met with loud and appreciative applause from his Mars Hill audience, reifying the "correctness" of his hypermasculine doctrine.

Mars Hill Church originally categorized their complementarian doctrine as an "open-handed" issue, meaning that it was not fundamental to a person's eternal salvation. Yet analysis of Driscoll's sermons show that a strict gender dichotomy was foundational to his theology, functioning as a "closed-handed" issue. For men, not being "manly" meant being neither a man nor a Christian. Driscoll's hypermasculine ideology was exemplified by a promotional video for the Resurgence titled "A Good Soldier." Using military imagery to emphasize the centrality of masculinity to his doctrine, in the video Driscoll walked through rows and rows of orderly gravestones at a national cemetery. As he walked, Driscoll explained the three keys to church planting included the man (a church planter), the message, and the mission. Selecting "the right man" is Driscoll's "most important variable," because only that variable makes a difference in the "leadership ability" and "quality of that senior leader, that founding pastor, that man who is to endure hardship, and to fight like a good soldier, to fight for sound doctrine, to fight for moral purity, to fight for families, to fight for truth, and to fight for the well-being of his family and his church family."[102]

For Driscoll, saving Christianity meant equipping men to "act like dudes" to take back the church and follow his lead. As Driscoll explained in his 2006 video for the Desiring God conference, "all this nonsense on how to grow the church" comes down to "one issue: young men. That's it. That's the whole thing," because it's the men who "get married, make money, make babies, build companies, buy real estate. They're going make the culture of the future." Therefore, Driscoll continued, by getting young men to the church "you win the war, you get everything—you get the families, the women, the children, the money, the business—you get everything. If you don't get the young men, you get nothing. You get nothing."[103]

Getting men into the church, however, was just the beginning. In the video for "A Good Soldier," Driscoll said once men are in the church, good leaders needed to know "what to do with them," since men wanted to know "how to get married," "how to have sex with their wife at least once a day," and "how to make money, buy a home," have children, pay their bills, father sons, encourage, love, and instruct daughters. The man chosen to lead the mission and teach men, Driscoll said, "must understand that his first priority is to gather men to—by God's grace—force them to become the kind of men that are needed for God's work and God's kingdom." Selecting the "right man" to plant a church would lead to women actually being loved, children being raised, and a city that has "an example of the difference that Jesus makes in the life of a man." Therefore, "the bottom line is to get the mission to get the men, 'cause if you get the men you win the war."[104] Driscoll's mission was not just to get men, but to get the right men; men able and willing to fight, not "Cabriolet-driving," "lemon-yellow-sweater-vest"-wearing losers "rocking out to the Spice Girls."[105] Driscoll's (and Mars Hill's) raison d'être was to remasculinize Christian men, reassert their God-ordained authority, and retake the church.

The Beginning of the End

Driscoll's deliberately confrontational style and his penchant for crude language made him one of the most admired and reviled figures within evangelical Protestantism.[106] Driscoll's rhetorical style and propensity to tackle controversial subjects made him an iconic "straight-shooter" to many young Christians, as well as a beacon for controversy for those who found his theology heretical and his style offensive. Driscoll regularly spoke at high-profile Christian conferences and appeared on the Christian Broadcasting Network, ABC's *Nightline*, *Oprah*, *The View*, Drew Pinsky's nationally syndicated radio program *Loveline*, and Fox News's online platform to address Christian America.

Locally, Mars Hill made Pacific Northwest history hosting more than 17,500 for their 2012 Easter service—baptizing nearly 700—at Century Link Field, home to the Seattle Seahawks.[107] The Mars Hill Church podcast continued to be ranked in the top ten Religion & Spiritual iTunes podcasts in five countries. The church had sixty-one elders and fifty-seven elder candidates. Three new campuses were scheduled to open in January 2014, with plans to develop two more campuses later in the year.[108] Mars Hill was developing a Bible college at their Bellevue (WA) campus in conjunction with Corban University to provide one-year certificates in Biblical Studies. The church was also partnering with Driscoll's alma mater, Western Seminary, to offer Master of Arts and Master of Divinity degrees. To accommodate the growth of their certificate and degree programs, the church was seeking at least

200,000 square feet of space in the Seattle suburb of Bellevue to create one large flagship campus. The fortunes of Driscoll and Mars Hill, however, were about to change.

Due to Driscoll's style and Mars Hill's doctrines, the colorful pastor and his church weathered several controversies over the years. Reflecting on 2013, Driscoll and Mars Hill had encountered a few hurdles. In May of 2013 former Mars Hill pastor Dave Kraft filed formal charges with Mars Hill's Board of Advisors and Accountability (BOAA) accusing Driscoll of being domineering, verbally violent, arrogant, quick tempered, and undisciplined.[109] While having a former pastor file charges against Driscoll was unusual, it did not seem to cause undue concern at the church, where the charges were eventually dismissed.[110] Several months later, Driscoll was in Southern California to speak at an Act Like a Man conference when he "crashed" the Strange Fire Conference at John MacArthur's Grace Community Church.[111] Driscoll did not attend the conference but took copies of his new book, *A Call to Resurgence*, to distribute to conference attendees in the church's parking lot. Claiming to have been accosted by the church staff, Driscoll tweeted, "Security confiscated my books." Grace Community Church's outreach pastor contradicted Driscoll's account, saying it was "nothing short of lying, absolutely shameful, and unbefitting of one who would take upon himself the calling of preaching the Truth."[112] Again, Driscoll's behavior at the conference was par for the course at Mars Hill.

By the end of 2013, however, Driscoll and his church hit a tipping point. Megachurch pastors rely on their charismatic authority to generate good will through trust. Once that trust is broken, however, the charismatic pastor "loses his magnetic effect" and the energy he once created disintegrates, sowing "chaos and disorder."[113] In November, Driscoll appeared on Janet Mefferd's syndicated radio program, where she accused him of plagiarizing portions of his book, *A Call to Resurgence*.[114] Driscoll denied the charges. Further investigation found examples of plagiarism in a number of Driscoll's books, including the *New York Times* best-selling *Real Marriage: The Truth about Sex, Friendship & Life Together*.[115] In the midst of the plagiarism scandal, it was discovered that *Real Marriage* had made the *New York Times* bestseller list due to Mars Hill's "gaming the system."[116] The church had funneled funds from their budget to pay public relations firm ResultSource to purchase thousands of copies of the book, inflating the book's sales to earn a spot for one week on the famed list. The revelation spawned an outcry from church members, some of whom accused Driscoll and the church of misappropriating church funds.[117] In a letter to Mars Hill, Driscoll apologized for the book-buying scheme, voluntarily retracted his status as a No. 1 *New York Times* bestseller, and pledged to stay off social media for the rest of the year.[118] Driscoll's apology, however, did not placate many members, nor former members, of Mars Hill.

Some members began looking more closely at the church's finances and found money designated for the church's international missions fund, the Global Fund, had been used for a variety of other church expenses. An internal church memo surfaced that stated a percentage of the Global Fund was used for some "highly visible" missions projects overseas, but that the "percentage should be flexible" and "not communicated to the public."[119] Mars Hill spokesman Justin Dean responded to this information saying, "Since donations given by the Mars Hill Global family were never intended to be designated solely for international efforts, we don't provide an itemized account of those funds."[120] Eventually Mars Hill issued an apology and offered to redirect previous donations to the Global Fund back to international missions.

The multiple revelations of plagiarism and diverted funds were taking their toll. In July 2014, Driscoll (on sabbatical) released a thirty-minute video to the church apologizing for not communicating as the church encountered significant criticism in the popular press and on social media. Driscoll then noted that, while he'd like to reconcile with the critics who had previously been part of Mars Hill, that these critics "remain anonymous and so we don't know how to reconcile, or how to work things out with people because we're not entirely sure who they are."[121] Driscoll's words set off an avalanche of former members organizing a variety of groups, including the "Dear Pastor Mark & Mars Hill: We Are Not Anonymous" Facebook group, with another group planning a protest to send a "strong message" to Driscoll, "that people he has harmed over the years are not unknown to him as he has claimed."[122] The firestorm building since the previous autumn exploded, and on August 3, 2014, approximately sixty-five protesters picketed Driscoll at the church's Bellevue campus carrying signs reading, "We are not anonymous" and "Question Mark."[123]

Between Driscoll's July apology and the August protest, blogger Wenatchee the Hatchet posted the 2000–2001 "Pussified Nation" thread, inciting more drama for Driscoll and Mars Hill. Driscoll was forced to issue another apology for the vulgar thread.[124] Events began disappearing from the Mars Hill calendar, including the "Jesus Festival" (a reward for having raised more than $2 million over and above the previous years' tithes), as did several of Driscoll's speaking engagements (Act Like a Man conference, Gateway Church Conference, and the Resurgence Conference).[125] Additionally, the release date for Driscoll's new book, *The Problem with Christianity*, was put off indefinitely.[126] The storm did not abate. Matt Chandler, then-president of the Acts 29 Church Planting Network (cofounded by Driscoll), sent a letter to Mars Hill alerting the church to the fact that Acts 29 had "no alternative but to remove [Driscoll] and Mars Hill from membership," because they believed Driscoll's behavior discredited the organization.[127]

On August 21, 2014, just two days before Driscoll was expected to return to preaching, psychology professor and blogger Warren Throckmorton posted a story stating, "On the heels of what was arguably the worst week in the history of Mars Hill Church, twenty-one former Mars Hill church pastors brought charges late last week against lead pastor Mark Driscoll."[128] Echoing charges made the previous year by former elder Dave Kraft, these twenty-one former pastors sent a letter to Mars Hill's three-member Board of Executive Elders (which included Driscoll) and BOAA charging Driscoll with twenty-five instances of "threatening, bullying, domineering, and 'shaming' behavior" during the previous four years.[129] The former pastors alleged Driscoll had created "a culture of fear" at the church, adding, "Pastor Mark is verbally abusive to people who challenge him, disagree with him, or question him."[130] In light of the letter and the myriad other scandals rocking Driscoll and the church, Driscoll stepped down from his preaching duties to take a six-week leave while church leadership reviewed the charges.[131]

On August 24, 2014, rather than returning to the pulpit, Driscoll addressed his church through a prerecorded message apologizing "for the times I've been angry, short or insensitive. I'm very sorry for anything I've done to distract from our mission by inviting criticism, controversy or negative media attention."[132] Driscoll promised to refuse outside speaking engagements and to postpone the publication of his next book.[133] The besieged pastor also stated that he was meeting with a "team of mature Christians" to provide counsel and to further his development and maturity.[134]

A week after the twenty-one pastors filed their charges, another nine pastors representing five Mars Hill campuses posted a letter questioning the church's transparency regarding finances, Driscoll's behavior at the Strange Fire Conference, the allegations of plagiarism, and the *Real Marriage* book-buying scheme.[135] These nine pastors asked Driscoll to step down from ministry, citing former BOAA member Paul Tripp saying that Mars Hill

Church's ministry culture was, "without a doubt, the most abusive, coercive ministry culture [he'd] ever been involved with."[136] Mars Hill leadership blamed increased "negative media attention surrounding" the church, for a decline in attendance and giving, and announced the closure of three church campuses with a fourth closure pending.[137] They also laid off 30 to 40 percent of the church's paid staff.[138] The church was in freefall.

The once thriving multisite megachurch that had weathered the controversies of Driscoll's strict theology could no longer sustain the fallout of these manifold scandals. With no clear resolution in sight, church leaders were forced to sanction Driscoll. Rather than submit to the church leadership's restoration plan for him, Driscoll resigned from Mars Hill Church on October 14, 2014, claiming "recent months have proven unhealthy for our family—even physically unsafe at times."[139] Driscoll stated that he was "an imperfect messenger of the gospel of Jesus Christ" and the Mars Hill investigation of the charges against him had shown no "criminal activity, immorality or heresy" that would disqualify him from ministry.[140] Mars Hill's leadership corroborated this, but added that Driscoll had been found guilty of "arrogance, responding to conflict with a quick temper and harsh speech, and leading the staff and elders in a domineering manner."[141]

Two weeks after Driscoll's resignation Mars Hill Church Executive Elder Dave Bruskas announced the dissolution of the church effective December 31, 2014. Individual campuses were told they could dissolve, merge, or become independent churches. The last sermon given at Mars Hill Church was delivered via video feed by Saddleback Church's Rick Warren. At midnight on January 1, 2015, the largest church in Seattle and Washington State, one that had encompassed fifteen campuses across five states, with an average weekly attendance of more than 12,000 people, was no more. Even the most vociferous critics were stunned by Driscoll's swift fall from grace and the imminent collapse of the church.

After Driscoll's resignation, many speculated he would rise again, just when and where were the mystery. Fans and critics didn't have long to wait. Five days after his resignation, Driscoll began his post–Mars Hill speaking engagements. While many of these early appearances were at low-key venues, Driscoll's history of misogyny ignited protests for two high-profile international conferences. Online petitions demanded that Brian Houston, pastor at Australian megachurch Hillsong, drop Driscoll from the program at the 2015 Sydney and London summer conferences. The protestors and petitions caught the attention of Australian media. The *Sydney Morning Herald* described Driscoll telling men that their wives were, in effect, "homes for penises." The *Herald* quoted a sermon, with Driscoll saying, "Ultimately, God created [men] and it is His penis. You are simply borrowing it for a while. Knowing that His penis would need a home, God created a woman to be your wife. And when you marry her and look down you will notice that your wife is shaped differently than you and makes a very nice home."[142]

Houston claimed the media coverage surrounding the controversy first alerted him to Driscoll's misogynistic rhetoric. Eventually, "amid a growing backlash in both Australia and the United Kingdom," Hillsong rescinded Driscoll's invitation to speak at the conference, rather than endorse or legitimate Driscoll's message about women or his abusive behavior.[143] Protesters applauded the decision but were stunned when Houston aired an interview with Mark and Grace Driscoll at the conference. Houston's claim of ignorance regarding Driscoll's gender rhetoric sounds naïve at best and disingenuous at worst, given that Driscoll's controversial complementarian theology and ribald rhetoric were a well-publicized cornerstone of his ministry.[144]

Driscoll continued his speaking circuit and created MarkDriscollMinistries.com, where he announced the 2016 launch of The Trinity Church in Scottsdale, Arizona. As Laura Turner from the Religion News Service described, Driscoll had "left a wake of destruction so severe that the entire network of churches he founded had to shutter its doors," but he was "back again, like a whack-a-mole."[145] On Easter Sunday (March 27, 2016) Driscoll preached his first service at The Trinity Church. At least four protesters attended the inaugural service, waving placards that read, "Trinity = Mars Hill" and "Where'd all the money go, Mark???"[146] Neither The Trinity Church nor Mark Driscoll Ministries mentioned Driscoll's time at Mars Hill Church.

Mars Hill Church's dissolution spawned the creation of eleven independent churches, as well as a host of like-minded congregations across the United States and internationally due to their involvement with Acts 29, The Gospel Coalition, and The Resurgence. Even as he reinvents himself, Driscoll continues to preach a hypermasculine doctrine, which continues to define him and his ministry. In 2017, Driscoll was a featured speaker at the annual James River Church's Stronger Men Conference billed as empowering and motivating men "to live out God's view of manhood and be the best husbands, fathers, and leaders God has called them to be."[147] The conference's promotional materials listed Driscoll as a "world-class communicator," appearing with "NFL Superstars" and a "UFC Legend," solidifying his place in a hypermasculine environment.[148] Connecting Driscoll to high profile, hypermasculine sports was not an anomaly, nor were these the only places where Driscoll's hypermasculine message resonated.

Mark Driscoll and Mars Hill Matter

Mark Driscoll and Mars Hill Church inhabit a unique and important niche in American evangelicalism. Driscoll's hypermasculine theology indelibly impacted twenty-first-century evangelicalism. What happened at Mars Hill under the leadership of Mark Driscoll matters. In 2021, *Christianity Today*, evangelicalism's flagship magazine, produced *The Rise and Fall of Mars Hill* podcast. Promoting the series, the magazine noted that the story of Mars Hill and Mark Driscoll remained influential because "so many elements of this story" influence evangelical culture today.[149] Throughout the series, host Mike Cosper asks the question, "Who killed Mars Hill?" While Cosper's question is complicated, the church's gender theology underlies much of the trouble because it hinged on masculine authority, which can quickly become authoritarian, especially in an autonomous church with little oversight of its leadership.

This book considers Mark Driscoll's gender rhetoric and how it impacted church members, to understand the appeal of his hypermasculine theology and how it became an important part of American evangelicalism. Driscoll's movement drew from earlier iterations of Christian masculinity movements but differed in substance and style. The data tell a complex and contradictory story of the messages given on how to be "real" Christian men and women. Seemingly antithetical to Seattle's liberal ethos, Driscoll's hypermasculine theology made his church thrive. Driscoll's neo–Muscular Christianity was built on a strain of American Protestantism decrying a crisis in masculinity and coalescing into a perfect storm of religious and political zeal to reclaim "traditional" masculine authority. This book makes sense of how and why a hypermasculine Christian movement emerged, was sustained, and continues to influence American Christianity and politics.

The availability of Driscoll's sermons and online resources led to thousands of pastors and church planters being "trained in a style of masculine reform carried out by shamelessly shaming—or conjuring fear of—religious, racialized, and sexualized 'others.'"[150] The effects of Driscoll's hypermasculine theology and the style in which it was presented highlight

Driscoll's "entrepreneurial drive, bullying tactics, and shameless humor," priming evangelicals' conviction that Donald Trump was their preferred presidential candidate.[151] After all, Driscoll's 2000–2001 online church forum, "Pussified Nation," preceded Trump's "grab 'em by the pussy" by more than a decade. Yet Driscoll's misogyny, bullying, and authoritarianism came with a cost, leading to the dissolution of his Mars Hill Church empire.

Chapter Outline

This book places the hypermasculine doctrine of Mars Hill Church in historical context, analyzing the rhetoric Mark Driscoll used to prescribe gender characteristics, roles, and relationships at Mars Hill Church, and how Mars Hill members responded to and interpreted his complementarian theology. Chapter 1 describes the process of how American religious organizations interact with (or against) the wider culture to formulate gender doctrines. Beginning with the upstart sects of Colonial American Protestantism, the chapter illustrates how social structural changes in the wider culture change interpretations of gender to form gender theologies that accommodate or react against the perceived dominant culture. The chapter situates Mark Driscoll and Mars Hill Church in a particular historic moment that facilitated the rise in hypermasculine theology.

The next three chapters address Driscoll's rhetoric regarding men, women, and families, respectively. Each of these chapters is organized in two parts. The first part of each chapter analyzes Driscoll's gendered rhetoric ("the talk") and then tackles how members of Mars Hill interpreted and negotiated his gender theology ("the walk"). Chapter 2 analyzes Driscoll's rhetoric constructing "real" Christian men. Driscoll targets feminism and the femininization of the church with portrayals of a hypermasculine Jesus and apostle Paul to show men how to be truly masculine. The chapter then addresses how that rhetoric both helped and harmed men at Mars Hill. Chapter 3 focuses on how a hypermasculine doctrine constructs roles and expectations for women as "homebuilders" and "helpers" to their husbands. Women's primary roles as wives, lovers, and mothers illustrate how their worth and utility is tied to their marital status. The chapter then describes how women negotiated the lived reality of these expectations. Chapter 4 discusses relationships between men and women through dating and marriage, as well as the central role of sex in marital relationships. The chapter discusses the repercussions of these arrangements in helping or hurting relationships. Chapter 5 addresses the consequences of what it means to be "real" men and women in the context of Mars Hill and explains the success of Driscoll's gender theology in creating boundaries that helped Mars Hill Church grow, at least to a point. The chapter also makes sense of how and why such a strict gender theology could be so successful in one of the nation's most liberal cities, and why the theology became the touchstone for a growing hypermasculine evangelicalism. The Conclusion ties Driscoll and Mars Hill Church's gender theology to our current political moment, Christian nationalism, and what it means for the future of American evangelicalism.

Data and Methods

The data for this project include sermons made publicly available from the Mars Hill Church website, interviews with then-members and former members of Mars Hill Church, and narratives from public Internet forums where then-current and former church members shared their stories of life at Mars Hill. Given the national controversy surrounding Driscoll's complementarian theology beginning in 2006, a random sample of Driscoll's sermons from 2006 were collected and analyzed to see if gender was indeed as central to the church's mission as the popular and local press reported. Analysis showed gender to be fundamental to Mars Hill Church's theology. As a "Bible-believing" church, sermon series at Mars Hill were based on books of the Bible. In 2006, for example, Driscoll preached more than thirty weeks on the New Testament book 1 Corinthians for the *Christians Gone Wild* sermon series. Given the centrality of gender to Driscoll's theology, based on his 2006 sermons, additional sermon series were collected that shed light on how gender and complementarian relationships were prescribed. Sermons chosen for analysis were preached between 2001 and 2012 and include sermons from the 2001–2002 *Proverbs* series, the 2006 *Christians Gone Wild* and *Vintage Jesus* series, the 2008 *Peasant Princess* series (based on the Old Testament book Song of Solomon), the 2009 *Trial* series, and the 2012 *Real Marriage* series from the book of the same name coauthored by Driscoll and his wife, Grace (see the Appendix for a list of sermons analyzed). Examples of Mark Driscoll's rhetoric are also taken from blog postings, Tweets, YouTube videos, and the Midrash thread "Pussified Nation." When the text generalizes themes found in sermons (i.e., "in Driscoll's sermons," "from Driscoll's perspective"), the generalization applies only to the sermons analyzed for this project. This project is not intended to be a comprehensive enumeration of the ways gender was preached at Mars Hill, but a glimpse into understanding how the church's hypermasculine doctrine was built and sustained over the time-period during which the selected sermons were preached.

Interview data were collected between 2009 and 2016 from twenty-six then-current and former members of Mars Hill Church. Additional narrative data come from two public Internet forums, We Love Mars Hill (WLMH) and Mars Hill Was Us (MHWU). WLMH included twenty-seven narratives, and MHWU included eighty-one narratives, from then-current or former members of Mars Hill. Interview and narrative data are denoted by first names—all pseudonyms—to provide privacy for the identities of interviewees and forum contributors. Generalizations to "Mars Hill members" and "former members" within this text refer to the narratives supplied by interviews and the Internet forums analyzed for this project.

Data were analyzed using the constant comparative method to code themes that emerged from the sermons and narratives.[152] Data included represent themes that emerged constructing masculinity, femininity, and relationships between men and women. The data from sermons, videos, blogs, and narratives have been lightly edited for spelling and punctuation. See the Appendix for a more detailed description of data and methods.

1

Evangelicalism and Gender

The Road to Mars Hill

Mars Hill Church's gender theology exemplified a strain of Protestant belief codified just a decade before the church's 1996 founding.[1] Building on complementarianism, Mark Driscoll's theology capitalized on an emerging call to make American Protestantism more masculine. Driscoll's theology demonstrates the dynamic relationship between conservative Protestantism and secular culture over time, illustrating how broad social processes instigate changes in social institutions, including religion. While American Protestant Scriptures haven't changed, their interpretations have. Scriptures are read through cultural lenses and interpreted in light of structural arrangements at given moments in history. Biblical interpretations, like cultures, are fluid and can be illustrated by a tale of two Baptist movements in American history.

A Tale of Two Baptists

Invigorated by the religious revivals in the mid-eighteenth century, a robust American tradition of piety was born. Waves of revival, spawned in part by preachers like George Whitefield and Jonathan Edwards, emphasized individual conversion with the assurance of salvation coming from the heart, rather than head.[2] Revivalists broke with Puritan orthodoxy, which equated Christianity to a hierarchical family with men in authority and women submitting to their leadership.[3] Instead, revivalists stressed the need for individual spiritual conversion and responsibility to God.[4] Convinced by the Revolutionary rhetoric of individual autonomy, the revivalists envisioned a new covenant—one that emphasized individual rebirth within a community that was related, not by biological ties, but by the grace of the saved. The revivalists' emotional and informal worship, combined with an open expression of visions and spiritual experiences, gave women and African Americans access to religion in new ways.[5] Within the bond of spiritual

Making Christianity Manly Again. Jennifer McKinney, Oxford University Press. © Oxford University Press 2023.
DOI: 10.1093/oso/9780197655795.003.0002

fellowship, revivalists affirmed that men and women, rich and poor, lettered and ignorant, were as capable as ordained clergy of discerning spiritual truth, leading to remarkably egalitarian communities when compared to the larger society.[6]

This revivalist spirit had significant implications for the Baptists, particularly in the southern colonies. These Baptists had "a strong antiestablishment streak" that included allowing women to preach.[7] In the mid- to late-eighteenth century Baptist women served along with men and enjoyed unprecedented access to the formal and informal channels of Baptist governance and authority.[8] Baptist women participated in the major decisions of collective governance including the election and dismissal of ministers, the admitting and excluding of members, the vociferous theological debates regarding the nature of conversion, and the qualifications for membership. The Baptist practice of allowing women to pray publicly with men in "mixed assemblies" scandalized the established Congregational and Presbyterian clergy.[9] The authority Baptists granted to women posed a challenge to the hierarchical Anglican, Presbyterian, and Congregationalist denominations.[10]

More than 200 years later, the Southern Baptist Convention (SBC), the largest Baptist organization in the United States, made headlines when they amended their Statement of Faith and Message after voting overwhelmingly to prohibit women from serving as pastors in the denomination, despite the fact that women were ordained and serving SBC churches.[11] The SBC revised their statement to say, "While both men and women are gifted for service in the church, the office of pastor is limited to men as qualified by Scripture."[12] The change in colonial-era Baptist theology to contemporary Southern Baptist theology represents the ways gender symbolizes an ideological divide within American Protestantism more generally. Colonial-era and contemporary Baptist movements both opposed "mainline" (established) religious cultures, using gender as a measure of orthodoxy. Yet colonial-era Baptists adopted *egalitarian* gender ideals, creating higher tension between them and the dominant religious culture, whereas contemporary Baptists adopt *hierarchical* gender ideals, to maintain higher tension between them and the (perceived) dominant religious culture. The key to understanding how and why these Baptist movements had such disparate gender theologies lay in the social structures they reacted against, or accommodated to, in those cultural moments.

Theologies reflect the social nature of religious organizations and how they function vis-à-vis the broader culture. Sect-church theory describes religious

organizations as existing on a continuum from rejecting the dominant culture (sects) to accepting the dominant culture (churches).[13] Rejecting the
dominant culture—or significant aspects of that culture—creates higher
tension between a religious organization and dominant culture. Accepting
the dominant culture—or the major aspects of that culture—creates lower
tension between the religious organization and the culture. Colonial-era
sects, including the Baptists, were inspired by the populist antiauthoritarian,
anti-intellectual, and visionary rhetoric that begat the American Revolution.
Beguiled by the promise of religious freedom, Protestant sects set themselves
apart from mainline churches by embracing the idea that anyone could be
chosen by God to preach the gospel—the poor, enslaved, uneducated, and
women. For these evangelical revivalists, "Nothing better symbolized their
countercultural identity than their willingness to allow large numbers of
women into the pulpit."[14] For contemporary Baptists and other conservative Protestants, nothing better symbolizes their countercultural identity
than their rejection of egalitarianism. For both colonial and contemporary
movements, gender functioned to protest the dominant culture of their re-
spective historical moments and signaled their distinctive religious identities
by maintaining a posture of higher tension to the mainline Protestant and
broader secular cultures.[15]

Sect-Church Theory, Tension, and Strictness

How and why religious organizations change their gender theologies can be
explained using sect-church theory and the concepts of tension and strictness. Sociologists use the concept of tension to distinguish sect from church
as ranging on opposite ends of a continuum of religious organizations.[16] In
this way sect and church represent ideal types of religious organization that
are useful in describing how sects *reject* the social environment in which they
exist, while churches *accept* the social environment in which they exist.[17] In
other words, sects are religious bodies with higher moral demands on their
members setting them apart from the culture at large. Churches are religious
bodies that adapt to the secular culture, imposing far fewer moral demands
that are at odds with the prevailing culture.[18]

Tension *between* a religious group and its sociocultural environment
is connected to the "strictness" *within* a religious group.[19] Higher tension
groups sustain norms and values that are significantly different (or perceived

as significantly different)—stricter—than those of the surrounding culture. This within-group strictness leads religious organizations to becoming exclusive, extensive, and expensive.[20] Strict Protestant groups have *exclusive* beliefs about who God is, what God is like, and what is required to be a good Christian. Exclusive groups recognize only one road to salvation and require a life-changing "conversion" experience for membership. Because the group's doctrines are exclusive, they impinge on all aspects of life, from defining who members associate with to how they spend their leisure time, making commitment to the group *extensive.* The exclusive and extensive nature of the group makes belonging to the group an *expensive* proposition, imposing nonnegotiable demands on members' beliefs and behaviors, limiting activities outside of the group.[21]

While it may seem counterintuitive, the higher personal costs of belonging to strict groups are balanced by higher personal satisfaction.[22] Members of strict religious groups contribute more money to their congregations, attend more services, have stronger beliefs, and are less involved in secular activities and other organizations.[23] The joy, energy, and excitement experienced by church members generates high levels of personal satisfaction and attachment to the church and church community.[24] The emotional energy produced by participating in the church reinforces the distinctive beliefs and practices of the group, creating meaning and identity for individual members to solidify their exclusive beliefs, practices, and promises. A church's strictness puts the group in higher tension to the outside world.[25]

The proliferation of megachurches and celebrity pastors in the American religious landscape has strengthened their impact in the social and political landscape.[26] Megachurches infuse group symbols—the Bible, family values, and theology—with emotional energy.[27] The catalyst for this energy is the charismatic senior/founding/teaching pastor, who defines the church's norms and expectations. The emotional energy produced within the group reinforces a pastor's claims of exclusive doctrinal truths and affirms the rightness of the extensive and expensive relationship to the church.[28] Historically, gender has played a critical role in strictness, putting strict churches in higher tension with the surrounding environment.

Charismatic megachurch pastor Mark Driscoll and his Mars Hill Church encapsulated the hallmarks of strictness with their innovative hypermasculine theology. Driscoll's and Mars Hill's gender theology stood in significant tension to Seattle's progressive culture. Driscoll's compelling, contentious, and charismatic persona reinforced a sense of his church's having the one and only true gospel, creating an energy that spurred remarkable growth. Understanding Driscoll and Mars Hill in the context of history, sect-church theory, tension, and strictness helps explain how and why their inno-vative hypermasculinity became indispensable for many evangelicals.[29]

Explaining Gender Theologies in Christian History

Like the opposing gender theologies of colonial and contemporary Baptist movements in American history, evidence exists of two predominant gender narratives in Christian history.[30] The most well documented, and perhaps criticized narrative, is the "tradition in which gender relations are organ-ized by the principles of hierarchy and subordination."[31] Sociologist Sally K. Gallagher describes this strain of belief citing early church fathers who mir-rored their own Greco-Roman culture, which was predisposed to misogyny. These church fathers stated that women did not bear the full image of God (Augustine), that women were the means through which Adam was deceived (Ignatius), that women were the devil's gateway (Tertullian), and that women were misbegotten men (Aquinas).[32] This narrative is the root from which today's evangelicals adopt "gender essentialism." Gender essentialism teaches that God created men and women differently—complementarily—with dif-ferent purposes and roles. While gender essentialism creates a hierarchy of authority, with men in authority over women, it paradoxically assigns equal worth to men and women. Gender essentialists interpret this gender ide-ology from the apostle Paul's letters, believing women should keep silent in the churches (1 Cor. 14:34), man is the head of the woman (1 Cor. 11:3), and women should learn in silence, neither teaching nor being in authority over men (1 Tim. 2:11–12).[33]

A second narrative also enjoys a long history. This narrative emphasizes partnership and mutuality between men and women and also relies on the apostle Paul's statement, "in Christ there is neither Jew nor Greek; male nor female; slave nor free" (Gal. 3:28).[34] Proponents of this narrative cite heroines who spread the good news of Christ, including Mary Magdalene, Philip's four daughters, and Phoebe.[35] They also argue that if women were forbidden from preaching, Paul would not have instructed them to cover their heads when praying or prophesying in public (1 Cor. 11:5), nor would he have given spir-itual authority to Priscilla in the teaching of Apollos (Acts 18:24–26), nor would he have named Junia an apostle (Romans 16:7).[36] Church fathers like

Tertullian ("woman is the devil's gateway") are also cited for challenging authoritarian models of marriage by urging mutuality between husbands and wives.[37]

Underlying these two gender narratives is the oft-overlooked social nature of religion—how religious groups function in regard to the broader culture. At any given moment in time, religious groups are negotiating their beliefs and practices in relation to other religious groups and the broader culture. Today we see this phenomenon in American Protestantism, with mainline and liberal denominations adopting increasingly egalitarian gender theologies, and fundamentalist and evangelical ("conservative") Protestants adopting increasingly hierarchical gender theologies. Since American Protestants draw from the same Christian canon, the question is how and why Protestants arrive at such disparate interpretations of gender.

Gender and American Protestantism in History

One of the most powerful mechanisms through which Protestants distinguish themselves from each other and the dominant culture is through their gender theologies. Gender has long been a dividing line between Protestant traditions, functioning as a central, salient, and effective element of boundary work.[38] For evangelicals, being *in*, but not *of* the world—an extension of the apostle Paul's teaching—justifies existing in higher tension to the secular culture.[39] Gender doctrines cannot be separated from the church and its authority, making them sacred and seminal to eternal salvation.[40] Many evangelicals believe in a God-ordained gender hierarchy assigning fundamentally different, if complementary, traits and tasks to men and women. While the gender hierarchy is interpreted by these evangelicals as a timeless continuity, gender ideals (and doctrines) change over time within and across cultures.[41] When social structures change, the reverberations are felt throughout all social institutions, including religion. Gender theologies are a prime example of how religious organizations respond to social changes.

A powerful predictor of changing gender ideologies is changing economic conditions. As the United States transitioned from an agrarian to an industrial economy in the nineteenth century, for example, gender ideals substantially changed (to "true women" and "self-made men," discussed below).[42] More than 100 years later, the transition from a postwar manufacturing economy to a service and information economy ushered in another significant change to cultural gender ideals (breadwinner/homemaker). During both transitions Protestants changed their gender ideals to maintain a desired level of tension to the culture. A historical perspective illustrates how social change influenced the way Protestants responded to the culture by rejecting or embracing new social currents. The following review examines the social nature of the shifts in American Protestant gender theologies, highlighting historical periods when social conditions necessitated reaction or accommodation to changing cultural gender ideals. This culminates in the twenty-first-century social conditions that created the context in which Mark Driscoll's and Mars Hill Church's gender theology was formed.

The Upstart Sects: Colonial- and Revolutionary-Era Gender Equality

Throughout American history Protestant understandings and practices of gender theologies have shifted as changes have occurred in the larger culture. Mainline denominations of the early nineteenth century—the Episcopalians, Congregationalists, and Presbyterians—followed a hierarchy/subordination interpretation of gender that restricted women's religious speech and forbade them to preach. This posture was succinctly stated in 1832 by the Presbyterian General Assembly, "to teach and exhort, or to lead in prayer, in public . . . is clearly forbidden to women in the Holy Oracles."[43]

Inspired by populist rhetoric, the evangelical "upstart" Methodist and Baptist sects rejected established religious denominations' gender doctrines and practices by including women in leadership and preaching. The upstart sects believed that religious authority came from heartfelt experience; since God communicated directly to believers, it was just as likely that God inspired women as well as men to proclaim the gospel.[44] Women participated in church governance, preached at meetings, and exercised their full rights as members of these religious bodies.[45] The widening of women's authority drew strident criticism from mainline denominations, many of whom argued for the silence of women at religious gatherings.[46] Maintaining strict standards of behavior (e.g., no drinking, no gambling, no profanity) and emphasizing the natural equality of all believers, the Methodists and Baptists created higher tension to the established religious and secular cultures.

The upstart sects' democratic, local, and autonomous organizations, as well as their use of persuasion rather than coercion for conversion, resulted in flourishing religious organizations.[47] By the mid-nineteenth century, however, the success of the upstarts broadened their fellowships; no longer were they religious outsiders. This broadening of their fellowships put pressure on the sects to soften the doctrines that set them apart from their larger social environment.[48] The Methodists, for example, increasingly exchanged local, uneducated clergy and democratic organization for an educated and professionalized clergy, as well as a centralized, denominational organization. Turning away from their radical roots, the Methodists adopted restrictive gender doctrines and even excommunicated some women who refused to stop preaching.[49] The southern Baptists were slower to accommodate to the mainline culture, even though they also lost their "outsider dissident" status.[50] Because they continued to rely on local (often bivocational) clergy (due to a belief that "ecclesial power resided in all members") and remained locally autonomous, the Baptists maintained important aspects of their sectarian status, allowing for continued growth.[51]

The Cult of True Womanhood and the Cult of the Self-Made Man

As America's agrarian economy gave way to an industrial market economy, a new gendered division of labor was born. Whereas an agrarian economy relied on families working together on farms or in trades, the industrial market economy privileged an emerging "separate spheres" gender ideology. The separate spheres ideal constituted men and women as fundamentally opposite, based on a biologically reductive essentialism. The separate spheres ideology awarded differential human traits to men and women, promulgating a Cult of True Womanhood and a Cult of Self-made Man. "True women" were ascribed the traits of piety, sexual purity, submissiveness, and domesticity and attached to the private sphere of the home.[52] Traits ascribed to men were consistent with the rough and tumble public sphere of the market economy: independence, self-control, competitiveness, and aggression. The allocation of differential human traits to men and women gave them authority in different social institutions. Women's "natural" piety gave them authority in religion and men's "natural" aggression gave them authority in business.[53] The Cults of True Womanhood and Self-Made Man were so pervasive that most Americans, religious or otherwise, adopted the ideologies as biological certainties, even though most Americans could not afford to follow them.[54]

Industrial gender ideals formed at the same time the upstart sects were becoming more successful. Recognizing the inconsistencies and accommodation to mainline and secular gender ideals, the Methodists were called back to their traditional revivalism and theology through the Holiness movement.[55] Advocating for gender equality, movement leader Phoebe Palmer penned a spirited defense of women preaching. In her 1859 book *The Promise of the Father*, Palmer wrote, "When the Spirit was poured out in answer to the united prayers of God's sons and daughters, did the tongue of fire descend alike upon the women as upon the men? How emphatic is the answer to this question!" The same spirit that fell upon New Testament women, Palmer contended, continued to fall upon "God's daughters" and "impelled them to testify to Christ."[56] The Holiness movement thrived, but the movement's ideals of gender equality did not reverse the Methodists' increasing adoption of a separate spheres gender ideology.

After the Civil War, Black Protestants found the industrial gender ideals of "true women" and "self-made men" inaccessible. Designated "laborers," a category casting them as less than fully human, Black men and women were excluded by the dominant cultural gender ideal.[57] Black families developed an alternative ideal, defining women by their resourcefulness, independence, and intelligence.[58] Because of these characteristics, Black women were not reliant on marriage to provide their primary identity, as white women were. Summarizing the alternative gender ideal for Black women in a 1912 speech to the Federation of Colored Woman's Clubs, Maggie Walker said, "every woman was by Divine Providence created . . . not for some man to marry, take home and support, but for the purpose of using her powers, ability, health and strength to forward the financial . . . success of the partnership into which she may go, if she will."[59] Black women embraced a threefold commitment to career, family, and social uplift, expecting to work for pay outside of the home, actively parent children, and work toward racial and gender equality.[60]

The pervasive embrace of the separate spheres ideology in white American and white Protestant cultures meant that husbands and wives looked remarkably different than their eighteenth-century counterparts.[61] Toward the end of the nineteenth century, as economic and other social structures changed, however, American Protestantism began to fracture and white Protestant men's perceived loss of power and "traditional" masculinity made the Victorian ideal of women's natural piety and morality suspect, pushing them toward a more masculine Protestantism.

Muscular Christianity and the
Fundamentalist-Modernist Controversy

At the end of the nineteenth century, industrialization, urbanization, and mass immigration were remaking American culture, and native-born white Protestants feared their way of life and faith were under siege.[62] As entrepreneurial capitalism gave way to consumer-oriented corporate culture, the Victorian codification of religion as feminine made white Protestant men feel their faith was "sissified and effeminate."[63] Women's authority in religion also threatened the dominance men had achieved in all other social domains.[64] To fully claim cultural dominance, white Protestant men sought to recodify the Victorian ideal of feminine piety to make religion manly.[65] Reshaping constructions of gender, the Muscular Christianity movement harnessed the Victorian ideal of bold and courageous masculinity to frame Jesus as a "brawny carpenter, whose manly resolve challenged the idolaters, kicked the money changers out of the temple, and confronted the most powerful imperium ever assembled."[66] Muscular Christianity portrayed Christianity as "no dough-faced lick-spittle proposition," according to Billy Sunday, a former professional baseball player. Sunday, a Muscular Christian disciple and preacher, embodied the movement, proclaiming, "I'd like to put my fist on the nose of the man who hasn't got grit enough to be a Christian."[67]

The rapid changes in American culture fueling Muscular Christianity also began to fracture Protestantism. While white Protestant men determined that women had "had charge of the church long enough," they diverged in how they conceptualized the utility of Muscular Christianity. "Modernist" Protestants sought to reclaim religious authority from women through the context of market capitalism. To align religion and business, modernists interpreted Scripture to be relevant to their modern context, which meant embracing the practices of good works over right doctrine.[68] This "Social Gospel" movement advocated for structural, rather than individual, transformations.[69] When taken to its logical conclusion, the Social Gospel movement had implications for gender, eventually leading modernists toward more egalitarian gender ideals.[70]

Alarmed by modernists and the Social Gospel movement, fundamentalist Protestants embraced an absolutist orthodoxy (right doctrine over good works) and continued to promote the "virile and heroic enterprise" of refuting the Victorian ideal of women's moral authority.[71] Fundamentalists characterized women's "natural" piety as a "dangerous inversion," threatening the natural order of creation. Yet fundamentalists continued to justify differences between men and women as biological, unabashedly asserting the rightness of male headship through an "absolutist, uncompromising, good-versus-evil" apocalyptic theology.[72] Countering modernist interpretations of the Bible, fundamentalists fashioned a theology of biblical inerrancy and highlighted Scriptures reinforcing strict gender roles, to justify removing women from religious authority. As Billy Sunday described, "Yes sir, woman is the battleground of the universe."[73]

While it may appear that fundamentalists were conserving biological distinctions to advocate for "traditional"—opposite—gender roles, there was "little that was conservative or traditional about" fundamentalism.[74] Defending an imagined past, fundamentalists equated modernist perspectives and an expansion of women's authority to "the last days and the rise of the Antichrist" and blamed them for—what they perceived as—feminizing the nation and the downfall of men.[75] By the 1920s, fundamentalists had successfully replaced the Victorian model of feminine virtue to define women as the psychologically and spiritually vulnerable sex, and to affirm men's "rightful position as religious leaders."[76]

The Great Depression, World War II, and Neo-Evangelicalism

On the heels of the divorce between fundamentalist and modernist Protestantism, the Great Depression threw the United States into economic and social turmoil. Within three years of the 1929 stock market collapse, unemployment tripled in the United States, industrial production fell by nearly 50 percent, and worldwide trade was at just one-third of its 1929 levels.[77] The Depression pushed women into the workforce, threatening Victorian and fundamentalist models of gender.[78] The essentialist attachment of men to industrial work meant that unemployment led to a loss of identity, demoralization, and self-medicating with alcohol for many men.[79] Yet, the equating of women's work outside the home with men's economic failure made a separate-spheres gender ideology attractive to many Americans. The nation's economic woes were often blamed on women, the Women's Suffrage Movement, and the passage of the Nineteenth Amendment, souring many on gender equality, even as more egalitarian attitudes had begun to supplant the Victorian separate spheres ideologies.

Modernist Protestants (increasingly defined as "liberal" or "mainline") continued to give women more latitude and larger roles within their congregations, mirroring the culture's changing gender ideals and practices. Mainline Protestants defended gender equality with a nonliteral reading of Paul's teachings, a Wesleyan perfectionist doctrine interpreting restrictions on women's leadership in the church as being swept away by the atoning death and resurrection of Christ.[80] Fundamentalists reacted decisively against ideological accommodation to changing economic and social constraints, rejecting modernist readings of the Pauline texts regarding women and women's roles.[81] Claiming a literalist reading of the Bible, fundamentalists doubled down on their strict, biologically essentialist theology that men had a natural aptitude for religion and were divinely equipped to defend Christian orthodoxy.[82]

The fracturing of Protestantism into fundamentalist and mainline factions also functioned to separate Protestantism's scriptural orthodoxy (fundamentalism) from social engagement (mainline). Hoping to bridge this gap and reunite orthodoxy with practice, a group of fundamentalist men gathered in the 1930s to bring fundamentalism out of its intellectual isolation and re-unify mainline activism with scriptural authority through "engaged orthodoxy."[83] These "neo-evangelicals," however, conflated fundamentalist gender doctrine with scriptural orthodoxy to maintain men's religious authority.[84] The Depression and World War II challenged fundamentalist and neo-evangelical ideals of gender, especially since fundamentalist and evangelical women were as likely to be working outside of the home as other women, and fundamentalist and evangelical men were just as likely as other men to be unemployed.[85] All of this changed during the postwar years, when a new cultural gender ideal was born.

The Long Decade of the Breadwinner/Homemaker

After nearly two decades of social and economic instability, the postwar "long decade" ushered in a breadwinner/homemaker gender ideal and a "golden age of marriage."[86] Buoyed by an expanding economy, the husband-as-provider/decision-maker with wife-as-nurturer/homemaker became the new American ideal.[87] Social historian Stephanie Coontz describes the new breadwinner family form as "a steamroller that crushed every alternative view," adding that, "By the end of the 1950s even people who had grown up in completely different family systems had come to believe that . . . a male breadwinner family was the traditional and permanent form of marriage."[88] American Protestants, mainline and evangelical, also saw breadwinner/homemaker as the traditional form of marriage, interpreting it as the self-evident God-ordained roles for men and women.[89]

As the postwar economy began to decline, so too did breadwinner/home-maker.[90] As real wages fell for men and wages for women increased, working wives became critical for families to maintain a middle-class lifestyle. With higher levels of education for women, compressed childbearing and rearing, and an expanding service economy, middle-class white women re-entered the labor force in striking numbers (working-class white women and Black women were already there). Responding to these changing social and economic conditions, mainline Protestants adjusted their theology, adopting more egalitarian beliefs and practices. Reacting against these social and economic changes, fundamentalists and evangelicals blamed working women for rising divorce rates, out-of-wedlock births, declining marriage rates, and the destruction of the American family.[91]

One of the most visible evangelicals during the long decade was Billy Graham. Graham feared that women reentering the workforce hastened the breakdown of culture and family. Too many women, Graham lamented, were " 'wearing the trousers in the family' despite the biblical principle 'that the husband be the head of the house.' "[92] Consistent with his fundamentalist background, Graham believed the Bible taught that women were to make the home as happy as possible, suggesting they could serve their husbands by keeping their houses clean, preparing husbands' favorite meals (on time), and attending to their dress and personal appearances—not working outside of the home. For Graham and other evangelicals, men and women had clear and absolute roles; any violation of these roles would create turmoil and spark God's anger.[93] Fundamentalist and evangelical Protestants were increasingly at odds with the secular and mainline cultures. The social upheaval of the 1960s and 1970s led fundamentalists and evangelicals to focus on the bread-winner/homemaker family as an antidote to the social chaos around them, crafting a "family values" platform that would transform them religiously, politically, and socially.

Family Values, Feminism, and a Crisis in Masculinity

The social upheaval of the 1960s and 1970s signaled a departure from a "traditional" þreadwinner/homemaker family form (white, middle-class breadwinner/homemaker), which heralded national decline from the perspective of fundamentalists and evangelicals. Sociologist Seth Dowland writes that the cultural revolutions of the 1960s rallied fundamentalists and evangelicals, who believed themselves to be the custodians of traditional American morality.[94] Worried that the civil rights movement, second-wave feminism, the sexual revolution, and gay rights showed the collapse of society, fundamentalists and evangelicals felt an urgency to conserve traditional values.[95] These conservative Protestants envisioned the traditional family—two heterosexual parents and their children—as the central unit of American society, and the nation's moral compass. Conserving social morality meant evangelicals stressing the necessity of men's authority.[96] Conservative Protestantism's gender essentialist theology hinged on hierarchy, attributing clear masculine "lines of authority" as necessary for successfully functioning families and society.[97]

To conservative Protestants, the second wave of the feminist movement, the Women's Liberation movement, proved a significant assault on traditional families and the nation. By usurping men's traditional places of authority, feminism destroyed the sanctity of families, and by default was destroying America. Feminism became conservative Protestantism's true "F-word." Conservative Protestants saw the evils of feminism embodied in the campaign for the Equal Rights Amendment (ERA).[98] Historian Kristin Du Mez explains that for evangelicals, "the ERA challenged the very foundation of the conservative Christian worldview: the idea that gender was a sacred, God-given certainty in an uncertain, fluctuating world."[99] Defeating the ERA became a rallying point for the emerging "family values" political platform and the way to stop feminism from destroying biblical femininity and forcing women "to be 'like men'—competitive and career-driven, sexually promiscuous—and, most alarmingly, for forcing them to take up arms in military combat."[100] For evangelicals, the ERA was evidence of gender chaos in the secular world; its passage would "not only 'masculinize' women but would also remove from men their obligations of provision and protection, rendering American defenses vulnerable."[101]

Rejecting gender equality and feminism outright, evangelicals made the case that "gender hierarchy and difference were not only the clear message of the Bible but unavoidably reflected in the physiological and psychological differences between women and men."[102] Popular conservative Protestant writers and speakers regularly lambasted feminism, describing it as "a subtle and pervasive poison, infecting the minds of Christians and non-Christians alike" (Elisabeth Elliott), an ideology meant to "destroy families, schools, morals, and communities across the nation" (Beverley LaHaye), and most colorfully: "Feminism is a socialist, anti-family, political movement that encourages women to leave their husbands, kill their children, practice witchcraft, destroy capitalism and become lesbians" (Pat Robertson).[103] For conservative Protestants, the only solution to restore "biblical" gender roles was to excise all things feminist and "draw a clear and absolute demarcation between men and women in almost every dimension of life."[104]

Closely related to concerns about feminism were concerns about sexuality. Just as feminism threatened the traditional family, so did homosexuality. Conservative Protestants expected men and women to honor their God-ordained sexual differences. Homosexuality sundered traditional understandings of gender and sexuality, disrupting the complementarity of men and women to form a holistic family. Just as the ERA galvanized conservative Protestants, gay marriage "struck at the heart of evangelical convictions about family."[105] Fighting feminism and the gay rights movement became focal points of the family values platform.[106]

Ostensibly, the fight against feminism focused on working women, who were transgressing their divinely ordained roles. The discourse, however, began to shift toward the deleterious effects of feminism on men and men's roles. Reinforcing the link between traditional family and masculine authority, Focus on the Family founder James Dobson blamed feminism for denigrating God's ordained masculinity, which threatened the health of the nation.[107] A "call to arms" was needed to reassert a Christian concept of masculinity, refute feminism, and reestablish a Christian nation by "defining and defending distinct gender roles" to provide "evangelicals a clear identity against secularists, feminists, and other liberals."[108]

Evangelical Feminism

The dire need for defending distinct gender roles was partially due to an emerging evangelical feminism. Growing alongside second-wave feminism, evangelical feminists questioned whether a gender hierarchy was part of God's original design, since it did not reflect the partnership modeled by the Trinity.[109] Basing their theology on both women and men being created in the image of God, evangelical feminists rejected gender essentialism to embrace egalitarianism.[110] The Evangelical Women's Caucus (EWC) served as the hub for evangelical feminism, advocating for the full participation of women in church ministries, as well as partnership in marriage.[111] These evangelicals saw feminism as a natural and logical extension of their faith.[112] EWC splintered in 1986 over a resolution to support lesbianism and gay rights. Dissenters of the resolution founded Christians for Biblical Equality (CBE), which retained the majority of members.[113] CBE bases their understanding of gender egalitarianism in Galatians 3:28, "There is no longer Jew or Greek, there is no longer slave or free, there is no longer male and female; for all of you are one in Christ Jesus" (NRSV). CBE's statement of "Mission and Values" asserts that the Bible teaches the "fundamental equality" of men and women, as well as all ethnic groups, economic classes, and ages. For CBE, leadership and "followership" are equally male and female. Evangelical feminist organizations continue to fight for gender equality within conservative Christianity, however, their membership remains "tiny," and their voices marginalized from the larger conversation.[114]

Conservative evangelicals characterized the evangelical feminist movement as rejecting biblical authority and accused practitioners as privileging feminism over Christianity.[115] Unable to dismiss the spread and influence of feminism, conservative evangelicals worked to discredit it. They claimed that egalitarianism undermined the authority of the Bible and that egalitarians were erasing differences between men and women (in function and authority) to distort God's ordained gender hierarchy, hurting families, and throwing the nation into utter social chaos.[116] As a direct response to feminism, both secular and evangelical, a contingent of conservative Protestants met to draft the Danvers Statement on Biblical Manhood and Womanhood in 1987. The Danvers Statement defended a gender essentialist understanding of men's and women's roles in church, home, and society. The statement codified "complementarianism" as the only viable Christian gender theology.[117] Complementarianism argued that hierarchy was embedded in gender, with men bearing the responsibility of authoritative teaching and leadership in the church and the home. Reestablishing a gender essentialist, complementarian theology, would strengthen families and the nation to reverse the "tragic" influence of feminism and gay rights on the culture, church, and home.

The drafting of the Danvers Statement was accompanied by the founding of the Council on Biblical Manhood and Womanhood (CBMW). Led by John Piper, CBMW's primary purpose was teaching husbands to "lovingly" lead their wives and teaching wives to "intelligently" and "willingly" submit to their husbands' authority. On their webpage, CBMW's "Statement of Faith" clearly restricts leadership roles in the church to men. Dowland explains how CBMW's faith statement differed from earlier generations of conservative Protestant gender ideals stating, "Whereas previous generations had relegated women to subservience through unspoken cues and social customs, conservative evangelicals opposed to feminism explicitly barred women from leadership roles through a particular reading of Scripture," fully institutionalizing "complementarian" theology as the only "biblical" theology.[118]

By the end of the twentieth century, American Protestantism was defined by its gender divide, hardening into complementarian and egalitarian factions. The rise of evangelical feminism signaled to evangelicals that their understanding of biblical gender norms must be preserved to maintain a proper hierarchy of authority. Justified by their definition of biblical inerrancy, conservative Protestants read Scripture as an absolutist text to argue for complementarianism, determining that feminism "demeaned the honor ascribed to motherhood by the Bible."[119] Biblical literalists fixated on verses that "ascribed authority to men" affirming the hierarchy (lines of authority) embedded within the creation.[120] Men, by God's design, were commanded to lead because they were better suited to leadership, in church and in the home.[121] Egalitarians interpreted Scripture as a radical message of gender inclusivity that rejected the patriarchal norms of first-century Judaism.[122] Clear battle lines had been drawn between these Protestant factions. There were, however, some surprises in how conservative Protestants interpreted and practiced their gender theology.

Headship/Submission, Egalitarianism, and the Promise Keepers

At the turn of the twenty-first century, social scientists and historians specializing in the study of gender and religion found that although conservative Protestant complementarians espoused gender hierarchy, by and large, their practices did not follow.[123] Recognizing the pervasiveness of, and need for, dual-earner families, evangelicals shifted their rhetoric to preserve distinctive hierarchical gender roles that allowed dual-earner families to align themselves with a religiously legitimated hierarchical gender theology. Evangelicals had subtly shifted their rhetoric from "breadwinner/ homemaker" to "headship/submission." This shift maintained the ideal of husbands' headship to allow evangelicals to remain distinct from the wider culture.[124] Even so, research illustrated that headship itself was largely symbolic, as most evangelical households practiced a more egalitarian division of labor.[125] The symbolic headship and practical egalitarianism of the headship/ submission ideal meant conservative Protestants affirmed two ideals of marriage: the ideal of husbands' headship (men being the spiritual leaders of the household and having the final authority in decision-making) and the ideal of partnership.[126] The affirmation of both ideals gave conservative and feminist evangelicals common ground. The ambivalence between rhetoric and praxis gave way to a wider acceptable range of gendered experience, particularly for men.[127]

The symbolic headship and practical egalitarianism evident in evangelicalism, however, generated voices within the tradition decrying a "crisis of masculinity." Within this shifting gender context, the Promise Keepers movement was born. Notable for their stadium events that drew thousands, the movement exhorted men to "take back" leadership within their homes and congregations.[128] Reflecting the ambivalence in evangelicalism over gender ideal versus practice, the movement broadened men's responsibilities to accommodate the changing social and economic realities of home life by helping their wives with unpaid household labor.[129] Sociologist John P. Bartkowski writes that, "Although many Promise Keepers would probably not see themselves as heirs to the egalitarian legacy of evangelical feminism . . . much [Promise Keeper] rhetoric has clearly been informed by biblical feminist critiques waged against 'unchristian' forms of domination and exclusion."[130] The movement's gender ambivalence may explain their rapid decline.

By the end of the twentieth century the rhetoric of strict gender roles had given way to a less aggressive division of gender, what W. Bradford Wilcox called "soft patriarchy."[131] This "soft patriarchy," in turn, provoked a reaction toward a hardline complementarian theology. The need to reassert an absolutist complementarian theology and practice led evangelicals to a push for a clearer division of labor in home and church. Toward this end, denominations like the SBC revised their statement of Faith and Message to take an official stance against women in pastoral leadership. Emphasizing this delineation between men and women—in ideal and praxis—the chair of the statement's drafting committee, Reverend Adrian Rogers, stated, "Southern Baptists, by practice as well as conviction, believe leadership is male."[132] The updated statement of Faith and Message also amended a passage on the family, to clarify the distinctive roles of men and women:

> The husband and wife are of equal worth before God, since both are created in God's image.... A husband is to love his wife as Christ loved the church. He has the God-given responsibility to provide for, to protect, and to lead his family. A wife is to submit herself graciously to the servant leadership of her husband.... She, being in the image of God as is her husband and thus equal to him, has the God-given responsibility to respect her husband and to serve as his helper in managing the household and nurturing the next generation.[133]

A push was underway to emphasize a stronger hierarchical gender essentialism expressing the equal worth of men and women *in essence* but not in practice.[134] Instituting this gender theology meant redefining masculinity and the relation of men to religion.

Neo–Muscular Christianity/ Hypermasculine Evangelicalism

Twenty-first-century evangelicals developed a "neo–Muscular Christianity." Like the earlier masculinity movement, evangelicals cast Jesus as "religious Rambo" and portrayed the Christian life as a "heroic quest" of spiritual manhood.[135] This warrior masculinity was an aggressive, testosterone-driven masculinity.[136] In 2001 three best-selling books revived James Dobson's call to arms for an uncompromising Christian masculinity. James Dobson's *Bringing Up Boys* derided feminists for emasculating men, making them "wimpified." Douglas Wilson's *Future Men* called for a "theology of fist-fighting" and recommended that boys be "trained in the use of firearms."[137] John Eldredge's multimillion-selling *Wild at Heart: Discovering the Secret of a Man's Soul* is arguably the most consequential of these books. *Wild at Heart* specified that God not only created distinctive gender roles for men and women but also created men and women with gendered souls—gender essentialism on steroids.[138] Eldredge's book proposed that God hardwired men to be wild and dangerous creatures meant to live out three essential desires: the desire to fight a battle, the desire to live an adventurous life, and the desire to rescue a beauty.

Eldredge's follow-up book, *Captivating: Unveiling the Mystery of a Woman's Soul*, coauthored with his wife Stasi, described the corresponding desires of a woman's gendered soul: to be romanced, to play a role in her own adventures, and to display her beauty.[139] *Wild at Heart* and *Captivating* not only propagated an absolutist headship/submission theology but also unabashedly placed men at the center of the Christian message, claiming a divine gender design that imbued men with authority and the traits of action, leadership, courage, and economic prowess.[140] Recovering this God-ordained masculinity was seen as redeeming Protestantism from the effects of feminism, and allowing men to take their rightful place in church leadership.[141] This neo–Muscular Christianity recreated strict gender doctrines to reinstitute opposition—ideological and practical—to cultural (and mainline Protestant) egalitarianism.

As evangelicals recodified headship/submission to recover a more muscular Christianity, terrorists struck the World Trade Center in New York City on September 11, 2001. The call to a more muscular Christianity was reinforced by the political rhetoric of a "war on terror." The growing conflation between evangelicalism and conservative politics primed evangelicals to be "more likely than other Americans to approve of U.S. engagement in a preemptive war, support military action against terrorism, and condone the use of torture."[142] Fifteen years after the fall of the Twin Towers evangelicals propelled Donald Trump into the presidency of the United States. While pundits and many religious commentators questioned how an "immodest, arrogant, foul-mouthed, money-obsessed, thrice-married man" could be supported by evangelicals, Trump was a logical conclusion to an evangelical Christianity saturated in a hypermasculine Christian milieu.[143] This is the historical context within which Mark Driscoll birthed his gender doctrine and Mars Hill Church.

Mark Driscoll and Mars Hill Church

The close of the twentieth century brought a strong reaction to the softening of conservative Protestant gender ideals. Within this context, Mark Driscoll cofounded Mars Hill Church with a theology based in complementarianism that responded to the "crisis in masculinity" by sharply departing from symbolic headship/practical egalitarianism. Driscoll serves as the touchstone for this hypermasculinity movement. Driscoll and the rise and fall of Mars Hill Church emphasize the social nature of religion and the importance of gender as a boundary marker between faith and secularism. Driscoll's hypermasculine doctrines helped Seattle's Mars Hill Church become one of the fastest-growing and most influential churches in the country. By creating a strict hypermasculine theology, Driscoll increased the tension between his congregation, the local Seattle culture, and other Christian churches.

Illustrated in his earliest teachings, Driscoll blamed feminism for the decline of American Christianity. In his 2000–2001 "Pussified Nation" thread from the Mars Hill forum, Midrash, Driscoll wrote:

> [S]o the culture and families and churches sprint to hell because the men aren't doing their job and the feminists continue their rant that it's all our fault and we should just let them be pastors and heads of homes and run the show. And the more we do, the more hell looks like a good place because at least a man is in charge, has a bit of order and let's [sic] men spit and scratch as needed.

Driscoll's gender theology created significantly more tension with the culture than the "soft patriarchy" of symbolic headship and practical egalitarianism. In a post–Promise Keepers era, with the theology of a warrior Christ gaining ground, Driscoll was no rogue itinerant preacher promoting a hypermasculine gender theology; he was, however, a leading voice in the movement. Driscoll stood apart in his flamboyant language, style, and reach. Driscoll's hypermasculine theology drew strict demarcations between the characteristics and roles of men and women. Driscoll's repackaging of masculinity, while foremost, also reconstructed femininity. The next chapters describe Driscoll's ideals of masculinity, femininity, and relationships between men and women, as told through his sermons. The chapters also show how members of Mars Hill Church interpreted and practiced the gender theology. Since Driscoll's mission centered on making men masculine, we turn to men and masculinity first.

2

Real Men (Don't Wear Sweater-Vests)

The rise and fall of Seattle's Mars Hill Church, helmed by Mark Driscoll, illustrates several contradictions. Considered one of the most literate cities in the country, Seattle is also politically and socially progressive. The hypermasculine Christianity preached by Driscoll and adopted by Mars Hill Church seemed at odds with the ethos of the city. Yet the unprecedented growth of the church, with Mark Driscoll as its brand, tells us something about the nature and success of the movement *because* of the liberal ethos of the city. Embracing some parts of the liberal culture while adhering to conservative theological doctrines set Mars Hill Church apart from both the Seattle culture and from other local churches, creating a unique religious niche for the church in the city. Driscoll's bombastic style and absolutist rhetoric created a clear, divine gender order that would polarize Seattle and the American evangelical community.

Driscoll's call for a strict gender-based division of labor in the workplace, home, and the church resembled previous cultural and Protestant "separate spheres" gender ideals, with a call to "Make (American) Christianity Great Again" or "Make Masculine Christianity Great Again." Historian Kristin Kobes Du Mez connected evangelical impulses toward hypermasculine doctrines for their embrace of Donald Trump, highlighting the "culmination of a decades-long embrace of militant masculinity . . . that has enshrined patriarchal authority . . . and functioned as a linchpin in the political and social worldviews of conservative white evangelicals."[1] While many commentators were surprised at evangelical support for Trump, Du Mez explained that evangelicals voted for Trump, not in spite of, but because of their beliefs.[2] Many evangelicals embraced Trump the same way they had embraced pastors like Driscoll, whose teachings "replaced the suffering servant of Christ with an image that more closely resembles Donald Trump" trading "a faith that privileges humility and elevates the least of these for one that derides gentleness as the province of wusses. Having replaced the Jesus of the gospels with an idol of machismo, it's no wonder many have come to think of Trump himself as the nation's savior."[3]

Making Christianity Manly Again. Jennifer McKinney, Oxford University Press. © Oxford University Press 2023.
DOI: 10.1093/oso/9780197655795.003.0003

Writing for *New York Magazine*, Ed Kilgore was not surprised evangelicals voted en masse for Trump, because "conservative evangelicals have a tendency to confuse Christianity with the patriarchal heartland American culture of the 1950s."[4] Driscoll's gender theology evoked the simplicity and nostalgia of a 1950s division of labor, with men as economic providers and women as homemakers. Driscoll's strict gender theology created significantly more tension toward the culture than the "soft patriarchy" of symbolic headship and practical egalitarianism that characterized late-twentieth-century perspectives of evangelical gender ideals. Driscoll's gender theology also stood in contradiction to a city seen by many as a bastion of social and political liberalism. Driscoll's message appealed to an audience of evangelical Christians seeking to reclaim an American Christian past that was counter to their perceptions of Seattle's liberal culture.

Driscoll's strict hypermasculine theology created an inflexible gender-based division of labor: "God made men and women equally important but gave them distinct roles in the church and home."[5] From Driscoll's perspective, hierarchical roles—man as head and woman as man's helper—are how the Bible ascribes authority. Driscoll's provocative rhetoric and gender theology influenced evangelical Christianity around the world. The success of Mars Hill Church can be attributed to Driscoll's flamboyant style and his focus on hypermasculinity, which helped mitigate real and perceived threats to American (Christian) masculinity due to economic and status declines.[6]

While his rhetoric constructed a very specific masculinity, Driscoll sometimes tempered his hypermasculine message so that all men could know that, by virtue of being male, they were the "glory of God." Even "tender-hearted" and "merciful" men had a place of authority in God's gender hierarchy—unless, of course, they were gay. Gay men had no authority in Driscoll's theology. Similar to the early twentieth-century Muscular Christianity movement, Driscoll reinterpreted men in the Bible as "warriors" and "ultimate fighters." Driscoll's hypermasculine Christianity constructed a hierarchical and heterosexual ideal rooted in his perception of Jesus's and the apostle Paul's masculinity. Holding himself up as a temporal example of true masculinity, Driscoll likened himself to a modern-day Paul, planting churches in pagan cities.

Men and women were attracted to Driscoll's gender theology. While Driscoll's message of salvation followed Reformed theology as part of the New Calvinist movement, men's salvation was evidenced by their adherence to and practice of his hypermasculine ideal. As Bartkowski stated, religious culture is not simply abstract, but is "rendered through the bodily practices of actual believers."[7] In light of the complex relationship between belief and practice, this chapter addresses the rhetoric Driscoll used to create the hypermasculine gender doctrine at Mars Hill Church and then illustrates how the rhetoric was interpreted and enacted.

The Talk: Make Christian Men Great Again

> God looks down and says, "I hate you, you are my enemy, and I will crush you," and we say that is deserved, right and just, and then God says, "Because of Jesus, I will love you and forgive you."[8]

From the beginning, Mark Driscoll's hypermasculine message was embedded in the ministries of Mars Hill Church. Driscoll's gender theology was evident in the now infamous "Pussified Nation" thread. Some contributors to the thread expressed concerns about the way the message was posed, but even when dissenting with the tone, most of those posting agreed with the overall message that men needed to "man up." In 2001–2002, Driscoll preached a sermon series on the Old Testament book of Proverbs, which he described as "a book written from men to men for the purpose of taking young men and maturing them into mature masculine men."[9] Despite the book's imputed origin and intent (from men for men), Driscoll promised that women would also learn from Proverbs: "There are things that pertain to women in Proverbs, but the thrust to the audience is very clearly male, even from a cursory reading of the book."[10] The series spoke to the roles of men with sermon titles like "Men and Masculinity," "Men as Husbands," and "Men as Fathers." Sermons for women included "Women and Femininity," "Women as Mothers," and "Women as Homebuilders." The strict gender roles Driscoll advocated, along with the church's rapid growth, began to draw censure and concern from the local Seattle and Christian communities. Driscoll's rising profile, coupled with his controversial gender theology, led to his being featured in a 2003 edition of the *Pacific Northwest Magazine*, broadening his regional reach.

It was in late 2006, however, when Driscoll solidified his national reputation, making headlines with his viral response to Ted Haggard's being forced to step down from the National Association of Evangelicals (NAE) and the Colorado megachurch he pastored. Driscoll's notorious response highlighted three elements of his ministry focus and style. First, Driscoll's comments were directed toward encouraging men, especially young men in ministry. Second, Driscoll's comments took an antiwoman turn, saying, "It is not uncommon to meet pastors' wives who really let themselves go; they sometimes feel that because their husband is a pastor, he is therefore trapped into fidelity, which gives them cause for laziness." Third, Driscoll seemed to revel in his acknowledgment that his views were often reviled: "At the risk of being even more widely despised than I currently am, I will lean over the plate and take one for the team on this."[11]

What caught the public's attention from the viral post was Driscoll's blaming women for men's sin. Driscoll's description of women "letting themselves go" and not being "sexually available" to their husbands, indirectly causing husbands to stray, brought considerable criticism. Much, if not most, of the early attention on Driscoll and Mars Hill Church regarded his rhetoric about women and their place in the home (and exclusion from church leadership). Driscoll's primary goal, however, was to empower men, who he felt had become emasculated by the culture and the Christian church. His charismatic style and male-focused theology led adherents to describe Driscoll as an "apostle" to men whose mission was "turning boys into men."

While local and national audiences debated the frequency, centrality, and ultimate impact of Driscoll's antifeminist rhetoric, there was only conjecture as to the pervasiveness of gender within Driscoll's doctrine (both inside and outside of the church). In an analysis of a random sample of Driscoll's 2006 sermons, gender was found to be a central component of his theology. In 2006 Driscoll preached two sermon series. The thirty-three-week *Christians Gone Wild* sermon series dealt with an excursive of the New Testament book of 1 Corinthians, while the twelve-week *Vintage Jesus* sermon series dealt with the questions that would best reveal who Jesus was. Both series emphasized a strict gender theology with a need for a warrior masculinity to counter a feminized church.

The Feminized Church

[If] Christian males do not man up soon, the Episcopalians may vote
a fluffy baby bunny rabbit as their next bishop to lead God's men.[12]

For Driscoll, the feminization of the church was directly responsible for the decline of Christianity. In a 2006 blog post, Driscoll communicated his perspective of the cause of the Christian church's decline. In the post, Driscoll blamed mainline churches pioneering the ordination of women, which led to the ordination of gay men, as the formula sure to destroy a denomination.[13] Driscoll contended that "pro-feminism" leaders and denominations were, by default, "pro-homosexuality" and promoted Christian decline.[14] In the blog post, Driscoll wrote that Episcopalians, not only had "gay bishops, a female Presiding Bishop . . . and a blessing of same-sex unions, but also a complete meltdown and fractured communion that can never be repaired."[15] For Driscoll, women's leadership in the church ushered in acceptance of homosexuality resulting in the feminization of the church, the emasculation of men, and the mass exodus of masculine men from the church. Thus, Driscoll's mission entailed reclaiming Christian manhood, which meant men needed to man up.

The Ultimate Fighting Christian Champion

> Paul was out making trouble [and Jesus] comes down from heaven and smacks Paul around, kind of like an Ultimate Fighter.[16]

Like previous Muscular Christianity proponents, Driscoll refashioned biblical men to set a precedent for his masculine-centered Christianity. Describing Jesus, prophets, and apostles as rough and violent men, Driscoll attempted to reverse the influence of feminism on the church and on men. In a promotional video recorded for John Piper's 2006 Desiring God conference, Driscoll described the apostle Paul, John the Baptist, and the Old Testament prophet Elijah as "pretty rough" dudes, who didn't look like "church guys" walking around "in sweater-vests singing love songs to Jesus."[17] Biblical men like David, he said, were "well known for their ability to slaughter other men," concluding, "I've got to think these guys were dudes: heterosexual, win a fight, punch you in the nose, dudes."[18] Driscoll needed to remasculinize the church by finding "innovative dudes" who would work on their trucks, shoot guns, make money, and "make the culture of the future."[19]

Driscoll indicted feminized pastors and churches for ignoring his ideal of a divine gender order. To emphasize his point, Driscoll developed a "riff" about the prototypical effeminate pastor. The effeminate pastor was described as a guy who, "shows up in the Cabriolet. He's got like a lemon-yellow sweater-vest, open-toed sandals. He's rocking out to the Spice Girls. . . . You know, not a big help."[20] The effeminate pastor was also "useless" at doing the real work of the church, which Driscoll saw almost exclusively as planting churches.[21] To build a church, Driscoll explained, "You've got to have a dude."[22] Dudes were "kind of like a pastor," but were "more like the UFC Ultimate Fighting version."[23] Whereas pastors in "normal" churches might photocopy well, a church planter had to be "a dude who can fight, and preach, and teach, and lead, and be courageous, and get something done to build a church, and to bring it forth out of nothing with God's help."[24] Driscoll's obsession with the church planter holding the highest calling and authority in the church meant that his examples of hypermasculine Christianity relied on characterizing the apostle Paul as "the dude." Channeling *The Big Lebowski*, Driscoll referred to Paul as "the dude" who fought the "freaks," "nut jobs," "weirdos," and "heretics" to become Christianity's first church planter.[25]

It's All about ~~Jesus~~ Paul

> If you're going to plant a church. . . . You've got to put your hands up, adjust your cup, and you've got to do your job. That's Paul. Paul's that kind of guy. So, he's the dude.[26]

Mars Hill Church's tagline, "It's all about Jesus," pointed to Jesus as head of the Christian church, as well as the titular head of Mars Hill. The core of Christian doctrine is in the saving death and resurrection of Jesus, who is one person of the three-person Trinity (God, Jesus, and Holy Spirit). In Driscoll's hierarchy of authority, God's authority (the Father) is followed by Jesus's authority (the Son), with Paul the church planter, subject to Jesus.[27] While God and Jesus existed within a divine realm, Driscoll used the fully human Paul as the example of Christian masculinity to follow.[28] Driscoll characterized Paul as a "man's man," admired for his willingness to "call people out" for the sake of the gospel. Driscoll described Paul as a "little Jewish guy showing up and saying, 'You [guys] are a bunch of babies.' "[29] When Paul met adversity from a culture that denigrated him or the gospel, Driscoll said Paul's response was unequivocal: "Those guys? Smack them around, smack them around!"[30]

In his *Christians Gone Wild* series, Driscoll paraphrased the Bible's story of Paul, found in the New Testament book of Acts. The book of Acts describes Paul's physical and metaphorical journey from the Jew, Saul, to the Christian, Paul. The book speaks of Saul's persecution of Christians, "ravaging the church by entering house after house; dragging off both men and women, he committed them to prison" (Acts 8:3). "Breathing threats and murder against the disciples of the Lord" (Acts 9:1), Saul traveled to Damascus to arrest Christians. On the road to Damascus, however, Saul was struck by a bright light that blinded him. He heard a voice asking, "Saul, Saul, why do you persecute me?" Saul asked, "Who are you?" and heard, "I am Jesus, whom you are persecuting" (Acts 9:5) in response. Jesus told Saul to enter the city, but "though [Saul's] eyes were open, he could see nothing" (Acts 9:8). For three days and nights Saul was without sight. Encountering the Christian disciple Ananias, Saul's sight was restored, he was filled with the Holy Spirit, and baptized into the Christian faith. Saul then began proselytizing for Jesus under his new name, "Paul."

Driscoll's interpretation of Paul's encounter with Jesus was a bit different. In his *Christians Gone Wild* series sermon "Pastor Jesus," Driscoll described Paul's conversion with an imaginative hypermasculine twist, saying that Jesus came "down" from heaven and "basically beats" Paul. Driscoll says, "I love that about Jesus." Paul was "making trouble" and Jesus came "down from heaven and smacks Paul around . . . like an Ultimate Fighter." Driscoll added, "I love that about Jesus, because you never know when he might show up and just knock you around a little bit." Continuing the story, Driscoll said:

> Jesus comes down from heaven, knocks [Paul] on the ground and blinds him for three days . . . which is a compelling argument for you to obey. Yeah, if Jesus came down and like punched you in the mouth and then made you blind for three days and said you're gonna be a Christian now and you're gonna be a missionary, after three days you'd be like, "Yeah, that's what I'm doin' now that I'm blind, and I would like not to be blind." So that's what Jesus does to him.[31]

In Driscoll's version of the story, Paul's conversion was a capitulation to a violent Jesus, which, for Driscoll, was a compelling reason to obey. Jesus's violence toward Paul undergirds Driscoll's hierarchy of masculine authority. Jesus used his divine power to coerce Paul into becoming a Christian, cementing violence as a masculine and Christian trait. Having been subject to Jesus's violence, Paul became an earthly authority—an ultimate fighter. Recognizing his status as subject to Jesus, Paul's response to Jesus (in Driscoll's words) was, "I wouldn't have taken this dang job if Jesus didn't come down from heaven, beat me up, blind me, and make me. Jesus had to whup me to make me take the job. It's not like I volunteered. . . . Jesus came down and punched me in the mouth and so I took the job."[32] Victimized by Jesus, Paul converts, accedes to Jesus's authority, and becomes "the dude." As "the dude," Paul was "not afraid of conflict . . . not afraid of being disliked . . . not afraid of a good fight."[33] Driscoll's recounting of the story of Paul highlights his hypermasculine Christian hierarchy: God, Jesus, and Paul. Paul, the first Christian church planter, becomes the epitome of nondivine masculine authority. As a successful church planter, Driscoll placed himself at the apex of a modern Christian power hierarchy that gave him authority over other Christian men (and women).

As heir to the first church planter, Driscoll described Paul in ways strikingly similar to himself. According to Driscoll, Paul was "not afraid of a good fight," and his mouth and attitude often got him into trouble. Paul was "always getting beat up, thrown in prison [or] kicked around. I mean the guy [was] always taking a beating."[34] Driscoll believed Paul's aggressive demeanor was part of a necessary skill set for "speaking truth" to the surrounding cultures. Church planters were "far more like a soldier getting ready for battle" because "the body count [was] really high in the church planting war."[35] Driscoll also described Paul as having a gentler spirit when it came to humble and repentant believers,[36] yet to be true to his vision of Paul, Driscoll's ideal church planter had to have a hard edge.

Setting himself and Paul apart from effeminate church pastors, Driscoll reinforced his hypermasculine ideal with a story of a church planter he described as the "least dudely dude" he'd ever met. In the *Christians Gone Wild* sermon "Church Planting in Corinth," Driscoll recounted a phone call he received from a church planter's wife. The church planter's wife called asking for Driscoll's help, because her husband "had a hard day." When Driscoll asked what her husband was doing, the woman replied that he was crying. "Really?" Driscoll asked, "What's that look like for a guy to cry? There's no crying in church planting. You . . . get up, you take your standing ten count, you adjust your cup, and you put your hands up, and you get back in the ring and you take your shots. You don't cry." Driscoll continued the story explaining that he drove to the church planter's house, only to find this least dudely dude laying "on the floor in the fetal position with a blankie," crying. Driscoll asked, "What happened?" The church planter said, "They were mean to me. They didn't like me. They rejected me." Driscoll responded, "Maybe they don't respect you. You have a blankie and you cry," concluding, "This does not inspire the best men to follow you into war." After admonishing the man for laying on the floor and crying in front of his teenage sons, Driscoll then looked at the man's sons and said, "Dig a hole. We're putting your dad in it. He's no good. We're done with him."[37]

This anecdote communicated that only "tough" men could be successful church planters. It also communicated a contradiction. Being a man was necessary, but not sufficient to being a successful church planter; even being a church planter was no guarantee of true Christian masculinity. Driscoll reinforced the necessity of being a man (or a boy), by shifting his attention to the church planter's teenage sons, rendering the church planter's wife invisible. The story also highlights that in the hierarchy of authority, not all men can be at the top; some men must be subordinate to others.[38] Driscoll expected other men to be subordinate to his authority, because Driscoll's masculinity was the litmus test for real Christian men. To strengthen his position of authority, Driscoll regularly mocked men who didn't meet his masculine standard. This was particularly true for men who aspired to leadership in the church.

Too Many Fools

I was reading in Samuel where there was Abigail, [a] sweet gal [who] married Nabal, which means "fool." [Nabal was] a complete imbecile . . . [and Abigail] tried to work around the fact that her husband was an imbecile. And I thought: We know a lot of people like that.[39]

In his quest to create men who could lead their churches and families, Driscoll derided the larger culture for sending the message that "men are idiots, men are imbeciles, men are incompetent, men don't achieve or redeem anything."[40] Driscoll assured men that this was not what God intended. Driscoll told his audience that Paul called men the "glory of God" and that the men of Mars Hill needed "to be cultivated and encouraged and nourished and instructed and exhorted and motivated and led."[41]

Driscoll complained that men had been deceived by a feminized church and culture that denigrated them. Yet Driscoll regularly disparaged men who do not meet his hypermasculine standard, regularly referring to men as "idiots," "imbeciles," and "complete jokes."[42] Driscoll often used sports analogies, appealing to Paul's writing to "fight the good fight" and to "run the race before us," to contrast true versus false masculinity.[43] Driscoll stopped short of Paul's including all believers in these metaphors, limiting leadership and the full inclusion and participation in his church to men following his lead. In one sermon Driscoll asked the men in his audience if they'd ever noticed the "one loud, obnoxious fat fan" sitting in the stands at sporting events, who yelled at the athletes on the field (e.g., "You're lazy. You can't run").[44] Driscoll said he'd like to see those "arrogant" "trash-talkers" in the middle of a football game have the running back go into the stands with the football to say to the fan, "Cool. Give it a shot."[45] Then he said, "I'd love to see that guy wet himself and spill his chili all over himself, you know? Because it's so much easier to criticize than it is to play." For Driscoll it was "easier to be a referee than an athlete," "easier to be a negative, critical Christian" than to be "a servant of Jesus Christ who gets something done."[46] Those guys? "All talk, no game."[47]

Like the "least dudely dude" he'd ever met, Driscoll regularly critiqued men who were, or aspired to be, pastors. In "Paying Your Pastors," from the *Christians Gone Wild* series, Driscoll jokes about men hoping to become full-time ministers, describing them as being "raised in the home-school co-op" and attending "Bible college." Driscoll said, "You're totally naïve" and "do not know what you're talking about." Fine-tuning his point, Driscoll related the story of attending a conference where "Pete" and "Repeat," a "couple Bible college guys" approached him to ask about becoming pastors. Driscoll described Pete and Repeat as, "just absolutely adorable," wearing "their little polo shirts," "their little shorts," and "their sandals," with "nice haircuts," "clean shaven" and carrying their Bibles. Approaching Driscoll, Pete and Repeat said, "Pastor Mark, we just wanted to ask you some questions about ministry. We're in Bible college. We're going to graduate in a few years, and we're so looking forward to serving the Lord." Driscoll's response? "These guys were so dumb!"[48]

Grumbling about how popular culture set men up as failures, Driscoll himself regularly ridiculed men, the Nabals, who could not live up to his standard. Driscoll's rhetoric infantilized other men as Cabriolet-driving, sweater-vest-wearing, Spice Girls–singing wusses, to create a masculinity that few could attain. Driscoll taught men to live up to an example that only he seemed to fully realize (at least by virtue of his rhetoric), setting up many Mars Hill men for failure. To meet the masculine standard proclaimed at Mars Hill Church, men were given opportunities to pursue leadership roles in the church or in the church planting field, as new Mars Hill satellite campuses and Mars Hill–influenced Acts 29 churches were created. Funneling Mars Hill men into leadership positions gave them status. Because very few could achieve Driscoll's level of success, however, most men were limited in what they could ultimately achieve. These men continued to be subordinate to other men in the church, who were subordinate to the church elders and ultimately subordinate to Driscoll.

The highest level of authority at the church, apart from Driscoll's, was that of elder/pastor. Over the church's existence, the ranks of the elders swelled from a handful of men to more than sixty men, many of whom were paid full-time salaries for the position. Following the dictates of masculinity championed by Driscoll, many Mars Hill men felt a need to signal their obedience to the standard, for example by sporting beards, wearing black, being married and having children, and being the sole economic providers within their families. One category of men, however, could never achieve masculinity at Mars Hill: gay men.

This Ain't Brokeback Bible Church

Jesus had loving friendships with men, but he wasn't gay.[49]

In his *Christians Gone Wild* sermon series, Driscoll compared Seattle to the New Testament city of Corinth, describing the latter as a place of "massive sexual perversion. They had transvestites, homosexuality, friends with benefits, strip clubs, cohabitating" and "crazy naked people everywhere."[50] In the series, Driscoll characterized Christian debates on homosexuality as "very intense," adding, "but it's also very clear in Scripture. Leviticus says, 'A dude should not lie with a dude, like a dude lies with a chick.' That's my translation."[51]

Driscoll used the word "gay" like adolescent boys use the word "fag" to reinforce heterosexual masculine privilege.[52] Driscoll regularly derided men who were effeminate. In a sermon on the "gifts of the spirit," Driscoll told men the gift of encouragement was primarily a woman's gift where, for example, they might send letters dotting the letter "I" with hearts or smiley-faces. For men who do the same: "You're gay. I hate to break it to you. It's a fine line, but like, if you send letters with like, hearts for the dotted 'I's, that is not the gift of encouragement. That's a guy who listens to a lot of Barbara Streisand and thinks Richard Simmons is a great guy."[53] In another sermon Driscoll defined himself as "flamboyantly heterosexual," saying, "I drive a truck and eat meat and watch ultimate fighting."[54] Driscoll then rebuked those who might think his description of "real men" was inconsistent with Jesus, saying,

"Really? [Jesus] was a hippie in a dress? . . . When he comes back on a horse with a sword to declare war on you, we'll talk about that."[55]

The Christian scriptures, for Driscoll, as for many evangelicals, stipulated the unnaturalness of homosexuality. Driscoll cautioned the men at Mars Hill, telling them that some homosexual men tried to rationalize their behavior, but they were guilty of sin and were not real men. As Driscoll explained in the *Christians Gone Wild* sermon "Changed by Jesus," "some dudes" justified their homosexual acts saying, " 'Well, if I'm the pitcher, not the catcher, then I'm not gay. Only the catcher is gay, not the pitcher.' "[56] But for Driscoll, "if two dudes are naked, it's gay, all right? It's dudes."[57] While he describes this idea as "the down low" where " 'I'm not gay because I'm not the receiving party,' " Driscoll turns to Paul saying that Paul teaches, "Giving and receiving partners in a homosexual relationship are both guilty of homosexual activity. Both are guilty of sin. Both are not fit for God's kingdom. They're rebelling against God's intention of one man, one woman, one flesh."[58]

Driscoll stressed the need for church leaders to avoid entanglements inappropriate for Christian men as role models, especially if it implied homosexuality. In the sermon "Pastor Jesus," Driscoll reassured his church he would never run away with his secretary. Driscoll told his church, "Paul travels with a guy," therefore, his own assistants were men. Referring to a question he'd recently been asked, "Pastor Mark, how do we know that you won't run off with your secretary?" Driscoll replied, "This ain't Brokeback Bible Church, I mean we're not . . . gonna do that." Because Driscoll's assistant was "a dude," he further clarified that, "furry is not my type," and "I know he's not gonna sleep with me 'cause I can take him." Driscoll assured the church that if he and his assistant were "travelling or strategizing, you can guarantee it's biblical; there's nothing weird going on."[59] Effeminate and homosexual men had no place in Driscoll's theology and the "tragic" or "partial" interpretation of Jesus as a "gay hippie in a dress" meant that Driscoll took pains to emphasize Jesus as a heterosexual warrior.

Jesus Is Not Rocking Out to the Spice Girls

You have been told that God is a loving, gracious, merciful, kind, compassionate, wonderful, and good sky fairy, who runs a daycare in the sky, and has a bucket of suckers for everyone because we're all good people. That is a lie.[60]

While the apostle Paul was described as an exemplar of Driscoll's hypermasculine Christianity, he was subject to the authority of Jesus. Driscoll believed that feminized churches and pastors had grossly misinterpreted Jesus as a "gay hippie in a dress, rocking out to the Spice Girls, driving around the Middle East in a Cabriolet, hoping to meet nice people to do aroma-therapy with while drinking herbal tea."[61] Driscoll described his experience with this "tragic" interpretation of Jesus stating, "Before I was a Christian, I was very disinterested in Jesus because I thought, 'Why give your life to a man you can beat up?!' That's what I thought. Because the pictures I'd all seen of Jesus—he had feathered hair, was wearing a dress [and] listening to a lot of Elton John."[62] Fortunately, Driscoll discovered a Jesus he could give his life to: a blood-smeared, tattooed-up, eyes blazing, slaughterer-of-nations. Drawing from the apocalyptic last book in the New Testament, the book of Revelation, Driscoll described Jesus by saying, "Now, this guy right here, I can't take Him, right? He's got a robe dipped in blood. Any guy who has blood as an accessory is tough, right? And it ain't His blood!"[63] Emphasizing his point of Jesus as Warrior, Driscoll continued, saying, "On His robe and on His thigh He has this name written: 'King of Kings, Lord of Lords'—tattooed down the leg of Jesus, right?! This is tattooed-up, white-horse-riding, blazing-eyes, all-seeing, sword-coming-to-slaughter-the-nations, robe-dipped-in-blood Jesus. Love that guy."[64]

Driscoll upended images of a Jesus who was "meek and mild" with those of a triumphant and victorious warrior. Driscoll claimed the former images of Jesus were "deficient," hurting men's ability to worship Jesus as the true warrior-king. Driscoll blamed the feminization of the church for this "very deficient picture of Jesus," as well as for the overall lack of men and mascu-line leadership in the church.[65] Driscoll claimed that a "growing crisis in Christianity" existed because men didn't "think much of Jesus," men were "not inspired by Jesus," the only men participating in church life were not "the most manly."[66] Driscoll lamented the state of men in the church saying that men who rejected Jesus had only a "partial view of Jesus" and "all they see is [a] humble, marginalized, Galilean peasant. They don't know that He's still alive, that He's King Lord God, He's triumphant Warrior, Victor. He's the kind of inspiring God that men should seek to be like, to pray to, to worship as the exalted, glorious, risen, ascended King of Kings and Lord of Lords."[67]

Highlighting Jesus as warrior, victor, and king did not exclude Jesus's divine characteristics of mercy and grace. Driscoll acknowledged Jesus's complexity in *The Peasant Princess* sermon, "My Dove," describing him as a strong man willing to do the "unthinkable," by suffering and dying for the sins of the world. As he died on the cross, Driscoll explained, Jesus interceded with God to forgive "his murderers" showing he was "tenderhearted" and "forgiving" with his final words, "Father, forgive them." Driscoll then addressed the men of his church about believing in this deficient and partial portrait of Jesus, saying Jesus "puts up with people like you and me" because Jesus is "patient, he's loving, he's gracious, he's merciful, he's kind." Driscoll told Mars Hill that no-one who went to Jesus saying, "I repent of my sin, forgive me," would be turned away because, "Jesus is tenderhearted and forgiving of anyone who repents.[68]

Driscoll intimated that these more feminine attributes of Jesus (patience, mercy, kindness) were due to Jesus's divine nature. For earthly men, however, a "tattooed-up" Jesus and a "rough and tough" Paul were Driscoll's primary examples of Christian masculinity. Mars Hill men were expected to be "strong men, courageous men, bold men. Men like Jesus."[69] Driscoll affirmed both Jesus's and Paul's complicated masculinities and told men to emulate Jesus and be "repentant," "humble," "aware of their own sin" and "willing to admit such wrong."[70] Yet Driscoll's overall message, in rhetoric and style, spoke to emulating a Jesus who was warrior-god. Men should evidence Jesus's divine traits, but as earthly men they must always be strong because the Bible "says 'act like a man.'"[71] Acting like a man meant being strong enough, "even in this church," to have courage and confront other men who were "not being nice to their wife and kids," or who weren't "working hard" or "being honorable."[72] Driscoll told the men at Mars Hill they needed to have "strength," and "boldness" in order to "put your finger" on that "guy's chest and say, 'Look, you're a Christian. You go to Mars Hill. You're a Mars Hill man. Don't treat your wife like that. Don't treat your kids like that. Don't work your job like that. That's not how we do things. That's not how Mars Hill men are. That's not how God's men are.'"[73]

Driscoll equated Mars Hill men with God's men, as if only the men at Mars Hill had the teaching, the strength, and the pedigree to be God's men. By accepting Driscoll's version of masculinity, Mars Hill men could be transformed from "average" and "ordinary" men, through an "extraordinary transforming event," when "in an instant," they "get a new body, and they're strong, and they're supernatural, and they don't die, and they don't get sick, and they live the life we all wish we could."[74] Driscoll gave his audience examples, asking, "Clark Kent becomes who? Superman. Peter Parker becomes? Spiderman. Bruce Wayne becomes? Batman. Diana becomes? Wonder Woman—tricky one, and she's fallen out of favor. And Bruce Banner becomes? Incredible Hulk."[75]

Driscoll appropriated characteristics of a hypermasculine Jesus to legitimate and reinforce a hegemonic or hypermasculine cultural ideal. By constructing a Christian masculinity that was a precursor to salvation, Driscoll gave an exclusive message to the men at Mars Hill and awarded himself a seat at the apex of masculine Christian authority. Since not all men were Driscoll, they had to compensate for their inability to reach the top of the gender hierarchy. If masculinity was equated with skill and success, far more men sat in the stands than played on the field.[76]

While sometimes contradictory, Driscoll's rhetoric constructed a hypermasculine ideal for Christian men reminiscent of the rhetoric from the early twentieth-century Muscular Christianity movement. Occasionally, Driscoll highlighted Jesus's divine characteristics like mercy, veering toward Jesus as "tender warrior," similar to the Promise Keepers movement.[77] Yet Driscoll's ideas of masculinity were not his own creation. He used superheroes and other tropes from popular culture (Ultimate Fighters, Mixed-Martial Arts) to bolster his version of masculinity, as well as to critique media depictions of false masculinity (e.g., men as "imbeciles" or the "dumb dad"). Using popular culture references as his benchmark, Driscoll claimed a hypermasculine Christianity, for which he seemed to have an exclusive market. Violating his call for Christian masculinity could have dire consequences; men's very salvation was jeopardized if they did not emulate Driscoll's version of masculinity. Therefore, Driscoll's rhetoric was not just talk. Driscoll's appeal lay in his ability to persuade others that his masculine Christianity was, in fact, the only true Christianity (leaving many men out). Men couldn't simply "talk the talk," they had to "walk the walk." For men at Mars Hill Church, the evidence of their regeneration and salvation lay in embodying Driscoll's hypermasculine ideal.

Walking the Talk: Boys Go In, Men Go Out

My guys have never said . . . to me, "We never talk. We never sit in a circle, and look at one another in the eye, and get to the heart." No, but we will watch a cage fight, standing shoulder to shoulder, eating chicken wings, and at the end we feel like that was quality time.[78]

Driscoll's rhetoric constructed an exclusive way to salvation. Driscoll was unapologetic about his focus on men and masculinity, stating, "We get a lot of criticism on this. . . . The criticism is Mars Hill is just too much about men. And you know what? Mars Hill is about men. . . . We see Mars Hill as a man factory; boys come in, men go out. Period. That's what we're about."[79] Members of Mars Hill had to evidence their commitment to Driscoll's ideal because they risked the eternal consequences of damnation if they didn't. There were also temporal consequences; the church practiced shunning for members who did not follow their theology.[80]

Mars Hill Church initially targeted young, college-aged men and women, who saw Driscoll's explosive style as authentic. Members of Mars Hill affirmed Driscoll's penchant for "speaking truth" about the perils of a feminized church and the need for men to "step up." Driscoll's clarion call was seen as countercultural, setting Mars Hillians apart not only from the liberal Seattle culture but also from other Christian churches (local and national), which had purportedly accommodated to a liberal, feminized culture. The core of Driscoll's "truth" was the need for men to reclaim their masculinity, and subsequently restore the Christian church and a divine gender order. Driscoll's confrontational approach was described as "fresh" and "raw." Writing on Mars Hill Was Us (MHWU), Ethan described Driscoll's style and Mars Hill Church as "all I was hoping for, a counterculture existing to worship and to reach the city. It was real in its approach—raw—and called men to move forward."[81] Another contributor to MHWU, Elijah, stated that hearing Driscoll "speak the truth so freely" about "the emasculation of the American church" was "heartening" and "a big draw for me as a young man just out of the military."

Driscoll's masculine-centered message positively affected many men at Mars Hill. Chandler stated on MHWU, "Having just turned 18 and trying to find my place in the world, I found Mark's pounding home of topics on masculinity to resonate deeply." Responding to what they perceived as a lack of direction for men, many at Mars Hill related how Driscoll's "straight talk" and focus on masculinity gave them a "framework" to become "responsible" men. Writing on a second Internet forum, We Love Mars Hill (WLMH), Parker noted that Mars Hill's masculine framework was important because "so many American men refuse or don't know how to grow up, because we don't have a ritual, a moment where our society tells us we're no longer a child." Many men felt Mars Hill's message of masculinity helped them become better men. Many women at Mars Hill agreed that the church's masculine focus was necessary and central to building up men and the church. Cindy, a woman in her late forties, told me, "Young men really respond to Mark" and that, there was "a real appeal . . . especially for young men, who haven't had anything to fight for."

There was a consensus from Mars Hill members that American Christian men were in trouble. One man I interviewed, John, said, "I'm a guy and I liked [Driscoll.] He's a man's man. He appeals to the testosterone in any guy, for sure. He called out the slackers and Seattleites," who weren't "stepping up to the plate in terms of their role . . . in dating or marriage." Driscoll's message appealed to John because he liked how Driscoll's "straight-up preaching style" called men out. John and his wife eventually left Mars Hill because the church didn't sanction women's leadership, but he agreed with the idea that men were not living up to their roles saying, "In Seattle, maybe everywhere, there's a need for men to step up. They're not getting married to women, they're fathering kids, and they're not doing anything. So [Driscoll's] telling them what they need to do."

Many appreciated Driscoll's focus on getting young men into the churches. Bill assured me that, "Most churches miss the boat on men. Men are just sitting on the sidelines and the churches are run by women." Attracting men to church was seen as the cornerstone of reviving Christianity; as Driscoll stated, "If you don't get the men, you get nothing."[82] Driscoll championed a hypermasculinity, but his mocking of men, coupled with his assumptions that men were failing illustrates a low view of men, where men could not attain true Christian masculinity until they encountered and adhered to his strict message.

Andrew seemed conflicted about the masculine focus at Mars Hill. Asked what he thought the mission of Mars Hill was, Andrew said, "I think the mission of the church is to train young men; teach young men the Bible." After a long pause, he continued: "No. That can't be right, can it?" Andrew seemed genuinely perplexed that Driscoll's focus on men could constitute the church's mission. He then explained that Driscoll had "a great persona and presence and resonates with aimless young men, and for whatever reason feels he has a heart for them. [Driscoll] draws them in, so God bless him for that burden and the work being done there." After another long pause, Andrew added, "I, however, am not a drifting young man."[83]

Driscoll's confrontational style and hypermasculine presentation were seen, at times, to overshadow the gospel message. Bill, a man in his early fifties, said Driscoll's masculine approach was sometimes "too much."

Describing Driscoll as "a former boxer and a manly man," Bill told me there was "a story that at one point [Driscoll] asked a bunch of guys to punch him in the face so that he could say he was taking hits for the gospel." According to Bill, Driscoll's hypermasculine actions and talk were seen as "rookie" mistakes. He believed that as Driscoll and the church aged, their message would mature. Yet he felt that Driscoll's hypermasculine rhetoric and style justified the goal, saying Driscoll appealed "to men and a very male environment." Sometimes however, Driscoll's rhetoric and style "overshadowed the church, especially combined with the church's stance on women in leadership," which then "overshadowed the message." Ultimately for Bill, however, it was important to teach men how to lead because most pastors "aren't leading the men and helping them do what they should be doing. So, that's a good thing Driscoll does." Another member of the church, Cammie, told me, "I don't always agree with [Driscoll's] methods, but I know his heart is there." Cammie believed that the church's mission "to train up men" was important, because "if a lot of men out there are apathetic and if they get on board, we'll have a stronger church. [Driscoll] wants to teach them to be leaders, bold, unapologetic about their faith and that will be a good core for the church."

While several former members reported leaving the church because of Driscoll's strict gender theology, few rejected it outright. I interviewed Tom, a former Mars Hill member who countered Driscoll's rhetoric from a theological perspective:

> Mars Hill is uniformly trying to turn boys into alpha male warriors, who were all buff and willing to physically fight for what is right . . . people are different and God puts different people—men—into places and they aren't warriors. David was a warrior, because God made him into one; but Boaz [and] Samuel, they weren't. So the way it was set up to be so biblical, it's not.

Tom critiqued Driscoll's "distortion" of Scripture, saying that Driscoll's making men the most important part of the Christian mission—and not just any man, but "a fighter, who is brash, bold and physical"—was simply not biblical. "Look at Rahab and what she did," he said. "She was a woman and a prostitute, and yet she's in Jesus' lineage." For Tom, Driscoll's teaching flew in the face of "all that is biblical" and showed "no sense of humility whatsoever" wanting to "change all the men in Seattle to be military men," who were "minions of the Most High Driscoll."

Women often blamed Driscoll's masculine-centric rhetoric for their leaving Mars Hill. These women were critical of the hypermasculine message. One woman in her early twenties, Kendra, explained to me how the church's exclusive messages about gender rankled her:

> The whole masculine Christianity is unique to Mars Hill, the masculine Jesus and theology. They spend a lot of time talking about what it means to be a man and they maintain the cultural standard using theology to justify why it's so awesome—and the best Christian sex ever! There was a riff that [Driscoll] always used, he could have put it to music, about a sweater-vest wearing, Cabriolet-driving guy, who was a euphemism for liberal Christianity and Mars Hill was definitely not that. They created a tension between the two and only Mars Hill was correct. Jesus had to be masculine and the gospel had been feminized. It's not just a male-friendly place, that is the only Christianity. Then Driscoll would say that any other way was wrong for allegorical reasons. Like you're going to discount someone's faith because they're wearing a sweater-vest? If you're not on board with Mark Driscoll, it sucks for you on judgment day because hell is hotter with a sweater-vest on.

Taking Talk Seriously

> Jesus has tender words for vulnerable societal outcasts who knew they were sinners and had harsh terrifying words for powerful proud arrogant authoritarian leaders. We were all enamored by what was flashy, loud, and eternal. That has caused deep harm.
>
> —Elena, MHWU

Many Mars Hill members reported that Driscoll's call to men was transforming. Aaron wrote on MHWU that he "truly became a Christian at Mars Hill" and Driscoll's focus on men, masculinity, and leadership allowed him to become aware of his "need for Jesus." Being at Mars Hill gave Aaron from MHWU the opportunity "to be a part of, and lead, several community groups" and "to serve on, and lead, several teams on Sundays." He became an intern, eventually joining the church staff, and was "blessed" by the many people he encountered there, helping him to grow as both a Christian and as a leader.

Other Mars Hill members, however, noted that there was a "dark flip side" to the church's masculine-focused teachings. Carson wrote on MHWU that, "Mars Hill was nothing short of amazing. I loved that they were aggressive and laid heavy burdens on men. It felt like the solution to all the problems I'd experienced . . . [but] the type of grace that was taught there had a dark flip side." The focus on men often meant putting young men on a fast track to leadership within the church. Putting men into the leadership by virtue of their being male was sometimes unpopular for members. On MHWU Aubrey wrote that Mars Hill was "too loose about who was given authority. For example, my now fiancé had only been a Christian for a couple months and they almost immediately put him in leadership." Bill told me that his community group of middle-aged couples was led by some "young kid" the Mars Hill leadership picked out, which the group didn't appreciate. Others, like Stella, noted on MHWU that friends were getting bad advice from the young men put into leadership, stating that, "many young men without wisdom or experience were being put in the position to counsel others and giving terrible advice, you just saw that this couldn't last forever."

One woman I interviewed was a business owner, who critiqued the work of the young men in leadership. Aimee, in her early forties, was irritated that the younger men in leadership "never" had "a backup plan." Aimee told me she offered her expertise to these young leaders for church events, but the men always turned her down, telling her they had it under control. Although she chafed under their leadership, Aimee said she reminded herself that the men were "all young guys" and that they were "the leaders of the church, and I have to be respectful, even if they're only twenty-three."

Another issue regarding young men in leadership at Mars Hill was their emulation of Driscoll. Several members and former members of Mars Hill observed the ways in which men at the church adopted Driscoll's brash style. John, a business executive, described a book Driscoll recommended to him extolling "true" Christian gender and family roles. At one point, John laughed out loud describing the book's content: "And another thing the book said, was that men should have facial hair. As if facial hair is some measure of how Christian you are! And I looked around and I saw a lot of men at the church with facial hair. That doesn't make sense." Yet, it did. The stakes at Mars Hill were high; a man's salvation depended on his ability to adhere to Driscoll's masculine ideal. A hypermasculine presentation signaled a man's acceptance of and adherence to Mars Hill's gender doctrine.

Cammie began attending Mars Hill in her early twenties, when she and her now-husband began dating. She explained that the couple's male friends at the church emulated Driscoll's speech and style. "All the guys say how much they love Driscoll and his teaching," she explained, "and even without noticing it, they start to lead the way he does, bluntly and harshly. They do this because the church teaches men to be the leaders and by emulating that theology." Emulating Driscoll included men using language that was "harsh." Elaborating on this, Cammie related a story about how a male friend responded to her female friend about a recent breakup. The man had what she called "a classic Mars Hill response," telling their friend she had not been "submissive enough" and needed "to repent of her sin." Cammie told me, "In most cases, outside of Mars Hill, people would just say they had a difference of opinion and broke up, but at Mars Hill everything is very spiritualized and often harsh." She said the way her "guy friends talk to each other is all about 'calling people out,' but that it's a harsh starting point. And it's an emulation of [Driscoll's] style." It was common for her to hear men say, "Well, I hope God convicts you on that and that you repent of your sin." Cammie and her husband saw a need for love and support as a step between hearing about someone's sin and "calling them out," but "that's how it is at Mars Hill," she said. "It's a strict and rigid approach."

One man I interviewed embodied the penchant for channeling Driscoll's rhetoric and style. In his mid-twenties, Austin aptly applied Driscoll's contradictory masculine rhetoric. He denied that a hypermasculine Christianity was the only to salvation but highlighted a Jesus who was "tough and wild," rather than "meek and mild." Austin explained the draw to, and success of, Mars Hill Church, saying, "There's a lot of wussiness in church and Mars Hill doesn't have a lot of that. It's not all about machismo or UFC stuff. There's a lot of that at Mars Hill, but . . . this is not Jesus who is meek and mild, but Jesus the victor who is tough and wild." I asked Austin what he meant by churches having too much "wussiness." Austin responded, saying:

Like the solution to trouble in a marriage is for the guy to get in touch with his sensitive side, or to be with kids . . . that just rubs me the wrong way. I'm not saying to do that is sin, but . . . when God asked [Jesus] to "take this cup" . . . he said, "Father, you're the man and I'll do your will even if it conflicts with mine." If we don't like it, too bad. If the church strays from that . . . it's about something else and something else is wrong and bad. . . . In last week's sermon there was a "come and see" element . . . but there was also "go and die." That's what the apostles were called to do [go and die, so] . . . you've got to get the men.

Austin mimicked Driscoll's style and language, almost reveling in the message that, "you've got to get the men." At one point in our interview, he mentioned that his wife was often irritated with the masculine focus at Mars Hill. Austin was able to agree that if the message went the other way—that "you had to get the women"—he would probably be irritated, too, "but that's the way it is."

Tough Love in Practice

This is rough and tough sort of a talk.

—Tom

Emulating a "harsh" style was consistent with reports that Driscoll used "tough love" to get his message across. Driscoll regularly told Mars Hill, "God uses hard words to produce soft people. And if all we ever get are soft words, we become hard people."[84] After the dissolution of Mars Hill, many men reflected on their adoption of Driscoll's language. On WLMH, Rowan wrote that Driscoll "set a high bar for men: a mix of 'hardline' complementarianism and a cultural caricature of himself. This was taught in a fairly graceless way with little regard for the changing power of the Holy Spirit working within us." Rowan added that he measured up to many aspects of the legalistic masculinity, but "realized soon enough that there were many aspects" he could not. Rowan said that he and "many others" at Mars Hill "mirrored much of what Mark taught. We'd get together to watch UFC fights and then have uncomfortable conversations afterwards as we realized none of us enjoyed it." The result of this was taking "brothers to task when we saw them not looking like the cultural version of 'men' Mark pressed us to look like. I wish I could say this was at least done in a generally respectful manner, but sometimes it wasn't."

It wasn't enough for men at Mars Hill to affirm the standards of masculinity. They had to signal to others that they adhered to the hypermasculine theology and that they held each other accountable to it. John described what he perceived to be Driscoll's rebuke of men not emulating his example:

One time I met up with [Driscoll] before a service and I was wearing a cardigan. And later that night in the sermon—I'm sure it was unconscious—but he started to say we're not a bunch of cardigan-wearing men. . . . He was like, "I wear all black" . . . and I thought, "He's insecure." That's not good in a leader. Here I was wearing the cardigan, but I didn't care, because I'm not insecure. It was at that point that he said I was arrogant and my wife shouldn't be working, so we had to decide if we should stay or leave. We decided to leave.

While many embraced Driscoll's rhetoric and style, there were tensions. Some described Driscoll's style as "violent" or "abusive." Church members disagreed on how to interpret Driscoll's rhetoric and expectations. Writing on WLMH, Matthew commented that in emulating Driscoll's style he had interpreted "talking to guys 'like a man' " as if "yelling at them was a biblically faithful way to call guys to repentance." On the same forum, Vincent wrote that he wanted to "apologize to people who see Jesus as a warrior with a whip or a judgmental dictator because of the example we set." Yet many expressed their approval of Driscoll's style to "call men out." On MHWU, Naomi described a sermon where "Mark screamed half the service, calling on men to step up and take responsibility and cursing at abusers and fornicators." Coming "from a long series of churches with mostly female leadership, because men were simply disinterested," Naomi said, Driscoll's preaching "was actually refreshing." Naomi "appreciated the fact that men were not allowed to slide under the radar" at Mars Hill, and that they were "called upon to step up and be leaders."

Others forgave Driscoll's tone and harsh demeanor because they believed him to be correct in his overall message. Andrew, in his mid-fifties, chose Mars Hill because of the focus on young men and masculinity. He struggled, however, with how Driscoll conveyed the message:

One Sunday Mark Driscoll warned that the next week he was going to "beat up" the men. And he did. He shouted at them. He was talking about men who batter their wives—yes, it's horrific—but shouting at the whole congregation as if it's a congregation of wife batterers is a little odd. So, what's he saying to me that I can learn from? I'm a husband, so I can see something that I can learn. But his tone was so harsh and that happens a lot. So, you had to gut it out and think, "I don't like the way he said it, but it was right in what he said."

Andrew concluded that Driscoll says, " 'Hard words make soft hearts and soft words make hard hearts.' So, he speaks hard words for the good of the people." On MHWU, Ava stated, "I probably ended up walking out on Mark about five times because of how he approached a few topics including mental illness, sexuality, and what it means to be a man. I found him to be insensitive and verbally abusive at times." Tom characterized Driscoll's harsh style as one of "tough love," saying Driscoll's rhetoric made clear you "can't love everyone. If you have to hurt someone to love them, then that's okay."

One woman commented on Driscoll's tendency to invoke violence in speech and behavior to appropriate hypermasculinity at Mars Hill. Referring to some of the church's earliest men's ministries, Kelsey talked about how Driscoll started a "fight club," based on the movie of the same name. She said, "If you look at the movie, they fight themselves to death. For Brad Pitt's character, he's playing out his masculinity through this brutal fighting. There are a lot of blogs out there that bring this up, asking shouldn't we be concerned if a pastor is using this brutal movie as a metaphor for his ministry?"

Many members of Mars Hill appreciated Driscoll's masculine focus. Even many who left the church were attracted to Driscoll's ability to speak forthrightly about the "weaknesses" that the culture and other churches had when addressing men. As Chandler wrote on MHWU, "[Driscoll's] teaching gave me a framework from which to understand the world (the framework given to me growing up did not work in 'the real world'), although I'd later find that framework to be flawed and fall apart. . . . It also served as an early way to develop my leadership skills."

The End of Men

> While I was copying what I saw exercised in the pulpit and repeating a process of shaming that various leaders did to me, that doesn't excuse my own sin in perpetuating it.
>
> —Rowan, WLMH

After Mars Hill closed, scores of people took the opportunity to denounce Driscoll's style and the church's culture. Men related their stories of how emulating Driscoll hurt them, other men, and the women in their lives. Rowan wrote extensively on WLMH about the damage inflicted on him and other men who emulated Driscoll's hypermasculinity. Rowan described how he "sought forgiveness" from the many men he had "shamed," by yelling at them or intimidating them for "failing to 'stand up as men' and not 'having their shit together.' " Rowan reported that he "copied" the behavior he saw "from the pulpit," which meant verbally abusing other men and insisting "they 'get their shit together' and 'just stop sinning.' " "Sometimes," Rowan wrote, his verbal abuse wasn't "even for something sinful, but something that just didn't fit Mark's cultural idea of a 'manly man.' "

Not adopting hypermasculinity had consequences for men because Driscoll's gender order was tied to salvation. Once the church collapsed and men reflected on their experiences, they saw Driscoll's equating his hypermasculinity as the only way to be God's men. Rowan wrote that the "things that stuck" with him were "the teachings that even as a Christian, God will abandon" men who "do not hold up" a "high standard, that God will cease to listen to our prayer." The idea of "God abandoning His people sunk into" Rowan's thinking and festered "for years."

The pressure to maintain the façade of fulfilling the masculine standard meant that many men had traits that countered the standard. Rowan noted, "I knew I did not measure up to Mark's standards and I quickly learned to hide my own sin from fellow Christians at [Mars Hill Church]." Carson stated on MHWU that he followed the program by "fundamentally changing" his "professional life due to the mentorship I received at Mars Hill." Yet when he couldn't "pull it all off" and sought counsel outside of Mars Hill, he "was made to feel implicitly like a failure and explicitly like a threat because I talked to someone outside Mars Hill." Owen wrote on MHWU that he'd "always felt like I don't fit in or measure up, so prolonged time at Mars Hill has left me with a very low view of myself. If everything Mark said about what it means to be a good Christian man is true, I'm a failure. Single, not tough, longtime struggler with addictions."

The dissolution of Mars Hill also allowed former members to reevaluate their attitudes toward homosexuality. As a nondenominational evangelical church, Mars Hill's antihomosexual stance was not surprising; most members of Mars Hill considered an antihomosexual stance a Christian directive. Aimee told me that, "Going to Mars Hill gave me the courage to say that I don't believe in things like homosexuality. It's a sin. Now I have the courage to stand up for those things." Theo, a man in his mid-twenties, appreciated that Mars Hill didn't give in to the culture on issues like homosexuality, saying Driscoll would "just tell you [that] you need Jesus because [if you're flaunting your homosexual lifestyle] you're in sin." Theo liked that

Driscoll wasn't "afraid to call it out, like other churches who just accept you and say it's okay." Some members who left Mars Hill reclaimed their identities as gay Christians. Colton, for example, explained on MHWU, "At this point, I am a Christian, and I'm gay . . . and I no longer consider those things to be mutually exclusive. This took a lot of studying and time (and prayer) . . . but my mental health has improved greatly and I'm sad about all the years I spent trying to fit someone else's mold at Mars Hill." Tom told me that Driscoll's antihomosexuality stance was the "final straw" for him. He said that Driscoll's approach was that people who were gay were going to die and go to hell unless they converted and repented. Since his brother was gay and Christian, Tom didn't buy Driscoll's argument. Another man, Logan, wrote on MHWU, "I no longer see things black and white. I have developed more compassion for others. I no longer believe that it's wrong to be gay."

While many reproached Driscoll, the Mars Hill leadership, and the church culture in general for perpetuating a false and damaging version of Jesus and manhood, this perspective was far from universal. Grayson, a man who attended Mars Hill until the church closed, wrote on MHWU that the hype over Driscoll was misplaced: "I started going to Mark's house . . . for a men's Bible study. His uber-macho/hyperbolic public persona practically disappeared. He revealed a man that was Christ-filled, caring and [a] compassionate man." Driscoll's focus on masculinity was not only resonant with men, but also with women. Kirsten, a woman in her mid-thirties, explained why Driscoll's focus on men was so important:

> I think Mark has always talked about . . . his desire to preach to young men, and to preach the gospel to them—one of the least likely people to show up at church and to hear the gospel. . . . I know that [at] our church . . . one of the biggest demographics . . . are young guys in the city of Seattle, which is a miracle. . . . My personal opinion is maybe that is why Jesus chose Mark, because he speaks in a way that attracts, that speaks to them in a very real way that they can understand. I feel the impact of that in our church and community. I feel like . . . when you reach the young men . . . that . . . impacts the families, and the wives, and the girlfriends, and the children of all those people in an enormous way.

As Kirsten describes, Mark Driscoll's hypermasculine theology impacted the Mars Hill community—men, women, and children.

Men Don't Have a Feminine Side

Men don't have a feminine side. They're men. Dogs don't have a cat side.[85]

Manhood and masculinity are not constants; they fluctuate over historical contexts and within the life-course of the individual. Even within the same culture, at the same historical moment, masculinity varies depending on race, class, age, sexuality, and region of the country.[86] As a social institution, American Christianity is not exempt from experiencing the reverberations of social change. When economic and social conditions changed in the 1960s and 1970s, power began to shift. The perceived loss of "traditional" masculinity produced a push toward a more masculine Christianity, embodied in Driscoll and his rhetoric.

Just as proponents of hegemonic masculinity fear the loss of male status in a changing economy, so did Driscoll fear a loss of male status in the church. Driscoll's hypermasculine men were held up as the example for the church, modeled on a hypermasculine Paul and Jesus. As with hegemonic masculinity, the intended effect of Driscoll's masculinity discourse was to put power, privilege, and control squarely into the hands of white, heterosexual Protestant men. Consistent with hegemonic and hypermasculinity is the capacity to exert control and/or to resist being controlled or dominated by others.[87] In claiming privilege, eliciting deference, and resisting exploitation, masculinity and manhood acts reproduce an unequal gender order within categories of men.[88] This unequal order for men, however, still allows them— by virtue of their biology—to be "the glory of God" in Driscoll's gender theology. For gay men, and women in general, there is no place of power in the church. While gay men are excluded from Driscoll's Christianity altogether, women have a clear role, complementing their husbands in the home. What are the keys to being "true" women at Mars Hill Church? How did Driscoll set women, their roles, and their characteristics apart from a male-centered Christianity? While his focus was on men, Driscoll's complementarian theology also relied on women following a clear script.

3

Real Women

Wives, Mothers, and Lovers

While the thrust of Driscoll's focus at Mars Hill Church was men and masculinity, women and femininity had their part to play in a hypermasculine, complementarian theology. Driscoll's gender-essentialist rhetoric rendered men's and women's differential traits and roles as biological (ascribed), but his rhetoric made masculinity and femininity something men and women had to achieve—men (re)learned Christian masculinity, as women (re) learned Christian femininity. In Driscoll's theology women had three primary roles: wives, mothers, and lovers. These feminine roles were attributed to the book of Genesis, where God separated the sexes, resulting in equal, but differential, spheres for men and women: "God creates the male and female and that makes them equal," Driscoll says, but women don't have to be "skilled in hand-to-hand combat" like men to be equal, likewise, men don't "need to give birth" to be equal to women. Though created equally in God's image, men and woman have "different domains."[1]

Recalling a white, middle-class 1950s breadwinner/homemaker gender ideal, Driscoll's theology assigned women to the home (homemakers) and men to the marketplace (breadwinners). Driscoll extolled these separate domains as God's design and as a place where men and women would find complete fulfillment. Men and women keeping, or returning, to their separate domains purportedly restored the institutions of family, the Christian church, and society. One of Driscoll's perpetual complaints about women was their conformity to the secular culture's feminist ideology. Driscoll asserted that women not attending to their homeward domain created a culture of chaos and decay. Driscoll often cited a New Testament passage from the book of Titus (2:4–5) as an imperative for women to be in the home.[2]

In Driscoll's interpretation of biblical texts, God created women as helpers to their husbands, making marriage the default position for women. Young women lived under the authority of their fathers until marriage, when they transitioned to being under the authority of their husbands. As wives, women

Making Christianity Manly Again. Jennifer McKinney, Oxford University Press. © Oxford University Press 2023.
DOI: 10.1093/oso/9780197655795.003.0004

become lovers, which leads to their becoming mothers, glorifying God by fulfilling their three callings—each of which happens in the home. The expectations for Christian women left no space for single women, nor did it leave space for women who worked outside of the home. In fact, women working outside the home (or desiring to work outside of the home) was evidence that they had been seduced by the feminist lies of the wider culture. In Driscoll's sermons, consistent with the broader conservative Protestant culture, feminism's influence on women in the church was a core concern for each aspect of biblical womanhood.

Conformed to the Patterns of This World

In Genesis 3 Satan comes and he engages Eve, not Adam.[3]

Driscoll's teaching on women's roles and their homeward domain relied on defining the wider culture as selling destructive lies to women, privileging the marketplace at the expense of the home. In his sermons Driscoll emphasized that men's and women's God-ordained differences were "much more than mere cultural conditioning."[4] Like other conservative Protestants, Driscoll blamed the feminist movement for undermining God's gender design, convincing women (and some men) that equality meant women working outside the home and men sharing household tasks. For Driscoll, these ideals perverted Gods' design because men did not "naturally gravitate" toward the home, nor did women "naturally gravitate" toward the marketplace.[5]

Driscoll indicted Betty Friedan (as well as Eve) for women's proclivity to be deceived. Not only did Friedan's *The Feminine Mystique* call the home a prison to which women were "shackled," Driscoll complained, it also told women that divorce would liberate them to leave their marriages, get out of their homes, and go to work.[6] Women adopting feminist values missed the "biblical value" of their homeward orientation, putting their self-fulfillment and autonomy above the needs of their husbands and children.[7] Driscoll lamented the loss of the "idyllic" 1950s world to the "anarchy and death" of the current culture, where women undermined the authority of their husbands.[8]

Driscoll also countered arguments that women's participation in the marketplace helped provide families with a necessary second income or built a stronger economy. These talking points simply reflected feminist propaganda, leading women to covet men's domain to prove their worth outside of the home and church. Addressing the women of Mars Hill, Driscoll said, "I'll tell you this, Ladies, you have nothing to prove. God made you in his image and likeness" because "identity comes in God creating you and Christ redeeming you."[9] Driscoll challenged the women at his church to see the ways in which they had been conformed to the feminist culture, knowingly or otherwise. In a sermon from the Old Testament book of Proverbs, Driscoll asked women to "fast" from television, radio, women's magazines, romance novels, and "false sermons" from the culture.[10] He then challenged them to read their Bibles to see that the wider culture was filled with "loud," "defiant," and "undisciplined" women.[11] Driscoll expected that women would realize the false gospel of gender equality was leading them to stray from God's designated domain. Believing feminist propaganda illustrated that like their mother Eve, women were easily deceived.

All about Eve

Eve meant well. She didn't mean to ruin the world.[12]

When Driscoll described women as coveting men's domain, he blamed Eve's original sin and a feminist culture for teaching women to be "the same" as men.[13] Driscoll interpreted Eve's encounter with the serpent in the book of Genesis as Eve choosing independence over obedience. Eve's choice for independence resulted in separation from God and her husband, Adam, and set all of womankind on the sinful path of seeking autonomy, rather than submitting to their husbands' authority. In Driscoll's version of the story, the serpent told Eve that if she were independent and autonomous, she would "be free," and then, like God, Eve could "make her own decisions" and determine for herself how the world should run.[14] These choices were not only Eve's "sins against the Lord," but also sins against her husband, leading to a "destructive independence."[15]

Eve's sin in the garden implicated all generations of women, tempting them to choose autonomy over submission. Yet Driscoll also charged Adam with sin in the garden—ironically making Adam and Eve equal in their iniquity. Eve's sin of commission was abetted by Adam's sin of omission. Adam, Driscoll told his congregation, sinned when he passively stood by, "hands in his pockets" and did nothing to stop Eve.[16] The original sins of Eve and Adam led to curses being placed on both women and men.[17] For women, the curse was "related to her homeward orientation," where women experience "great pain" in childbirth and a desire to "rule over" their husbands.[18] For Driscoll, Eve's sin and the curse on women is the root from which gender wars, chaos, and conflict in home, church, and society arise. Thus, it was Eve who ruined the world. "Some women sin obviously," other women sin "with good intentions," Driscoll said.[19] Even with good intentions, women cause "conflict and difficulty" in their marriages, putting them in the "same position as Eve."[20] Independence and autonomy make women not trust their husbands and think, "I'm going to just lead, make my own decisions, be a total feminist . . . get a Women's Studies degree . . . get a job and forget him."[21] This sinful attitude hurts women and hurts their marriages.

With a twist on the infamous Karl Marx adage that religion is the opiate of the masses, Driscoll argued that feminist culture was an opiate to women. Feminism, in effect, created false consciousness. In the sermon "Women and Femininity," Driscoll noted that women were prone to accept "deceptive" teachings and "false instruction." If women would attend to Scriptures applied "specifically to the ladies," they would see their "great propensity" toward conforming to "the pattern of this world," Driscoll said. To redeem themselves and be reconciled to their rightful domain, women needed to accept their secondary place in the order of creation and ask God, "Where have I been deceived, like Eve?"[22] The first step in this process of reconciliation was in recognizing that women were made from, and for, men.

Woman Was Made for Man

So God creates the woman, Genesis 2, to be his helper.[23]

Complementarian theology derives from text in Genesis 2, where God says, "It is not good that the man should be alone; I will make him a helper as his partner" (NRSV). After God creates the animals in the fields and the birds of the air, none are found suitable to partner the man. So, God causes "a deep sleep to fall upon the man" (NRSV), takes one of the man's ribs, and from that rib makes woman.[24] This second account of the creation story in the Bible casts woman as the helper and partner of man. Therefore, complementarians determine that hierarchy is embedded in gender relationships to extrapolate that woman, being made helper to man, comes under the authority of men. Complementarians like Driscoll relegate women to their father's authority and then to their husband's. Explaining these relationships in a sermon, Driscoll uses an example from the Old Testament book of Deuteronomy. Paraphrasing the text, Driscoll states that if a young woman commits adultery, she would be put to death at "the steps of her father's home" because "that body" (her body) was "under the jurisdiction of her father."[25] Shifting to familial authority after women marry, Driscoll asked the women of Mars Hill, "When you get married, Ladies, who does your body belong to?" "To your husband," Driscoll replied, "and his body belongs to you."[26] While Driscoll notes that wives and husbands are equally responsible to give their bodies to each other in marriage, based on text from 1 Corinthians 7, his emphasis is on women's submitting—bodily—to husbands, which is cause for men's enjoyment.[27] Apart from giving of their bodies sexually, as lovers, Driscoll's expectations of women's submission revolved around their being respectful.

Respect is a key component of women's submission. In "Women and Wives," Driscoll encouraged women to be respectful with gentle and submissive spirits, which diminished the desire for women to live "in a man's world." Living in a man's world only incited husbands into competition. Driscoll warned women that acting like men (e.g., working outside of the home) would cause husbands to treat wives like men, crushing them. Women needed to cultivate a fear of the Lord to make them good wives, mothers, and lovers because, "More than anything, Ladies, that's what a man loves." If a husband knows his wife fears the Lord, he knows "she'll be a good lover," mother, and wife. How do women learn to fear the Lord? By learning "in quietness and full submission."[28]

Silence and Submission

> So, when you think of submission, sometimes all you think of is all
> the husband's making his wife do terrible things.[29]

Women in conservative religions often find submission to be a place of power, rather than subordination.[30] Sociologists Sally K. Gallagher and Christian Smith report that conservative Protestant women benefited from gender hierarchies proscribing men as economically and spiritually responsible for wives and families. Gallagher and Smith found "male headship provides both emotional and material benefits to women," who can hold men to a higher standard, giving them a sense of security and stability.[31] The women in Gallagher and Smith's research were aware that adopting strict gender roles made them economically vulnerable, yet were relieved, in some cases, to have someone else ultimately in control.

While many conservative Christians proclaim a "headship/submission" ideology, they are much more egalitarian in practice.[32] For Driscoll's theology, however, women's submission was often equated to silence, making men and women decidedly unequal in both theory and practice. Even though Driscoll claimed he did not equate submission with silence, he repeatedly emphasized that women should "speak in appropriate tones, at appropriate times, in appropriate ways."[33] While this definition of submission permitted women to speak, there were significant constraints on when, and how, they could speak. For Driscoll, women should be strong enough to "bless" not "curse," "restrain" rather than "unleash," "control themselves when they could be moody," "withhold when they could gossip," and "speak temperately when they could be loud."[34] Using his wife, Grace, as an example, Driscoll said, "My wife has never once raised her voice to me. She has never spoken ill of me," because the "safest place she is, is with me. Because there is no one that cares for her like I do."[35] By keeping to their homeward domain in submission and silence, women protected themselves and their families.

Driscoll reinforced an ideal of women's silence through a number of anecdotes. In a *Christians Gone Wild* sermon, "One Body, Many Parts," Driscoll described visiting a small congregation where a woman provided music during the service: "This gal started singing and I just about died," he said. "I mean I've been in car wrecks. I played football. I was a catcher in baseball. I have never sustained an injury like this. This was the most deep, penetrating, painful, excruciating injury I've ever sustained—just listening to this woman." Driscoll elaborated on the woman's "incredibly horrendous" singing explaining, "I can't sing at all, okay? I sound like I got captured by Al-Qaeda when I try to sing. But I could have done a duet with this chick and we would have been just fine." Driscoll said that when the service ended, he approached the church's pastor asking, "What's up with the special music gal?" When the pastor said that the woman "really loves the Lord," Driscoll replied, "You can shut up and love Jesus . . . and she should. She shouldn't even talk." Even for women who "really love the Lord," silence, especially in church, was their best course of action.[36]

Not being silent could be interpreted as not being submissive. In another *Christians Gone Wild* sermon, "Under Authority Like Jesus," Driscoll compared the first-century city Corinth to Seattle, saying citizens of both cities had forgotten that God made two sexes, male and female, resulting in "gender confusion" where women were "all feminists" and "dudes" were "all effeminate." Rejecting God's gender hierarchy, feminists usurped men's authority, making them akin to strippers, prostitutes, or lesbians—"disrespectful, disgraceful, and shameful."[37] Driscoll used an analogy to describe these women, comparing them to "a gal in a short skirt and a belly-showing shirt" wearing a "push-up bra" and "clear heels," who takes off her wedding ring and steps onto the stage during a worship service to ask, "Hey, can I lecture?" Driscoll's response to the hypothetical woman was swift: "No. No. You can't. You can sit down and take notes, but you can't say anything." When the woman replies, "Well I want to lead." Driscoll says, "You're going to Hell. We don't want you to lead anybody. . . . You're going to get up there, put a big stainless-steel pole on the middle of the stage and everybody'll think they came to the wrong place."[38] This analogy equated women speaking to being shameful and reinforced women's need to speak in the prescribed appropriate ways. Driscoll reminded the women at Mars Hill to "fear the Lord" and understand their place under the authority of men.[39] This headship/submission gender relationship reflected God's design in appointing men to care for women. When women were respectable by submitting to God and their husbands, they realized their value and their role as homebuilders.

Homebuilding

When I say "homebuilding," just use the word "ministry." It's a synonym in the Scripture.[40]

Driscoll's complementarian theology evoked a nostalgic era of family, where women understood the honor of being homemakers. Citing a 1968 Gallup Poll, Driscoll claimed American women once understood their God-given homeward orientation "to have four children, be married, and stay home with their kids."[41] Embracing their ordained homeward domain did not mean women were "chained" to a sink doing "dishes for the next fifty years."[42] To the contrary, embracing their homeward domain was women's full-time ministry. Being in the home allowed families to thrive. Driscoll emphasized that women's domain was the home, not the workplace.

Antifeminist evangelicals blame working women for a host of society's ills. Driscoll was no different, lambasting working women for causing high divorce rates, children growing up without fathers, and women's and children's high poverty rates. Driscoll refuted "myths" of feminism, telling his congregation that working women did not strengthen the economy, help families economically, or create better workplaces. Driscoll argued that unless a woman made "over $60,000 a year" she was "netting zero" due to the costs of childcare.[43] Driscoll claimed that women trying to "reinvent the workplace" had instead "burdened the economy," causing juvenile delinquency, crime, and children being in therapy or on medication—a "complete social collapse"—because women were not fulfilling their roles by looking after their homes.[44]

After listing the numerous ways working women were hurting families and society, Driscoll asked his audience a series of rhetorical questions: "Is it a sin for a woman to have skill?" "Is it a sin for a woman to know how to make money?" "Is it a sin for a woman to get educated?"[45] While the answer to each of these questions was "no," none of the questions directly dealt with whether it was a sin for women to work outside of the home. Yet, the context and tone of Driscoll's sermon communicated, minimally, that working outside the home was a risk for women. Driscoll commented that "a lot" of the "ladies" were told not to marry until they'd established their careers, because their husbands would "probably" leave them, which meant thinking, "You need to be able to take care of yourself," which fueled divorce.[46] Working women made men think, "You don't need me? Fine, I'm out," because if men don't feel women need them, "they will leave."[47]

It may not have been a sin for women to have a skill, know how to make money, or get educated, but the subtext was clear: women choosing to work risked the very things ushering them into God's kingdom—their marriages and children. Driscoll stated that women rejecting their homeward orientation and domain distorted the marketplace, creating a need for maternity leave, on-site childcare, and sexual harassment laws, which meant women had created a workplace where they were "incapable of operating in a competitive environment" with men.[48] Yet this narrative is at odds with the historic record.

Throughout history, most men and women worked together at home, producing what could not be purchased.[49] Industrialization changed the nature of family and work, separating them into distinct spheres.[50] Driscoll's theology relied on the cultural ideal of a breadwinner/homemaker ideology, which even at its height was unattainable for most American families.[51] Driscoll's theology evoked a mid-twentieth-century white, middle-class cultural family ideal as the only biblical ideal, blaming feminism for women rejecting their homeward orientation. Specifically, Driscoll blamed older women for not properly mentoring younger women on their homeward responsibilities, saying, "There are not a lot of godly older women," because previous generations of women "believed a number of lies," resulting in them not being "very godly."[52] Even for women who had begun their married lives as homebuilders, once their children had been raised, Driscoll opined, many "ran off" to the marketplace: "I'm not saying that it is sinful for a woman to do that, but" younger women could use "some practical discipleship from older women."[53] Older women disciplining younger women could blunt the influence of feminism, and help those women focus on their homeward domain and become wives of noble character.

Women as Wives: The Proverbs 31 Woman

In Proverbs, wisdom is a lady. She's like a beautiful, sweet, glorious wife.[54]

For many evangelicals the phrase "Proverbs 31 woman" calls to mind the epitome of biblical womanhood.[55] The book of Proverbs describes the archetype of woman, saying, "A wife of noble character, who can find? She is worth far more than rubies" (NIV).[56] As the definitive model for the Christian wife, Mars Hill women were expected to emulate the Proverbs 31 woman, described as a "crown" and "glory" to her husband, "strong," "wise," "helpful," and "in every way a blessing."[57] Like the woman in Proverbs, Mars Hill women needed to be "priceless." The ubiquity of the Proverbs 31 women in evangelical ideology is difficult to overstate. Yet as Driscoll extolled women who exemplified the Proverbs 31 woman, he also stated these kinds of women, like godly older women, were hard to find. What defines Driscoll's version of a Proverbs 31 wife?

A Wife of Noble Character

This is the woman of women. This is this awesome great gal.[58]

The noble/excellent/capable wife of Proverbs 31 (depending on the English Bible translation) is notable for the honor she brings her husband. The Bible says that her husband "lacks nothing of value," and she "brings him good, not harm all the days of her life" (NIV). Driscoll described the Proverbs 31 woman as "skilled and competent" in her homeward domain, making her a "treasure" to her family.[59] A Proverbs 31 woman "can do it all" with "pleasant words."[60] Drawing from the example of the Proverbs 31 woman, Driscoll told the women of Mars Hill, "Ladies, you want to be righteous? The foundation of your home has to be righteousness, holiness, love for God, and obedience."[61] One more quality that made the Proverbs 31 woman enviable and an exemplar of biblical womanhood: her silence. "Let me ask you this," Driscoll said, "does this woman say a word? She doesn't say a word," rather, "her whole life preaches. She is a sermon."[62] The epitome of biblical womanhood, for Driscoll, was a homebuilder who preached without saying a word. The Proverbs 31 woman had "wisdom, instruction, and knowledge."[63] Women not embodying these qualities were a disgrace.

Disgraceful Wives

[A] disgraceful wife is like decay.[64]

Not all women were Proverbs 31 wives; some were like a disease. Driscoll told his audience it was easy to spot men without Proverbs 31 wives because these men looked like they had an "incurable disease," adding, "and sitting next to him is that disease. She's wearing a ring."[65] Driscoll said the book of Proverbs stated, "many women" are like that (a disease), and those women "bring death."[66] These "loud, quarrelsome, ill-tempered" women were "a death" and "a cancer."[67] These "screaming, yelling, threatening, plate-chucking" wives attacked their husbands through sheer volume.[68] Husbands despised these wives, because they put husbands in a no-win situation; if a husband yelled back at his wife "and beats her, then he is mean." If a husband "takes it," then "he is weak. He can't win." Driscoll told wives at Mars Hill, "You want to decay your husband? Yell at him. You want to do it extra quick? Do it in front of his friends."[69]

Two consequences for being a disgraceful wife were implied by Driscoll. First, by enticing her husband to attack her, verbally or physically, a disgraceful wife was picking a fight she could not win, getting her husband's "adrenaline rushing . . . angry and hot."[70] These "mouthy, difficult wives" declared war against their husbands, stoking conflict, undermining the authority of their husbands, and undermining their marriages.[71] If a woman did win an argument, she would "despise" her husband as "a weak coward."[72] Second, disgraceful wives "made husbands not want to come home."[73] These outcomes represented a cause-and-effect relationship. Driscoll warned the women of Mars Hill about choosing the path of disgrace, saying, "loud women dig their own graves" and then "scream all the way to their death."[74]

How to Undermine a Marriage

> Some women . . . are like a dripping faucet. They make you feel like a prisoner of war. They decay your bones and it's like a hurricane in your house that you can't get to settle down.[75]

For complementarians, women fulfill their ordained roles through marriage. While being single is not a sin, Driscoll's gender theology left little room for single women. As people under the authority of husbands, women policed themselves (and other wives) to make sure husbands were happy. This could be a significant amount of pressure for women. Driscoll saw men and women as innately different, where women were built for men, not vice versa. Women believing the cultural lie that men and women were "the same" undermined their marriages. Using his wife, Grace, as an example of biblical womanhood, Driscoll explained, "My wife helps me. It's gonna sound terrible [but] the way I help my wife is by leading our family. She is built to help me. She understands that."[76]

For Driscoll, wives needed to understand their place in the creation order—under the authority of husbands. Upending the order of authority put everything at risk, destabilizing women's identity as wives, a crucial identity. Like his riff for the Cabriolet-driving effeminate pastor, Driscoll developed a riff of negative characteristics describing women and wives from the book of Proverbs, repeating the riff within a variety of sermons over more than a decade. Driscoll addressed these negative examples of attention-seeking and manipulative wives, saying, "They speak and flatter" men to "manipulate" them, and nothing "disrespects, demeans, and incites a man" like these behaviors—but some wives just "love the attention."[77]

Disgraceful wives, especially women who were unfaithful or abandoned their husbands, drove husbands to act like "caged animals."[78] These husbands felt "trapped" and frantically tried to find reasons to "biblically divorce" their wives to "escape" their marriages.[79] Driscoll again invokes a cause-effect relationship, asking his church, "Does it justify any of the sin? No," but if women are "decaying" a husband's "bones," husbands are "going to look for a cure," which can sometimes mean getting "rid of that which is causing him ill."[80] The burden was on women to control themselves and to keep from "enticing" or "inciting" husbands to physical or verbal violence, to be crowns and not decay, in order to maintain their status as wives and mothers.

Women as Mothers: Saved through Childbearing

> Your wife will be like a fruitful vine within your house; your sons will be like olive shoots around your table.[81]

In the 2002 *Proverbs* sermon series, Driscoll reiterated God's plan for women to be mothers. By bearing children, women were blessed to follow in the steps of Mary, the mother of Jesus. As mothers, women's primary responsibility was in raising children "for the purposes of God's glory."[82] Driscoll painted a stark picture between God's plan for women as mothers and an imagined feminist secular culture, telling Mars Hill, that American society had created "birth control, abortion, daycare, foster care, whatever," to "avoid having children" or to "avoid the hard work of raising" children because society sees children "as the curse."[83]

Driscoll told the women at Mars Hill, "Biblically, you'd be hard pressed to not choose being a mom" and "you'd be hard pressed to justify anything that looks like the contemporary American family."[84] Again, Driscoll repudiated an imagined secular, contemporary American family, saying working mothers had relinquished their duty to raise children to professional daycares and nannies, effectively abandoning their ministry. This dereliction of duty negated God's design. Due to their "natural instincts" Driscoll didn't care if a woman had "more degrees than Fahrenheit," her place was at home parenting her children, not hiring professional childcare workers.[85] Driscoll told women it was "foolish," trying to work eight hours a day, with an hour commute to work each way, to spend "two quality hours" with their "kids every night" in order to "instruct them."[86] Working women "missed every opportunity . . . the day afforded"; they "missed all of those teachable moments."[87] Good mothers, Driscoll said, weren't "talking to the clown" (grabbing fast-food) to get dinner for their families after work.[88] Good mothers took their divine role of motherhood seriously, doing their work—ministry—at home.

Driscoll praised motherhood, but sometimes belittled mothers. Not unlike his denigrating of men (Nabals), Driscoll did not respect women, even when they chose full-time motherhood. Complaining that organizations like the National Organization for Women (NOW) publicly attacked the roles of wives and mothers, encouraging women to be independent from their husbands and children, Driscoll asked his audience, "When does mom get to go on CNN? Well, she doesn't. She's just mom. She doesn't know anything. She doesn't have a degree. She's not a PhD candidate. . . . She's just mom."[89] From Driscoll's perspective, women entered the workforce for recognition, via performance reviews, raises, and promotions. Christian women—Mars Hill women—needed to find their identities and worth in Christ, but also through their children. Good mothers had children who would not abandon them after their husbands died (as an aside, Driscoll added, "Am I saying you're gonna kill" your husbands? "Indirectly perhaps. But you will likely outlive them").[90] While Driscoll told women their identities were found in Christ, he also told them their children's identities were dependent on "the poor or good training" of their mothers.[91] "Righteous" mothers had good children, but "foolish, stupid, rebellious" mothers had children just like themselves.[92]

Mothers were also expected to practice "God-centered parenting," rather than "child-centered parenting."[93] The latter type of parenting was characterized by Driscoll as giving children whatever they wanted instead of what they needed, which was a "recipe for death."[94] Mothers believing their children's hearts were "basically good," would seek to "encourage" their children's self-esteem, resulting in "nation that looks like ours: people who are reprobate but think they're really pretty wonderful."[95] Instead of nurturing a child's self-esteem, mothers needed to discipline their children, because "If you don't discipline your children, you hate them."[96] Undisciplined children were the kind of children who were called to the principal's office, became sex offenders, or ended up in prison—a "complete disgrace."[97] Biblical womanhood was fraught with opportunities to become a disgrace. One ordained role for women, however, allowed them full freedom of expression: lovers.

Women as Lovers: You Should Do That Twice

She gets the last word in the book. She speaks first, last, and most.[98]

A vital part of a woman's homeward orientation was being a good lover. Once married, women could be sexually free with their husbands: "You should be enjoyable," Driscoll told wives.[99] Lamenting the "tragic" message taught by many Christian churches that sex was wrong or vile, Driscoll interpreted multiple Bible passages as mandating sexual liberation within marriage. Yet his teaching on wives' sexual freedom highlighted husbands' pleasure. Driscoll cited Proverbs 5:19 ("A loving doe, a graceful deer—may her breasts satisfy you always, may you ever be intoxicated with her love" [NIV]), and asked, "What does that assume, Ladies?" that husbands have "access to your breasts," because wives should be "free" with their bodies in marriage.[100]

Driscoll also referenced Proverbs 31:22 as an example of women's sexual freedom ("She makes coverings for her bed; she is clothed in fine linen and purple" [NIV]) asking the men at Mars Hill, "when your wife dresses nicely is that a ministry? Yes!"[101] Dressing well was part of a wife's ministry to her husband, allowing him to say, "What a cute wife I have! I like that!"[102] If wives objected, telling husbands, "I don't like being a sex object!"[103] Driscoll responded, "If that's your husband, you should be glad that you're a sex object. I have never heard a man say, 'My wife just wants me for my body.' That's his goal! It is an honor when a husband looks at his wife and finds her to be lovely."[104]

Driscoll was adamant about women sexually pleasing their husbands. "When you have a lovely wife, and a lovely home, and a lovely bed," Driscoll told husbands, "You have a lovely life."[105] Addressing the men in his congregation, Driscoll asked, "How many men think that a beautiful woman, with a beautiful table, with a piece of meat, and maybe a nice glass of wine or a nice beer is a ministry? Amen! That's a ministry."[106] In his colorful fashion, Driscoll equated having a beautiful wife to having "a hunk of some animal flesh" and "an import beer" (and "not a lite beer, 'cause we don't sin against God!").[107] While seeing women (wives) this way was described as "an honor," these sermon exchanges objectified women.

Objectifying Wives

I love your feet, I love your legs, wow, that's amazing, the petting zoo
is now open.[108]

As the Proverbs 31 woman served as the standard for homeward-oriented
wives and mothers, the Old Testament book Song of Solomon provided
Driscoll an exemplar for women as lovers.[109] In the Song of Solomon, two
lovers speak openly of their sexual desire for one another. Driscoll seemed
captivated by the woman narrator's sexual liberation, noting that she speaks
"first," "freely," and "frankly" about her sexual desire.[110] In 2008, Driscoll
preached *The Peasant Princess* sermon series on the Song of Solomon.
Throughout the series Driscoll faced significant criticism for his objectification of women, as well as his graphic sexual instruction targeted toward women. In response, Driscoll explained, "We're not talking about
objectifying women like pornography does. We're talking about husbands
being captivated by their wife. And she doesn't see this in any abusive
way."[111] At the same time, Driscoll's interpretation of the book sounded remarkably like an adolescent boy's gleeful encounter with his first Playboy
magazine.

In *The Peasant Princess* sermon "Dance of Mahanaim," Driscoll
paraphrased Song of Solomon 4:5, where the man says to the woman, "Your
two breasts are like two fawns, like twin fawns of the gazelle that browse
among the lillies" (NIV). Driscoll interpreted the verse as saying the woman
was "unclothed, dancing for her husband," when the man proclaims, " 'Oh,
your breasts are like small, furry woodland animals."[112] In other words,
Driscoll said, the man is saying the woman's breasts are "perky, they're
frolicking, they're fun, they're playful," and they're found in a petting zoo,
which means (for husbands), "the petting zoo is now open!"[113] Driscoll reinforced his masculine-centered interpretation by then exclaiming, "All
Scripture is God-breathed and profitable. And all the men said? Amen!"[114]

Two years before *The Peasant Princess* series, Driscoll preached a sermon,
"Good Sex, Bad Sex" in the *Christians Gone Wild* series. Like the later
Peasant Princess series, the "Good Sex, Bad Sex" sermon drew from Song of
Solomon and instructed women about the pleasures of sex and their respon-
sibility to be sexually free with their husbands. Departing from his concern

that wives be silent or speak appropriately, Driscoll extolled the woman in Song of Solomon for speaking freely about her sexual desires, saying, "This is the kind of talking we need to have." Wives should tell husbands, "Honey, this is what I want. This is what I like. This is what I need," and husbands would respond, "finally, a conversation I'm listening to," because husbands were praying to Jesus, asking, "make her a little freaky! Amen!" Driscoll's rhetoric communicated that too many wives were not open and free with sex, and their hesitation was not "biblical." He complained that too many women told their husbands, "Don't touch me," "No, that's my body." "Stop grabbing my butt," to which husbands could "biblically" respond, "That's not your butt, that's my butt."[115]

While Driscoll reminded his audience that men were responsible for sexually pleasing their wives, he spent significantly more time in the "Good Sex, Bad Sex" sermon addressing wives' sexual duty to husbands, reiterating that, "The wife's body does not belong to her alone, but to her . . . husband."[116] Practically, this meant if a husband wanted to undress his wife and have her put on her "pajamas on in front of him because he likes to see" her, then she should do that.[117] If a husband wanted to "bathe together, that's what you're doing, because" his wife's body was "his body, and he wants to see it, and he likes to touch it, and he likes to enjoy it."[118] Driscoll complained that some would describe his take on marital sex as "sexist"; his response, "No, that's sexy."[119]

Driscoll's teaching on wives' sexual service to husbands became one of the most controversial aspects of his theology. Responding to critics taking him to task for his stance on women not having authority over their own bodies, Driscoll made two concessions. First, he clarified that there were circumstances allowing a woman to say, "No," to her husband: "I'm not saying that there aren't extenuating circumstances sometimes that would cause the marriage to benefit from a break," however, "the typical pattern of a marriage is, 'I belong to you, you belong to me. I serve you, you serve me.'"[120] Second, Driscoll clarified that sex in marriage was not simply about wives satisfying husbands, but husbands also satisfying wives to make sure wives were "having good sex all the time."[121]

While Driscoll's rhetoric seemingly put wives on equal footing with husbands, the decisively gendered nature of his doctrine put men's sexual desires at the center of his teaching. Consistent with his other teachings, the consequences of not being sexually free were different for men and women. Though Driscoll indicated men could distort sexual desire by consuming pornography or through "un-godly" masturbation, his instruction focused on women. Wives who were not sexually free undermined their marriages, just as disgraceful wives did. Driscoll told women if they weren't sexually free, they were putting their husbands in a "very difficult circumstance," because if a husband initiates sex and his wife "continually rejects him," that "destroys him," and leaves him vulnerable to other women who were "happy to make up the difference."[122] Driscoll linked infidelity to wives not being sexually free, saying, "Why do most men go out and have sex with women they're not married to? Because those women will do things that their wives won't even talk about."[123] Wives denying husbands sex was not an option: "Ladies, do you think you have the right to deny your husband sexually? You don't."[124] In a familiar pattern, Driscoll told his audience that denying sex to husbands does not excuse infidelity, yet implies the opposite: "Does that excuse infidelity? No. Does that excuse adultery or lust? No. But is there a cause-and-effect relationship?" Yes, "most certainly."[125]

Even when he holistically applied 1 Corinthians 7:3–5 to husbands (wives and husbands equally serving each other's sexual needs), Driscoll's expectations were primarily on wives submitting to their husbands' sexual desires. For all his talk about liberating wives' sexually, husbands' desires were preeminent. What did wives and husbands fulfilling their "duty" mean, Driscoll asked, "It means what every dude in this room hopes it means."[126] Driscoll told men they could pull out a list of sex acts they wanted to try and if a wife said, " 'I don't do that,' " a husband could say, " 'I've got a verse. . . . We're biblical. We're a Bible believing family, especially when it counts, you know? And this counts,' so the wife says, 'Well, I don't do that.' Well, you should, twice!"[127]

Driscoll relied on a gender essentialist "boys will be boys" understanding of men's sexual needs and desires. In "Dance of Mahanaim," from the *Peasant Princess* series, Driscoll explained, "all men are visual, with the exception of dead men." For Driscoll, men could not help but notice beautiful women. The secular culture "assaults men with images of beautiful women," Driscoll said, with men deriving "physical pleasure from . . . observing a beautiful woman." The pleasure men receive is hardwired into them, "hormonally," and therefore, not "a sin" for men to notice beautiful women; "he can't help it." The sin comes when a man "lusts" after the beautiful woman with "sinful desires." Wives shouldn't judge husbands: "Don't judge your husband for being a dude," Driscoll said. Instead, women needed to be "visually generous" lovers to help their husbands: "Men see the world in terms of combat and sport," where allies and enemies engage. Men want to "crush" their enemies to win, so wives need to reassure husbands, "frequently," by telling them, "I'm on your team," and by being visually generous. What did visual generosity entail? When wives changed clothes, for example, they didn't "go in the other room and shut the door." When wives bathed, they didn't "go in the other room and lock the door."[128] Even though men were "naturally" visual, and women needed to understand their husbands' predisposition for noticing beautiful women, Driscoll also explained—possibly to mollify his critics—that God gives a man a "standard of beauty."

Standard of Beauty

A woman who loves . . . God, she's beautiful no matter what she looks like.[129]

Driscoll's teachings on sex objectified women. The idea of God's standard of beauty being a wife contradicted Driscoll's statements that men could not help noticing beautiful women. With masculinity at the center of Driscoll's theology, women's value was inherent to their relationships with men. Driscoll reminded his church that God made woman for man. What God didn't do, Driscoll said, was bring men "a line of women and then let the man choose his favorite."[130] Instead, God "brought one woman" and that woman "was a wife."[131] A man's wife was his "standard of beauty."[132]

While Driscoll's views were misogynistic at worst and paternalistic at best, gender relations were negotiated through men's needs. Driscoll told Mars Hill that men were given a standard of beauty by God, who didn't ask Adam, "Well, what do you like? Tall, short, white, black, Asian, young, old, long hair, short hair, skinny, formerly skinny?"[133] At the same time, Driscoll explained that men had "snapshots" of beautiful women housed in their memories and revisited like a "rolodex in the brain."[134] Thus, in practice there was a standard of beauty apart from men's wives. Wives could fight this "natural" process by being "visually generous" to husbands. Not being visually generous could result in a husband's infidelity.

Driscoll's advice for wives to be visually generous, combined with the messages they received from his pulpit about being beautiful ("when you have a lovely wife . . . you have a lovely life") provoked critique. In spite of Driscoll's conceptual "standard of beauty," his rhetoric underscored the need for women to "keep themselves up." In a 2008 *Vintage Jesus* sermon, Driscoll referenced the film *Talladega Nights: The Legend of Ricky Bobby*, saying, "If you went to see that film, [Ricky Bobby] really loves baby Jesus" and "repeatedly prays to baby Jesus" thanking him "for my smokin' hot wife."[135] Driscoll said, "That's become a recurring theme in our house. My wife, for example, came out the other day and said, 'How do I look in these jeans?' I said, 'Thank you Jesus for my smokin' hot wife.'"[136] While this anecdote elicited significant laughter from the audience, it illustrated the larger framework from which many women at Mars Hill felt pressure to conform to a conventional beauty standard.

Driscoll reinforced a standard of beauty, and his expectation that it was incumbent on wives to look attractive, when he told a story about how husbands had "jurisdiction" over wives. In his "Good Sex, Bad Sex" sermon, Driscoll told his congregation, "I have some jurisdiction over the appearance of my wife." Driscoll related that when they married, his wife, Grace, had long hair. After having a baby Grace had cut her hair short. Driscoll said, "She came home and she says, 'How do you like my hair?' 'What hair? It's all gone.' I was so sad." While some women can look nice with short hair, Driscoll said, he preferred Grace with long hair because her long hair "was just beautiful, lovely," and made her look "like a wife." Cutting off her hair made her "look like a nun," when he needed "a wife." Driscoll continued, saying, "My wife's beautiful. I love looking at her . . . I'm always looking at her. Yeah, and some of you say, 'Well, that's terrible.' Well, no . . . it's good. You know, the wife wants to please her husband, wants to share her body with her husband, wants to give herself to her husband, wants to be the object of desire for her husband."[137]

Driscoll's functional beauty standard was evident throughout his teaching, where he regularly invoked a cause-and-effect relationship when telling women the consequences of not following his interpretation of the Bible's expectations for them. This cause-and-effect relationship was referenced by Driscoll in his infamous blog post explaining Ted Haggard's drug use and solicitation of male prostitutes. In the post, Driscoll implicated Haggard's wife for his behavior, stating that wives who were not sexually available to their husbands, or who "let themselves go," may not be sinning, but "may not be helping [husbands] either."[138] When describing the disgraceful wives from the book of Proverbs, Driscoll warned, "Ladies, don't just think that because you marry a Christian man, he's just going to put up with it," reinforcing women's need to follow his formula for being wives who were crowns, mothers who were dedicated, and lovers who were sexually free and lovely.[139]

Husbands had a part to play in their wives' attractiveness. For husbands complaining their wives were "not very sexually alluring," Driscoll told them, "Love her until she becomes more lovely."[140] As the "glory" of a husband, wives (and their loveliness) reflected their husbands' work. If a wife had "places where she needs cultivation . . . that is the man's responsibility."[141] Husbands cultivating wives reaped "a good return," with wives who became "more lovely every day."[142] Driscoll may have placed the responsibility on men to cultivate their wives, but wives who were not lovely and respectable reflected husbands' poor cultivation. Women felt additional pressure because to appear unlovely was a visual cue condemning a husband's cultivation, which was disrespectful to their husbands and to God.

Walking the Talk: Women Speak

> I have begun to realize that God loves me even though I am a woman. And that he gave me a mind and a voice, and I should be able to use them as the Holy Spirit leads.
>
> —Eleanor, MHWU

Mark Driscoll's gender doctrine was central to Mars Hill Church. How women interpreted and internalized the church's gender doctrine varied; some felt freed, others felt trapped. Women at Mars Hill actively supported the church's gender doctrine, reporting that it freed them from an expectation to work outside of the home, allowing them to concentrate on being full-time wives and mothers. One woman I spoke with, Anna, said "I liked everything [Mars Hill was] subscribing to . . . it was freeing and it was exciting to hear that . . . I get to stay home with kids . . . it was exciting for me because I wanted all those things." On We Love Mars Hill (WLMH), Alice wrote that "hearing almost every Sunday that my sole purpose could be mother and wife gave me a sense of joy and relief at the same time. I could have everything I had always wanted, and it was all justified because they are noble callings." Yet over time, Alice also found something was missing: "Me! I forgot about me. In all the years I attended Mars Hill, slowly over time I became somebody completely different and not all for the better." Kirsten had the opposite reaction to the church's gender doctrine, telling me that quitting her job to be a full-time mother "was really hard for" her at first. Then she realized that caring for her son "the way he needed" her to care for him had taught her "a lot about trusting God" and "God's desires" for her, as a woman.

While Mars Hill had a poor reputation in Seattle for their gender doctrine and its impact on women, Bill told me it was not surprising so many women were drawn to the church because, "There are a lot of traditional women in Seattle." The "woman issue," he said, was "a minor issue." Mirroring Driscoll's rhetoric, Bill told me, "The real issue is not about women. It's about passive men who are just sitting around lost and confused." For women, however, the "woman issue" was central to their identities. Cammie told me that she had to question Mars Hill's teachings because, "For me, as a woman," the gender theology was "a primary issue, because it defines who I am as a human being, and what my role is in the church and as a wife."

Regardless of their career aspirations (or lack thereof), women at Mars Hill wanted to be good wives and mothers. Because the church's gender doctrine held that women, especially mothers, should not "covet" the man's domain by working outside the home, many women with careers felt they couldn't stay at the church. One professional woman, Faith, left the church when it wouldn't support her career. Reflecting on the church's theology for women and families, Faith told me it was "too easy." She said, "As a woman you don't have any responsibilities. You don't have to worry about your career. You know what to do. In some ways it is good practical advice." Ironically, after leaving Mars Hill and having her first child, Faith quit her professional job and became a full-time mother. Describing the "mom's group" at her new church, she said:

> My friends [in the group] are all totally over-educated and having a really hard time with the transition to motherhood. We sort of joke—but it is not really a joke—that instead of going to law school and medical school, we should have studied "home-ec." It would have given us the skills we need to do what we are doing. Instead, we are clueless, fumbling. We are used to being experts, now [we're] completely out of our element, running households poorly and raising children blindly. If we had studied "home-ec" and [stayed at] Mars Hill, we could feel like we knew what we were doing. It would be a lot more comfortable in a lot of ways.

As much as Faith believed Mars Hill gave women an easy "playbook" for being wives and mothers, some Mars Hill women struggled to live out the church's theology. In practice, even women who supported Mars Hill's gender theology found living out their "God-given" roles was difficult. Some women used Driscoll's rhetoric of being conformed to the feminist culture and attached to the "idols" of the marketplace to make sense of their struggle to follow his doctrine. For others, these issues seemed an almost insurmountable stumbling block to their ability to faithfully live into the gender doctrine.

A Desperate Housewife Comes Clean

> Every morning I woke up dreading the day and how I would fill the hours.
>
> —Darla

In 2007, Mars Hill launched the Reforming the Feminine blog. One of the first posts illustrated how women actively managed their interpretation and application of the church's gender doctrine.[143] In the post, "Darla" described being blessed by the birth of her first child, writing that the first month of being a mother was "wonderful," with "friends and well-wishers" providing meals and support.[144] When her maternity leave ended, Darla quit her job to be a full-time wife and mother. The reality of being at home, however, created significant dissonance for her. Darla writes that she had been waiting for the chance to "finally leave the workforce." Having listened "week after week" to the encouragement of her Mars Hill church family to serve her husband and love her children, she writes, "Yes, yes, I thought. That's what I want!" Darla "longed for" the "freedom, to do what God had truly designed" her to do. The teachings of Mars Hill resonated for her: "We are plowing a counterculture!" "It is a high honor to be a wife and mother!" Yet, Darla says she was "filled with resentment, bitterness, and discontentment." She felt "miserable" and "isolated." She missed her work friends, her commute, and the Starbucks drive-through.

As she transitioned into her new role as a stay-at-home mom, Darla's husband was offered a job at Mars Hill. Describing the job as an "amazing opportunity" and answer to prayer, Darla was also "seized with fear." How could she keep up the façade of being a "happy housewife" with the church watching? Darla was sure she'd "buckle under the pressure," with her church family recognizing how much she "loathed" being at home. Darla feared the repercussions for her husband, if people at the church found out—would they see it as her "husband's inability to shepherd his wife"? Darla rehearsed what she thought she knew in her head, "This is what I wanted, right? This was the calling that God had made me for. I was designed to be a mother to my child, a helper suitable to my husband." While she believed these things in her head, Darla didn't feel it in her heart, writing, "I was so disgusted with the ugly and horrendous condition of my heart that I couldn't tell anyone, not even my husband. It was a secret sin that I harbored within myself."

"Sick" of her sin, Darla "confessed" her feelings to her husband, who "was shocked and hurt." Mimicking Driscoll's rhetoric, Darla wrote, "It wasn't enough to be valued by God and to have my identity in Christ. I wanted the world to value me. I didn't want to be appreciated for scrubbing toilets and changing diapers. I wanted to be validated by a paycheck and the empty praise from others 'in my field.' " Darla resented being relegated to the home, which "was hard" on her marriage.

At her husband's request, Darla submitted her story to the Mars Hill blog, but was concerned about the church's reaction: "Would they be in-dignant? Separate themselves from me? Did anyone else struggle with sin the way I did? Certainly, no one I knew. All the ladies I had encountered had joyfully submitted themselves to God's will in their lives." Darla feared the consequences of her confession, especially the consequences for her husband's job at the church. Surely her husband would lose his job when people realized "what a wretched wife" she was. This spiraled into Darla thinking her family would have to find a new church, sell their house, and her husband having to work "60-hour weeks stocking shoes at Nordstrom while I tidied our immaculate tent city campsite." And what about the mission of their church? Mars Hill members "were here to glorify Jesus and the God-given roles that he had designed" for women and men.

Darla closed her post by saying she wishes she was "a triumphant woman of God who had answered her calling and had peace with the Lord." Unfortunately, she was "still a sinner," desiring "affirmation in the eyes of the world"; she was "still rebellious towards God's will for" her life. Darla had faith that God would ultimately transform her into the wife and mother he intended her to be. Yet Darla's story illustrates the difficulty some women encountered when trying to conform to Mars Hill's gender doctrine—even for women who wholeheartedly believed in the church's doctrine.[145]

As women reflected on their time at Mars Hill, they noted the difficulties in reconciling who they were and how people at the church responded to them within the black and white teachings of being "homeward oriented." Alice explained on WLMH, "I was raised to be a loving, tolerant, independent woman and I had to learn at an early age how to be strong. I've always been a peacemaker, creative with big ideas and strong opinions," but those "qualities did not fit in well at Mars Hill." On the same forum, Delilah wrote, "Because I was a woman, the pastors and coaches didn't feel completely comfortable meeting one on one with me," making her feel "like a burden" whenever she asked for help. Lucy stated, "Sitting and listening to that teaching every week, I felt like I didn't fit in and something was wrong with me." When she found she "disagreed with Driscoll's interpretation of scripture," Lucy reports on Mars Hill Was Us (MHWU), her husband questioned her faith, asking, "Are you even a Christian? You just don't agree because you don't want to follow that part of the Bible." Women struggled to negotiate their place in the church. For women who were not married, or who did not have children at home, they questioned how, as women, they could serve. Savannah wrote on WLMH that she "felt that there was no outlet" for her "to serve others" at the church, "especially as a woman."

Is It a Sin for a Woman to Have a Skill?

> Another thing I started noticing is. . . . Nobody had any career, which
> also seemed strange to me, because I was a professional.
>
> —Faith

For women, being single or not yet having children was seen as a temporary state. Yet without being wives or mothers, the role of women at the church was not clearly defined. Many women at Mars Hill were college-aged students, who were in school. Many other women were post-college age and working outside of the home, either before they were married or before they had children. Driscoll's gender rhetoric often cast women's education or work outside of the home as "not necessarily a sin," but his message was mixed. These contradictions were highlighted in a *Proverbs* sermon where Driscoll recounts a conversation with a Christian woman who told him she was going to college. When Driscoll asked her why she was going to school, she said, "Well, so I can get a good job." Driscoll asked her if she ever wanted to be married. "Yes," she replied. "Then why are you going to spend all these years getting your education if you want to be married?" Driscoll asked. The young woman told Driscoll she was going to college, "Just in case some day my husband divorces me, then I'll have a good career to fall back on and take care of myself." Driscoll said, "Here is a woman who is getting her divorce lined up before her husband. . . . That is tragic."[146]

Driscoll concluded the story with, "Am I saying women shouldn't go to college? That's not what I'm saying at all."[147] The quote communicates that women are to be married, which supersedes getting a college education, thus, why would women "spend all these years" in college? On WLMH, Hailey describes excitedly telling a pastor at Mars Hill that she'd been accepted into a Master's program at a regional seminary. The pastor responded in a way she said she'd never forget, asking, "Why are you going there? Don't you realize that [school] is full of feminist propaganda? Won't your decision to pursue a higher degree simply put your husband in debt? You need to rethink your priorities." Hailey had heard the criticisms of "the chauvinist culture" at Mars Hill, "but at that moment the truth of it all became real" to her.

For Mars Hill women, it was not just getting a higher education that was disputed. On WLMH, Ellie commented that when she and her husband began attending Mars Hill, they didn't have any children, so she "didn't make a huge fuss about Mark constantly pressuring women to be stay-at-home mothers." Eventually, however, "the way Mark preached on the roles of men and women" became "a major point of concern," because she felt "called by God to become a teacher and was in school to do just that." Ellie didn't really believe Driscoll thought being a stay-at-home mother was "really the path God called all women to," because she trusted her call to teach. She concludes, "Sadly, now I see that [Driscoll's] views on gender roles are completely unbiblical and only further his control over his own family as well as his church 'family.'" The church's doctrine and Driscoll's rhetoric was compelling, as Stella wrote on MHWU, "I grew up . . . surrounded by strong women in leadership roles. I got to Mars [Hill] and was somehow quickly convinced that all of that was wrong. That my mom shouldn't have been working when I grew up."

Many women at Mars Hill worked outside of the home. The cost of living in the Seattle-Metropolitan area made living on one income difficult. Yet, the church's gender doctrine communicated that once women married, particularly when they had children, they should no longer work outside the home. Leah wrote on MHWU, "I started a business during my time [at Mars Hill], and that was widely treated like a cute hobby. I had many people ask me, assume, and tell me I should shut down the business when we had kids." Aimee and her husband were in their mid-forties and had no children. She told me that she didn't "have any problem with women working," in general. She did, however, have concerns about mothers working, saying: "I feel if you work and have kids and are paying for day care, does that even make sense for you to work? I think when a woman is working and it has a negative impact on the family . . . it is not really making that much sense . . . I consider that to be wrong." When clarifying what would make a negative impact on the family, Aimee told me, "when you are working for the love of money, or the love of independence, or the love whatever it happens to be." Echoing Darla's story, some women, particularly mothers, at Mars Hill were susceptible to, or suspected of, "coveting" the "marketplace," which was interpreted as harming families. Even for stalwart believers, motherhood could be fraught. For many women, even married women, however, motherhood was not an immediate option.

Infertility: "I'm Not Pregnant, What Am I Going to Do?"

Motherhood was central to a woman's identity at Mars Hill. Driscoll's gender-essentialist theology relayed that God built women to have a natural predisposition toward motherhood. Driscoll's urging of women to be "homeward oriented" relied on women becoming mothers, fulfilling one of their primary duties to "raise children in the way they should go." Single women were urged to prepare themselves to be good wives and mothers. Married women were expected to become mothers. Ellie wrote on WLMH that, "Over time, we were influenced by the pressure we heard from the pulpit on how we need to have children because they are a blessing . . . and it is biblical to not use birth control." This rhetoric was powerful enough that the more Ellie and her husband attended church, the more they "thought about having children and so [they] changed [their] plans and got pregnant." As women embraced the gender theology at Mars Hill, they wanted to experience the joy of being wives and mothers. Once married, there was an expectation that children should quickly follow. One woman I interviewed expressed how important it was for women to become mothers at Mars Hill. Anna explained:

The day after I got married, I was, "I want babies now!" After getting married, that is the first [thing] everyone would talk about, "When are you having kids?" Geez, the families that got pregnant on their wedding nights, God bless them, those were the ones that really earn their tickets to the Mars Hill heaven. They were the most godly. . . . I did stay home for a while, and

I thought, "Here we are, I'm at home now. [My husband] is out working. Here we go. We are on the road to babies."

Unfortunately, Anna and her husband struggled with infertility. She told me of her struggles, saying, "every month that went by without being pregnant . . . felt like a waste. It felt like I was just waiting for that next month to come along so I could be pregnant, and I could start to fulfill what I understand as God's desire and purpose for my life."

Struggling with infertility can be a wrenching experience. For women at Mars Hill, the strict gender theology added a layer of anxiety to infertility. Anna told me, "I remember this one girl," who was recently married, "crying in the bathroom" at church "saying, 'I thought that I was going to be barren. . . . We have been trying to have kids for nine months and I finally just got pregnant.' I remember her saying those words, 'barren, barren.' It was like, who even says that?" Leah also recounted, on MHWU, a difficult story of experiencing "a really tough two years of infertility while at Mars Hill," writing, she was "still working through with a counselor the bullshit people told me about my infertility" when she attended Mars Hill. Leah describes being told she "was being selfish" by grieving and to "put on a happy face" when she attended the baby showers to which she was invited, because she "was a bad friend for not attending." Leah wrote, "I was told that if I was hurting and grieving not being able to be a mother, it was because I didn't trust God and didn't believe enough." For women like Leah, not being able to live into Mars Hill's gender theology could be devastating.

For Anna, Mars Hill's gender theology began to fall apart when she couldn't have children; then her marriage faltered: "This idea of this family, everything was just gone." The strain on Anna's marriage impacted her husband, who decided he couldn't meet Driscoll's standard of a "manly man," causing him to pull away from the church and their marriage. He became verbally and physically abusive. Anna said, "Slowly all of those things that I had been hoping for and I had been led to believe would happen for me, the husband and the kids, and that model Christian lifestyle was not happening for me at all." Leaving her husband, Anna was initially supported by the pastors at Mars Hill. In the end, however, she was counseled to go back to her husband and save her marriage; she couldn't:

That was a really lonely place to be and it felt really scary to feel banished from a church and to feel like everybody—all of your old . . . friends—were looking at you as a failed Christian. It wasn't because I [didn't believe] in God . . . or anything like that, but because I couldn't even make my marriage work. That for them was the key for why I was failing as a Christian . . . I couldn't just have a couple of crappy things happen to my marriage. It had to be in some way I was sinning, or he was sinning, or we weren't glorifying God.

Anna left Mars Hill feeling judged by the church for being "a failed Christian" because she couldn't have children and couldn't keep her marriage together. In Mars Hill's gender theology, these were the roles endemic to her "nature" as a woman. Having "failed" at being a wife and mother, she had to rethink the church's gender theology: "It has taken me quite a while to restructure my thinking on that, because obviously I don't have kids today and my life still has purpose. I'm not married anymore, and my life still has purpose." Women feeling judged at the church encompassed more than experiencing infertility. In order to be successful wives and mothers, women felt they needed to adhere to the church's beauty myth.

Show the World You Are Loved

Everyone can . . . see that [Grace Driscoll] is so well taken care of, because her body is so good, her hair is perfectly highlighted, and she has the perfect face [to show] the world that she is loved by a man.

—Anna

Driscoll's rhetoric consistently impressed on listeners that a man's wife was his standard of beauty. While this rhetoric seemed to release women from the expectations of the wider culture's "beauty myth," women at Mars Hill had reason to fear if they did not meet a cultural beauty standard. Driscoll regularly highlighted the cause-and-effect relationship between women "letting themselves go" and a husband's infidelity (or divorce). Women not being beautiful could reflect two things. A woman who "let herself go" could be seen as a "disgraceful" wife, or it could reflect a husband who was not "loving" her enough to "cultivate" her. Either of these scenarios put pressure on women to appear beautiful. This rhetoric had an impact. One college-aged woman, Esther, shared her concerns about Driscoll's rhetoric, stating that she did not consider herself a "beautiful" woman. Esther understood Driscoll's

rhetoric to mean that her (hypothetical) husband would ultimately be unfaithful, which would be her fault because she was not beautiful. Therefore,
she "might as well not get married," since the marriage would ultimately fail.

Aaliyah reported to WLMH that when she suspected her husband of
cheating on her, the Mars Hill Church elders told her she "needed to change,"
advising her that she had a "good husband" and to "fix [herself] up and be
more [sexually] available." So, she "did just that." Aaliyah wrote, "I believed
what was preached numerous times over the years about how a woman
should look, so much to the extent that I thought I was being a good wife by
starving myself, so that I'd be pleasing for my husband to look at, almost to
the point of my death just after the birth of my second child." Ellie also shared
on WLMH, that after the birth of one of her children she feared her husband "would start watching porn or something, because of Mark's teaching
on keeping your husband satisfied to keep him from sinning." She wrote, "I
specifically remember a sermon where [Driscoll] blamed the wife of a pastor
who committed adultery for 'letting herself go.'"

Driscoll's standard of beauty also relied on women submitting to their
husbands. As Anna described, Driscoll's teaching on women "started to
bubble over—women's roles, how to take care of a man, how to please a man,
how to dress for a man"—and Driscoll would point out his wife as the perfect example, saying, "look at her, look at how wonderful she is. My wife has
never so much as raised her voice to me." Unwittingly, Anna alluded to the
impact of Driscoll's rhetoric that women reflect their husbands' cultivation.
She told me that the church had women read how to be a "Christian wife" like
"the Proverbs 31 woman." At the same time, Driscoll pointed to his wife "as
an example of how a woman should keep her body, hair, face, all of these . . .
things . . . because . . . everyone could see how much she is loved." Anna said it
was important for women to look attractive, to reflect well on their husbands.

She Doesn't Say a Word

Women needed to be given a voice.

— Eleanor, MHWU

In *The Beauty Myth*, author Naomi Wolf wrote that the qualities considered
beautiful in women function to prescribe behavior, not appearance.[148]
While women seek to meet the beauty myth in appearance, they lose their

independence and power. The beauty myth counteracts the economic and political gains women have made, functioning as a mechanism of social control that halts or reverses women's advancement. Driscoll's "standard of beauty" functioned as a beauty myth. Women could interpret Driscoll's rhetoric as an imperative, fearing a husband's infidelity. Driscoll characterized the Proverbs 31 woman as a beautiful and righteous woman, extolling her silence. Driscoll used his wife, Grace, as an example of a beautiful woman, who had never raised her voice to him, linking beauty to submission and quietness, if not outright silence. Many women at Mars Hill felt silenced. For example, Sadie wrote on WLMH that her time in a women's prayer group "was spent mostly talking about how we could please our husbands, submit to our husbands, or 'serve them well,'" resulting in women who "seemed oppressed, stifled, and silenced." Eleanor stated on MHWU that at "a Bible camp that many of us at Mars Hill attended, a new rule was created in which women could no longer speak at all during communion, even in the very informal setting we had at camp. The women there accepted this." Women accepting their silencing "with heavy hearts and fearful obedience" was a condition of being under the authority of men and in congruence with the church's gender hierarchy.

Women transgressing the church's gender hierarchy were quickly sanctioned. On MHWU, Abigail described the negative impact Driscoll's teachings had on her, referring to his "abusive attitude toward women— which was cloaked in being 'doctrinally sound,'" writing, "When Mark and I disagreed on something, he decided to write an open letter to my husband telling him, 'Shut your wife up, or I'll shut her up for you.'" Abigail described receiving "anonymous emails from several men in the church, one of whom said that I was, 'an adulterous whore' for trying to 'take Mark down.' Another said that he understood that I did these things because I was mentally ill." Abigail and her husband left the church and were shunned by the Mars Hill community, epitomizing the negative repercussions of women not showing their submissiveness through silence or by not speaking in appropriate tones, at appropriate times, or in appropriate ways.

Women struggled with understanding when to speak and when to stay silent. Amelia wrote on MHWU, "I was both consciously and unconsciously indoctrinated that women just aren't supposed to be 'heard' as much as men. My husband was often asked to speak for us in various circumstances and I didn't understand why I couldn't speak my own mind or even have a different opinion than him." Writing on the same forum, Leah stated, "It was made really clear that women were not to speak up. . . . If I brought up questions in a group setting, I was shut down." Even in women's ministries, the church's leadership could silence women. Delilah explained on WLMH that she wanted to start a women's Bible study, but was told by the church's leadership, "that women couldn't get together to read the Bible without more oversight . . . they seemed very concerned that the theology would go bad. A church doesn't feel comfortable with women reading the Bible together? They need oversight and guidance?"

Women who did not (appropriately) submit to men at Mars Hill were perceived as "disgraceful." As noted previously, when one woman told her husband that she disagreed with Driscoll's interpretation of Scripture, her husband questioned her Christian faith, accusing her of not wanting to follow the "biblical" roles of women. The pressure to submit or be silent was felt by many women. Lydia wrote on WLMH that through prayer, she heard Jesus tell her to "flee Mars Hill," but she didn't share this with her husband, because she was already "accused of being an unsubmissive wife." When Hailey returned to Mars Hill after spending some time away, she found, "People were afraid to question the severe complementarian theology Pastor Mark encouraged through his *Peasant Princess* and *Real Marriage* series." Writing on WLMH, Hailey said she knew women at Mars Hill who "were afraid to deny sex to their husbands, women who were afraid to pursue passions outside the home, and women who were afraid to speak about the neglect they experienced from husbands." These women thought "any unhappiness they felt was because they weren't praying hard enough, didn't know how to submit to their husbands well enough, didn't have hearts that were right enough. . . . They didn't have a voice."

Spiritual and Physical Abuse

[Driscoll] verbally lambasted the elders . . . for not keeping their wives in line.

—Julia, WLMH

Internalizing the teaching of submission at Mars Hill meant that when they experienced abuse, women may not have defined it as such, seeing abuse as a corrective to not being submissive enough.[149] One woman related a story to me of a couple who sought counseling because the husband and wife were concerned that the wife was not submissive enough. As she told the story, Diana began to cry, explaining that the couple's strategy to make the wife more submissive was to tear out pages from the Bible with verses about wives submitting to husbands. Each day, the wife would eat one of the pages, believing that literally ingesting God's commands for wives to be submissive might have the necessary effect.[150]

Women reported experiencing men using their authority to bully or abuse them. Olivia reported on MHWU that the way she "saw women being treated was really harmful, mentally and spiritually. Some of it was sexual harassment," she wrote, "and some of it was bullying because of a misinterpretation of Scripture." Olivia continued, saying she saw "faithful women serving behind the scenes who were yelled at over misunderstandings because the men felt it was their right." Many women felt the negative repercussions of Mars Hill's gender doctrine. Everleigh wrote on MHWU that, "Mars Hill enhanced the fear I already had and encouraged it, along with self-hatred, religiosity, and self-punishing." Delilah stated on WLMH, "women have fallen by the wayside in favor of men. On paper, Mars Hill is complementarian, but it has been taken too far and has tread into misogynistic waters." Stella reported to MHWU, "I was always somebody who worried about doing the right thing in God's eyes . . . and unfortunately Mars Hill was the exact type of place to prey on my insecurities and get me to spend years thinking that I wasn't good enough, and that my unwillingness to submit to my husband was a sin." She said, "I still cringe when I hear the word 'submission' in any context." Liesl told me, "I am tired of being told that I am practically worthless because of my gender. And even more tired of not knowing what to do about it." Once Mars Hill Church imploded, there was a reckoning, and the process of healing began for many women.

Woman Was Made for Man: Reprise

Mark's take on the scriptures . . . his preferences . . . were taught as actual gospel. I ate it all up. I grew my hair out.

—Isabella, MHWU

Mark Driscoll created an empire through Mars Hill Church to reach and train men. The church's gender theology put men first. Women at Mars Hill

were not surprised at the church's gender doctrine; many embraced it. Mars
Hill Church's gender theology was not as "out there" as many wanted to believe. The iconic breadwinner/homemaker roles of the long decade continue
to serve as an American cultural touchstone. Americans, generally, ascribe to
biological essentialism, where males and females are seen as fundamentally
different due to biology.[151] Subsequently, men and women are seen as different, with opposite characteristics and roles.[152] For Driscoll and Mars Hill,
these differences were cast as God's divine design, making them seem imper-
vious to cultural changes over time.

While many women thrived in this environment, many others struggled.
Even women, like Darla, who believed in the church's separate spheres theology, grappled with actively embodying Mars Hill's prescribed gender
roles. Living a separate spheres ideology, however, incurred costs. The mar-
ketplace/homebuilder (breadwinner/homemaker) theology rested on the
assumption of biological or religious determinism. Even within the context
of the American Christian church, that is not what the evidence shows.
Historical evidence illustrates a dynamic gender ideology that changes as
sociocultural conditions change; gender, even in God's economy, is not
static. For women, Mars Hill Church's strict gender theology could be
repressive.

Cindy told me that she and her husband had chosen to attend Mars Hill
because it was a church filled with "young people," especially young men.
In their late forties, Cindy and her husband appreciated Driscoll's mission
and wholeheartedly supported the church's teaching. Yet as she reflected on
the dynamics of the church's mission to men, she told me that she felt that
women at Mars Hill were "really weighed down under a huge burden of what
a good Christian wife is supposed to be," saying:

> There is a very heavy emphasis on getting married and then having chil-
> dren, and pretty consistent teaching about the role of women. Sometimes
> they just see that done without a sense of . . . grace and . . . the individu-
> ality of women, and how they express themselves and live. I just felt, es-
> pecially some of these younger women that I would see—young moms
> that so dearly wanted to do it right—it felt like the way it was being taught,
> especially maybe with young Christians, especially maybe new Christian
> couples, and the sense there is this right way to do marriage, and children,
> and roles of men and women, that didn't allow for much grace. Kind of a
> heavy burden to bear.

Not every woman at the church could embody the Proverbs 31 woman, even when she tried. As she watched her desire for children slip away, heralding the end of her marriage, Anna felt the weight of being "a failed Christian," coming to the conclusion that Mars Hill was "dangerous" for women: "Women don't really have a place, and if they do, it is a diminished role. Mark would also say the roles are equal, they are different. It is true, the roles are very different for many women. . . . Women were not allowed to go to any kind of leadership without the permission of their husband. . . . I really truly believe that a lot of women felt very powerless, so very powerless."

At the end of each weekly sermon, Driscoll prayed for his congregation. As he closed one of his 2002 *Proverbs* sermons, addressing the roles of Christian women, Driscoll prayed for the women at Mars Hill, that they "not fall into the common sins of quarrelsome, ill-tempered, gossiping, loud-mouth, divisive, tearing down, disrespectful, unloving, foolishness." But instead, that they would have wisdom, strength, prudence, and helpfulness, as well as fear of the Lord, a love for what was holy, "a desire to learn the Scriptures, and be obedient," so as not to "dishonor" their husbands in front of their children, and thereby tear down their own homes.[153]

Harnessing a strict separate-spheres theology of men in the marketplace and women in the home, Driscoll's rhetoric created a clear divergence in gender roles. Ascribed to creation and God's original intent for men and women, the church's complementarian theology was indispensable to their message of salvation. While many women thrived with the clarity and freedom the church's theology provided, other women struggled to fulfill the theology's requirements—even when, like Darla, they desperately sought to live it out. Women's only avenue to fulfill their purpose was through a complementarian family. Only when married women were wives, mothers, and lovers could they realize their purpose and faith. Family at Mars Hill was a scriptural imperative. How did these complementarian families function in practice? The next chapter addresses the unique features of Driscoll's ideal family and the implications for living into his ideal.

4

Real Family

Dating and Marriage

Mars Hill Church's hypermasculine theology was one of its most controversial elements. Like other conservative Protestants, Driscoll contextualized individual salvation through the prism of the nuclear family, consisting of husbands who led and wives who followed. The focus on complementarian family norms made gender salient and specific in relationships between evangelical men and women.[1] Conservative Protestants believe that complementarian family norms constitute the moral foundation of church and society, and thus cannot be dispensed with.

In the late twentieth century the American cultural gender ideal shifted from breadwinner/homemaker toward dual-earner families. Evangelical ideals shifted as well, to a headship/submission ideal that maintained the symbolic nature of the complementarian family, while also accommodating the economic shifts making dual-earner families more necessary. As conservative Protestants adhered to a theology of men's spiritual headship and women's submission, they mostly functioned as practical egalitarians.[2] Conservative Protestants understood this shift to mean a husband's symbolic spiritual headship was not equated to his having final authority or status as a primary breadwinner in the family.[3]

Driscoll's rhetoric and mission rejected symbolic headship/practical egalitarianism, returning to a nostalgic, golden era of family, where men were expected to be breadwinners, lest they were "denied the faith." Driscoll's rhetoric reiterated a clear gender hierarchy: "the man is the head and the leader of the home . . . the wife is to respect and follow the leadership of her husband."[4] In Driscoll's hierarchy, men had authority in all spheres, including the home. Driscoll repeatedly told men that if they wanted the respect of other men, their wives, and their children, they needed to "pay the bills," "make the money," and "feed the family."[5] Men being economic providers was an imperative for Driscoll. Men who balked at his strict theology were told to "look at the condition of marriages and families" in the secular culture "and ask if

Making Christianity Manly Again. Jennifer McKinney, Oxford University Press. © Oxford University Press 2023.
DOI: 10.1093/oso/9780197655795.003.0005

it's working."[6] To Driscoll, any man who was not a breadwinner was "just a loser."[7]

In conjunction with the publication of *Real Marriage: The Truth about Sex, Friendship, and Life Together*, cowritten by Driscoll and his wife, Grace, the 2012 eponymous sermon series served as the broadest dissemination of Driscoll's beliefs regarding dating, marriage, and family. Mars Hill Church extensively marketed the *Real Marriage* series, urging Mars Hill community groups to purchase the curriculum for their weekly meetings and sending publicity materials to thousands of churches to participate in the series. The church's website claimed that more than 2,000 churches had signed on to be part of the Real Marriage Campaign.[8] Not surprisingly, the book and sermon series garnered controversy, especially the chapters and sermons on sex, which recapitulated much of Driscoll's previous sermon material from the Song of Solomon.

Many of Driscoll's critics noted that his anger, especially toward women, had been tempered in the *Real Marriage* sermons. The late author and blogger Rachel Held Evans wrote that she was pleasantly surprised that Driscoll did a "much better job of emphasizing mutuality in sexual relationships," than in the past, but added that he continued to reduce "the Song of Songs to a sex manual, instructing wives to be 'visually generous' with their husbands."[9] If more than 2,000 churches did subscribe to the series, Driscoll may have chosen a more measured approach to his teaching. Indeed, the sermons for *Real Marriage* were significantly shorter than his usual weekly sermons.

Marriage is central to a complementarian theology. Driscoll consistently told his church that, "statistically, more than 90 percent of you will marry."[10] As part of the evangelical "family values" tradition, Driscoll upheld an essentialist gender nature as the bedrock of the complementarian family, constituting the moral foundation of society.[11] Within the complementarian family, men and women have different roles to play, as designed by God, within opposite domains. Mars Hill Church's gender theology, however, was a strict complementarianism that gave men ultimate authority over even the women's domain of the home. Driscoll's rhetoric placed men's authority and leadership at the fulcrum of a Christian family, a force countering the influence of a feminized secular culture.

As previously described, Driscoll justified his masculine-focused theology by interpreting Genesis 2, where God created Adam/man before Eve/woman, making Adam/man as "the head and leader of the family."[12] Eve/woman was created as "man's helper, spawning the institution of marriage," which is "one man, one woman, and one covenant."[13] Driscoll characterized Genesis 2 as describing a "covenant marriage," which prescribed separate domains for men and woman, wherein men and women "work together in a complementary fashion, like a right hand and a left hand; that the man is to be the leader, and . . . the woman is to be the helper."[14] Driscoll's idealized family, based on a heterosexual ideal, presupposed a "Christian" process of dating, often referred to as "courting," leading to marriage and children. Much of Driscoll's mission to young men was spent preparing them to date in order to marry.

Singleness and Dating

You gals, you hit thirty then you're like, "I'M THIRTY, I'M SINGLE, I'M FREAKING OUT!"[15]

Mars Hill Church was a magnet for young evangelicals, a significant number of whom were single. When he embarked on the *Real Marriage* series, Driscoll encouraged singles to attend and learn the principles of marriage, with the added benefit that they "might even find a spouse."[16] Just because there were hundreds of couples married each year at Mars Hill, Driscoll told singles—especially women—not to feel pressure to marry. While some circumstances allowed for singleness, marriage was God's ideal. Closing one *Real Marriage* sermon, Driscoll said, "I pray for those who are single, Lord God, that they would see how incredibly selfish they are. Their money is spent on them, their time is devoted to them, all their worries are about them."[17] From Driscoll's perspective, singleness was temporary, since marriage was God's design. How did singles get to be married? Courtship and dating.

Courtship and Dating

The dude needs to figure out what the dude wants to do.[18]

Like many conservative Protestant churches, Mars Hill Church addressed dating through the lens of "courtship." In his 2006 *Christians Gone Wild* series, Driscoll preached the sermon, "Divorce and Remarriage," which tackled the church's perspective on courtship, describing it as pursuing someone "if you're very interested in them, and they're dad approves, and their mom approves, and their friends approve." For men, "You don't just get a gal, you gotta go through her dad, and his gun, and her brothers, and their guns, and mom," and her friends, church, and theology. Courtship at Mars Hill hinged on men. Driscoll addressed the men in his church saying, "Gentlemen, it all rides on you. You will need to initiate, the woman will respond. You will need to propose, she will accept or decline." Before initiating, however, men had to determine whether they were "called" to marriage. Driscoll described how a man needed to ask himself, "Do I believe that I am called to a life of singleness, or do I think that I am going to burn in hell 'cause I can't help myself" because "I'm a guy who has certain desires." Driscoll told men that if they didn't think they were "built for singleness, you're not built for chastity," but were "supposed to be a husband, and a dad, and a dude," then dudes needed "to figure out" what they should do.[19]

"Dudes" at Mars Hill were accorded the opportunity to determine if they were called to singleness. Yet Driscoll's rhetoric communicated that men were more likely to have "certain desires," making a call to singleness unlikely. Therefore, men pursued women, obtaining permission—from her father (and his guns) and then her brothers (and their guns), and then her mother, friends, and the church. Driscoll recognized women's dependence on men, saying, "the ladies" could "feel that they are in this powerless position whereby if you don't make up their mind, they are just confused and wasting time with you," so "do the ladies a favor, and be a man about it, and figure out what you want, and get it done."[20] Once a man decided he was called to marriage, and initiated a relationship with a woman, Mars Hill Church members were expected to enter into the church's premarital process, ensuring members married "the right person, at the right time, in the right way, for the right reasons."[21] By default, the complementarian theology at Mars Hill meant courtship was gendered.

Courtship for Men

Marriage is for men, it's not for boys.[22]

In order to "take a wife," men needed to take financial, spiritual, and economic responsibility by "doing well in school, figuring out your career, moving out of your parents' house, worshipping God, taking responsibility for yourself."[23] Driscoll emphasized men's need to "be men" in order to marry: "You are a man first and then you take a wife, but you better know what you're getting into. Lots of men naively walk into marriage and realize that it's a lot more Genesis 3 and a lot less nudity and fruit."[24] Men taking responsibility was portrayed by Driscoll as countercultural. Driscoll complained that American men were taught to extend their adolescence to "take advantage of women," be "into pornography" and "abdicate" their responsibilities.[25] Taking responsibility meant men guarding their hearts against lust, pornography, and inappropriate sexual relationships. Men who felt called to be married needed to put themselves in a position where they could "get married sooner [rather] than later," so as not to fall into sin.[26]

Only men who had proven their responsibility were eligible to pursue courtship at Mars Hill. In addition to securing the permission of a woman's father, however, men needed permission from the pastors at Mars Hill to court/date. The latter could be accomplished through the mentoring of a community group leader or in the context of the premarital process at the church, where courting couples were assigned married couples as mentors. The church wanted younger men under the authority of older men, because Driscoll thought younger men didn't really know what they were doing: "No, you don't," Driscoll said.[27] While men took responsibility, women's roles in courtship were quite different.

Courtship for Women

Ladies, you should not be chasing men, men should be seeking you.[28]

Women at Mars Hill hoping to marry had to wait for men to initiate the courtship process. By fearing the Lord and walking in holiness, women should eventually have a husband, home, and children. Yet even for women following this formula, there was no guaranteed success. In a sermon on courtship, Driscoll highlighted the lack of power women had in the courtship process, saying if "a guy doesn't wanna marry you, you pretty much aren't getting married, right?"[29] For courtship and dating at Mars Hill, women had two directives: maintain their chastity and marry men they respected.

First, women had to reject the sexually liberated secular culture. In dozens of anecdotes, Driscoll warned single women not to use sex to create relationships. In one example, Driscoll compared some women to prostitutes saying, "they are cheap," "easy," and "quick."[30] These "sexually promiscuous" women wrongly think having sex with a man means "he will love her, which is insane," because if men loved these women, they would marry them.[31] Second, women must respect the men they married: "If you don't respect him, don't marry him."[32] Driscoll said too many women thought they could love, care, and fix their husbands, but they would eventually realize, "It's not love, it's death . . . if a man can't swim on his own, don't go out to save him, let him drown."[33] For his complementarianism to work, Driscoll needed women to follow the courtship process by waiting for the right man to pursue them, "The whole society really is riding on this issue of women having enough wisdom."[34] Women who were "easy and cheap" and settled for "B-grade men," would get men who "rise to the level of expectation."[35]

No Sex for the Single Girl (or Boy)

You're not free to be . . . sexually active [and] not married.[36]

Driscoll was notorious for his sex-positive advocacy within marriage. Driscoll contrasted sexually active women—cheap, easy, and quick—with Mars Hill women, whose "desires [were] toward godly things until you get married, and then toward your spouse."[37] Driscoll related a story about a woman at the church who was living with her boyfriend. The woman told Driscoll his ideas on sex outside of marriage were "old school," "old-fashioned," and "negative," to which Driscoll retorted, "You're an idolater."[38] The woman explained she was a Christian, but Driscoll disagreed, telling her she had "turned her back on Jesus," because sleeping with her boyfriend meant her bed was "a pagan altar," her boyfriend a "pagan priest," and her body a "living sacrifice."[39] Driscoll referred to sex outside of marriage as "an act of worship" to "a demon god," illustrating "deep sin" and "rebellion."[40] Driscoll was adamant that sex outside of marriage was not acceptable for Christians, yet there were subtle differences in how he addressed men versus women. For example, in a Q&A session following a *Real Marriage* sermon, a man asked how to confront a friend living with his girlfriend. Driscoll replied, "Be tough," because "1 Corinthians says that fornicators go to hell."[41] Going to hell is dire for Christians, but Driscoll had a solution for the fornicator. Because "Jesus died for our sins," the man's transgression could "be forgiven."[42] Driscoll condemned sex outside of marriage for both men and women; Driscoll's rhetoric, however, extended forgiveness to men.[43] Presumably, Jesus died for the sins of women, as well, but Driscoll's redemption did not always encompass women.

Consistent with evangelicalism's "purity culture," which often places more of a burden on women, Driscoll's theology held men and women differentially accountable for sex outside of marriage.[44] In the *Real Marriage* series (and book), the Driscolls were lauded for their openness about their own marriage. In the sermon "Sex: God, Gross, or Gift?" Driscoll humorously recounted a story describing the couple's sexual activity before marriage. Driscoll disclosed that when he and Grace met, they were not virgins and were having sex while they dated. Driscoll was a new Christian, while Grace "was not walking faithfully with the Lord." At a college Bible study, a pastor introduced Driscoll to a new "F-word." The pastor read from a Bible passage that said "fornicators" would not inherit the kingdom of God and Driscoll thought, "Wow, that's a big deal. Boy, I really feel bad for those fornicators" but wasn't sure what a fornicator was. Driscoll called the pastor to say he had a friend who might be a fornicator and asked for a definition. That pastor asked, "Is your buddy sleeping with his girlfriend?" When Driscoll said, "Yes," the pastor replied, "They're fornicating." Driscoll objected, asking if the pastor was sure. When the pastor said he was sure, Driscoll said, "They love each other!" It was "still fornicating," said the pastor. "Well, they're going to get married" Driscoll said. "Still fornicating," replied the pastor. Driscoll even tried reasoning with the pastor that since the couple had already slept together, it was "too late," to stop. Still the pastor said it was wrong to fornicate. Finally comprehending the gravity of the situation, Driscoll told the pastor he'd let his friend know he was a fornicator. With his quick wit, Driscoll shifted his attention and story back to directly address his audience saying, "So, I called Grace—my 'friend'—I said, 'We are fornicating.'" As the daughter of a pastor, Grace knew that she and Driscoll were fornicating and agreed they should stop. Driscoll said that by the grace of God they did stop fornicating and the couple were married between their junior and senior years of college: "Some people are like, 'Why'd you get married so young?' Some reasons."[45]

Driscoll's story highlights two subtle demarcations. The first is between non-Christians and Christians. As a non-Christian, Driscoll, ostensibly, did not know it was a sin to "fornicate." As a new Christian, there was grace for him; once he learned that fornication was wrong, he stopped having sex with Grace. Jokingly referring to Grace as his fornicating "friend" holds her, as a Christian, accountable for the sin. Rhetorically, there was another demarcation: gender. Grace, as a woman, was held more accountable for having sex before marriage. Drawing from an essentialist theology, Driscoll communicated men could not help their biologically based sexual desires, but women could and should. In another anecdote Driscoll described a friend from college, saying, "I'll never forget this buddy of mine in college. He loved Jesus. He was a virgin—to me that was like a unicorn. Like, I'd heard about them, but I had never seen one. I didn't know they were real. I thought these were mythical creatures."[46] The underlying context conveyed that men's sexual activity was understandable and forgivable. In that same sermon, Driscoll used Jesus as an example of sexual fidelity, saying, "We look at the Lord Jesus, and he was single and died a virgin—which is maybe one of his miracles."[47] The explicit content of Driscoll's message of saving sex for marriage was at odds with his implicit message that being a male virgin was "miraculous" and as rare as a "unicorn." Driscoll seemed to see men having sex before marriage as more rule than exception, whereas women having sex before marriage made them "cheap" and "easy."

Real Marriage

Every marriage is implicated by the first marriage.[48]

"It's a very serious matter to be married," Driscoll told Mars Hill, because the story of a wedding in Genesis "quickly moves to a war."[49] In Driscoll's interpretation, once Adam and Eve were married Satan moved from attacking God to "assaulting a husband and wife," putting Christian marriages on "the frontline" of the "battle."[50] Within this scenario, Driscoll introduced a dual hierarchy for men, one on earth and one in heaven, putting man in the center of a cosmic hierarchy, where God was "above him and creation beneath him."[51] In this hierarchy, man was subject to God, with creation subject to man. God saw that man didn't "have a partner" and God answered with "a wife."[52] While Driscoll told his audience that men and women were equal, his theology positioned men in authority over women: "Within marriage, the man is the covenant head" and God gives him an "additional burden" for "the well-being of his family."[53]

In order to be covenant heads, God had created a process for men to follow. First, men left their mother and father. Leaving his parent's home symbolized a man's journey to a new family. Fulfilling his responsibilities allowed a man to "find a woman, love her, and then enjoy the fruit of marital union," at least until sin entered the world.[54] In Genesis 3 Adam and Eve sinned. Eve was tempted by Satan and Adam stayed silent, resulting in men and women being cursed.[55] Men were cursed by having wives who didn't "immediately or easily respect" them, making it "increasingly more difficult" for him to "feed his family."[56] Women were cursed by not trusting their husbands and becoming "thorns" in their husbands' flesh by wanting to "rule over" them, "boss" them around, "manage," "manipulate," and "control" them.[57] Like Eve, women were responsible for their sins, but husbands were also responsible for wives' sins. Driscoll said that husbands would "stand before God" to give an account for themselves, as well as giving an account for their wives and children, who were under their authority.[58] Whereas some Protestant theology consigns gender inequality to the fall, Driscoll asserts that hierarchy was embedded in God's design from the beginning.[59] Therefore, by virtue of creation, men have authority over wives and children because they are "covenant heads."

Every Covenant Has a Head

Within marriage, the man is the covenant head.[60]

In Driscoll's gender hierarchy men were "covenant heads," who were subject to Jesus (who was subject to God), and women and children were subject to men.[61] In his 2012 *Real Marriage* sermon, "Men and Marriage," Driscoll described men being empowered by the Holy Spirit to act like Jesus toward their wives, so that wives were "cherished," "nurtured," "loved," "pursued," and "forgiven," reflecting a husbands' "investment." Ultimately, Driscoll said, a husband was responsible for "the management and the well-being" of the marriage covenant. In the sermon Driscoll attempted to reconcile his contradictory rhetoric of gender equality with men's headship over wives. Struggling to articulate the contradiction, Driscoll described a company's CEO, a nation's president or king, a sports team's coach or general manager, and a military unit's highest-ranking officer as ultimately responsible for the success or failure of their ventures. Why? "Because they're the head." While others may have some responsibility, being in the highest authority meant these men "bear the most responsibility."[62] It's not surprising Driscoll relied on icons of secular masculine culture to illustrate authority. Driscoll denigrated the wider culture, except in areas where men were given power or authority. Driscoll used scriptural references to legitimate a secular order of masculine authority, telling his audience that the Bible mandated wives' submission to husbands, interpreting scriptures as saying, "the man *is*, the husband *is*, the head of the wife."[63] The only question was whether a husband was "doing a good or a bad job," with wives serving as "referees."[64]

Wives may be referees, but they were cautioned about "ruling over" husbands. During the Q&A for the "Men and Marriage" sermon, Grace Driscoll reiterated her husband's complementarian position, stating that wives were "helpers" and husbands were to "lead" and "teach" women "what respect means." Grace told women to encourage husbands, but "not in a motherly or patronizing way" because "it could sound like nagging." Grace reinforced the centrality of men within Driscoll's theology in her closing prayer, thanking the "Lord" for giving men his "Word" to instruct them on how to lead. She also prayed that men would desire "to lead this next generation, to lead a new legacy of boys into men," who love and honor God, and respect women to lead them "well."[65] Grace's call for men to "respect" women reversed one of Driscoll's key directives in marriage, where men were to love wives, and women to respect their husbands.

Driscoll's theology gendered love and respect. In his *Proverbs* series, Driscoll asked the Mars Hill "Ladies" if they felt being loved was more important than being respected. He then asked the men if they felt respect was "way more important than love?" saying, "That's a guy. Men and women are different in that way."[66] Driscoll was interpreting verses from the New Testament book of Ephesians and told women their job was "to respect and honor" their husbands, and to encourage them.[67] Men's goals "should be to make enough money" to "provide" for their families, so their wives "can have children."[68] This latter directive to men functioned as the cornerstone of Driscoll's expectation for men in families.

The Role of Men in Families

> It doesn't matter how much beer you can drink, or how much meat you can eat, or how loud you can belch. That does not make you a man. A monkey can do that.[69]

At the beginning of the *Real Marriage* series, Driscoll asked the men in his congregation to take a literal stand for serving as leaders and taking a "sacred oath" to publicly commit to loving their wives and families. Driscoll recited each line of the oath, with the men in the congregation repeating him:

> My church will be served by me.
> My wife will be loved by me.
> My wife will be served by me.
> My family will be led by me.
> My wife will be prayed over by me.
> The Bible will be opened in our home by me.
> And my grandchildren will worship the same God as me,
> because my children will worship the same God as me.[70]

Driscoll then directed the men to lay hands on, and pray over, their wives, who "desperately" wanted husbands to lead their families.[71] The need for men to be good leaders in their families meant that Mars Hill Church held "men to a high standard."[72] Drawing on "the essence of masculinity," Driscoll reiterated the need for men to take responsibility.[73] Unironically, Driscoll said, "We live in a day where masculinity is defined by some sort of ridiculous machismo," but that masculinity was ultimately about men taking responsibility: "You may not be big. You may not be tough. You may not be able to win a thumb-wrestling match, let alone a cage fight, but if you take responsibility, you are a good head and you are a masculine man."[74] As covenant heads, men's lives were to reflect being in a relationship with Jesus, their spouses, their children, and as workers. Driscoll made a point of saying that being a "worker" was not the most important role for a man, despite the fact that he regularly derided men who were not family breadwinners as being "worse than an unbeliever."[75] Men who were not breadwinners could not financially support their wives' homebuilding.

The Role of Women in Families

Ladies, you were built to be a what? A helper.[76]

Chapter 3 detailed women's roles in Driscoll's gender theology. As helpers to their husbands, women were created to be wives, mothers, and lovers. Using verses from the book of Ephesians (5:22–33), Driscoll defined the role of women in families as submitting to their husbands because husbands were the "head of the wife."[77] By submitting to husbands, wives were "respectful," facilitating their husbands' becoming "respectable." According to Driscoll, there were two ways women could approach respectability. They could "nag and disrespect," their husbands, "never" getting the results they hoped for, or they could "pray" for husbands, "instead of just nagging" them; they could "respect" them, helping them to "become more respectable."[78] Driscoll asked the women in his audience if they respected their husbands and then said, if they were honest, every wife would have to say, " 'I've got room to grow.' "[79] Driscoll's 2012 *Real Marriage* series called out two types of disrespectful wives: those who are silent and compliant and those who are loud and contentious.

Disrespectful Wives

She wants to tell him what to do, boss him around, she wants to manage and manipulate and control and cajole the man.[80]

In "The Respectful Wife" sermon from the *Real Marriage* series, Driscoll seemed to walk back his stance on women being silent, telling his congregation that wives who were "too silent and too compliant" were disrespecting Jesus and their husbands. Driscoll said women thinking they should "just shut up" and do what they're told was a misinterpretation of submission that was enabling, not helping, husbands. At the same time, Driscoll reiterated that "loud" or "contentious" wives were creating a "hostage situation" for husbands, who couldn't "beat" their wives, but had to "take it," making husbands "wusses." Loud wives drove their husbands away: "I'm not saying it's right" but "it's inevitable." Yet wives didn't have to speak to show disrespect. Driscoll reminded women that their sin was "not just what we say or do. It's also what we think." Driscoll cautioned women on their proclivity to be conformed to the wider culture, saying, "disrespect" in their heads would "reside" in their hearts and come out in their "speech." Driscoll emphasized the need for wives to pray, telling them prayer would "condition" them to speak better of their husbands, rather than the "nagging, gossiping, busy-bodying, bitter brigade, sometimes called the women's prayer circle." Driscoll reiterated the ways women were disrespectful to their husbands: "Are you a nag?" "Are you quarrelsome?" "Are you manipulative? Do you play him like a puppet?"

Driscoll concluded one rant telling women, "You're a joke, but you're not funny."[81]

Driscoll reminded women that husbands needed to be encouraged and respected. "Ladies," Driscoll said, "your husband needs you" not to condemn him because Satan and his enemies were "already doing that!"[82] Wives needed to be encouraging and careful not to point out a husband's faults, failures, flaws, or he "will think that he lives with his critic or his mother, neither of which is ... motivating for him to grow in godliness."[83] While some women had the gift of encouragement, Driscoll noted, some needed "to grow in that gift."[84]

Being a wife was tricky in Driscoll's theology; wives had to encourage, without enabling; respect, but not nag; speak, but not too loudly. During the sermon Q&A for "The Respectable Wife," a woman from the audience said she had "lost respect and trust" in her husband because he refused to lead and lacked "a desire to step up." She asked what she should do. Driscoll said to tell her husband that she loved him and wanted to follow him, but he had to lead and let her know how to come alongside him. The woman needed to assure her husband that she wasn't going to do his job or take his role. Not assuming the responsibilities of her husband meant that it might be incumbent on the woman "to let some things fall apart." Driscoll expressed frustration that the woman had to ask her question at all. He scolded the men of Mars Hill saying, there was "no reason ... not to know how to lead," since "an army of men" at the church were happy to help, teach, and train other men to lead. "The men of Mars Hill," Driscoll said, "have this deep in their DNA. They want to be good men—God's men"; and they wanted other men to be good men and God's men. A Mars Hill man wanted to be "a different kind of man" who raised "different kinds of sons. That's deep in the heart of the men of this church." Driscoll believed that only weak men thought "leadership skills ... come from the man fairy."[85] Men needed to find other men from which to learn how to be good covenant heads, to allow women to be homebuilders, to facilitate the unique benefit of marriage: sex.

"Friend" with Benefits

This is my lover and this is my friend.[86]

Real Marriage addressed the role of sex in marriage, drawing from earlier sermon series, particularly *The Peasant Princess* series. Referring to the Song of Solomon, Driscoll commented that he couldn't "think of a more beautiful definition of marriage—lover and friend—or to use our language, 'Friend with Benefits.'"[87] For Driscoll, sex was the "distinguishing aspect of marriage" and a gift created by God binding husbands and wives together.[88] The gifts of sex accrued via "chastity before marriage" and "fidelity in marriage," resulting in "two servant lovers who are friends and obey the Word of God, and live within their freedoms, and enjoy one another."[89] The primary reason for sex, according to Driscoll, was pleasure.[90] Sexual pleasure, however, existed in two phases: sex before sin and sex after sin.

Sex before Sin

God created our bodies for sexual pleasure and called it very good![91]

In his characteristic "bro" style, Driscoll described the "first account of sexual relationship" in Genesis.[92] Repeating his interpretation of the order of creation, where God created a helper suitable to Adam, Driscoll abruptly stopped to say it was a "big day" for the "ladies" because they "just got made" and were "going to get married nekked . . . that's a big day!"[93] In the marriage covenant men and women "become one flesh" through consummation: "God was glorified. They were satisfied. That's sex before sin."[94] It was important for Driscoll to underscore the idea that God created sex for pleasure (at least for people who were married) because he believed that a consequence of original sin distorted the goodness of sex, which was emblematic of sex after sin.

Sex after Sin

[A]ll sex outside of heterosexual marriage is a sin.[95]

"God created the body and he created the passions and pleasures of the body for marriage," Driscoll told his audience.[96] Sex before sin, however, was short-lived. After sin entered the world, the role of sex in marriage was distorted, and "we do great destruction to our own body, to the hardwiring of our own brain, and to our ability to really enjoy our spouse, and to be faithfully devoted to them."[97] Driscoll described how sin distorted God's gift of sex, which was rooted in how men and women had "diametrically opposed perspectives on sex and marriage."[98] Driscoll said that some see sex as a "the most important thing in the world" (god), while others see sex as "dirty, nasty, vile, and wrong" (gross).[99] Sex "can be a false god" and "done in a way that is gross," Driscoll said, but "ultimately sex is a gift."[100]

Driscoll listed the numerous ways that sex outside of marriage was distorted by sin, including homosexuality, bisexuality, erotica, bestiality, swinging, prostitution, incest, rape, polyandry, sinful lust, and pedophilia, among other things.[101] These acts were characterized by Driscoll as idolatry: "You know what porn is? Idolatry. You know what fornication is? Idolatry. You know what adultery is? Idolatry."[102] When people asked him about "tolerance and diversity,'" he replied, "What about God, who says, 'It's not about your sexual orientation; it's about my glory?'"[103] Directly addressing homosexuality, Driscoll cited a passage from the New Testament book of Romans (1:26–27) using the English Standard Version (ESV), "For this reason God gave them up to dishonorable passions. For their women exchanged natural relations for those that are contrary to nature. And the men likewise gave up natural relations with women and were consumed with passion for one another."[104] Driscoll included homosexuality as idolatrous, concluding that committing homosexual acts meant "being a pervert" and "desiring" and "doing disgusting things."[105]

Driscoll demarcated the distortions of sex, explaining that the culture tended to see "sex as god," whereas the church tended to see "sex as gross."[106] He also gendered the two perspectives, associating sex as god with men and sex as gross with women. Regardless of the competing narratives (culture/church, men/women), Driscoll said the Bible presented sex as a profound gift within marriage: "If you remain pure and you're with your spouse" you will be "connected to them, to desire them, to be satisfied with them, to long for them, and in marriage that's wonderful."[107] By following his directives, couples fulfilled God's desire for them to be servant lovers to each other.

Servant Lovers

Ladies, will there be times that you don't feel like making a meal? Men, will there be times when you don't feel like earning a living? Sure. You'll do it. Why? Because you have a duty.[108]

In the *Real Marriage* series, Driscoll relied on his previous teaching from the Song of Solomon as his guide to marital sex. At the beginning of each sermon in his 2008 *Peasant Princess* series, Driscoll expressly told his congregation that the book's narrators were married, justifying their sexual relationship. The text itself never states whether the man and woman were married. Driscoll's interpretation, however, only fit his theology if the man and woman were married—otherwise, the text illustrated what he considered sex as idolatry. Driscoll actively undercut arguments regarding the fact that the text does not state the couple are married, by casting critics of his perspective as the "sex as gross" crowd.

Driscoll also revisited his interpretation of 1 Corinthians 7:3–5, which held husbands and wives mutually responsible for sexually satisfying each other. The gender differentials, however, were striking. As described in Chapter 3, Driscoll expected wives to be "a little freaky" with sex and be open to their husbands' desires, including doing things they didn't want to do ("So the wife says, 'Well, I don't do that.' Well, you should, twice."). Yet this "equality" and mutual satisfaction were decidedly gendered. Husbands' fulfilling their wives' sexual needs meant: "When she comes in and says, 'I want to cuddle,' the dude's like, 'Cuddle? I don't want to cuddle. He will be doing what? Cuddling."[109] In another example, Driscoll said if a wife wanted her husband to "get up out of bed" to "get her a snack when you're watching a movie at midnight," will he? "Yes."[110] Driscoll's interpretation of men's versus women's sexual desires were not commensurate; wives being "a little freaky" in bed and letting husbands treat breasts as "the petting zoo is open," was quite different from husbands cuddling wives and getting them a midnight snack.

The consequences of not being sexually free were different for men and women. Driscoll explained that God gave "sex for protection," because marriages without "frequent, good sex" made husbands "vulnerable" to sexual "temptation" and "danger."[111] Husbands not attending to their wives risked wives making an "emotional connection" to another man and devastating the marriage.[112] The ramifications for men and women were different. Perhaps Driscoll's attaching women to "sex is gross," meant they bore a greater burden of accommodating husbands, since men were considered biologically prone to making sex their god. Driscoll blamed the wider culture for catering too much to women. In an effort to shift power back into the hands of men, Driscoll explained that culture encouraged everyone to "assume that women are superior to men," pressuring "men to understand women, to sympathize with women, to empathize with women."[113] That was

"all well and good," Driscoll said, as long as wives understood "the visual nature of men, the sexual nature of men, the aggressive nature of men, the way
that men are men."[114]

Husbands could ensure their sexual needs were met by being "verbally
generous" with wives.[115] Encouraging wives with positive comments and
assuring wives that sexual desires were solely for them would result in the
sexual freedom men craved. By "capturing the heart," mind, and soul, men
could "capture the body."[116] What seemed like equality in sex was simply
women's submitting to husbands' sexual desires. The aim for Driscoll was for
men to use a variety of strategies to "capture" a wife's body. Men's pleasure in
sex was primary. Driscoll's instruction, at best, gave women agency in sex, at
worst it gave men the power to manipulate women to obtain sex. As the covenant marriage unveiled the benefits of sex, one logical outcome—apart from
pleasure—was children.

Having Children

God calls [children] a blessing. They teach us so much.[117]

Complementarians believe motherhood is one of women's primary roles. As
covenant heads, however, men bear responsibility for their wives and children. Citing sociologist W. Bradford Wilcox, Driscoll told his congregation, "Statistically, it has been proven that Christian daddies are the best."[118]
Driscoll then contrasted this to the secular culture, telling men they wouldn't
get very much encouragement "to be selfless, chaste before marriage, faithful
in marriage . . . generous to their family with their money, and the values of
God. Those are the values that are nurtured and encouraged within Christian
churches like ours."[119]

In the Q&A following the *Real Marriage* sermon "Can We ?", the Driscolls
addressed the question, "Can we marry without the intention of having children?" Grace Driscoll responded to the question saying, "I used to believe
that everyone should have kids, no matter what, and I believe that everyone
should desire kids, because that's what God commands—to be fruitful and
multiply."[120] Driscoll joined his wife in the discussion, taking a familiar jab
at the wider culture's expectations of dual-working parents, guessing that
some couples should not have children, "because you're selfish and you
both have your careers, and you don't want to be inconvenienced."[121] Grace

concurred, reinforcing that a principle role for women was in raising children. Therefore, "to not want to have kids is, I would say, selfish, because children are a blessing."[122] Grace elaborated, saying, "Women are saved through childbearing," but quickly backpedaled to say women were not "saved eternally" by childbearing, but "redeemed, day after day after day through raising our children."[123] The Driscolls assured their audience that Mars Hill Church had "tons of couples" who initially did not want children, but "worked through that issue" and were "thankful" and "blessed" by the children they had.[124] Similar to the Driscolls' understanding that sex was a cornerstone to marriage, so was having children.[125] Women built their homes by mothering. Without a father's authority, however, a mother's work was in vain.

The Importance of Fathers

Every child should have a fulltime youth pastor, and his name should be "Dad."[126]

Consistent with his essentialist gender theology, Driscoll's expectations for how men father were gendered. In describing praying for his sons versus his daughters, Driscoll said, "When I held my daughter for the first time, I prayed for her health, her salvation, and her husband."[127] For his son, Driscoll prayed for a wife and salvation, but also "for him to be a godly man and a good Christian so that he can know the gospel and love and cultivate a woman to look like [the] Proverbs 31 [woman]."[128] Driscoll's masculine-focused theology portrayed men's failures to father sons as sundering God's hierarchical gender order: "It should begin with dads teaching boys. Some of the reason why we have young men that are lost, and they're weak, and they're soft, and they're confused, or they're rebellious, or they're defiant, or they're dangerous is because their dad didn't do his job."[129]

Driscoll regularly regaled his audience with tales of his five children. Illustrating his own efforts to train his sons in the gender hierarchy, Driscoll told a story of how one of his toddler sons once put his boots and coat on to go "bye-bye" with his mother.[130] Driscoll told him he needed to "stay here with Daddy." Driscoll's toddler son told him, very firmly, that he had to go. Driscoll asked his son, "Well, why do you have to go?" His son said, "I will protect [Mom]." Driscoll asked him, "How are you gonna protect her?" His son replied, "I'm a tough guy." Driscoll addressed the church saying, "that's good," because his son's idea is, "I love Mommy and we need to keep an eye on her. She's valuable." Driscoll said, "if at two he gets that, then at sixteen he won't curse her out and smack her around the house. Right?"[131] Driscoll's son was learning the "order of creation," where men (even toddler boys) had the authority to protect women. Without men's protection, women were vulnerable to the violence of men, even to the violence of their sons, who could grow up to curse them and smack them around. In Driscoll's complementarian theology, women needed men to be mentored in Christian masculinity to save them from violence.

When Dad was doing his job, a mother's job was made much easier. Even when Driscoll charged women with primary parenting, mothers' work was seen as less valuable than that of fathers: "Because if Mom is trying to love the kids . . . and Dad never picks up his Bible, he is undermining all of her efforts."[132] Men reading their Bibles modeled Driscoll's gender hierarchy, where children "go to their father for a question, he goes to his Father for the answer," cementing masculine headship and authority.[133]

Since Driscoll's theology held men accountable for their wives and children, what happened when children misbehaved? A question posed during a *Real Marriage* Q&A asked, "If a child grows up and makes bad decisions relationally, is that always a reflection on the father?"[134] Driscoll responded that it was, but explained that there were examples in the Bible "where godly parents have children who act in" ungodly ways, so a father may not be at fault.[135] Men may bear some responsibility, by virtue of their role as covenant heads, but there was not a direct cause-and-effect relationship between fathers and children's behavior. In fact, in a *Peasant Princess* sermon, Driscoll said fathers "can be forgiven for almost anything."[136] Relating a story of a "daddy who grew up beating his daughter—very physically violent."[137] This man "got saved, met Jesus, was repentant," and now takes his daughter to lunch each week. Driscoll explained this was the father's way of showing how he "should have been loving" and "spending time" with his daughter after he'd "stolen those good memories and hours from" her.[138] So now the father gives that time back to his daughter because he's "really sorry." Driscoll described this as "an example of restitution."[139]

Similar to Driscoll's forgiving men who had sex before marriage, this example reinforced the idea that men's mistakes could be forgiven. Fathers modeled the hierarchical nature of Driscoll's gender theology, but children going astray was not all their responsibility, nor was their abusive behavior if they were repentant. The rhetoric Driscoll used for mothers was different.

Driscoll described mothers' failures as creating children who were a "complete disgrace." Fathers—even abusive ones—had a special role to play in parenting, especially for their daughters.

Dads and Daughters

[I]f you are blessed as a man to raise a little girl, you have been given an amazing honor.[140]

Driscoll often spoke about the special bond between fathers and daughters. In *The Peasant Princess* sermon "I Was a Wall," Driscoll said, "Do you know what's one of best things that a little girl can have? A dad who walks like Jesus." In the sermon, Driscoll took the wider culture to task, saying, "Too many gals don't have a dad. Some do have a dad; he's a drunk, he's a pervert, he's the porn guy, he's violent, he's abusive, he's a molester." In a familiar pattern, Driscoll equated non-Christian men, and possibly non–Mars Hill men, with violence, reinforcing the need for girls and women to be protected. Part of this protection included men actively participating in their daughters' courtship. In his sermon, Driscoll described how the father–daughter relationship should work, with fathers not being "overbearing," with "all kinds of slavish rules," yet also not permissive—for example, fathers shouldn't just "put" their daughters in a "car with some guy," letting "her go wherever he takes her, to do whatever he wants." Instead, that guy needed "to come honor" Driscoll, because "that's my daughter and I love her. That's biblical protection and oversight."[141]

In "I Was a Wall," Driscoll also explained that fathers were expected to train daughters "to be attractive but not seductive." Driscoll described being "very scared" when attending dinner parties, Bible studies, or other events where little girls walk up to "perfectly strange men" asking "to be held, picked up, or [climbing] right up [to] sit on his lap." Little girls doing those things weren't getting their father's affection, Driscoll said, adding "Daddy needs to give that." A daughter's not receiving a father's affection was "in a very dangerous position, as a little girl, with men who are abusive."[142]

Men not actively parenting their daughters by giving them affection had daughters who were "sexually loose," "promiscuous," "in pornography," and working at "strip clubs," or in "massage parlors."[143] To avoid promiscuous daughters and protect them from abusive men, Driscoll emphasized using violence to maintain a daughter's chastity and her relationships. "Everything looks different when you have a daughter, right, dads?"[144] Driscoll said, "I would take everything I've learned from watching CSI on how to hide a body," and "would use it."[145] Driscoll's rhetoric was laced with warnings for women's unchecked sexuality, while encouraging the use of violence to maintain a father's authority over daughters.

Fathers were tasked with monitoring daughters, because Driscoll believed daughters without fathers, or with inadequate fathers, grew up to be "doors" (promiscuous), not "walls" (chaste).[146] Men needed to model the divine gender hierarchy to their daughters, in order to stop them from "craving male attention," so that they can be good helpers to their husbands, rather than disgraceful or disrespectful wives. As previously noted, a consequence of wives' disrespect was divorce, Christian men didn't have to "put up" with disgraceful wives.[147] Disgraceful wives who precipitated divorce were a cancer to men.

Divorce

There's way too much divorce.[148]

In the *Real Marriage* sermon "Friend with Benefits," Driscoll addressed divorce, saying there were occasions when the Bible allowed for divorce. What tended to happen, he said, was people could have "sin in their life, be married to someone" and think they've "married the wrong person" ("They never think, 'I'm the wrong person'"). Driscoll complained that couples told him, "God wants me to be happy!" to which he replied, "God wants you to be holy," reminding them Jesus "didn't hang on the cross" because the Father wanted him "to be happy." People "fall out of repentance," Driscoll said, "but they don't fall out of love." When people say they've fallen out of love they are abdicating their responsibility to their spouse. Driscoll told them not to follow their hearts, because hearts "can be deceptive, and deceitful, and wicked." Driscoll said that some marriages were difficult because some spouses were difficult, making life "painful" and "arduous," because these spouses were "stiff-necked," "hard-hearted," "stubborn," and "tough." God isn't punishing "you, but he's sent you on a divine mission to serve," pursue, love, forgive, and help their difficult spouses. In this process, Driscoll expected some spouses to realize "they're not the only sinner in the marriage," God was sanctifying them, too.[149]

One reason for divorce was adultery. Driscoll told his audience that while adultery constituted one condition for divorce, at Mars Hill he had helped couples forgive and reconcile.[150] In fact, Driscoll reported he'd seen divorced couples "come to faith in Christ in repentance" and subsequently officiated their remarriages.[151] Driscoll clarified that he was not saying there weren't conditions for divorce and remarriage, but it was better for people to ask if there were ways they had contributed "to the devastation of the marriage."[152] Again, Driscoll subtly shifted expectations for men versus women caught in adultery. In a *Peasant Princess* sermon, Driscoll told the story of a man who had committed adultery, Driscoll said the man took a business trip, which caused his wife anxiety. Deflecting his responsibility, the man told Driscoll, "Well, Christians are supposed to forget."[153] Driscoll countered him saying, "Jesus doesn't come with a side of amnesia. You still remember things. It doesn't work like that. 'Oh, you beat me? I don't even remember that.' No, we remember. We just choose to not hold it against someone."[154] Driscoll "remembered" the man's sin, but at Mars Hill it was not held against him once a man repented. Women's sins (adultery) were a different matter.

Driscoll warned the men at Mars Hill about divorce in "The Little Foxes," a sermon in *The Peasant Princess* series. In the sermon, Driscoll told men, "particularly you single guys," to be aware of "no-fault" divorce laws because wives could betray them. Describing how men who loved their wives, went to work, worked hard, provided, and had kids with stay-at-home-wives could find that those wives would leave. A woman could meet "her soulmate on-line," have "an emotional affair," hook-up "with some guy," run "off with the kids," file "for divorce," get "half of everything" a man owned, including the kids, "because custody generally goes to the primary caregiver, and if your wife stayed home, she's primary caregiver."[155]

Driscoll furthered his point in "The Little Foxes" sermon by following his cautionary tale with an example of his "buddy" who "loved Jesus, loved his wife, loved his kids, worked his job." This buddy's wife stayed at home to take care of their kids but rejected her husband's authority. When her husband was "out working hard," she ran around on him, "met her soulmate" (some "underemployed guy"), filed for divorce, and took "half" of his buddy's money, "and his kids." Now, Driscoll said, his buddy picks up "his kids from a house that he paid for, from a man that stole his wife and children." Driscoll concluded his anecdote, telling the men at Mars Hill, "You guys need to be very careful that you're looking for a good life and a good wife and not just a good time."[156] Driscoll painted women as a threat to men's success as covenant heads. Women being conformed to the wider culture, as well as their promiscuous nature, made them a threat to men's authority. It was difficult not to see Driscoll's hypermasculine theology as a reflection of his own biography, reading his marital struggles into the lives of millions of Christians.

The Driscolls Survived and So Can You

This is unfair. I deserve better.[157]

In "New Marriage, Same Spouse," the first sermon in the *Real Marriage* series, Mark and Grace Driscoll spoke of their foibles and successes in marriage. The impetus for the *Real Marriage* book and subsequent sermon series was a secret that negatively impacted the Driscolls' marriage. The story the Driscolls shared illustrated the roles of men and women in a complementarian marriage, while highlighting the damage women can cause to their marriages. In the sermon, Driscoll described the couple's premarital process, where a pastor told them to share their sins with each other. Driscoll recounted asking, "All of it? What about the nasty stuff?" and was told, "You've got to share all your sin." While Driscoll thought he and Grace had shared everything during their premarital counseling, Grace hadn't told him one thing. At this point in the sermon, Driscoll referred his audience to the *Real Marriage* book, which detailed the secret Grace kept from him. In the book, Driscoll writes he awoke one night to a vision of Grace being unfaithful. In the vision, Driscoll "saw in painful detail Grace sinning sexually during a senior trip she took after high school when we had just started dating."[158] Driscoll said the dream was so clear, "it was like watching a film—something I cannot really explain but the kind of revelation I sometimes receive."[159] The next morning, Driscoll asked Grace if what he had seen in the vision was true. It was. Grace took responsibility for her "act of sin," and for hiding it from her husband, saying, "This set up our life on a foundation of dishonesty."[160]

Resuming the "New Marriage, Same Spouse" sermon, Driscoll told his audience that when Grace confirmed the incident in the vision he felt "humiliated" and his "pride was really damaged," saying he was "a very proud man, in the worst sense of the word." He then said, had he known her secret, "I wouldn't have married her." As a Christian pastor with a pregnant wife, Driscoll felt the couple had to stay together, "But at that point," he "responded sinfully," "shamefully," and "bitterly." Driscoll interrupted his story to ask the audience, "What's your secret?" which he said would be a recurring theme throughout the sermon series. Without spouses sharing their secrets, he said, marriages could not flourish. Driscoll picked up the thread of his story, explaining that instead of responding to Grace's secret "biblically, humbly, graciously," he became embittered against God, thinking, "I'm a godly man. I read the Bible, I pray, I study, I serve, I give. . . . I'm a hard driver, big-time performer. Don't I deserve better than this?" Not only was he bitter against God, but Driscoll was also embittered against Grace, for "many years."[161]

In that first sermon of the series, Driscoll confessed to his congregation that for a decade he and Grace were in a "very lonely place," where his words often "brought death and not life." Yet Driscoll's words were not directed solely at his wife, but at a worldwide audience as he generalized from his own life experiences and inclinations to all men and women, making sure to put men (particularly church planters like himself) at the apex of his gender hierarchy. Driscoll apologized to his church saying that as he struggled in his marriage, his tone became "chauvinistic" and "harsh," which he regretted. Driscoll addressed those who had been at Mars Hill during that time, asking for their "forgiveness" and saying that "by the grace of God," he hoped to "set a better example."[162]

Driscoll's apology notwithstanding, the example had been set; a hypermasculine gender theology impacted all areas of the lives for the people of Mars Hill. Some thrived under Driscoll's teaching, some rejected the teaching outright, others tried and failed to adhere to the doctrines. Regardless, Driscoll's hypermasculine, complementarian theology made a mark in how Mars Hill members interpreted biblical texts regarding family and how they practiced or failed to practice the church's ideal.

Walking the Talk: Relationships in Practice

Mark had read some sort of research book about [how] . . . Gen Y . . . didn't know how to be a loving husband or a wife, they didn't know how to be a man or a woman, they didn't know how to be a family, and so Mars Hill felt like that was part of their mission.

—Kendra

Mars Hill Church promoted a success sequence for men defined by completion of a degree, obtaining a career position, marrying, and having children. The sequence is most possible for white, middle- to upper-middle class men and women, the same demographics that defined the average Mars Hill Church member. Driscoll's gender theology was built on a nostalgic breadwinner/homemaker ideal with race- and class-based assumptions. The church stressed men's taking responsibility via a success sequence, which theoretically resulted in women's success, as well. The success of the sequence at Mars Hill was varied. For some, marriage and children did not always result from following the church's gender doctrine.

Singleness: Second-Class Citizens

Because I was single, I felt second class.

—Delilah, WLMH

Being single at Mars Hill Church could make people feel like "second-class citizens." The church's complementarian theology was about heterosexual families: men and women marrying and having children. While Driscoll occasionally told singles they shouldn't feel pressure to marry, the church's mission and rhetoric contradicted him. Singles felt the pressure. Theo, a single man in his mid-twenties, told me that it was a "problem" that Mars Hill's theology "assumes . . . that I need to get married and have a family. If I am not doing that, then what am I doing? Obviously, I am strong enough to know that I don't need that yet, but there are plenty of . . . single guys, single women even, who are thinking to themselves, 'Well [what do I do] in the meantime?'" Theo paused, and then said, "Yeah, that's hard."

Like Theo, Kendra felt "totally fine being single," telling me, "I didn't feel inadequate in my life, or like that was a deficit in my life." For many others, being single could be like being "on the Junior Varsity team of Christianity," where singles were seen as "automatically less mature due to their singleness," as Matthew described on We Love Mars Hill (WLMH). On the same forum, Rowan stated that several leaders asked him, "So, you're successful and have your shit together, but are single and appear to be pursuing no one . . . what's up with that?" Rowan said, "This confirmed what I knew all too well: as a single guy in his mid-twenties, I was a fish out of water" at Mars Hill. For single women there was a dual hardship. Not only were they single, but they could do nothing but wait in hope that a man initiate the court-ship process. Even women in committed relationships could feel secondary to their boyfriends and fiancés.

The men and women at Mars Hill Church, by and large, understood and accepted the church's gender doctrine. As Cammie told me, single women at the church "subscribe to the belief that when they do find someone, and they do get married, that they want the man to be the leader in the relation-ship." Cammie also made sure that I understood that these beliefs weren't confined to Mars Hill: "I think that comes from even outside of Mars Hill," that "traditionally, culturally" men being relationship leaders "is the inter-pretation. I think Mars Hill furthers that and maybe even takes it one step up." While they may have accepted men as leaders in theory, single women at Mars Hill were sometimes surprised at how this functioned in prac-tice. For example, Kendra found dating at Mars Hill to be a problem. She described the single men at Mars Hill as "pursuing" women for marriage. After being asked out by several men, she told me, "I was like, 'Nope. No thank you, you're really awkward.' It just felt like [men] have all the power in this situation, like we just heard a sermon that gave it all to [them], and so if I don't say, 'Yes' [to dating] then I'm either asexual or a bitch." Even though Driscoll reported that women had the right to accept or decline a man's romantic attention, in practice, saying "no" to a man could be a problem.

The significance of men having "all the power" as covenant heads im-pacted single women in other ways. For example, Driscoll's emphasis on the role of men, especially fathers, in preparing daughters for marriage meant that single women were encouraged to seek out a "male head," to provide them "covering" before entering relationships. Kelsey, a newlywed in her early thirties described this process, telling me that single women at the church "felt like they needed to find a male head, who was married, within the church that would give them permission" to date. These male mentors were given "permission to directly talk to the men they were dating, espe-cially if they were that serious." Not all single women at the church sought out these mentors, but for women who did there was a "Christian cache," and "a sense that that's the right thing to do, and that you're setting yourself up for a really good marriage and good relationships if you've got a head covering of a man that, for lack of a better word, sanctions the fact that you can date this guy." Having a surrogate "head" meant women were "getting another spir-itual father from the church."

Single women also reported feeling secondary to the men they were dating. As part of the premarital process at Mars Hill, couples were assigned married couples as mentors, but met within gender-segregated groups; the two women meeting separately from the two men. Maddie told me these meetings were frustrating because her mentor "always brought [everything] back to [her boyfriend]." Maddie's story encompasses the hallmarks of a "classic courtship" at Mars Hill. Maddie moved to Seattle after graduating from college and immediately began attending Mars Hill Church. She liked the church and its complementarian theology, which "was in line with a lot of other churches" she had attended. Maddie said she "felt really good about what [Driscoll] preached" because it "aligned with what I interpreted Scriptures to say and what I had been taught growing up." Maddie met a man in her community group, who made his intentions to pursue her clear, telling her, "I want to date you and I date to marry someone." The man felt "called" to become a church planter, and asked Maddie if she would "follow him wherever he went." She thought that was "really romantic" and agreed.

The couple began the premarital process at the church, being mentored by the young married couple who led their community group. In her gender-segregated mentoring sessions, Maddie felt her mentor was too concerned that she didn't understand the honor it was to follow her fiancé into the mission field. Maddie had a professional job and her mentor was concerned she was "too independent" to commit to marriage with a church planter. What was worse, she told me, was that after her boyfriend's sessions with his mentor, he would question her commitment to follow him. One night, waiting for her fiancé to finish meeting with his mentor so the couple could join her parents for dinner, Maddie received a call from him. Her fiancé said he didn't believe she was ready to follow him in anything he wanted to do, and he broke up with her over the phone. Maddie was devastated. "In retrospect I can say that that language could have been a telling sign—it was just about following him. It wasn't about our marriage or our plans or more specifically the Lord's plan for us," Maddie told me. After several months of coming to terms with her broken engagement Maddie said, "I didn't really see any of the real explicit contradictions to what I understood and believed the church was teaching until I was no longer engaged."

The resources the church put into mentoring dating couples was part of the larger oversight of the church regarding singles. Writing on Mars Hill Was Us (MHWU), Aubrey described how the Mars Hill leadership was "way too involved in everyone's lives," adding, "Accountability is a good thing, but seriously, why did everyone have to talk to a pastor or community group leader first, before they went on a date?" While women were ostensibly more highly monitored in the courtship process, men also felt the oversight for singles was too much. On MHWU, Simon shared his concerns with the church's oversight regarding dating, saying he had an acquaintance, "who was exactly the kind of man Mars Hill wanted men to be" (dedicated to Jesus, with a career, and ready to start a family), but who had been forced to go outside of Mars Hill to find "potential mates." When the acquaintance approached women at the church, "he had to run a gauntlet of questions like, 'What are your intentions with this lady?'" The young man decided to stop "pursuing any relationship with women in the church" and looked "elsewhere."

While men could feel the pressure of being single and of being monitored by the church as they began dating relationships, the process of oversight also differed for them. The leadership at Mars Hill was male, which meant that single men benefited from multiple mentorship opportunities. Evan described how he benefited from Mars Hill's mission to get men married, on MHWU, writing that a Mars Hill pastor decided to help Evan "find a wife." Evan explained that after a church worship service, the pastor "went around the room, pointing at ladies he had seen me interacting with," asking, "What about her?" "She talks too much." "What about her?" "I think she has a boyfriend." Eventually, the pastor pointed out Clara, who he eventually married.[163] Evan said he and Clara dated for about six months before he proposed, and they were married ten months later, "and in the world of Mars Hill, that's a long engagement." They were pregnant "about ten months after that."

The process that helped Evan find Clara and start his family seemed positive to him at the time, but at some point, "those blinders started coming off. I saw things a little more clearly. The attitude of finding a wife seems strange to me now. It seemed more like hunting than pursuing. Clara always jokes that I stalked her." Mars Hill Church empowered men to be heads/leaders in their churches and families. Women could feel that men had "all the power." Men were adjured to "pursue" women and to "take" wives. Even women who accepted the gender theology at Mars Hill were surprised at being treated as secondary to their boyfriends and husbands. Another area of oversight that could frustrate singles at Mars Hill was their teaching on sex outside of marriage.

I Kissed Dating Goodbye

"Oh, me and my girlfriend are almost married so we are having sex [but] we still love Jesus." Mark would . . . say, "You are straight sinning."

—Theo

Singles who wanted to date were expected to adhere to the church's policy on (no) sex outside of marriage. When she described dating at Mars Hill, Kendra laughed, telling me that Driscoll was "always preaching" that, " 'If you're sleeping with your girlfriend, then that's sin. Break up. Go home and breakup with her, send her a text message right now,' like 'She's gonna be pissed,' and 'She's gonna hate this church, and hate Christians, but you're gonna breakup with her.' " Driscoll's rhetoric highlighted his "countercultural" stance, by juxtaposing a sexually promiscuous secular culture with Mars Hill's gender doctrine. Driscoll regularly told the men in his audience that having sex before marriage was practicing for divorce. The concern was not just about intercourse before marriage, but of other kinds of physical intimacy.

One of the most influential evangelical "purity culture" books was Joshua Harris's, *I Kissed Dating Goodbye*. Published in 1997, the book influenced a generation of evangelicals to focus their dating (or courtship) only on someone they expected to marry. As indicated by its name, the book also counseled that couples should not share physical intimacy before marriage, including kissing. Taking the lessons from Mars Hill and books like Harris's, Maddie and her fiancé waited until they day they were engaged for their first kiss. The next day, however, Maddie's fiancé told her, "We can't [kiss again] until we are married." Maddie felt rejected and ashamed. At the same time, the pastor mentoring her fiancé instituted a rule at his Mars Hill campus that couples could not kiss before marriage. Maddie said her Mars Hill campus was, "90 percent, if not more, college-age students [and] he made a rule that you couldn't kiss before getting married! To me that is just absolutely insane." Maddie told me, "It was really shameful for me. It felt like a lot of shame on me, and it made me feel like [our kissing] was gross." Maddie says that she now recognizes that wanting to kiss the man she loved was "a natural and healthy desire," and the no-kissing rule was not biblical, but at the time, the emphasis on physical purity made her feel guilty and wrong.

While Driscoll rebuked singles, regardless of gender, for having sex out-side of marriage, his tone and rhetoric were different when dealing with men versus women. Driscoll could find reasons why or how men could be forgiven for having sex outside of marriage. He seemed to believe that men's sex drive could not always be contained. That expectation was never accorded to women. When Driscoll related the story of Grace's "secret" he blamed the secret on the poor quality of the early years of his marriage, saying, "Had I known, I wouldn't have married her." Grace's having sex with another man when she began dating Driscoll disqualified her from being married to him. Delilah relayed a similar experience on WLMH. Describing herself as someone "with a past," Delilah wrote, "It was clear that I was lesser not solely because of my past, but because I was a woman with a past." The pastor responsible for mentoring Delilah's boyfriend told him "he could be a 'righteous man' and choose to end" the relationship because of Delilah's past. "The point was clear," she wrote, "I was damaged goods and if he wanted to end things, he should do so quietly."[164]

Marriage in Practice

It seems like everyone at Mars Hill Church is anxious to be married.
—Valerie

Mars Hill Church's mission to make families stronger by making men better husbands and fathers offered practical advice to men and women on suc-cessfully achieving a complementarian marriage. Driscoll's family ideal was reminiscent of the breadwinner/homemaker ideal, which many Americans believe to be the "natural" family form. Yet, Driscoll's complementarian family was treated as counter to the wider culture, making it seem unique and making people at Mars Hill feel they were singled out for their faith, similar to sociologist Christian Smith's argument that evangelicalism thrives when evangelicals feel persecuted for adhering to their faith.[165] Theo laughed when he described Driscoll's telling a story about walking around Seattle with his growing family and saying, "Yeah," in Seattle, "when you see a family of three kids, husband, and wife walking down the street, people start staring at you and you look like a zoo." Driscoll regularly joked from the pulpit about how Seattleites rudely asked about his five children, facetiously responding, "Yes, we breed. It's fun."[166]

Many families benefited from the support Mars Hill provided to them. Kirsten, a woman in her late thirties, told me that, after getting engaged, she and her husband decided to make Mars Hill their church home. They started the premarital class, met regularly with a pastor, and then were married by an elder at the church. Once married, Kirsten and her husband joined the "young-marrieds Bible study," which "was great, because there were just other married couples. We talked about . . . things that come up in the first year of marriage." The church's support for young married couples was so compelling, Kirsten and her husband decided not to move out of state, where her husband was planning to finish his education. "The biggest thing that swayed us to stay [in Seattle] was being a part of Mars Hill. We just couldn't imagine being married and not having the support" of the church. Once they had their first child, Kirsten quit her job to become a stay-at-home-mom. She said, "I was involved in a woman's group for a little while, just to get some support as a mother, and try to figure out how to do that." Later, she and her husband experienced a marriage "crisis," but again, the support at Mars Hill saved their marriage because, "we had people that were there to support us and to walk through that with us. That is what the body of Christ should be."

Kirsten told me that staying at home with her kids was what God had called her to do: "I'm not willing to let somebody else raise my kids. . . . If that means I stay home with them, then that's what that looks like. . . . I'm not really willing to change my priorities for a job. I feel like that would be not trusting God for providing for us and sacrificing my children for finances."[167] Kirsten and her family benefited from the church's focus on homebuilding because she could seek advice from older women at the church, as well as taking classes on parenting, and participating in moms groups: "I guess the mission of the church has impacted the mission of our family," she told me.

Kirsten's story illustrated what Faith described in Chapter 3. As a woman who had left Mars Hill because the church wouldn't support her career, within a few years Faith found herself a struggling stay-at-home mother. Saying that she and her overeducated friends were running households poorly and raising children blindly, Faith recognized that she would now benefit from Mars Hill's complementarian theology. Women at Mars Hill might flounder, like "desperate housewife" Darla, but they had support and status.

Apart from the programs and groups geared toward mothers, Kirsten described the support she felt from Mars Hill's mission to make men better husbands and fathers: "There is this undeniable—just weightiness— that a father has in his family. I saw this in my husband . . . where his

actions . . . impacted our whole family, and our marriage, and our relationship." Consciously or not, Kirsten utilized Driscoll's idea that mothers could
love children, but if fathers were not leading in the home, it wasn't enough: "I
could do that on my own as much as I can, but when you don't have . . . both
parents doing that, I think it doesn't hold the same weight." Kirsten considered
her husband's role crucial to raising their sons. She channeled Driscoll's rhetoric of boys being prone to becoming abusive without a father's guidance: "I
have two boys, and I feel like, gosh, as a parent, the damage that they could do
if they grow up to be rebellious and boys who use women and don't protect
them, who have kids and abandon them . . . that could impact generations."
Having their father present, to Kirsten, meant her sons would learn to "love
Christ and to protect women and to value them and cherish them and have
sons who do the same thing."

Mars Hill Church's emphasis on family and the role of men as husbands
and fathers was positively experienced by many men, as well. Theo, who
was single, explained to me that Mars Hill emphasized "doing family right."
Drawing on gender essentialism, Theo said that how men love their children
and wives "speaks volumes, because . . . most men struggle with . . . laziness, a
hardness of heart. It is harder," he said, "for God to get into the hearts of men
than it is for women," which is why he thought Driscoll's mission to preach to
men was so important:

> Men need it more, so let's preach to the fathers, so they can get themselves to-
> gether, because when a father loves the family, it turns it around. . . . Women
> can love their kids . . . they are gifted at that, but when a man changes . . . it
> is such a drastic change, that it can really change the way that the family is
> perceived, the way that the kids are interacting with each other, and I think
> just the whole family dynamic gets a lot better when the father is changed.
> So that is the whole . . . desire and the teaching of Mars Hill.

Several men expressed that Mars Hill had made them better husbands and
fathers. For Bart, writing on MHWU, Mars Hill "helped me truly save my
life and become a better father, husband, and overall child of God." Dylan
told a charming story of meeting his wife at Mars Hill on MHWU, saying
it took him "well over a year to finally get enough courage to ask her out."
Once they did go out, Dylan said, "I sometimes kick myself in the rear for not
asking her out sooner! I mean, what in the world was I waiting for, right?"
He then wrote, "Time and again, the Lord has been faithful in showing me

that I wasn't ready for marriage. There were so many areas of my life and in my heart that Jesus wanted to do some work." Dylan concludes that, by God's grace, "Jesus did a work in me . . . and changed me in the deepest places of my heart before I married her. I am thankful for the way Jesus worked through the men and women of Mars Hill Church to help me prepare for marriage and to better understand the meaning of marriage."

Mars Hill Church's complementarian family ideal worked for many, but not all families. Not following the church's prescribed gender roles could have significant consequences. Most people who could not countenance the gender hierarchy left the church. Some believed the church's gender theology was more elastic than it was. Others didn't interpret the gender theology as significant until their circumstances changed. Embodying Mars Hill's complementarian family ideal was important; it was a visible symbol of a person's commitment to being part of the Mars Hill family. Veering from the expectations of the gender theology had consequences.

Only for So Long

If you decide to leave, decide well, and with finality.

—Chase, WLMH

Mars Hill was a dynamic church with 15,000 adherents at its height. Members (and some former members) loved Driscoll's charismatic persona and his straightforward preaching. Most members at the church embraced its distinctive gender doctrine. People who could not tolerate the church's teaching simply didn't stay. Others tried staying at the church but found they could not make it work. One career-oriented woman, who loved "everything else" about Mars Hill, eventually left the church over conflicts with gender. In her mid-thirties, Faith talked about how much she and her husband enjoyed attending Mars Hill. Over time, however, the church's expectation that she quit her career to be at home and have children, made it impossible for the couple to stay. Rather than confronting her, pastors at the church met with her husband telling him, "You guys are in sin because of the way you are living." Faith's husband traveled extensively for work, which was "sinful" because it impacted their sex life. Faith told me, "[Pastor Mark] was such a literalist. He would quote scriptures to [her husband] like, 'Well, you have a sexual obligation to your wife. How can you be fulfilling this sexual obligation when you are gone?'" Faith said Driscoll "also said at some point, '[Women] are saved through childbirth.' So the fact that you have no children—what does that mean? Does that mean I am not saved, I guess? I don't know." The couple eventually left Mars Hill when Faith's husband was told, "Your wife needs to submit to you" and that the church "would not support" her career. When I spoke to her, Faith was wistful about all of the other things Mars Hill did well (worship, community), and told me how much she and her husband wished they were still there.

Others successfully adopted the Mars Hill complementarian ideal, at least initially. Sadie wrote on WLMH that complementarianism wasn't "a belief" she'd "previously held." But the theology "was presented well. Men and women are different. We do different things and have different qualities." Sadie and her husband had "chosen, for this season" of their lives, "traditional roles (where he works and I stay home with our children)," and "complementarian roles seemed to affirm" their choices. Like other women, Sadie "respected that men were trying to step up and participate." At some point, however, Sadie became "uneasy" and "began to have some serious concerns" about what she called the "elitism" at the church and a "belief in the clear perfection of their doctrine." Sadie says, "Many women referred to themselves as 'Daughters of Eve'" and that problems in marriage were attributed to sin. Not understanding "the headship teaching" meant that her community group leaders "showed irritation" when she spoke up or challenged them in the group, as her "vocal participation" was considered "out of line." She wrote, "To veer from the expectations of complementarian relationships as Mars Hill defined them was considered SIN."

Similarly, Ellie described on WLMH how her family had been living within the church's prescribed family form. When Ellie's husband lost his job during the recession, however, she and her family no longer met the church's complementarian ideal. Ellie explained, "I was told by church leaders that my husband wasn't doing enough and wasn't fit to be a father or husband since he had no job. As if all his other godly qualities are worthless because of the economy!" The pull of the church's theology was so powerful, that Ellie said, "Unfortunately, I agreed with the church and started to resent my husband for not having a job. I did this because I believed [Mars Hill] knew God's plan for our marriage, even though at my core I felt differently."

Some people referenced the *Peasant Princess* (Song of Solomon) and *Real Marriage* sermon series as changing their understanding of complementarianism. Natalie wrote on MHWU that she and her husband wanted to find a church within which to raise their family. While her family formed "deep friendships" within her Mars Hill congregation, Natalie reports that the "Song of Solomon and *Real Marriage* series nearly ruined" her marriage. During the *Peasant Princess* series, Natalie and her husband were told they "weren't having enough sex (according to the guidelines presented by Mark) and our sex life wasn't passionate and exciting enough (according to guidelines), we were in sin and not upholding biblical teachings on giving our bodies to each other." The *Real Marriage* series compounded this, sending the message that Natalie's marriage was "dysfunctional" and she and her husband should "be confessing and repentant of our hidden sins." Natalie said, "When we explained that we thought our marriage was functional and happy, and only had 'minor' sins to confess to the group, we were labeled as being unwilling to allow Jesus into our lives."

It took Natalie's family years to "recover" from the accusations and "the damage they caused in our marriage. At the time we started to truly believe we were dysfunctional because everyone said we were. We became suspicious of each other, wondering what the other was hiding that the rest of the church could surely see." Not long after the *Real Marriage* series ended, Natalie's family left the church and feared they would be "accused of abandoning the church because [they] wanted to continue in [their] dysfunctional marriage." Like Natalie, Conner and Luna also noted the negative consequences they endured from the sermons and teachings on marriage. Conner stated on MHWU that, "The *Real Marriage* series placed an unneeded stress on my marriage that heightened expectations where they did not need to be and I am still reaping the consequences." Luna reported on MHWU that she and her husband "nearly got divorced and are still feeling the repercussions of [Mars Hill's] teaching on marriage."

For many, Mars Hill's hypermasculine complementarian theology had an ugly underbelly. Women reported experiencing a darker side to the teachings that, as Kendra described, gave men "all the power" in relationships. Nora succinctly stated this on MHWU by saying, "My boyfriend turned ex-husband treated me badly using teaching he picked up at Mars Hill." Several men confessed to internalizing the church's hypermasculine teachings, negatively impacting their wives in the process. Lucas wrote on MHWU that his wife "never fit the [Mars Hill Church] mold for relationships." Instead of encouraging his wife to be who God made her, Lucas said, "I would use Scripture to lord over my wife, thinking I was justified in the eyes of God for Pharisaical self-righteousness." Evan struggled with addiction, and his wife was told that his addiction "was her fault." Evan concluded on WLMH that, in hindsight, "a lot of the stuff preached about honor and chivalry [at Mars Hill] turns out to be chauvinistic and misogynistic." Another man, Vincent, stated on WLMH that he pressured his "brilliant and hard-working wife to give up her dream of law school and have a baby and be a stay-at-home mom as soon as possible," when he "allowed others to take verses from the Bible out of context" to "rob" his wife of her dream: "I only added pressure on her. It was wrong and I'm terribly sorry."

Some women attributed a darker side to the hypermasculine theology taught at Mars Hill, claiming Driscoll's teachings had led to physical abuse. On MHWU, Addison described the church's response to her abusive husband. Several months after relocating to help build a new Mars Hill campus, Addison's husband became physically abusive. One night, pastors from the church picked her up and gave her a place to stay. When Addison pursued a divorce, none of the pastors tried to dissuade her, supporting her decision to leave the marriage. While she says she, "could not have made it during that time without [the pastors'] support and love," Addison blamed Driscoll for teaching "that men should take charge and be leaders," allowing "men like [her] ex to twist it into control and abuse their wives."

Tina also described her experience with her physically abusive husband. Writing on MHWU, Tina's account of abuse was unsettling in how it mimicked Driscoll's rhetoric regarding the cause-and-effect relationship incurred by disrespectful wives. Tina describes her abusive husband, qualifying his abuse as being exacerbated by her own actions: "I was naive and very unwise in the way I conducted myself. I tried to argue with him when he was drunk and would raise my voice at him. That instigated him physically assaulting me." Tina recognized her husband's abuse was not her fault, but still took some responsibility for it, when she concluded, "I'm not saying it's my fault, but I definitely made my fair share of mistakes, too." Unlike Addison, however, when Tina reached out to the pastors at Mars Hill, she reports they "immediately began pushing [her] to reconcile with [her husband]. But there was no way that was going to happen. I knew I had to get away." Eventually, Tina says, she was "put on church discipline and shunned."

In Chapter 3, Anna spoke of being a "failed Christian" because she couldn't make her marriage work. As the marriage faltered, Anna's husband had become physically abusive, spurring her to leave him. Anna's mother wouldn't help her leave, telling her, "This is a problem you need to fix with your husband. I am not going to be your crutch.'" Anna went back to her husband and blamed herself for her husband's abuse, telling me:

> I started reading *The Power of a Praying Wife* [and] . . . *How to Find a Hero in Your Husband*, all of these books [and] I thought . . . "It is kind of your fault. If you were to pray for him in the right way, he wouldn't have these problems" [or] "This is not just him, this is a you thing. You need to be the good wife." That kind of actually fell right along with, and in line with, what Mars Hill had been teaching, that a woman has to prop up her husband. If she is not doing that, of course the husband is going to falter.

Anna wanted to meet with a pastor at Mars Hill, but she told me, "Mars Hill had a policy at this point [that] a woman could not go to the Mars Hill elders, or go through counseling, without the permission of her husband." A married friend at the church, who was concerned, made an appointment for Anna. The elder who met with Anna was supportive: "He said, 'You can't go back to him.' He said, 'That is a very abusive relationship. That is a damaging relationship.'" That was the first time Anna realized, "I was submitting myself to abuse, because I thought that that was what I was supposed to do. I thought that I was supposed to be the good wife who kept the marriage together, the good wife who, in spite of all the negatives, made it positive." Unfortunately, the supportive elder was replaced by one who told her to go back to her husband. Having no money and no resources, Anna did go back, only to find her husband was involved with another woman. Anna divorced him and left Mars Hill.[168]

Mars Hill Church's gender theology taught a strict, hypermasculine complementarianism. Driscoll told the men at the church that they were not to abuse their wives. Yet, hypermasculinity exaggerates men's physical prowess and is laced with implied or actual violence. Minimally, Driscoll's rhetoric regularly invoked violence and his speech was often abusive, even when he preached against men being abusive. In Chapter 2, Andrew described Driscoll's preaching and tone as having "a harsh edge." Andrew also described a Sunday service where Driscoll "warned that the next week he was going to beat up the men. And he did. He shouted at them." Reflecting on this Andrew commented that Driscoll's "tone was so harsh and that happens a lot."

Driscoll's tone and his linking of violence to masculinity made Mars Hill Church's complementarian theology distinctive. Holding himself and his wife, Grace, up as examples of the proper Christian couple and family meant that the men and women of Mars Hill could emulate them and feel they were on the right track. Cammie talked about how her "guy friends" at Mars Hill mimicked Driscoll's tone and language "whether they would admit it or not." Driscoll's rhetoric and style were so relentless, she said, "I don't know how you could go there and not start to emulate that or start to think those things. Either you are going to go there and you are going to be completely on board, or you are going to go there and [be] completely turned off by it."

Cammie's concerns were best illustrated by Austin, who told me most churches had too much "wussiness" in them. Austin described his wife as, "super-gentle and sweet as apple pie." He also said that she was trying to teach him that he was being " 'rough for the purpose of being rough,' which is retarded." She told him, " 'You know, come on, you just wanna be rough around the edges, as opposed to just [being] abuseful [sic].' " But Austin was struggling on where to draw the line, because he knew he needed to be masculine ("maybe it's just sinful, like . . . there's a masculinity to it"), but he also underscored that it was he, not his wife, who had the power. Austin assured me his wife agreed with the church's doctrine of men being leaders, "she just wishes it was delivered differently, I think."

Teaching that men were "heads" of wives gave them power, which could have catastrophic consequences for women. Trying to shift a husband from being "abuseful" to just "rough around the edges" was not always successful for wives. Eleanor alluded to her concerns that the church's theology could lead to abuse, writing on MHWU, "I began to fear the idea of marriage, because I didn't know if I would ever meet a man I could obey. A close friend of mine married an abusive boyfriend because she thought his behavior was just that of a Christian man ruling her with biblical authority." Because Eleanor was considered "divisive," her friend was "no longer allowed to speak" to her, which was a concern because she has heard her friend "may be suffering physical abuse."

Like Eleanor's friend, some women who reported being abused by husbands believed enduring physical abuse was simply part of God's gender design, where women submitted to a husband's correction. Given the passive role women played in Mars Hill's version of courtship and the centrality of their roles as wives and mothers, it is not surprising that women married men who could be abusive. Waiting on a man to initiate a relationship could mean that accepting any man was a better option than remaining single and losing the ability to fulfill God's calling as wife and mother. This is true especially in an atmosphere where a woman saying "no" to dating a man made her "asexual" or "a bitch," and maybe not a good Christian woman. While some men could interpret Driscoll's rhetoric of headship and submission, taking it to extremes, other men went through a revolution in their thinking about headship and submission.

You Say You Want a Revolution

The other thing was that the man must find a job that gave him enough such that he can take care of his family if the wife doesn't work. I am thinking this is not necessarily biblical.

—Tom

Some husbands were confronted with the discrepancies between men's and women's experiences at Mars Hill. Kelsey met her husband, Will, in graduate school and began attending the church when they started dating. Kelsey struggled with Driscoll's gender theology. She talked to Will about how women were being "side-lined" at the church; he didn't see it, asking her if she was "making it up." After struggling in their first year of marriage, the couple joined a Mars Hill pastor and his wife for dinner. During the dinner, Kelsey questioned the church's gender theology. The discussion became confrontational, and the pastor looked at Will and told him he should divorce Kelsey. The pastor was serious. He told Will that the church had made a mistake in sanctioning a marriage where the wife would not submit to authority—not the church's, the pastor's, nor her husband's. Kelsey and Will left the dinner shaken.

Will was determined to reconcile with the pastor and continued to attend Mars Hill, with Kelsey accompanying him only occasionally. After several months of trying to reconcile with the pastor, who would not meet with him, Will went to the church's elders. Without any reconciliation and his continued quest to meet with the pastor, Will was asked to step down from his leadership position at the church and eventually asked to leave the church. Will continued to attend Mars Hill, believing he was following the church's protocol for reconciliation. As he tried to understand his experience at the church, Will met with a friend, who told him, "Look, Kelsey's seeing some things that are very true." The friend related stories of attending Mars Hill with women friends who felt the church distorted biblical texts relating to women. In light of Kelsey's experience, his friend's counsel, and the church's refusal to follow up with him, Will was finally convinced. "Enough," he said, and left Mars Hill.

John had a similar, though less traumatic, experience. He and his wife started attending Mars Hill after relocating from the Midwest. They loved the church and its "edginess." Over time, John's wife started to become more and more uncomfortable at the church, telling him, "I don't know about this church." John didn't understand her concerns, even when his wife would say, "Listen, [Driscoll] is saying that I shouldn't work at all, and my goal should be . . . to start having kids right away and raise a family and stay home and do that and support you in any kind of career that makes . . . money." John didn't believe his wife, telling me, "It was kind of shocking, and I was [like], 'No, that's not true. That is too extreme. I've never heard anything like that.'" More and more, however, John's wife would return from a women's Bible study to relate what she was hearing. Eventually the couple decided to leave Mars Hill: "I don't disagree that a woman should submit to her husband," John told me, "but you have to read the whole passage, too. What is the guy's side? To love your wife . . . part of loving my wife is making sure that she functions with the skills that God has given her . . . which allows her to take the role beyond the home." John interpreted the same Scripture with a different lens than Driscoll, leading the couple to leave Mars Hill, to give John's wife the option of pursuing her calling in a career.

Jared also described how he and his wife loved Mars Hill. Jared started attending Mars Hill with his college friends. When he and his wife began dating, she joined him at the church. As they dated, his wife began to question Mars Hill's gender theology. Her questioning led Jared to critique what he was hearing. Jared told me that he started to go through "a revolution" in his perspective on women and the church: "We loved so much that was going on there," but "at the same time," his "involvement started to wane because" he couldn't picture himself raising his family there. Jared said he "couldn't justify having a daughter who felt like they couldn't fully use their gifts if God called them to [not] trust them on [issues of gender] but trust them on everything else." Jared and his wife left the church because they wanted to be at a church they could support and that would support them "100 percent."

Successful Sequence?

I really wanted a family, a husband, and children, and I wanted security.
—Tina, MHWU

Driscoll's complementarian theology was attractive to many. Having clear domains and roles for men and women reflected an iconic decade of an anomalous American family form. Harnessing the language of being countercultural helped Mars Hill create a sense of solidarity for church members. Many men, women, and families benefited from the support systems and resources at Mars Hill. The formula for successful marriages, however, could not be sustained by all couples. The assumptions Driscoll's gender theology relied on required that husbands earn a wage that supported a wife and children. Even for people who believed Driscoll's theology, their economic situation could be prohibitive to achieving the ideal. Emily reported on MHWU that "because of financial hardship," she and her husband were forced to relocate, so her husband could join the military to "afford to support [the] children" they wanted to have, in order to live out the church's complementarian theology.

Other couples found that as they considered the ramifications of the church's complementarian theology, the requirements were too strict or had proved too destructive to their marriages. Others simply moved away from the church's convictions to allow women more autonomy and independence, seeing a discrepancy between what Driscoll taught as biblical versus what they thought was "mandated" by the Bible. Several people spoke of becoming egalitarian in their marriages, regretting the roles they had submitted to at Mars Hill. Some simply left the church, devastated that the church's success sequence did not work. Anna captured the heartbreak for the latter group, who believed that following the church's theology would lead to fulfilling God's purposes for their lives:

We believed this lie of all we had to do was commit our lives to God, commit our lives to church, get married and have kids and then our life would be this wonderful community and this big apple tree that has beautiful blossoms and produces beautiful fruit every new season. I truly, truly believed that once I got married and once I had babies, that my life was fulfilled, that my purpose had happened.

For better or for worse, Mars Hill Church's complementarian theology left its mark on its members. Following the dictates of the complementarian doctrine could be very positive. Kirsten, for example, felt her husband's taking authority had made a real difference in the lives of their sons. For others the church's complementarian theology could result in people, like Anna, feeling they had failed as Christians. Regardless of the outcome, the church's complementarian theology was consequential.

5

Real Consequences

Thriving in one of the most liberal cities in the nation, Mark Driscoll and
Mars Hill Church pioneered a hypermasculine complementarianism within
American evangelicalism. Like previous Protestant masculinity movements,
Driscoll's hypermasculine theology could only exist given certain historic
and sociocultural conditions. Over time, as social conditions changed—
and Driscoll's antics became more notorious—the church's strictness led
to significantly higher costs for some church members. The monitoring of
members and their adherence to the church's doctrines also ratcheted up the
church's strictness. Failure to adhere to the church's theology was interpreted
as sin, lack of faith, or "rebellion" for individual members and the practice of
shunning impacted more and more families. Driscoll's authoritarian leadership and the increasingly widespread monitoring and sanctioning of church
members forced some members to grapple with a gender theology they
could no longer practice and an institutional structure that was no longer
supportive. Posting on Mars Hill Was Us (MHWU), Ryan enumerated the
church's failings: "consolidation of power," "public lying," "financial malfeasance," "exorbitant salaries," "shady book deals," "the character assassination
of anyone who ever spoke out," and a "growing call" for change. For years the
church had successfully balanced the tenets of strictness to hold the right
balance of tension with the culture. Increasingly, however, the church's exclusive doctrines and extensive commitments made the church too expensive.

Strictness and Mars Hill Church

"Strict" churches are paradoxical. They hold exclusive doctrines and generate
extensive commitments from members. These characteristics can create
strong congregations, bringing significant rewards to individual members.
Thousands of Mars Hill members enjoyed Driscoll's high-energy preaching,
unapologetic demeanor, access to the church's community groups, programs,
original music, cutting-edge technologies, and scores of other resources.

Making Christianity Manly Again. Jennifer McKinney, Oxford University Press. © Oxford University Press 2023.
DOI: 10.1093/oso/9780197655795.003.0006

Actively participating in the church and adhering to the churches exclusive doctrines created strong community ties to like-minded evangelicals, leading to extensive commitments to the church family. Over time, however, the relationship between members and the church could sour, making a costly faith less worthwhile.

Exclusive

Mars Hill Church maintained exclusive beliefs about what was required to be a good Christian. Driscoll's teaching and persona were compelling, with members seeing his hypermasculine theology as a powerful rebuke and correction to the secular culture and more mainline ("feminized") churches. Commenting on the appeal of Mars Hill's exclusive doctrines, Cindy, whose family joined Mars Hill because of its masculine focus, told me Mars Hill had put a "stake in the ground" drawing people to Driscoll and his message. Given the "relativism in our culture," Cindy said, Mars Hill's popularity lay in its having "clearly put a stake in the ground that said, 'There are some things that are true and right, and you can trust and believe in,' giving a certain order to things." Cindy thought that message especially drew "people who felt kind of lost." When people wondered, " 'Is there anything worth believing and actually hearing?' 'You bet there is!' " Cindy saw "young men, 18 to 35, really responding to Mark Driscoll," because, "he will stand up unafraid and say, 'This is what we believe!' and 'This is what the Bible says,' even if it runs very against the culture."

Based on my interviews and the people writing on the Mars Hill forums, men did respond to Mars Hill in the ways Cindy described. Several men writing on MHWU expressed these sentiments. Ethan, for example, described his time at Mars Hill as, "all I was hoping for—a counterculture existing to worship and to reach the city. It was real in its approach, raw, and called men to move forward." Similarly, Elijah reported that he, "knew that Seattle was (and still is) a pretty liberal city," and it "was heartening to hear a preacher speak the truth so freely" regarding "sexuality, cohabitation, the emasculation of the American church, etc." Noah also noted the positive impact of Mars Hill's exclusive teachings, saying, "The truths" Driscoll shared from Scripture had "powerful impacts" on his life. "One of the most powerful things" Noah learned was "men taking responsibility for their actions."

Women responded positively to the exclusive nature of Mars Hill's theology, as well. Aimee told me Mars Hill theology had "really no gray" areas. The church, she said, was "staying true to [a] belief system, and the gospel, and not letting the world change you." Aimee loved the clarity of Mars Hill's theology, saying, "I am a person who loves guidelines, loves rules, and it makes my life easier, so I was happy to abide by [Mars Hill's] rules." Alluding to the tension between Mars Hill and the wider culture, Aimee excitedly told me, "We are not politically correct!" The lack of political correctness was a significant draw to Mars Hill. Another woman, Aria, wrote on MHWU that "a lot of people were offended by [Driscoll's] teachings," because he was "real" and "didn't sugar coat anything." Yet those were the "very things" keeping Aria "coming back" week after week.

Setting a stake in the ground, Mars Hill's exclusive doctrines, as well as the manner in which they were delivered, set the church apart from the wider culture, as well as other Christian churches. Mars Hill's doctrines were often interpreted as the only Christian truth, making salvation contingent on both believing and practicing the doctrines. Many Mars Hill members believed Driscoll taught a capital "T" truth. Tina wrote on MHWU, for example, "I immediately knew I had heard the truth when the gospel had been preached at [Mars Hill]." While many people described how they encountered "the truth" at Mars Hill, others critiqued the sense that the church had "the only truth." Writing on MHWU, Stella described an "underlying vibe" at Mars Hill, "not necessarily directly stated from the pulpit, but somewhat implied, that [Mars Hill] was the only church in Seattle preaching the truth and not being wimpy about things." Another MHWU contributor, Isabella, stated frankly, "Mark Driscoll's take on the Scriptures . . . were taught as actual gospel." Kendra explained to me that Mars Hill charted out "what was black and white, and what was right and wrong," to be "precise with the boundaries of sin." Mars Hill members, Kendra said, didn't always "realize" that the church taught "an interpretation" and "a very Mars Hillian form of theology."

The church's exclusive doctrines, delivered in Driscoll's energetic, unapologetic, and politically incorrect approach made members feel empowered. Members of Mars Hill felt transformed as they forged a counterculture in the city, recognizing and appreciating how the church's exclusive doctrines put them in tension to the city. Writing on MHWU, Colton described this feeling: "I remember Mark yelling at the crowd . . . I don't remember what [about], but he pointed at the door, and said something to the effect of, 'If you don't like it, there's the door.' Strangely, I was hooked. I liked that someone was going to preach without a concern for what others thought." Driscoll provided clarity that Mars Hill was distinct from the wider culture, and "If you don't like it, there's the door!" Adhering to Mars Hill Church's exclusive doctrines created a tribe, a family, fostering the extensive commitment that characterized membership at the church.

Extensive

Mars Hill Church's strict doctrines impinged on everything from who church members associated with to how they spent their leisure time. The high levels of commitment required by the church created strong in-group boundaries that helped sustain the church's norms and values. Many members at Mars Hill were thankful to be with like-minded others. Simon expressed this dynamic, writing on MHWU, "I had not found a 'tribe' where I felt I belonged," but "Mars Hill seemed to be the kind of place" where he could find that home. On MHWU, Elias also described how he "loved worshipping with others" who were like him and pointed to the relationship between the church's strictness and tension to the secular culture, saying he learned to be strong in his "convictions," at Mars Hill, "even though the whole country" was "moving in an opposite direction" to his beliefs.

The extensive commitment to the church created insiders and outsiders. Not only was the secular culture counter to Mars Hill, other Christian churches, and even some Mars Hill Church members, were suspect. In a *Christians Gone Wild* sermon, Driscoll asked his church, "Is Mars Hill your family?" If not, "then there's something tragically wrong with you. Maybe you're not even a Christian. Maybe you're just like Judas sent in on the team to just cause trouble."[1] Driscoll made distinctions between those at the church who were faithful members and those who weren't (the "Judases"). Driscoll warned the church that some members were threats to the church. He explained, "There's a lot of people who say they're a Christian and they're not."[2] These people are "lying or deceived" and Mars Hill members needed to be aware of them, because there are "always a few Judases in the bunch."[3] Driscoll was adamant that some at Mars Hill were really outsiders, "In this church there are people who love God and are living new lives" and there are "people who aren't living new lives, which indicates that they don't love God."[4]

Kelsey felt she'd been labeled a "Judas" after questioning the church's complementarian doctrine, which was interpreted by a pastor as disloyalty to the church. Kelsey told me, "[The pastor] did say to me that he didn't think we believed in the same Jesus. I would agree with him that we don't believe in the same Jesus, but he meant that he believed in Jesus, and I didn't." Questioning the church's doctrines demonstrated not only a lack of commitment at Mars Hill, but also the perception of being apostate, a "for us, or against us" dynamic, as Rory said on MHWU, or, as Zoey from MHWU described, a sense that some members were "potential enemies, rather than family."

The dynamic of being part of the Mars Hill family—an insider—versus being a potential enemy, was illustrated by Kirsten. Mimicking Driscoll's language about being part of the Mars Hill family, Kirsten explained to me how aggravating she found it when "outsiders" criticized Driscoll or Mars Hill. "It's weird and sad how [outsiders] don't understand" Mars Hill, Kirsten said. Kirsten described how her brother, who didn't attend Mars Hill, would make comments "about what Pastor Mark said in a sermon—and he didn't even hear it. Someone else told him, and he has to tell me, and it's very critical, negative," Kirsten complained. "He's never even been to Mars Hill! Why does he care? When you're not a part of the family, why do you care?" These strong in-group boundaries were created by the extensive commitment to the Mars Hill family and their adherence to exclusive doctrines. An unintended consequence of this insider/outsider dynamic were costs associated with monitoring other church members, to make sure they were truly part of the Mars Hill family. For those who fell short, sanctions could be costly.

Expensive

Mars Hill Church imposed nonnegotiable demands on its members' behavior. In meeting these demands, members enjoyed being part of the Mars Hill family, which provided rewards—high personal or family satisfaction, belonging to a group of like-minded others, and access to resources. While the church's strict doctrines and extensive commitment put members in tension to the secular culture, they also highlighted members' awareness of internal threats. Driscoll warned church members about the destructive nature of threats coming from inside the church body. At one point Driscoll asked his church, "How in the world does a church like Mars Hill defend [and] protect itself" from "deception coming in, leading to the destruction of the church" by "people that are deceived and claim to be Christians?"[5] Driscoll's message was so pervasive, these "wolves in sheep's clothing" became a cautionary tale of insiders posing a threat to the well-being of the church. Kelsey described the dynamic of labeling people "wolves" as part of a larger process at the church, saying being a member at Mars Hill "may cost you friends, loved ones, family members, [and] lovers." This strategy, she explained, created "a distrust between the people in the pews," because "when Mark Driscoll talks, there's a divide between those who are Christian and those who aren't. You are never sure who's next to you in the pew—if it's a believer or not, so you better watch out."

Church members were aware of the consequences of not being "on mission." In the fall of 2007, Mars Hill fired two popular elders for not supporting a proposed leadership reorganization at the church. Executive Elder Jamie Munson sent a letter to church members informing them that one of the fired elders, Paul Petry, was to be treated as "an unrepentant believer."[6] Munson's letter stated, "While the treatment of an unrepentant believer may seem harsh, it is actually motivated out of love and care for the individual and the rest of the church."[7] Munson referred members to the church's statement on "Church Discipline," which read, in part, "Although rejection and disassociation may seem harsh, these responses are simply a means by which the individual in question may come to an acknowledgment of their sin and repent."[8] Accordingly, unrepentant believers were to be treated "as if they were enemies of the gospel," which meant treating them "like an outcast" and an "outsider."[9]

The day after the pastors were fired, Driscoll infamously referred to them as being "off mission" and bragged about a "pile of dead bodies" behind the "Mars Hill bus," saying, "There is a pile of bodies behind the Mars Hill bus, and by God's grace it'll be a mountain before we're done. You either get on the bus or you get run over by the bus. Those are the options. But the bus ain't gonna stop."[10] Being part of Mars Hill Church required an allegiance to their exclusive doctrines and extensive structures, making the church expensive.[11] Members had to be willing to sacrifice friends and family if the church deemed them "wolves." In the wake of the church's 2014 scandals, writing on We Love Mars Hill (WLMH), Silas described how church leaders were "visiting community groups" and "labeling anyone who speaks out" about the scandals as "divisive" and "wanting to tear down the church." Silas noted how those speaking out were labeled "wolves" and pointedly stated that a recent sermon, titled "Empowered by the Spirit to Face Wolves," gave Mars Hill members, "the picture." These practices created a culture of fear at Mars Hill, because wolves were excommunicated through the church's practice of shunning.

Shunning

The shunning process at Mars Hill stripped members from access to any Mars Hill resources, and members in good standing were expected to stop communication with "unrepentant believers." Shunned former members of Mars Hill reported spending "years in isolation, cut off from friends, sometimes suffering deep clinical depression, nightmares, disillusionment and shattered faith."[12] Former members referred to the church as having a culture of fear: "At first, many people feel embraced, as if by family, perhaps the family they dreamed of but never had. But somewhere along the way, the hug turns into a stranglehold, a vice-grip that tightens every time a person asks a question, voices an opinion or stands up against mistreatment or abuse."[13]

Several contributors to MHWU acknowledged the impact of this insider/outsider culture of fear at Mars Hill Church. Chandler described his experience of being labeled a "wolf" by people he had "been good friends with for years," writing, "Most of my friends went to Mars Hill and most of them cut off all contact with me fairly quickly." Watching friends and family being labeled wolves and shunned reinforced the culture of fear, and some members strategized how to leave the church without incurring the negative consequences. Carson described how his family left the church "as quietly" as possible, after having "watched a number of folks get their reputations smeared if they raised too many issues or didn't accept very basic explanations and pleas to 'just trust the leadership.'" Leah reported how her family argued for months about leaving Mars Hill and how she "felt sick walking into the church." But Leah's husband was "nervous about leaving" after they "watched dozens" of friends leave and seen "the cruel things said to them, and about them." Amelia's experience was similar, as she described how "incredibly hard" it was to leave, and how her family "felt judged and shunned by some" when they disclosed their departure.

The culture of fear was tied to the church's authoritarian leadership, which was gendered. Driscoll's authority was attributed to his masculinity. In his booklet *On Church Leadership*, Driscoll describes how those under a pastor's authority need to obey that authority, writing, "Pastors need the people in their church to obey them and respect their God-given authority so that their work does not continually resemble a series of kicks to the groin."[14] In 2014, roiled by the controversies engulfing the church, Mars Hill members and former members expressed their concerns with Driscoll's authoritarian leadership. Again, those writing on MHWU described the church leadership's penchant for authoritarianism. Lilly stated, "If you disagreed, or challenged something, you were dismissed as being divisive and the matter was never considered. The open-handed issues that were actually closed-handed is-sues like complementarian [versus] egalitarian. Things they disagreed with were so talked down that you were essentially a heretic for holding a different viewpoint." Liam described how the leadership at Mars Hill "was very heavy-handed," giving "a tone of 'shut up and do as you're told' instead of working with people." Morgan said the church had "an 'obey your lead-ership and don't question the authority' attitude." Chandler described the church's "authoritarian theology," saying, "It touched everything including ideas of gender, ideas of masculinity/femininity, gender roles, relationships," and "conceptions of truth/certainty/meaning and ethics." Chandler's char-acterization was prescient. As members and former members questioned the authoritarian nature of the church and its leadership, many also began to question whether what they had learned from Mars Hill's exclusive doctrines was really true.

Reevaluating the exclusive truth claims preached at Mars Hill, Emily explained the dissonance she felt, writing on MHWU, "Once all of the allegations came out, I started questioning everything I believed and what doctrine I had put into my life. Was what I believed Bible-based or Mark [Driscoll]-based?" On the same forum, Vicki wrote that Mars Hill had taught her "everything could be answered and explained," but then she realized that wasn't "how the gospel works in the real world," and she "had to throw the whole thing out and start building truth of [her] own." Morgan posted on MHWU that, "The preaching . . . seemed to be more about Mark's personal views than the Bible." Having left Mars Hill after her marriage crumbled, Anna was familiar with this reevaluation of Driscoll's teaching and the church's exclusive doctrines, telling me, "It took me quite a while . . . to figure out what was godly and was Mars Hilly. It was, 'What does the Bible actually say about this?' and 'What is Mars Hill saying?' I thought they were one and the same. It just took me a while to realize that they weren't, they just weren't the same."

Being a member at Mars Hill Church was complex. People became members because the church was life-giving, fresh, exciting, no-holds-barred. Members were positively impacted and enjoyed Driscoll's bold style and energetic preaching. Whether they had left years before or were grap-pling with the repercussions of the 2014 scandals, then-current and former members of Mars Hill reflected on the good that had come from their time at the church. Men reported the positive impact of Driscoll's preaching. Dylan, for example, wrote on MHWU that before attending Mars Hill he had not been "a godly man," but that, "God used the preaching of Mark Driscoll and the men of Mars Hill Church" to help him see his sin, repent, and set his life in a new direction, for which he was "eternally grateful." Women's descriptions of Mars Hill's benefits often related to their husbands. On MHWU Stella wrote, "I was struggling with being [at Mars Hill], but we stayed because my husband was getting things out of the preaching. Thankfully the things he was getting were all good and inspiring him to be a better husband and person, so I was willing to sit through church for him."

Mars Hill's exclusive doctrines and extensive community made commitments rewarding, but the nature of those commitments to the doctrines and the community also made them costly. Like other charismatic leaders, Driscoll's control of the church's theological narrative effectively communicated that his doctrines were the only acceptable biblical interpretation.[15] The strictness characterizing the church brought the benefits of group solidarity and access to church programs and resources, however, it also stripped members of those resources, as well as access to their families and friends if they were perceived as divisive ("wolves"), which was equated to questioning the church's doctrines or questioning the church's authoritarian leadership structure.

When Strictness Fails

Leveraging the hallmarks of strictness can generate high levels of commitment to, and personal satisfaction from, church involvement. The positive energy generated from involvement helps to concretize the perceived truth of the church's practices and promises. Mars Hill's doctrines were interpreted as "the truth," as Bill told me, "Whether that's with a little 't' or a big 'T.'" Because the church was "straightforward" with their doctrines, Bill said, they could be "very in your face" and "uncompromising" about the exclusive nature of their beliefs.

Following the Mars Hill Church doctrines, including the hypermasculine gender doctrine, was nonnegotiable and attached to eternal salvation for members. Following these doctrines, however, could lead to diminishing returns. Eventually, strict groups can reach a point where the costs outweigh the benefits.[16] To maintain members, strict groups must adjust "to social change," not becoming "too deviant, but not embracing change so fully as to lose all distinctiveness."[17] As social conditions changed, both inside and outside of the church, maintaining the strict hypermasculine gender doctrine became too costly for many members.

Gender as Testing Ground

For nearly twenty years Mars Hill sustained an optimal level of strictness, resulting in explosive growth and creating an energetic and committed community. As an alternative to the "soft patriarchy" characterizing American evangelicalism at the end of the twentieth century, Driscoll's strict hypermasculine complementarian theology created a distinctive footprint, setting Mars Hill apart from Seattle's secular culture and from other Christian churches. Mars Hill Church's unique style borrowed elements from Seattle's liberal culture, known to locals as a place for beer-drinking and "tatt'ed" up members, yet with a theologically conservative gender doctrine. Bradley, a church staff member, explained Mars Hill's unique mix of cultures to illustrate the tension between Mars Hill and the outside world. Being "culturally liberal and theologically conservative," he told me, "confused people," because being "seen as super hip and extremely cutting edge, pushing the limits of the general culture . . . makes everyone a friend and an enemy at the same time." This unique market niche spurred tremendous growth for Mars Hill.

The church's growth, however, could not be maintained. As the church grew, doctrines seen as "open-handed" became "closed-handed" and the internal monitoring and sanctioning of members grew. The 2008 economic recession, for example, made it more difficult for church members to live into the gender doctrine. Church members like Ellie, from WLMH, whose husband lost his job, found the complementarian theology untenable given her family's new economic reality. The church, however, did not accommodate to these external economic constraints.

Others also found that the church's doctrines and promises came up short. Reflecting on his time at Mars Hill, Rowan, who had participated in mimicking Driscoll's hypermasculine persona by watching UFC fights and shaming men who did not meet the Mars Hill Church standard of masculinity, found himself seeking forgiveness from other men at the church for his past behavior. On WLMH, Rowan said the hardest thing for him to process from his time at Mars Hill was his own "response to [Driscoll's] shaming of men—shaming of me—from the pulpit." Emmett, also writing on WLMH, described feeling "shamed" and "emasculated" when he and his wife sought counseling at Mars Hill, saying the experience was "a graceless assault on my dignity, faith, and manhood." Even for those following Mars Hill's prescribed complementarian path, the costs of maintaining strict gender roles became too high. Many became disillusioned as they saw friends and family struggle.

When the church collapsed in 2014, many former members indicated embarrassment for belonging to a church with such a strict gender doctrine. Vicki reported on MHWU that she felt "embarrassed," having "been a part of an organization that treated women as less than men and didn't allow people in positions of leadership based on their gender or orientation." Lucas also reported on MHWU that Driscoll's "harping on gender roles had a negative effect" on him, and he wasn't sure why Driscoll "chose that issue," saying, "I thought I did at the time, but I am not sure now." Kendra told me that when she thought about Mars Hill's "really rigid gender roles," she found them to be "subversive and damaging." Kendra said, "not only do you get a whole gender paradigm handed to you, it has the nice icing of God all over it," a "dangerous combination," she concluded.

While Mars Hill's strict doctrines created group solidarity, not following the doctrines was blamed on individual sin. As Cammie described, the culture of Mars Hill often centered around "calling out" individual sin, which she characterized as "harsh." Others pointed out this tendency as well. Alice shared on WLMH "how harmful [Driscoll's] preaching was to [her] husband," writing of her sadness at what her husband experienced "as a result of being told almost every Sunday" that he wasn't "man enough," while being asked to adhere to "unrealistic expectations." Women also experienced feeling they weren't enough. Olivia wrote on MHWU that the bullying at the church "took a huge toll after a while," and that, as a woman, she was treated "as an afterthought" who was "attached" to her husband.

The constant monitoring and sanctioning of church members exacerbated the church's culture of fear. Writing on WLMH, Hailey described members being "afraid to question the severe complementarian theology Pastor Mark encouraged," and how Mars Hill's "chauvinistic culture" negatively impacted "the marriages of people [she] knew and loved." Hailey wrote that women at the church thought "any unhappiness they felt was because they weren't praying hard enough, didn't know how to submit to their husbands well enough, [or] didn't have hearts that were right enough." Many women did not speak up for fear of their own "failings" being made known to other members of the Mars Hill community, because the consequences of not following Mars

Hill's strict complementarian theology could be severe. Hailey's description of women feeling that they were "not enough" resonated with stories told by other women, who were afraid of gaining weight, for example, because it could lead to a husband's infidelity or to a divorce, a recurring theme in Driscoll's teaching. Even as she strove to be a good Mars Hill wife, Darla's not embracing her roles of wife and mother was characterized as "disobedience." In a blog post Darla wrote of her fear that her sin would result in her husband being fired from his staff position at Mars Hill, leading her family into home-lessness. Olivia summed up her time at Mars Hill, writing on MHWU, "The entire time I was [at the church], I always felt that I was not doing enough, giving enough, or producing enough." Complementarian gender doctrines can be fraught for women, who lack authority and access to resources, which can make them feel isolated as they struggle to live into their roles.

Dysfunctional Doctrine

Driscoll's hypermasculine theology could be dysfunctional for men and women, albeit with different consequences. Though Driscoll specifically preached against husbands abusing wives, his hypermasculine persona could be perceived as verbally abusive. In his 2009 "Marriage and Men" sermon, Driscoll "called out" men who were not taking responsibility in relationships. After listing a number of ways men fell short, Driscoll pointed out how—even in the context of sitting in the auditorium and listening to the sermon—some Mars Hill men were pretending he wasn't talking about them. Suddenly, Driscoll began screaming, "HOW DARE YOU? WHO IN THE HELL DO YOU THINK YOU ARE? ABUSING A WOMAN. NEGLECTING A WOMAN. BEING A COWARD! A FOOL! BEING LIKE YOUR FATHER ADAM. WHO DO YOU THINK YOU ARE? YOU ARE NOT GOD. YOU ARE JUST A MAN." Driscoll continued to scream, telling Mars Hill men that if they abused women, they were robbed of their mascu-linity, because there is no excuse for Christian men to abuse women.[18]

Driscoll was well known for yelling in sermons and for relying on violence—spoken or implied—as a mark of Christian masculinity. Violence is one means that allows men to maintain their authority.[19] Men who fear they are not "man enough" may turn to violence to prove their masculinity.[20] This has serious repercussions for women within complementarian relationships because they are under the authority of men. In an earlier chapter, Anna described her husband's physical abuse, linking his abuse to his fear of never measuring up to Driscoll's standard for Christian men. Anna told me:

> My husband . . . would constantly say, "I don't fit the mold of the role of the man that Pastor Mark is talking about. I am not a huge beer drinker. I don't eat a ton of red meat. I'm not out there hunting and shooting and killing. I am not this big, gruff wilderness man that Mark tries to portray as being the modern-day spiritual leader of a household." He felt very, very diminished as a man, because he did not see himself as this kind of person, and this was the example of what a godly man looked like.

Driscoll's hypermasculine theology could blur the line between men maintaining their "God-given" authority versus men committing abuse.[21] Studies examining gender norms and violence have found that "traditional gender ideologies increase the risk of violence," because women are subordinated to men's authority.[22] Intimate partner violence may not be interpreted by women as abuse, but as their own weakness, spiritual inferiority, or failure (failing their families, failing God).[23] Women experiencing violence may believe "they are called by God to endure the suffering" and to forgive their abuser.[24] Religious organizations that use "exclusively male language" and exclude of women from certain roles and responsibilities in the church can exacerbate men's violence.[25] For women who are defined by their domestic roles, maintaining marriages "for better or worse, until death do us part" is a primary duty.[26] The pressure to maintain masculine authority can result in perpetrators' abusive behaviors being defended, with victims pressured to forgive their abuses and to not involve law enforcement agencies.[27] Given the hypermasculine rhetoric and practice expected of the men at Mars Hill, regardless of Driscoll's warnings against abusing women, it may not be surprising that men who felt they could not live up to the church's ideal of masculinity may have turned to violence to assert their authority.

To be clear, Driscoll was outspoken in telling men abuse was not tolerated at Mars Hill, not least because it robbed them of their masculinity. At the same time, the church's hypermasculine theology put men in authority over women. This power imbalance, Driscoll's sometimes negative rhetoric toward women (disgraceful, loud, decay, a disease), and his use of "cause-and-effect" rhetoric could have led women and men to believe violence was a logical consequence of women's not fully submitting to a husband's authority. In Chapter 4, Addison (MHWU) blamed Driscoll's teaching ("that men should take charge and be leaders") for allowing men like her ex-husband "to twist it into" controlling and abusing their wives. Tina also reported on MHWU experiencing abuse, while mimicking Driscoll's rhetoric regarding the cause-and-effect relationship incurred by disrespectful wives, blaming herself for inciting her husband to violence. Anna also blamed herself, initially, for her husband's abuse, thinking if she had prayed hard enough, or prayed in the right way, or had been a good wife, then the abuse wouldn't have happened. Anna also cited her understanding of Mars Hill's doctrine as saying, "a woman has to prop up her husband. If she is not doing that, of course the husband is going to falter." For one couple, having a wife eat pages of the Bible to literally internalize her submission seemed utterly normative. Mars Hill Church's hypermasculine theology could leave marks, visibly and invisibly.

Plowing a Counterculture

The sociocultural conditions that helped construct Mars Hill Church's and Driscoll's hypermasculine gender theology as normative are part of the dynamic relationship between religious organizations and the broader culture. Strict churches seek to maintain tension to their sociocultural environment, which means holding beliefs and practices at odds with that culture. While Driscoll's hypermasculine complementarian theology was at odds with Seattle's progressive ethos, it was not wholly countercultural. By and large, Americans see gender differences as rooted in biology, and a breadwinner/homemaker family ideal as "traditional."

Since the Industrial Revolution and the birth of an American expectation of separate spheres gender ideologies, differential traits and roles for men and women have been attributed to biology.[28] Often, research on the biological determinants of gender difference were efforts to demonstrate the inferiority of women to men.[29] Similarly, Driscoll's rhetoric of men and women being equal, yet having different roles, recalls a mid-twentieth century shift in gender ideology when sociologist Talcott Parsons argued that women were not inferior to men, the two simply occupied different social roles; women managed the family's internal relations and men managed the family's external relations.[30] Though Parsons rejected the popular biological arguments for sex role differences in favor of learned gender patterning, he took for granted that sharply different gender roles were normative.[31] Yet the breadwinner/homemaker ideal, in practice, was short-lived, even as it endures in American culture as the iconic standard of family life.[32]

At Mars Hill, however, complementarian theology was taught and perceived as countercultural. Given the monitoring and sanctioning at the church, signaling belief in the complementarian doctrine meant striving to live as economic provider/homebuilder. Toward that goal, Mars Hill committed to paying their elders a family wage, so they could serve as exemplars of the complementarian family to the members of Mars Hill, as well as to the city of Seattle. As Seattle's cost of living skyrocketed, living in the city on a single wage became more and more difficult.[33] Adding suburban campuses could help ameliorate cost-of-living issues, but for many rank-and-file church members in the Seattle metropolitan area, the cost of living made adhering to the church's complementarian theology a challenge. The church's complementarian theology tied economic provision to men, which is risky because the marketplace is volatile.[34]

Masculinity, Economic Provision, and Protection

In their research on Protestant men and masculinity, Hoover and Coats found men expressed a "remarkable consensus" in defining masculinity through provision.[35] Yet the men Hoover and Coats interviewed were ambivalent about how provision worked in practice. While most of the evangelical men interviewed were the primary breadwinners in their households, they accepted the idea that women should have the option for work and career. Experiencing tension between financial provision and a need to provide emotional and spiritual support to their families, the men Hoover and Coats interviewed felt that choosing to invest in their careers disadvantaged their ability to provide support at home. While these evangelical men used the language of headship to describe their identities as men, they were conflicted about how their leadership should work. These men felt keenly the lack of practical guidance from their churches on navigating the realities of dual-earning households within the context of headship. Evangelical churches had not provided the resources they felt were needed to learn how to be biblically masculine, without diminishing women. While these evangelical men sought resources to more clearly articulate how to be masculine, they were "not looking for a 'Mixed Martial Arts Jesus.' "[36] The ambivalence these evangelical men felt about how to be masculine within the context of headship may help explain why so many other men and women seek out churches like Mars Hill. Driscoll gave clear guidelines as to how to be masculine Christian men (and feminine Christian women). Even so, cultural conditions make it very difficult to live into the strict division of labor advocated by pastors like Driscoll.

Defining masculinity apart from economic provision is a return to earlier epochs of family and gender relations. Social historian Stephanie Coontz writes that the modern dual-earner family "represents a return to older norms, after a very short interlude that people mistakenly identify as 'traditional.' "[37] For most of human history men and women worked together as economic partners on family farms or in household businesses. Not until the nineteenth century did capitalist production replace home-based production, creating a new division of labor where (white) husbands and older children specialized in work outside the home and (white) wives specialized in household and childcare labor at home. This nineteenth-century gender specialization represented a transitional stage in history, "when households could no longer get by primarily on things they made, grew, or bartered, but could not yet rely on purchased consumer goods."[38] Subsequently, masculinity was identified with economic activities and femininity with nurturing. These arrangements are often seen as the "natural" way to organize family, yet the arrangements are neither "natural" nor Christian.

Legitimating a culture's gendered division of labor often relies on claims of an essentialist (biological) ideology. While gender essentialism has been a recurring narrative to explain conservative Protestantism's complementarian theology, it was not specifically a Protestant purview. Biological essentialism has been used across many cultures and religions as a legitimation of gender stratification, where deviation from cultural gender norms is attributed to a distortion of nature.[39] Yet gender is socially constructed, varying over time within and across cultures. Social psychologists Cecilia Ridgeway and Shelley Correll explain gender as a "system of social practices for constituting people as two significantly different categories, men and women, and organizing social relationships of inequality on the basis of that difference."[40] Categorizing men and women into distinctive groups and assigning different human traits to each is so routine, it becomes an invisible process.[41] Inequalities based on this invisible process impact all social institutions to produce and organize gender inequalities. Driscoll's "countercultural" gender theology reinforced gender stratification.

Following a cultural script, Driscoll defined gender differences as biologically based and, therefore, God-ordained. Driscoll consistently used his children as illustrations of these difference. An anecdote from the Introduction, for example, described Driscoll telling Mars Hill his sons like to pee in the yard and his daughters liked to go shoe shopping, because that's how God intended it. Driscoll's examples sometimes linked violence to boys, making protection through violence a seemingly biological trait. Describing his young son's penchant for carrying a (play) sword around, Driscoll recounted to Mars Hill a time when his sword-wielding son went to a doctor's appointment. When the doctor asked why he brought a sword to the appointment, the young boy replied, "To kill bad guys."[42] Driscoll underscored the link between biology and gender juxtaposing his daughter (who apparently didn't "pack" weapons) with his son, saying boys and girls were different "biologically, chemically, hormonally, spiritually."[43]

Because biological essentialism is embedded in American ideas of gender, Mars Hill members who disagreed with Driscoll's gender theology still described differential gender roles as natural. John, for example, believed that men and women naturally gravitated toward different roles. Where John disagreed with Driscoll was in believing there was a scriptural mandate for these differential roles. John explained, "I think the vast majority of people are going to fall into those categories," where men are "going to work at a fulltime job" and women "are going to get pregnant and have kids." Most families, John believed, "fall right into Mars Hill's views and they are going to be fine with that." John accepted biological differences. John's argument with Driscoll's theology was a lack of "a biblical mandate" for these roles, concluding, "I don't think you can use Scripture to dictate that as a norm. I just don't see it."

Gender and Culture

While institutional and individual practices allocate privilege and advantage to incumbents of some social positions, the same practices subordinate and disadvantage others.[44] Western presumptions about men's greater status and competence become salient for individuals within social institutions. This presentation is done within the context of interactions that legitimate particular ideologies regarding "the rightness and necessity of their arrangements, practices, and social relations."[45] The cultural production of two distinctive genders functions to organize inequalities between men and women. Gender inequalities become embedded within societies, social institutions, groups, and internalized by individuals.[46] Assumptions about men and women's different traits and skills "shape behavior and serve to differentiate men and women," making the hierarchical dimension of gender inequality "particularly consequential" by privileging men and subordinating women.[47] While men ostensibly benefit from this structure, women can also benefit because these gendered scripts allocate security, provision, and protection to women.[48] Of course, these benefits for women are dependent on an economic system that can support single-earner families.

As one such social institution, evangelicalism adds a unique dimension to the legitimation of gender ideals, justifying them as part of the sacred order. Organizations exist in a changing environment, to which they must adapt, requiring the realignment of goals and the internal rearrangement of the organization itself.[49] Mars Hill could not do that. By insisting that Driscoll's hypermasculine theology had a "biblical" mandate that represented God's divine design of men and women being radically different, Driscoll demanded men separate themselves from anything associated with the feminine. This separation can represent an anxiety expressed through "hostility toward anything even hinting at 'femininity.'"[50]

Masculinity

Defining and enacting gender is social. Masculinity requires a complex framework of ideas that put great importance on positions of power and wealth over others and the social relationships that generate men's dominance over others.[51] Biological sex is an obvious criterion for social differentiation, leading to economic, political, and social inequalities between genders.[52] In the context of masculinity and power, the capacity to exert control and/or to resist being controlled or dominated by others is an essential element.[53] Hegemonic masculinity, and the power associated with it, are generally enjoyed by very few men, yet it requires all men (and women) to position themselves in relation to its normative ideal.[54] In the 1990s, scholars challenged hegemonic masculinity by addressing masculinities at the intersections of race, class, and sexual orientation, to focus on men from marginalized groups, whose alternative masculinities threatened white, middle- and upper-class, heterosexual men.[55] In light of these changes, white, educated, heterosexual, and affluent men adapted, while still maintaining the arrangements giving them power.[56]

Driscoll and Mars Hill Church harnessed these social-structural arrangements with their hypermasculine theology, reinforcing the cultural ideal of masculine power and justifying that power with the authority of God. While this appropriation was not new in American culture or Protestantism per se, it did represent a shift within twenty-first century Protestantism that was characterized as counter to the wider cultural ideal of gender equality. This ideal shaped perceptions of masculinity for men and women at Mars Hill Church. Attached to a theology that declared complementarianism as God's only acceptable gender arrangement, the theology ascribed power to men. This gender theology is not a core Christian tenet, but as one sanctioned by Mars Hill's exclusive doctrine, it functioned to legitimate men's position of power over other men, as well as over women. This legitimation was illustrated on a Mars Hill forum. Referring to Driscoll's "Pussified Nation" thread in his post on WLMH, Jason, for example, acknowledged, "Here were a bunch of disaffected young men feeling power for the first time, especially over women! And it was sanctioned by Jesus Christ himself!" Men's power over women was crucial to the hierarchy, especially since all other men at Mars Hill were cast as submissive to Driscoll's masculinity.

A man is not inherently masculine—he must achieve and consistently demonstrate masculinity.[57] This requires not only the subordination of women to men but also the subordination of some men to other men, since all men cannot occupy positions conferring hegemonic masculinity.[58] While Driscoll's hypermasculine theology elevated men over women, it also created dilemmas for men. On the one hand, it claimed that masculinity was God-ordained and essential to the nature of all men. On the other hand, it taught that masculinity had to be achieved. The theology also created hierarchies among men, putting some men into precarious positions: were they man enough to meet God's requirements?

Like the economic and social changes that presaged previous religious masculinity movements, the perceived loss of power in "traditional" masculinity produced a push toward a more masculine Christianity.[59] Driscoll's appropriation of hypermasculinity illustrated that masculinity was not part of a biological or essential human nature. If masculinity were a matter of simple divine biological order, there would be no need for Driscoll to teach men how to be masculine. Driscoll's theology exemplified a need to reclaim men's status, which he effectively enacted through the teaching of "biblical" gender roles within his megachurch. Like the twentieth-century Muscular Christianity movement, Driscoll's hypermasculine theology sought to retain power, privilege, and control for white, heterosexual, Christian men. Driscoll did this unabashedly, baptizing his hypermasculine doctrines as God's design for men (and women), countering social change to restore men's power and privilege with a nostalgic gender order.

While Driscoll defined men by their domain in the marketplace, he also gave them authority in the home. Bringing men back into the home has advantages. Wilcox has written extensively on the positive impact engaged evangelical fathers have on their homes and children.[60] The balance of being "soft patriarchs," who provide spiritually or financially for families, however, can be risky. The shifting nature of work, where dual-earner couples are more and more necessary to support families economically, means men need alternative ways to prove their masculinity. At some level, Driscoll's hypermasculine theology provided this alternative to men. While Driscoll focused his rhetoric on men as economic providers, he also stressed the need for men to be "tough and wild." Driscoll's gender theology provided men with a primary identity as "masculine." As long as they took responsibility at home, Driscoll conceded, men were masculine. Turning his own masculine tropes around, Driscoll described how some men drove trucks, shot guns, and beat women, but that didn't make them men. Real men "take responsibility," by loving their wives and children—even men who drive hybrids ("God bless you, we'll pray for you!").[61] Even as he reassured the men whose masculinity was suspect (hybrid drivers), Driscoll explained that as long as they provided for their families—economically, emotionally, or spiritually— they were masculine.

Yet Driscoll often maintained his masculine authority on the basis of violence, with his bloodied-robe-slaughterer-of-nations-Jesus laying the foundation for his hypermasculine doctrine. Idealizing an ultimate fighting masculinity, men were at the mercy of more dominant, violent men, as were women. Describing his young son's penchant for wanting to protect his mother, Driscoll casually noted that if his son recognized his mother as valuable, when he grew up, he wouldn't "smack her around." Driscoll also seemed to think that masculine authority meant as long as he could physically "take" others, he was in charge. In describing images of Jesus as a hippie-in-a-dress, Driscoll rejected Christianity, because he couldn't believe in a God he could "take." Driscoll's Jesus wore a robe splattered with blood ("and it's not his blood!") to legitimate masculine violence.

When Driscoll spoke of men's responsibility to love their wives, however, his tone could be harsh. Disgraceful and disrespectful wives, for example, could incite husbands to violence. Driscoll's language was laced with violence, even when speaking against it, reflecting the idea that men were naturally violent. Driscoll's harshness was noted by several people in interviews and on the forums. Kendra told me that Driscoll's sermons "were really biting" and "he was just really blistering," becoming "like Rambo at the front of the room, like he just like really didn't give a shit about what most people thought at that point." Cammie also commented on Driscoll's tone, saying he was "harsh," but people like that, as if going "to church to be yelled at . . . is a great thing." Cammie said that men at Mars Hill emulated Driscoll, having "this need to call somebody out . . . it just comes from a very harsh starting point . . . in large part . . . [the men] . . . lead in the way that [Driscoll] leads, which is very harsh, even offensive at times." Driscoll's harsh tone and blistering speech often targeted feminism, which he considered the original sin.

Feminism as Original Sin

The social nature of religious organizations responding to changing cultural conditions is less a reflection of "biblical" rules and more a reflection of the tension inherent in organizations and institutions responding to those cultural shifts. In the midst of changing social conditions, people often reach for a nostalgic past to reclaim a time where things seemed more stable. Whenever men have felt threatened by social change, they have often resorted to arguments based on natural differences implied by biological sex to maintain a status quo that privileges them.[62] The solution to the "crisis in masculinity," however, cannot be resolved by reviving a separate-spheres family system.[63]

As a response to the "softening" of Christian patriarchy that led to more egalitarian practices, Driscoll created a theology that reaffirmed male hierarchy and hegemonic masculinity, utilizing hypermasculinity to exaggerate men's physical and sexual prowess. This hypermasculine style was rooted in antifeminism. Antifeminist movements erupt when changing social conditions are perceived to threaten men's privilege and power. Driscoll's antifeminist theology was similar to other antifeminist movements (e.g., white supremacy, nationalism, Men's Rights movements). These movements see themselves as "victims" of feminism and seek to limit women's authority by expecting women to be in the home, supporting their husbands by building and keeping beautiful homes and raising children.[64]

In his work on white supremacist men, sociologist Michael Kimmel found these men believed their "rightful" power had been co-opted by minorities, including women. White supremacist men attack other (white) men "for becoming feminized (thus unsettling the natural order)," complaining they are "sissies and weaklings . . . limp-wristed . . . slack-jawed" men who, "while still heterosexual in theory and practice, have not even a vestige of the old macho spirit."[65] Instead, white supremacists encourage other white men to reassert "their place in the natural hierarchy" and saturate their websites with images of "warrior-like men"—a successful strategy for recruiting young white men.[66] Driscoll never overtly espoused white supremacist views. His antifeminist rhetoric and his admonitions against a feminized church and effeminate "church boys," however, were strikingly similar to the antifeminist rhetoric of the white supremacist men Kimmel interviewed.

Like other masculinity-focused movements, Driscoll's complementarian theology fixated on hypermasculine men as a means to stop the degrading of men's power by returning women to their "natural roles" in the home. Some women at Mars Hill understood this. One woman on MHWU, Luna, wrote that Driscoll's teaching "permeated throughout community groups and staff and I became 'lesser' as a female across the board. The part of me that was strong and capable used to be valued and was appreciated in the leadership role I had. Then it became the very thing that was used against me because 'I was preventing my husband from leading.'" Driscoll claimed that God and biology had created men for headship, normalizing men's power. In one sermon, Driscoll asked his audience if they had ever taken classes in anthropology or sociology that attributed gender differences to the culture. "Don't blame it on the culture," Driscoll said, masculinity and femininity were reflections of creation.[67]

Not only had feminism led to a mass exodus of men from the church, Driscoll claimed, it had also led to homosexuality and the effeminacy of men who remained in the church. According to Mars Hill's outspoken pastor, feminism says, "men have ruined the world and women will fix it."[68] Worse, for Driscoll, was "Christian feminism," which was "the battering ram on the church door" that opened "the way for homosexuality" by denying "the basic

Biblical tenets that we were made equal but distinct as male and female, with differing God-intended roles in the church and home."[69]

Driscoll blamed feminism for the decline of Christianity because feminism preceded acceptance of homosexuality and both were "cancers . . . eating away at many liberal denominations."[70] He adjured Christian men to "man up soon," before liberal denominations like the Episcopalians voted "a fluffy baby bunny rabbit as their next bishop to lead God's men."[71] Asking if "a causal connection between a critical mass of female clergy and a mass exodus from the churches, especially among men, would be difficult to establish, but is it entirely a coincidence?" Driscoll cited sociologist Rodney Stark's and historian Philip Jenkins's arguments for the success of strict churches in gaining adherents, contending that churches "growing robustly" did not ordain women.[72] While strictness seems to result in gender conservatism, sociologist Kevin Neuhouser illustrated that strictness in a Latin American context resulted in women having more equality within the Pentecostal church because the key to strictness is being in higher tension to the society. Neuhouser described how Brazilian culture's macho ethos gave way to Pentecostal women having more power, because the church's more egalitarian ideals stood in significant tension to the larger cultural gender ethos.[73]

Fearing their loss of power to women meant that men must prove they were "men among men."[74] The constancy and frequency with which men reassure themselves of their masculine status "indicates a preoccupation with the obverse—'that men were in danger of being called something else: unmanly, a mollycoddle, as sissy, even a pansy. Whereas manhood could be achieved, it could also be lost; it as not simply a quality that resulted naturally and inevitably from one's sex' and it's dependent on women being secondary, not competing with men."[75] This illustrates that masculinity and femininity aren't essential, but relational. Driscoll refuted the necessity of feminism, claiming that women were not an oppressed group as a majority of Americans, they lived longer than men, and were more likely to vote and "control the government."[76] What the women's rights movement had accomplished was "strategically" creating women as a separate category, so they did not have to compete with men.[77]

Driscoll sought a return to a more "traditional" gender order, using the ultimate authority of a sovereign God to sanction his theology. Nostalgia for a family form that resurrects a separate spheres gender ideology as the only traditional option creates a vigorous antifeminist movement.[78] Members of evangelical churches like Mars Hill may not see themselves as in league with other masculinist movements, but each seeks to "Make America Great Again," by returning to a nostalgic past, where men have authority and women know their (secondary) place in home, church, and society.

Conclusion

Question Mark

The collapse of Mars Hill Church on the heels of Mark Driscoll's abrupt resignation, did not signal a collapse of the hypermasculine theology that made Driscoll notorious. Nor was the church's collapse the end of a "Make Christianity Manly Again" campaign. In fact, by the 2016 presidential election, the hypermasculine theological movement Driscoll had done so much to popularize had expanded beyond the religious sphere into politics to help elect Donald Trump.

In the wake of the 2016 presidential election, historian Molly Worthen described Donald Trump's "authoritarian machismo" as being "right in step with a long evangelical tradition of pastor-overlords who anoint themselves with the power to make their own rules—and, in the event of their own occasional moral lapses, assure their followers that God always forgives."[1] Even after four years of Trump's crudeness, ribaldry, and sexually inappropriate comments, 76 percent of white evangelicals voted for Trump in the 2020 election. White evangelical support for Trump illustrated a "strong preference for leaders who demand unquestioning obedience—and who, like Trump, consider disagreement a form of disloyalty."[2] Trump's display of unapologetic masculinity was seen as key to restoring an evangelical-friendly political and religious order.

Trump's loss to Democrat Joe Biden in the 2020 election was a blow to white evangelicals. As he fabricated tales of a "stolen" election, Trump repeatedly blamed "weak" men, like Mike Pence, for not doing their job to restore him to the presidency—juxtaposing his masculinity with their failed (weak) masculinity. Trump famously used this tactic on the late Arizona Republican Senator John McCain, saying, "He was a war hero because he was captured. I like people who weren't captured."[3] Trump's tactics were successful, with 60 percent of evangelicals believing Trump's assertions that the election had indeed been stolen.[4] Registering his disdain for evangelicals' support

Making Christianity Manly Again. Jennifer McKinney, Oxford University Press. © Oxford University Press 2023.
DOI: 10.1093/oso/9780197655795.003.0007

for Trump, former president of the SBC's Ethics and Religious Liberty Commission, Russell Moore commented, "The church of Jesus Christ ought to be the last people to fall for hucksters and demagogues, but too often we do."[5]

Evangelicals' faith in Trump as the epitome of masculine authority was not unprecedented. Masculinity has long been embedded in the political discourse of the United States, where candidates strategically symbolize their masculinity while simultaneously emasculating their opponents.[6] In many ways, the 2016 election between America's first female presidential candidate, Hillary Clinton, and Trump was a referendum on gender hierarchy. Trump's hypermasculinity created the perfect foil to Clinton's feminism, which was on full display during the 2016 campaign. During her husband's campaign for the 1992 presidential election, Hillary Clinton famously rejected traditional gender roles, defending her choice to have a career, saying, "I suppose I could have stayed home, baked cookies and had teas, but what I decided to do was to fulfill my profession, which I entered before my husband was in public life."[7] Trump's "Make America Great Again" was not only about making men great again (white native-born, heterosexual, "fist-pounding, gun-toting guy-guys"), but also about putting women (and maybe "nasty woman" Hillary Clinton particularly) in their place.[8] Clinton personified an assault on traditional gender and family roles, making her anathema to evangelicals.

Refuting Clinton and bolstering traditional (white male) authority, Trump supporters reified this hypermasculine authority by wearing t-shirts with slogans like "Trump That Bitch" or "Donald Trump: Finally Someone With Balls." Sexism toward Clinton was a cornerstone of Trump's campaign: "[I]f Hillary Clinton can't satisfy her husband," Trump asked supporters, "what makes her think she can satisfy America?"[9] Trump's statement emphasized the importance of traditional gender roles and relegated women's authority to sexually satisfying their husbands, and finding Clinton falling short. Trump's statement recalls Driscoll's mandate for wives to sexually satisfy their husbands ("I have a verse!"), with the threat of a husband's infidelity or divorce if they didn't. Trump's statement also implied that America was male and that electing Clinton would leave Americans unsatisfied. This latter sentiment was blatantly displayed by Trump supporters wearing shirts or carrying placards reading, "Hillary Sucks But Not Like Monica." For many white evangelicals, Trump's sexist language and masculine bravado were familiar due to pastors like Driscoll.

It should be no surprise evangelicals placed their trust in Trump's brag-gadocio. Mark Driscoll and his hypermasculine theology became a conduit to legitimate a God-ordained social order that glorified men's power. Men reasserting their masculinity hoping to restore a Christian America were key for Trump's political success. Post-Trump, Republican Senator Josh Hawley of Missouri asserted that, "The crisis of American men is a crisis for the American republic."[10] The emphasis on, and necessity of, masculine au-thority is "critical to understanding American evangelicalism today, and the nation's fractured political landscape."[11] Just as Trump has inspired "copycat" politicians, who are remaking the Republican party in his image, Driscoll's success as a preacher with an "insult comic" vibe[12] has also remade the evan-gelical landscape, spawning a number of copycat pastors and commentators who embrace his hypermasculine theology and emulate his style.

Evangelicalism and Hypermasculinity

While Driscoll's iconic style set him apart from other evangelical pastors during his time at Mars Hill Church, his success changed the formula for what was acceptable to say and preach for evangelicals. Many evangelical men have taken their cue from Driscoll's irreverent and sometimes bawdy style, emphasizing a hypermasculine persona and rhetoric. Emulating Driscoll's bravura, for example, former Council on Biblical Manhood and Womanhood president Owen Strachan regularly tweets about the necessity for Christian men to be truly masculine. In February 2020, Strachan posted a thread complaining about contemporary masculinity, beginning with an appeal to the apostle Paul (as Driscoll often did), tweeting, "Men today are often soft, weak, passive, unprotective. But physical discipline is key for men. Hear Paul: 'I batter my body and make it my slave' (1 Cor 9:27). Christic man-hood is protective, sharp, watchful. The man who is willfully soft physically is often soft spiritually."[13] Strachan followed with a tweet stating Christian men needed to stop making excuses, reject softness, do hard things, be first in battle and last in retreat, be watchmen on the wall, protect women and chil-dren, fight evil, and bleed for the truth.[14] Strachan finished the thread calling men to take "hits" for the gospel: "Biblical men take hits for the truth. Who today will suffer for the gospel? Who will be persecuted for righteousness' sake? Who will endure hatred for Christ? Who will suffer injury to overthrow evil? Who will be unpopular to be faithful? Who will bleed for the truth?"[15]

In a since-deleted tweet, Christian writer and political commentator Matt Walsh depicted a hypermasculine Jesus, tweeting, "Jesus was extremely aggressive toward evildoers. Insulted them, yelled at them, shamed them, beat them with whips. The Mr. Rogers version of Jesus is a modern invention completely."[16] Commenting that Walsh's interpretation did not square with the original language or context of the passage, sociologist Samuel Perry wrote, it was clear Jesus did not beat (or whip) people, "But authoritarians like Walsh LOVE a Jesus who hurts people."[17] Echoes of Driscoll's style, rhetoric, and theology can be seen in these examples, as can his mastery of social media in order to stoke both support and derision.

While men like Strachan and Walsh attempt to capture the evangelical imagination of "biblical manhood" and a hypermasculine Jesus, other evangelical pastors bolster complementarianism by chastening women. In 2019, John MacArthur, for example, criticized popular Christian speaker and author Beth Moore. MacArthur said, "Women need to get themselves under control and realize they are not to speak in a church." MacArthur explained, "When women take over a culture, men become weak; when men become weak, they can be conquered."[18] In another example, a spring 2021 sermon from Baptist pastor Stewart Allen Clark went viral. Channeling Driscoll's rhetoric, Clark castigated women, saying, "Why is it . . . after they get married, [women] let themselves go? I'm not saying every woman can be the epic . . . trophy wife of all time, like Melania Trump." Clark suggested women needed to practice "weight control" or husbands might divorce them. Paraphrasing 1 Corinthians 7 (a familiar verse from Driscoll's teaching on sex), Clark reminded his congregation that wives "no longer" have "all the rights" to their bodies, saying, "So, whenever she's not in the mood, take out your Bible."[19]

Like Driscoll, these men adhere to a strict complementarian doctrine. The soft patriarchy that characterized late-twentieth-century evangelicalism spurred a backlash movement that created hypermasculine evangelicalism in the twenty-first century. While Driscoll's brazen style was unique at the time, his authoritarian leadership and adherence to an exclusive set of doctrines, including complementarian theology, were not. Driscoll was at the vanguard of the Young Restless and Reformed Movement (YRRM) that fully institutionalized a strict complementarian theology with the drafting of the Danvers Statement and founding of the Council on Biblical Manhood and Womanhood in 1987. Driscoll's rhetoric, style, and entrepreneurial spirit (cofounding Acts 29, for example) helped put YRRM and their theology on the map.

YRRM: Masculinity, Hierarchy, and Authority

As a celebrity pastor within the Young Restless and Reformed Movement (YRRM) Driscoll was emblematic of the hierarchical leadership and complementarian theology that were movement-standard. Male hierarchy and authority are deeply embedded in YRRM/New Calvinism, with complementarianism interpreted as an exclusively correct and absolutist Christian doctrine. The conflation of "Calvinism" with "Christian" was noted by the 2009 *Time Magazine* article naming New Calvinism one of the ten ideas changing the world, stating, "some of today's enthusiasts imply that non-Calvinists" may not be Christian.[20]

In his ten-year retrospective of YRRM, Collin Hansen alluded to this tendency by ascribing the movement's growth to young evangelicals not hearing biblical truths from their parents or churches, implying non-YRRM churches did not preach "biblical," and thus not Christian, truths. Hansen lamented that YRRM sometimes "willingly overlooked immaturity, even explicitly ungodly behavior and speech," focusing too much on "worldly success—at the expense of character."[21] This description seemed to encompass Driscoll without directly naming him, but could easily envelop a man like Trump (barring his lack of New Calvinist credentials), helping explain his popularity with so many white evangelicals. Hansen wrote of the necessity of submitting to (masculine) authority, writing, "Does your theology lead you to submission to authorities in your home and in your church and in your community?" Hansen's question is intriguing. For complementarians, authority is embedded in masculinity, but a chain of command implies multiple levels of authority. Some men must submit to other men in the hierarchy. Submission, however, is embedded in femininity. This juxtaposition creates dissonance for men.

In *Christianity Today*'s 2021 podcast *The Rise and Fall of Mars Hill*, host Mike Cosper interviews several former Mars Hill staff and elders. In one episode, "The Brand," a former Mars Hill staffer commented on Driscoll's immaturity as a young thirty-something leading a megachurch.[22] Had Driscoll submitted to the authority of more mature pastors/elders/men, he believed, things could have turned out differently. But Driscoll couldn't submit to another man. Based on his taxonomy of masculine authority, Driscoll's submitting to another man would feminize him and diminish his authority. Driscoll often told Mars Hill, "Jesus is the senior pastor." This statement seemingly positioned Driscoll as submissive to the authority of a (divine) male. This structure is tricky, however, because Jesus is not physically present in a temporal realm. Similar to the complementarian position on gender that holds men and women equal in essence (sometimes phrased as equal "in God's eyes"), women do not hold authority in the earthly/temporal realm. In the same way, Jesus may be the author and savior of the Christian faith, but as a divine being, does not physically inhabit a position of authority on earth. In the physical world, there is always a physical man sitting in a position of authority over other men. Driscoll's success as purveyor of his own megachurch empire, allowed him to sit at the apex of authority, making it impossible for him to submit to another man, or even an elder board.[23]

While authority is embedded in this twenty-first-century YRRM church hierarchy structure, it is mutually reinforced through a variety of institutions. As a "biblically inerrant" strain of evangelicalism, New Calvinism claims its doctrinal authority comes from a literalist interpretation of the Bible. How the Bible is interpreted imbues authority to the text. One of the most popular English Bible translations among evangelicals is the English Standard Version (ESV).[24] The ESV was created to counter the perceived influence of, and accommodation to, the secular culture and feminized churches. Previously, the most popular English Bible translation for evangelicals was the New International Version (NIV). When the NIV underwent revisions in the late-1990s, to use more gender-inclusive language, a backlash movement formed. Accusing NIV publisher Zondervan of accommodating to the feminist culture, evangelicals wedded to complementarian ideology, including Wayne Grudem (cofounder and past president of the Council on Biblical Manhood and Womanhood), negotiated with Crossway to revise the Revised Standard Version (RSV). This revision became the ESV, which was published in 2001.

The ESV was strategically revised to "secure readings of Scripture that preserved male headship," combatting liberal, feminist, and secular cultures.[25] The ESV editorial team systematically changed the biblical text of the Revised Standard Version (RSV) to emphasize complementarian interpretations of gender, masculine authority, and feminine submission.[26] In an analysis of these revisions, Samuel Perry found that editors manipulated the text, introducing text nonexistent in the RSV to reinforce men's ecclesial authority.[27] Perry states that ESV editors "intentionally" changed the text to "make various verses and passages about gender roles in the family, gender roles in the church, and masculinity and femininity more agreeable to complementarian interpretations."[28] The New Calvinist doctrine of biblical inerrancy means that evangelicals relying on the ESV as their primary Bible translation come to understand complementarianism and masculine authority (as well as feminine submission) as the literal word of God.[29]

These strict beliefs about complementarianism and masculine authority are also bolstered within families. In line with Driscoll's admonitions that mothers practice "God-centered parenting," where disciplining children is an imperative, New Calvinist parents demonstrate hierarchical authority within their homes, as well as their churches. Sociologist Lydia Bean writes in her book, *The Politics of Evangelical Identity*, "It is impossible to overstate the value" some evangelical churches place on "socializing children" through "an authority-minded approach to parenting." This approach to parenting instills obedience to authority in children.[30] Authority is from parent to child, but also from husband to wife. Thus, the hierarchy of authority is emphasized multiple ways within the home. The focus on masculine authority and hierarchy becomes embedded in home, church, and Scripture, mutually reinforcing obedience to a "chain of command" as a form of obedience to God.[31] Together, these institutions (family, church, Bible) emphasize exclusive doctrines and extensive commitment to those doctrines as integral to salvation. These doctrines and commitments are often strengthened through megachurches like Mars Hill, which have proliferated in the United States since the 1970s.

Megachurches, Charisma, and Masculine Authority

Driscoll's notoriety and influence owes much to his media-savvy strategy in building his megachurch empire, which spread his message across multiple continents. According to Warren Bird and Scott Thumma, "What happens in large churches today both models and shapes the landscape for most other churches tomorrow—for better or for worse."[32] Megachurches like Mars Hill, and what they teach, matter. Evangelicals are becoming increasingly concentrated in megachurches, making them more visible, and changing the nature of religion and politics.[33] The decline of mainline Protestantism and rise in the "nones"—people claiming no religious affiliation—can intensify the visibility of evangelicals,[34] especially evangelical megachurches, creating higher tension—and a seemingly insurmountable chasm—between evangelicals and the secular culture. Megachurches are not a historically new phenomenon, however, their proliferation in the United States after the 1970s has made them a "distinctive social phenomenon."[35]

In *High on God: How Megachurches Won the Heart of America*, Wellman, Corcoran, and Stockly link megachurches with a particular gender theology, writing that the power structures dominating and subsequently fueling megachurches "*depend on* a gender ideology of clear gender/sex distinctions and roles, including female submission to a male leader."[36] While most megachurches do not explicitly demand "the subordination of women to men . . . or the demand that by right, men have all rights over women," these researchers found that patriarchal structures are "preferred, reinforced, and expected," and are "portrayed as fulfilling a divine plan, even if women's sub-jugation and men's domination is not made explicit."[37] Wellman, Corcoran, and Stockly explain that these arrangements give "paramount leadership to men without having to boast about it or deny it, or even put it into bylaws. Thus, it can deny any accusations of sexism, making it all the more insid-ious."[38] Men and women can benefit from these arrangements because they provide clear roles for both. Men are tasked with leading the church and their families, which enables women to "create stable homes, to be protected finan-cially and otherwise, and in the long run to sustain order in the community."[39]

Megachurch founders are charismatic figures who often become the focus of attention in their churches.[40] These men confidently present a "sense of certainty that they have the one and only truth," often based on a "vivid" and literal interpretation of the Bible.[41] Many megachurches are autonomous (nondenominational) with pastors sitting outside of denominational or ec-umenical authoritative organizations, and few megachurch pastors have any "guardrails to keep them on track."[42] Because of their autonomy, megachurch pastors can become authoritarian and foster an insider/outsider dynamic at their churches.[43]

The ability to create the bond between charismatic leaders and their constituents takes significant talent and emotional intelligence.[44] Charismatic leaders are seen as divinely inspired, "set apart from ordinary men" as evidenced by their exceptional abilities.[45] Charismatic leaders are experts in relaying messages that are "arousing, moving, and applicable, but *not* intellectually taxing."[46] The lure of charismatic pastors and their megachurches is in how powerfully members experience a sense of the di-vine. This same dynamic is at work with men like Trump, as well as Driscoll. Within the context of worshipping at a megachurch, just like convening with like-minded others at a Trump rally, charismatic leaders are able to transport followers to a place of transcendence and meaning. Charismatic leaders cultivate relationships between themselves and their followers that create a sense of being part of a tribe or family that is set apart. Much of the allure of charismatic men like Driscoll and Trump is in their seemingly superhuman (masculine) authority.

Charisma is tied to masculine authority, and for evangelicals bridges their religious preferences and their political preferences. Gendered ideas regarding authority "exert considerable influence on political thinking."[47] Views of a masculine God directly impact perceptions of power and authority shaping political beliefs.[48] Masculine images of God and belief in traditional gender roles lead to preferences for male leadership, including male political candidates.[49] Images of a masculine God may also involve images of a vengeful God, meting out "righteous punishment" to destroy his enemies, which legitimates taking harsh stances toward "those perceived to be wrongdoers or social outsiders."[50] The punishment of outsiders or wrongdoers takes on added significance when legitimated by a supernatural God.[51] These ideas would be familiar to those who see Jesus as a "warrior-god," for example, with a "sword in his hand and a commitment to make someone bleed."[52] The understanding of masculine authority, legitimated by a hypermasculine (vengeful, warrior) God was familiar to white evangelicals, influencing them to support Donald Trump, who promised to rout their enemies. Charismatic leaders, religious and political, convey a sense that they have the answers—exclusively correct beliefs, which require strong (extensive) commitment. Followers are rewarded by becoming part of a tribe, or family, of like-minded believers. These dynamics are at work within Christian nationalism, which overlaps with the religious and political concerns of white evangelicals.

Christian Nationalism

Evangelical megachurches can function as "certainty enclaves," protecting individuals from the dissonance and uncertainty raised by "liberal" culture.[53] Internalization of these dynamics—hypermasculinity, charisma, authoritarianism—in the context of faith communities helped propel Trump into the White House. Driscoll and Trump both sought to restore a declining society by embracing the hierarchical order of the patriarchal family, placing family, religion, and national power back into the hands of white, heterosexual men. These are also the core beliefs and concerns of Christian nationalists. In their book, *Taking Back America for God*, sociologists Andrew Whitehead and Samuel L. Perry write that Christian nationalists "connect America's very survival as a civilization with its adherence to traditional definitions of the family, traditional gender roles, and heterosexuality."[54]

Waging a campaign to restore families and heterosexual gender roles meant waging a war against feminism, a movement making evangelicals feel displaced and marginalized.[55] In the late-1990s a survey of American Christians found that 66 percent of evangelicals saw feminism as hostile to their values and morals.[56] In a PRRI and *The Atlantic* post-2016 election poll, 64 percent of evangelicals agreed "society as a whole has become too soft and feminine," illustrating evangelicals' experiencing "intense gender anxiety in recent years."[57] This gender anxiety was magnified during the 2016 US presidential election.

For evangelicals, Democratic nominee Clinton's gender disqualified her from the race. Trump's masculinity, juxtaposed to Clinton's "wrongly aggressive feminism" reinforced his appeal.[58] Here was an opportunity to elect a "real man" to the White House.[59] Trump's candidacy provided an opportunity to not only destroy Clinton—the "epitome of everything wrong with feminists"—but also push back against feminism.[60] Many evangelicals were enlivened by the virile potency embodied in Trump's words and actions, seeing his blatant sexism as "refreshing," as they cheered his putdowns of Clinton.[61] In postelection analysis, political scientists found that hostility to women, more than affinity for authoritarianism, predicted voter support for Trump, leading to the conclusion that, "Trump's toxic masculinity was a deep part of his appeal."[62]

Populist movements often presume a nostalgic male-dominant and racially homogeneous past where women and minorities are blamed for taking jobs and breaking up the family.[63] Christian nationalism is both gendered and racialized, which is how so many white evangelicals found themselves in the company of white nationalists and proponents of antifeminist movements in supporting Donald Trump. Fighting against threats to families and the nation—nontraditional gender roles, same-sex marriage, and immigration—helps preserve these movements' American identity and their ideal of America.[64] By appealing to these issues and ideals, Trump was taking America back to a nostalgic 1950s to "Make America Great Again." For those feeling devalued by mainstream politics, Trump became both warrior and hero.[65]

These ideals are also codified by evangelicals within their complementarian theology, which is foundational to a "God-and-country Christian nationalism."[66] Researchers find significant overlap between hypermasculinity, Christian nationalism, and forms of white supremacy.[67] Christian nationalists seek to preserve or return to a "mythic society," where "traditional hierarchical relationships (e.g., between men and women, whites and blacks) are upheld."[68] Along with gender, race has been central to the formation of white evangelicals' cultural and political identity, overlapping with white nationalism, which sees America as an inherently white and conventionally Christian nation.[69] After eight years of Barack Obama's presidency—where his citizenship and his faith were questioned by Christian and white nationalists—Trump was cast as a restorer of the proper relationships between the nation's perceived Christian foundation (for evangelical and conservative Protestants), as well as a restorer of "proper racial (white)" foundations of the country.[70]

Because evangelical churches tend to be racially homogeneous, assumptions of masculine authority often invoke a traditional, but invisible, white masculinity. Two-thirds of American evangelicals are white, which can render race invisible within white evangelical churches.[71] In his work on whiteness and Christianity, Robert P. Jones is careful to convey that most white Christian denominations and most white Christians have "taken pains" to distance themselves from slavery, laws enforcing racial segregation, and overt racism. Even so, Jones writes, norms of whiteness "have become deeply and broadly integrated into white Christian identity, operating far below the level of consciousness."[72] Whitehead and Perry write that, "Americans who embrace Christian nationalism, particularly if they are white, remain committed to the belief that *real* Americans—or at least the 'good kind' of Americans—are native-born, white Christians."[73] Whitehead and Perry also find a "powerful link between Christian nationalist beliefs and believing that God's people must fight wars for good," which requires good Christian men to lead the charge.[74]

Like Christian nationalists, white supremacists exaggerate a gender binary and can enact a "toxic form of hypermasculinity."[75] While this is often packaged as a return to traditional masculinity, it's a reaction to social reorganization that amplifies voices of women and other minorities.[76] Because white men have traditionally held positions of power and wealth in American culture, most white men feel entitled to these social goods.[77] Men who lack the means of accessing this power and wealth can feel a sense of aggrieved entitlement, becoming reactionary and nostalgic in their politics, hoping to "restore" what they feel they have lost.[78] These men "look backward" to a past that was "more responsive to their needs."[79] Expressions of hypermasculinity, coupled with beliefs concerning the need to "fight wars for good" can also lead to violence.

Trump's 2016 election emboldened nationalists.[80] Trump's losing the 2020 election was a terrible blow to them. Stoking emotions with false claims of a "stolen" election, Trump told supporters at his "Save America" rally on January 6, 2021, "We fight like Hell. And if you don't fight like hell, you're not going to have a country anymore."[81] Christian nationalists were conspicuous at the rally and attack on the Capitol. Banners proclaiming Christian faith were rife at the insurrection, with many participants' rhetoric reflecting "an aggressive, charismatic and hypermasculine form of Christian nationalism."[82] One woman praying in a group shouted, "This is our moment, Lord, this is our moment to take back the country. This is our moment to fight . . . with you as our weapon. You are our fighter." Another person shouted, "We fight for God, and God fights for us."[83] At the insurrection, white evangelicals, Christian nationalists, and white nationalists found common ground. As Trump biographers Brody and Lamb described, Trump had indeed become "the ultimate fighting champion for evangelicals,"[84] and they, in turn, became his ultimate fighting champions. Trump's rhetoric, coupled with the Christian nationalist belief in fighting for good—to reclaim the "real" Americans—had real consequences.[85]

The assumption that men need to reclaim/reassert/retake their places in a "natural hierarchy" can lead individual men toward violence, as well. In March of 2021, Robert Aaron Long killed eight people, including six Asian women, at two massage parlors. An active member of his Southern Baptist Convention (SBC) congregation, Long said he targeted the massage parlors because he was struggling with a "sex addiction" and wanted to "remove the temptation."[86] While his church denounced Long's "wicked act" as antithetical to their beliefs and revoked his membership, the church's beliefs about sexual morality could be a riff on Driscoll's. Long's pastor, Jerry Dockery, had regularly targeted feminism and changing gender roles as the work of Satan in his sermons. In a September 2020 sermon, for example, Dockery told his congregation, "Radical feminism has engulfed our culture like a tsunami." Invoking the same enemy as so many other masculinist movements, Dockery blamed feminism for social dysfunction, saying, "We're now striving for gender neutrality, for gender fluidity, you name it. It's just gender whatever-you-want. And I would say to you that this is blatant . . . guidance, direction and strategy of Satan to oppose and usurp the authority of God."[87] Seeing women as a "temptation," Long felt he had the right to "remove" them.

Rhetoric and symbols from hypermasculine Christianity and Christian nationalism can be appropriated by other groups hoping to return America to white patriarchal authority. White supremacists, for example, us the imagery of "warrior-like men" to recruit young white men into their organizations.[88] On June 17, 2015, twenty-one-year-old Dylann Roof killed nine church members at Emanuel African Methodist Episcopal Church in Charleston, South Carolina.[89] Before the attack, Roof published a 2,500-word manifesto weaving together white supremacy, nationalism, and hypermasculine Christianity.[90] Roof wrote, "I see some people who seem to use Christianity as an excuse for not doing anything. They tell themselves they are being pious, but they are really being cowardly." Roof concluded that Christianity didn't need to be a "weak cowardly religion." Instead, he believed there was "plenty of evidence to indicate that Christianity can be a warrior's religion."[91] Similarly, in 2019, nineteen-year-old John Earnest killed one worshipper and injured three others in an attack on a Poway, California, synagogue. Earnest had written a letter explaining his belief that Jewish people deserved to die and that their deaths would glorify God. His letter also wove white supremacy into "cogent Christian theology."[92]

Overwhelmingly, most men are not violent. These young men were activated by rhetoric that laid the groundwork to make violence a plausible solution to reclaim what seemed lost—their power as white men. The tribal mindset that infuses groups, particularly those who follow a charismatic leader, sets insiders apart from outsiders. Outsiders can be cast as enemies. A hypermasculine, warrior-god mentality can be appropriated when a situation seems to require violent action as a way to reclaim the power and status men feel they're due. When these men don't receive the rewards of their dominant race and gender categories, they can feel—in Driscoll's words— "conned," "trapped," or that women are "ruling over them."[93]

A Reformission Rev Apologizes

In his 2012 *Real Marriage* sermon series, Driscoll apologized for a "season" in his ministry in which he was harsh and chauvinistic. In the *Real Marriage* book, Driscoll describes his bitterness against his wife, Grace, and God, writing that after they married his "previously free and fun girlfriend was suddenly [his] frigid and fearful wife."[94] Driscoll felt "conned" by God because Grace was controlling their sex life, "ruling over" him.[95] Driscoll reports he "grew more chauvinistic," which affected his preaching "for a season."[96] During the *Real Marriage* sermon series Driscoll apologized to his church and pledged to set a better example. The apology, however, blamed Driscoll's wife, Grace, for his actions. While he apologized, Driscoll took no responsibility.

Former Mars Hillians were of two minds as to how Driscoll's behavior had changed over time. Some Mars Hill members thought Driscoll's rhetoric had gotten progressively worse; others believed it had gotten progressively better. In 2012, when Driscoll publicly apologized for the "season" in his life where his tone had been "bitter" and "chauvinistic," his timeline would explain the misogyny inherent in the 2000–2001 Pussified Nation thread, as well as his 2001–2002 *Proverbs* sermon series. The season, however, was reportedly over by 2008, when he preached *The Peasant Princess* series on the Song of Solomon. Yet, *The Peasant Princess* series was rife with his objectification and sexualization of women. While his tone and words were, to some extent, less harsh in the 2012 *Real Marriage* series, Driscoll resurrected his "riff" on disrespectful wives, spoken almost verbatim from the 2001–2002 *Proverbs* series.

In the *Real Marriage* book, Driscoll reinforced his hypermasculine doctrine repeating the same homophobic comments he had regularly used throughout his preaching at Mars Hill. In describing the Catholic church he attended growing up, for example, Driscoll wrote the church had "a priest who seemed to be a gay alcoholic. He was the last person on earth I wanted to be like. To a young man, a life of poverty, celibacy, living at the church, and wearing a dress was more frightful than going to hell."[97] Driscoll contrasted this priest with the pastor at the church he attended in college, who he described as "different." His college pastor "had been in the military, had earned a few advanced degrees," was smart and humble. "He bow hunted. He had sex with his wife. He knew the Bible. He was not religious. In that church I met other men who were very godly and masculine."[98]

In the end, it was Driscoll who could not meet his own standard of men taking responsibility at Mars Hill. In October of 2014, with the scandals rocking the church, Mars Hill's leadership had no choice but to "discipline" Driscoll, using the process of church discipline he had designed. Rather than accepting the plan of restoration, Driscoll resigned from the church. Former

Mars Hill members writing on Mars Hill Was Us (MHWU) were brutal in their commentary, calling Driscoll's masculinity into question by branding him a coward. Chandler wrote, "Like the coward he is, Mark ran off (he made a stop at the bank on the way) while proclaiming his innocence." Miles wrote, "The way Mark Driscoll left the church . . . was one of the most cowardly, lamest things I've ever seen and probably will ever see." Luna said, "Mark Driscoll is a coward and I struggle not to hate him for what he's done." Ryan may have summed the situation best when he described Driscoll's abrupt departure from the church as the "final betrayal from a man who refused to submit to the very discipline he always preached as necessary as a Christian."

In their work on American megachurches, Wellman, Corcoran, and Stockly use Mars Hill as a negative example, and Driscoll as a cautionary tale about the destructive behavior that can result from autonomous structures and authoritarian leadership, writing:

> What amazed many of us who witnessed this slow train wreck was [Driscoll's] ability to maintain the loyalty of followers, as they rationalized and justified his immoral an abusive behavior. Perhaps more than anything, the ability of "followers" to withstand and put up with the "bad behavior" of charismatic figures is a testament to the power charisma has over its followers. It underlines the need and desire for figures who "have the answer," who can anticipate the longings and desires of the hearts of their followers . . . that lets them know they are known and understood, and that there is an answer.[99]

Driscoll's "bravado and machismo . . . rallied and seduced many to his side, both in loyal attendance and millions in donations," yet despite "clear financial and administrative malfeasance, he and his spectacular celebrity profile escaped relatively unscathed to Scottsdale, Arizona."[100]

The Trinity Church: Same Stuff, Different Day

In Scottsdale, Driscoll reorganized, starting Mark Driscoll Ministries (now Real Faith) and launching The Trinity Church, which started meeting on Easter Sunday in 2016. The launch of The Trinity Church gave Driscoll a somewhat fresh start. In 2018, Driscoll announced a partnership with evangelical publisher Charisma House, whose publication of *Spirit-Filled Jesus: Live by His Power* marked the end of Driscoll's five-year hiatus from publishing.[101] In 2019 Driscoll appeared on Matt Brown's weekly podcast *The Debrief Show*, and said, "I don't hold to the five points of Calvinism. I think it's garbage . . . it's not biblical."[102] Driscoll then described men in the YRRM as "little boys with father wounds," which fit with the rest of the podcast, where he spoke about the importance of fathers and how a father's image impacts a person's image of God.[103] Even though Driscoll seemingly dispensed with Calvinism, he continues to focus on men, masculinity, and a gendered hierarchy of authority at The Trinity Church.[104]

Five years into his Arizona ministry, however, reports of authoritarian leadership, shunning, and financial malfeasance at Trinity began to surface online. Christian investigative journalist Julie Roys posted several of these reports, including a two-part interview with former security team members from The Trinity Church. In the interview, former director of security at the church, Chad, described a meeting where staff were briefed on a "spectrum of trust, from a zero to a ten. The higher you are on the spectrum, the more access you get" to the Driscolls. Chad was told he was "like an eight," rather than a ten because his wife "may be like a six." He was also told that another security team member's rating was "even lower," because that team member "couldn't get his wife under control. He's not leading his family well. He's not leading his house."

The hierarchy of authority at Trinity, like Mars Hill, is predicated on an essentialist gender order. Chad was told, "as men, we're pretty logical. You know, we approach things from a logical way, but women, women are way too emotional. . . . And if the men can't get their wives under control, then we have to reassess where they fall on this spectrum of trust." The extensive commitment to the church's exclusive doctrines is clearly displayed in this exchange, as are the costs. Men unwilling or unable to properly lead their houses by getting their wives under control risk losing access to the Driscolls or being expelled from the church.

In Roys's interview, Ben, another former security team member, responds to the accusation that he "can't get his wife under control," by appealing to the masculine authority proffered by Driscoll's gender theology, while impugning the masculinity of men holding positions of higher authority at the church. Ben says, "If you're accusing me of not leading my household, well, by all means pull me aside and let's have a conversation." But the church's leaders didn't speak with Ben directly, who noted, "Cowards talk about people; they don't talk to people. And that's what we have going on here." Again, Ben appeals to masculine authority, saying, "At the very least just be a man and say what it is."

The assumption of masculine authority, coupled with the expectation of trust in that authority, is common with charismatic pastors. When the bond between charismatic pastor and member is broken, the "tension between expectation and reality elicits instability and doubt."[105] Grove City College psychology professor and blogger Warren Throckmorton published several open letters on his blog in a series called, "Postcards from Phoenix," in the summer of 2021. In an open letter included in the "Postcards" series, former Trinity member Jolie writes, "Looking back over the years, there were many things that gave us pause. However, because of our close ties with the Driscoll family we ignored many red flags."[106] In her "postcard," another woman, Kim, describes the depth of trust in Driscoll's leadership, saying, "We even bought in when [Driscoll] said from the pulpit, 'Don't believe everything you read online' and how evil the media can be, which we all have seen to be true." Now that she is no longer at the church, however, Kim laments that those remaining at Trinity, "say things like, 'none of these situations affected me or my family personally,' or 'he is just such a good teacher,' or 'look how much fruit there is at the church' or 'these people just don't like Mark.'" Kim seems at a loss to explain how others at the church aren't influenced by Driscoll's authoritarianism, writing, "I don't know how this can't impact you knowing that your pastor, who is supposed to be your shepherd and actually protect his sheep, is in actuality harming many of the sheep in his care." Kim asks, "how can you ignore the stories of those who have experienced abuse? I know the answer everyone is being told to give is, 'It's all lies,' but what would be their motivation for lying?"[107]

This plea indicates the immense trust charismatic pastors enjoy. A pastor's "charisma generates deep trust from followers and may cause them to ignore the negative qualities in their leader," until that trust is broken, as it was for these former members of The Trinity Church and Mars Hill.[108] The reverence for masculine authority is so engrained in the broader evangelical movement, that the system—seen as God-ordained—cannot be questioned. Any abuses caused by patriarchal authority are reduced to individual sin, leaving the system in place.

"You Are Just a Man"

Misuses of authority are often dismissed as simply individual errors, rather than looking at the systems within which individuals make their choices. This was true for Driscoll and Mars Hill, as well. John Piper, for example, described the fall of Driscoll and Mars Hill as "a colossal" victory for Satan, but he also reminded followers that, despite their flaws, God "still used people to 'speak gospel truth.'"[109] One of the men I interviewed had an ambivalent relationship with Driscoll and Mars Hill Church. Bill admired Driscoll and accepted his hypermasculine doctrine, saying that other churches had "missed the boat" on men. Yet Bill chafed under Driscoll's authoritarian leadership, primarily because he was excluded from holding a leadership position at Mars Hill, since he didn't subscribe fully to Reformed doctrines. Bill recognized Driscoll's brand-building, and quite presciently told me, Driscoll "may be Reformed today, but if he became non-Reformed tomorrow he would be just as, if not more, popular. It's not about his message. It's about Mark Driscoll." Bill then said, "It's good for [Driscoll] to be a surfer now, so he can ride this wave. But it won't last forever."

America's religious landscape is changing. Driscoll's brand of evangelicalism helped shore up a nostalgic view of a Christian nation with strong families, by seeking to reclaim men's power within American Protestantism as a bulwark against social change. The unsettling economic effects of postindustrialization and globalization lead to people seeking security.[110] Religion that seeks to reclaim nostalgic ideas of order by adhering to a separate spheres ideology can help men, as well as women, feel safe.[111] Reviving a strict complementarian family to reinforce masculine authority, however, cannot resolve these larger structural issues.

Driscoll's authoritarian leadership and hypermasculine theology sowed the seeds of Mars Hill's destruction, creating an environment where all others were subject to his authority and unable to check his destructive impulses. History is being repeated at The Trinity Church, where trust in Driscoll's charisma and (ultimate) male authority leads to members submitting to a seemingly increasing authoritarian structure. Former Mars Hill member Henry described Driscoll's leadership and its impact on Mars Hill, writing on MHWU, "A gifted man of little character destroyed the church he helped create because men of character failed to stand up to him in time." Henry added, "It was truly a sad day when Seattle saw a man destroy the work of his own hands rather than simply humble himself and do the right thing."

Why did "men of character" fail to stop Driscoll? The members of Mars Hill Church believed in patriarchal authority, with Driscoll holding the position of ultimate authority at the church. Church members who did not follow Driscoll's dictates were expelled from the community. Driscoll's authoritarian leadership was embedded in the structure of Mars Hill Church and could not be extricated from the initial success and subsequent growth of the church. Mark Driscoll was the Mars Hill brand. In sickness and in health, Mars Hill's fortunes were tied to Driscoll, as are those of The Trinity Church.

Driscoll is one man, and Mars Hill and The Trinity Church are just two congregations. The fall of the Mars Hill Church empire at the hands of Driscoll does not, however, mean the end of hypermasculine theology within American evangelicalism. Driscoll and Mars Hill Church provided a template from which to understand how a hypermasculine religious movement dovetails with an increasingly mainstream evangelical political movement. White evangelicals will continue to attend churches like Mars Hill, support pastors like Mark Driscoll, and vote for politicians like Donald Trump, who promise to "Make America Great Again," because they see the movement as making "Making Christianity Manly Again."

APPENDIX

Data and Methods

Data for this project include fifty-seven sermons preached by Mark Driscoll between 2001 and 2012, as well as twenty-six interviews and 108 narratives from two online forums created in 2014 and 2016. Given the national controversy surrounding Driscoll's complementarian theology beginning in 2006, when his blog post regarding Ted Haggard went viral, a random sample of sermons from 2006 were collected to see whether gender was as central to the church's mission as the popular press reported. Analyses of these 2006 sermons showed gender to be a fundamental aspect of Driscoll's theology. Additional sermons dealing with gender and relationships between men and women were subsequently chosen for analysis. The sermons analyzed include: eight sermons from the 2001–2002 series *Proverbs*, twenty sermons from the 2006 *Christians Gone Wild* series, six sermons from the 2006 *Vintage Jesus* series, ten sermons from the 2008 *The Peasant Princess* series, two sermons from the 2009 *Trial* series, and eleven sermons from the 2012 *Real Marriage* series (see Table A.1 for a chronological list of sermons analyzed).

Mars Hill Church widely disseminated their weekly sermons. An average of approximately 250,000 people listed to the weekly sermon, and 15 million sermons were accessed each year.[1] The sermons were a Top Ten Religion & Spirituality podcast in the United States, United Kingdom, Canada, Australia, and New Zealand. Sermons were available to download from the Mars Hill Church website in audio and video formats and they were made available for streaming or download on a variety of podcast websites and apps. Sermons used in this analysis were transcribed from audio files. Seven sermons from the *Christians Gone Wild* and *Vintage Jesus* series, as well as both sermons from the *Trial* series, and all *Real Marriage* sermons were transcribed by Seattle Pacific University undergraduate students or alumnae. Transcriptions for the remaining *Christians Gone Wild* and *Vintage Jesus* sermons, as well as the *Peasant Princess* sermons, were transcribed by a professional transcription service, and funded by a Seattle Pacific University SERVE grant. Sermons from the 2002 *Proverbs* series were transcribed by a professional transcriptionist.

Sermon data (as well as the data from the interviews and online forums) were analyzed using principles borrowed from Glaser and Strauss's constant comparative method.[2] The constant comparative method requires data to be examined closely to compare similarities and differences in the concepts represented within the data. Data were coded using "open coding," whereby the data were initially analyzed line by line from transcripts. The coding generated concepts that allowed for making comparisons using whole documents (a broader approach to open coding) to label the concepts emerging from the data. Concepts were grouped into categories (themes) representing particular phenomena in the data. The themes that emerged from the data regarding masculinity, femininity, and relationships between men and women are represented by the subheadings within each of the chapters describing the data.

Table A.1 List of Sermons Analyzed

Series: Sermon	Date Preached
Proverbs: "Covenant and Headship"	October 21, 2001
Proverbs: "Men and Masculinity"	October 28, 2001
Proverbs: "Men as Husbands"	November 4, 2001
Proverbs: "Men as Fathers"	November 11, 2001
Proverbs: "Women and Femininity"	January 6, 2002
Proverbs: "Women as Homebuilders"	January 13, 2002
Proverbs: "Women as Wives"	January 20, 2002
Proverbs: "Women as Mothers"	January 27, 2002
Christians Gone Wild: "Church Planting in Corinth"	January 8, 2006
Christians Gone Wild: "Pastor Jesus"	January 15, 2006
Christians Gone Wild: "Boasting about Jesus"	January 29, 2006
Christians Gone Wild: "Servants of Jesus"	February 12, 2006
Christians Gone Wild: "Humble Like Jesus"	February 26, 2006
Christians Gone Wild: "Power from Jesus"	March 10, 2006
Christians Gone Wild: "Changed by Jesus"	March 26, 2006
Christians Gone Wild: "Our Resurrection Bodies"	April 9, 2006
Christians Gone Wild: "Jesus' Resurrection"	April 16, 2006
Christians Gone Wild: "Good Sex, Bad Sex"	April 23, 2006
Christians Gone Wild: "Divorce and Remarriage"	May 14, 2006
Christians Gone Wild: "Paying Your Pastors"	June 4, 2006
Christians Gone Wild: "Resisting Idols Like Jesus"	June 18, 2006
Christians Gone Wild: "Glorifying God"	July 16, 2006
Christians Gone Wild: "Under Authority Like Christ"	July 23, 1006
Christians Gone Wild: "One Body, Many Parts"	July 30, 2006
Christians Gone Wild: "Spiritual Gifts, Part II"	August 13, 2006
Christians Gone Wild: "Spiritual Gifts, Part IV"	August 27, 2006
Christians Gone Wild: "Spiritual Gifts, Part V"	September 10, 2006
Christians Gone Wild: "A Pastor's Love"	September 24, 2006
Vintage Jesus: "Is Jesus the Only God?"	October 8, 2006
Vintage Jesus: "What Did Jesus Accomplish on the Cross?"	October 22, 2006
Vintage Jesus: "Where Is Jesus Today?"	November 5, 2006
Vintage Jesus: "Why Should We Worship Jesus?"	November 19, 2006
Vintage Jesus: "How Did People Know Jesus Was Coming?"	December 3, 2006
Vintage Jesus: "Why Did Jesus' Mom Have to Be a Virgin?"	December 17, 2006
The Peasant Princess: "Let Him Kiss Me"	September 21, 2008

Table A.1 Continued

Series: Sermon	Date Preached
The Peasant Princess: "Sweet to the Taste"	September 28, 2008
The Peasant Princess: "The Little Foxes"	October 5, 2008
The Peasant Princess: "His Garden"	October 12, 2008
The Peasant Princess: "My Beloved Friend"	October 19, 2008
The Peasant Princess: "My Dove"	October 26, 2008
The Peasant Princess: "I Was a Wall"	November 2, 2008
The Peasant Princess: "Dance of Mahanaim"	November 9, 2008
The Peasant Princess: "Do Not Awaken Love"	November 23, 2008
The Peasant Princess: "Into the Fields"	November 16, 2008
Trial: "Marriage and Women"	March 15, 2009
Trial: "Marriage and Men"	March 22, 2009
Real Marriage: "New Marriage, Same Spouse"	January 15, 2012
Real Marriage: "Friend with Benefits"	January 22, 2012
Real Marriage: "Men and Marriage"	January 29, 2012
Real Marriage: "The Respectful Wife"	February 5, 2012
Real Marriage: "Taking Out the Trash"	February 12, 2012
Real Marriage: "Sex: God, Gross, or Gift?"	February 19, 2012
Real Marriage: "Disgrace and Grace"	February 26, 2012
Real Marriage: "The Porn Path"	March 4, 2012
Real Marriage: "Selfish Lovers and Servant Lovers"	March 11, 2012
Real Marriage: "Can We?"	March 18, 2012
Real Marriage: "Reverse-Engineering Your Life and Marriage"	March 25, 2012

Narrative Data

Narrative data analyzed for this book include interviews and contributions to two online forums. Interviews were conducted between 2009 and 2016, with twenty-six then-current or former members of Mars Hill Church (thirteen men and thirteen women). By talking with people about their experiences with the church, individual stories began to fill out the larger picture of the themes within the sermons. Interviewees were recruited using snowball sampling. Interviewees must have actively participated at Mars Hill Church for a minimum of six months. Each participant was provided with, and signed, a copy of the Seattle Pacific University Institutional Review Board-approved informed consent. The semistructured interview schedule consisted of seven questions:

1. How would you describe your religious background prior to attending Mars Hill Church?
2. What attracted you to/interested you in attending Mars Hill Church?

3. How have you participated with the church?
4. What do you see as Mars Hill's mission to Seattle?
5. How is Mars Hill distinctive from other Christian churches?
6. What else would you like for me to know about your experience with Mars Hill Church?
7. Why did you decide to leave Mars Hill? (asked of former adherents)

Of the twenty-six people interviewed, twelve were then-current members and fourteen were former Mars Hill members. Respondents ranged in age from twenty-two to fifty-four years (with a mean age of thirty-five). Twenty-four respondents identified as white and two identified as Asian/Pacific Islander. Four respondents had high school diplomas, seventeen had Bachelor's degrees, and five had Master's degrees. Fifteen respondents were married, ten were single/never married, and one was divorced. All of the interviewees had grown up in a church or had converted to Christianity prior to participating with Mars Hill Church. Prior to their joining Mars Hill, twenty-one respondents had belonged to evangelical churches, three to mainline Protestant churches, and two to Catholic churches. Interview data are denoted in the text by a pseudonym for each interviewee's first name.

Additional narrative data were taken from two online forums, We Love Mars Hill and Mars Hill Was Us. We Love Mars Hill (WLMH) contributors posted their stories in the fall of 2014. The twenty-seven contributors included fifteen men and twelve women. Created in 2016, Mars Hill Was Us (MHWU) included eighty-one contributors: thirty-eight men, thirty-nine women, and four people who did not identify their gender. Contributors on MHWU identified themselves by full names, first names, initials, as "private," "regular attender," "member," "group leader," or "staff." Data from these Internet forums are denoted by pseudonyms for first names, along with the forum in which contributors posted.

Notes

Preface and Acknowledgments

1. Richard Perkins, *Looking Both Ways: Exploring the Interface between Christianity and Sociology* (Grand Rapids: Baker Books, 1987), 169.

Introduction

1. Kristin Kobes Du Mez, *Jesus and John Wayne: How White Evangelicals Corrupted a Faith and Fractured a Nation* (New York: Liveright, 2020), 3; Molly Worthen, "A Match Made in Heaven," *The Atlantic*, May 15, 2017, https://www.theatlantic.com/magazine/archive/2017/05/a-match-made-in-heaven/521409/.
2. Public Religion Research Institute (PRRI), *Dueling Realities amid Multiple Crises, Trump and Biden Supporters See Different Priorities and Futures for the Nation: Findings from the 2020 American Values Survey* (Washington, DC: PRRI, 2020), 32.
3. PRRI, *Dueling Realities*, 32.
4. Du Mez, *Jesus and John Wayne*, 263.
5. See John P. Bartkowski, *Remaking the Godly Marriage: Gender Negotiation in Evangelical Families* (New Brunswick, NJ: Rutgers University Press, 2001); Seth Dowland, *Family Values and the Rise of the Christian Right* (Philadelphia: University of Pennsylvania Press, 2015); Du Mez, *Jesus and John Wayne*; Sally K. Gallagher, *Evangelical Identity and Gendered Family Life* (New Brunswick, NJ: Rutgers University Press, 2003).
6. Du Mez, *Jesus and John Wayne*, 249.
7. Jerry Falwell Jr., "Falwell Jr. on Trump: We're not electing a pastor-in . . . ," interview by Anderson Cooper, *Anderson Cooper 360*, CNN, June 1, 2016, https://www.youtube.com/watch?v=G42VEGGmliQ.
8. Kristin Du Mez, "Donald Trump and Militant Evangelical Masculinity," *Religion & Politics*, January 17, 2017, https://religionandpolitics.org/2017/01/17/donald-trump-and-militant-evangelical-masculinity/.
9. Emma Green, "Franklin Graham Is the Evangelical Id," *The Atlantic*, May 21, 2017, https://www.theatlantic.com/politics/archive/2017/05/franklin-graham/527013/.
10. Peter Wehner, "The Deepening Crisis in Evangelical Christianity," *The Atlantic*, July 5, 2019, https://www.theatlantic.com/ideas/archive/2019/07/evangelical-christians-face-deepening-crisis/593353/.

11. Jerry Falwell Jr. (@jerryfalwelljr), "Conservatives & Christians need to stop electing 'nice guys.' They might make great Christian leaders but the US needs street fighters like @realDonaldTrump at every level of government b/c the liberal fascists Dems are playing for keeps & many Repub leaders are a bunch of wimps!" Twitter, September 28, 2018, https://twitter.com/jerryfalwelljr/status/1045853333007798272.

12. Wehner, "Deepening."

13. Du Mez, *Jesus and John Wayne*, 271.

14. Gerardo Marti, *American Blindspot: Race, Class, Religion, and the Trump Presidency* (New York: Rowman & Littlefield, 2020), 7.

15. Marti, *Blindspot*, 7.

16. Du Mez, *Jesus and John Wayne*, 256; Marti, *Blindspot*, 214.

17. Marti, *Blindspot*, 214.

18. Wehner, "Deepening."

19. Andrew L. Whitehead and Samuel L. Perry, *Taking America Back for God: Christian Nationalism in the United States* (New York: Oxford University Press, 2020), 16.

20. Dowland, *Family Values*, 17, 131.

21. Du Mez, *Jesus and John Wayne*, 272.

22. Whitehead and Perry, *Taking America*, 17.

23. Frances Fitzgerald, *The Evangelicals: The Struggle to Shape America* (New York: Simon & Schuster, 2017), 629.

24. Fitzgerald, *Evangelicals*, 629.

25. *New York Times*, "Transcript: Donald Trump's Taped Comments about Women," October 8, 2016, https://www.nytimes.com/2016/10/08/us/donald-trump-tape-tra nscript.html; Philip Rucker, "Trump Says Megyn Kelly Had 'Blood Coming Out of Her Whatever,'" *Washington Post*, April 8, 2015, https://www.washingtonpost.com/ news/post-politics/wp/2015/08/07/trump-says-foxs-megyn-kelly-had-blood-com ing-out-of-her-wherever/.

26. Du Mez, *Jesus and John Wayne*, 265.

27. Charles S. Corprew III, Jamaal S. Matthews, and Avery DeVell Mitchell, "Men at the Crossroads: A Profile Analysis of Hypermasculinity in Emerging Adulthood," *Journal of Men's Studies* 22, no. 2 (Spring 2014), 105.

28. Du Mez, *Jesus and John Wayne*, 10.

29. Marti, *Blindspot*, 217.

30. *Church Leaders*, "John MacArthur: Mark Driscoll Paved the Way for Donald Trump," March 23, 2016, http://churchleaders.com/daily-buzz/276029-john-mcarthur-mark-driscoll-paved-way-donald-trump.html.

31. Max Weber, *The Theory of Social and Economic Organization*, translated by A. M. Henderson and Talcott Parsons (New York: Free Press, 1964), 358; Lorne Dawson, "Crises of Charismatic Legitimacy and Violent Behaviors in New Religious Movements," in *Cults, Religion and Violence*, ed. David G. Bromley and J. Gordon Melton (Cambridge: Cambridge University Press, 2002), 81–82.

32. Megachurches are defined as having a sustained weekly average of attendance of 2,000 or more people (including adults and children). See Hartford Institute for Religion

Research, "Megachurch Definition," accessed February 13, 2022, http://hirr.hartsem. edu/megachurch/definition.html.

33. James K. Wellman Jr., Katie E. Corcoran, and Kate J. Stockly, *High on God: How Megachurches Won the Heart of America* (New York: Oxford University Press, 2020), 124.

34. Wellman, Corcoran, and Stockly, *High*, 72, 85.

35. Wellman, Corcoron, and Stockly, *High*, 28.

36. David Eagle, "Historicizing the Megachurch," *Journal of Social History* 48, no. 3 (Spring 2015), 591.

37. Du Mez, *Jesus and John Wayne*, 194.

38. Du Mez, *Jesus and John Wayne*, 197.

39. These states were Washington, Oregon, California, and New Mexico.

40. Mars Hill Church, *It's All about Jesus: Annual Report, 2013*, accessed October 1, 2014, http://www.marshillchurch.org/media/mars-hill-quarterly/mars-hill-church-ann ual-report-fy13.

41. Donald Miller, *Blue Like Jazz: Non-Religious Thoughts on Christian Spirituality* (Nashville, TN: Thomas Nelson, 2003), 134; Jack Jenkins, "How Evangelicals Are Protesting the 'Rush Limbaugh of Christianity,'" *Think Progress*, August 5, 2014, http://thinkprogress.org/lgbt/2014/08/05/3467250/mark-driscoll-protest/;   Jason Mollinet, "Church Reeling after Founding Pastor Calls Women 'Penis Homes,'" *New York Daily News*, September 10, 2014, http://www.nydailynews.com/news/natio nal/church-reeling-pastor-calls-women-penis-homes-article-1.1934308. In his 2021 podcast, *The Rise and Fall of Mars Hill*, host Mike Cosper notes that many evangelicals were introduced to Driscoll by Donald Miller's naming Driscoll the "cussing pastor" in his book, *Blue Like Jazz*. Cosper states he found few instances of Driscoll's cursing in sermons, yet the weekly podcast introduction includes a sermon clip where Driscoll yells, "Who the hell to you think you are?!" See Cosper, "Who Killed Mars Hill," June 21, 2021, produced by Mike Cosper, *The Rise and Fall of Mars Hill*, 60:00, https://www.christianitytoday.com/ct/podcasts/rise-and-fall-of-mars-hill/who- killed-mars-hill-church-mark-driscoll-rise-fall.html.

42. *Christianity Today*, "Avatar: 'The Most Satanic Film I've Ever Seen,'" Gleanings, February 26, 2020, https://www.christianitytoday.com/news/2010/february/ava tar-most-satanic-film-ive-ever-seen.html; Janet I. Tu, "Yoga 'Demonic'? Critics Call Ministers' Warning a Stretch," October 8, 2010, https://www.seattletimes.com/ seattle-news/yoga-demonic-critics-call-ministers-warning-a-stretch/#:~:text= %E2%80%9CShould%20Christians%20stay%20away%20from,for%20a%20lit tle%20demon%20clcla.%E2%80%9D; Sharon Hodde Miller, "Much Ado about Mark Driscoll," Her.Meneutics, *Christianity Today*, July 15, 2011, https://www.christ ianitytoday.com/ct/2011/julyweb-only/much-ado-about-mark-driscoll.html; Gina Meeks, "Mark Driscoll Angers Twitterverse with Tweet about Hell," *Charisma News*, January 15, 2014, https://www.charismanews.com/us/42428-mark-driscoll-angers- twitterverse-with-tweet-about-hell.

43. "The Driscollizer," The Mark Driscoll Insult Generator, accessed June 24, 2015, http:// driscollize.me.

44. Lori Leibovitch, "Generation: A Look inside Fundamentalism's Answer to MTV; the Postmodern Church," *Mother Jones*, July 1, 1998, http://www.motherjones.com/polit ics/1998/07/generation.

45. Jesse Benjamin, "Mark Driscoll Kicks His Own Ass," *The Wittenburg Door*, July 1, 2008, http://www.wittenburgdoor.com/driscoll-kicks-own-ass.html.

46. See James K. Wellman Jr. and Katie E. Corcoran "Religion and Regional Culture: Embedding Religious Commitment within Place," *Sociology of Religion* 74, no. 4 (Winter 2013), 496–520.

47. Driscoll's conservative theology certainly stood in contrast to Seattle's progressive political and social culture. Even so, Driscoll constructed Seattle as an "imagined secular." In her work on evangelicals and gender, Sarah Diefendorf defines the imagined secular as "a world full of nonreligious individuals who push for access to abortion, trans rights, gay rights, deviant sex, and marriages void of God." See Diefendorf, "Contemporary Evangelical Responses to Feminism and the Imagined Secular," *Signs: Journal of Women in Culture and Society* 44, no. 4 (Summer 2019), 1004.

48. Mark Driscoll and Grace Driscoll, *Real Marriage: The Truth about Sex, Friendship & Life Together* (Nashville, TN: Thomas Nelson, 2012), 5.

49. Driscoll and Driscoll, *Real Marriage*, 5.

50. Driscoll and Driscoll, *Real Marriage*, 6.

51. Driscoll graduated from Washington State University in 1992 with a degree in Speech Communication and holds a Masters of Exegetical Theology degree from Western Seminary.

52. Driscoll and Driscoll, *Real Marriage*, 8. The verse Driscoll cited was Romans 1:6, which describes that through the grace bestowed by Jesus Christ, Christians, "including yourselves . . . are called to belong to Jesus Christ" (NRSV).

53. Driscoll and Driscoll, *Real Marriage*, 8.

54. Erica C. Barnett, "Cross Purposes," *Seattle Weekly*, May 4, 2006, http://www.thestran ger.com/seattle/cross-purposes/Content?oid=32140.

55. Mark Driscoll, *Confessions of a Reformission Rev.: Hard Lessons from an Emerging Missional Church* (Grand Rapids, MI: Zondervan, 2006), 132. See also James K. Wellman Jr., *Evangelical vs. Liberal: The Clash of Christian Cultures in the Pacific Northwest* (New York: Oxford University Press, 2008).

56. The name "Acts 29" symbolizes the continuation of church planting described in the New Testament book of Acts, which has twenty-eight chapters. The Acts 29 network has planted hundreds of churches around the world. See James S. Bielo, "Act Like Men: Social Engagement and Evangelical Masculinity," *Journal of Contemporary Religion* 29, no. 2, 233–248.

57. The Gospel Coalition, "About," accessed January 20, 2022, https://www.thegospelco alition.org/about/.

58. Warren Cole Smith and Sophia Lee, "Changing Course?," *World Magazine*, July 25, 2014, http://www.worldmag.com/2014/07/changing_course; Mark Woods, "Decline and Fall: The Slow Erosion of Mars Hill," *Christianity Today*, November 4, 2014, http://christianitytoday.com/decline.and.fall.the.slow.erosion.of.Mars.hill/   42568. htm?print=1.

59. Libby Anne, "Pastor Mark Driscoll Called Women 'Penis Homes,'" *Love, Joy, Feminism* (blog), September 8, 2014, https://www.patheos.com/blogs/lovejoyfemin ism/2014/09/pastor-mark-driscoll-called-women-penis-homes.html?utm_source= twitterfeed&utm_medium=twitter; Dee, "Queen Esther Was Not a Slut: The Harsh Treatment of Women in the Old Testament," *The Wartburg Watch* (blog), August 3, 2015, http://thewartburgwatch.com/2015/08/03/queen-esther-was-not-a-slut-the-harsh-treatment-of-women-in-the-old-testament/.

60. Collin Hansen, "Pastor Provocateur," *Christianity Today*, June 3, 2007, http://www.christianitytoday.com/ct/channel/utilities/print.html?type=article&id=50001. Hansen currently serves as vice president of content, and editor-in-chief of The Gospel Coalition.

61. Keith Hinson, "Motions: GCR Task Force Endorsed," *Baptist Press*, June 25, 2009, http://bpnews.net/bpnews.asp?id=30774.

62. Collin Hansen, *Young, Restless, and Reformed: A Journalist's Journey with the New Calvinism* (Wheaton, IL: Crossway Books, 2008), 136.

63. Du Mez, *Jesus and John Wayne*, 199. Traditional Calvinist doctrines maintain "five points" that are often referred to by the mnemonic TULIP: the total depravity of man, unconditional election, limited atonement, irresistible grace, and perseverance of the saints.

64. Du Mez, *Jesus and John Wayne*, 200.

65. Du Mez, *Jesus and John Wayne*, 200; Molly Worthen, "Who Would Jesus Smack Down?," *New York Times Magazine*, January 11, 2009, http://www.nytimes.com/2009/01/11/magazine/11punk-t.html.

66. Jared Oliphint, "John Piper's Twelve Features for the New Calvinism," *Reformed Forum*, March 17, 2014, https://reformedforum.org/john-pipers-twelve-features-new-calvinism/. Writing for the *New York Times*, journalist Mark Oppenheimer described the growth of Calvinism among Protestant denominations and noted its controversy. In the SBC, for example, approximately 30 percent of churches considered themselves Calvinist, while nearly twice as many were concerned about the influence of Calvinism within the denomination. See Oppenheimer, "Evangelicals Find Themselves in the Midst of a Calvinist Revival," *New York Times*, January 3, 2014, http://www.nytimes.com/2014/01/04/us/a-calvinist-revival-for-evangelicals.html.

67. David Van Biema, "Ten Ideas Changing the World Right Now: The New Calvinism," *Time Magazine*, March 12, 2009, http://content.time.com/time/specials/packages/article/0,28804,1884779_1884782_1884760,00.html.

68. Mark Driscoll, "Time Magazine Names New Calvinism 3rd Most Powerful Idea," *The Resurgence*, March 12, 2009, http://theresurgence.com/2009/03/12/time-magazine-names-new-calvinism-3rd-most-powerful-idea; Mark Driscoll, "More Thoughts on Time Magazine and New Calvinism," *The Resurgence*, March 12, 2009, http://theres urgence.com/2009/03/12/more-thoughts-on-time-magazine-and-new-calvinism.

69. See Gallagher, *Evangelical Identity*.

70. Driscoll, *Confessions*, 66–67.

71. Driscoll, *Confessions*, 67.

72. While the office of pastor or elder was limited to men, women at Mars Hill Church could serve as deacons.

73. Mark Driscoll, *On Church Leadership* (Wheaton, IL: Crossway Books, 2008), 41.

74. Jen Smidt, "Complementarian Relationships in Marriage," in Mars Hill Church, *This Is Mars Hill: 2010 Annual Church Report*, 21, accessed October 1, 2014, http://marshill.com/2011/02/20110130_mars-hill-church-annual-report-fy10_document.pdf

75. Driscoll, *Church Leadership*, 48.

76. Worthen, "Smack Down?"

77. Jenkins, "Evangelicals Are Protesting."

78. Barnett, "Cross Purposes."

79. Barnett, "Cross Purposes."

80. Mark Driscoll, "Pussified Nation," *Midrash*, December 5, 2000, available at Matthew Paul Turner, "Mark Driscoll's Pussified Nation," MatthewPaulTurner.com (blog), July 29, 2014, https://matthewpaulturner.com/2014/07/29/mark-driscolls-pussified-nation/.

81. Joel Connelly, "Dozens Protest Mars Hill Church after Leader Resignations and Mark Driscoll Apology," *Seattle Post-Intelligencer*, August 3, 2014, http://blog.seattlepi.com/seattlepolitics/2014/08/03/mars-hill-church-protest-mars-hill-resignations-mark-driscoll-apology/.

82. Janet I. Tu, "Pastor Mark Packs 'Em In," *Pacific Northwest Magazine*, November 28, 2003, http://community.seattletimes.nwsource.com/archive/?date=20031128&slug=pacific-preacher30; Mark Driscoll, "Above All Earthly Powers: The Supremacy of Christ in a Post-Modern World," *Desiring God: 2006 National Conference*, available at "Church Needs Dudes," YouTube video, posted by Josh Brage, 1:54, August 14, 2006, https://www.youtube.com/watch?v=lex6orNNzTs. Driscoll's account of Mars Hill being mostly young, single men was challenged the following year in a *Christianity Today* article written by Collin Hansen ("Paster Provocateur"), who reported that Mars Hill's largest demographic was single women. In the book *Real Marriage*, Driscoll amended his original claim, stating that Mars Hill had "a higher-than-usual percentage of guys" (xiii).

83. Mark Driscoll, "Evangelical Leader Quits amid Allegations of Gay Sex and Drug Use," *The Resurgence*, November 3, 2006, http://theresurgence.com/md_blog_2006-11-03_eangelical_leader_quits.

84. *Seattle Post-Intelligencer*, "Mars Hill Pastor Responds to Uproar over Blog Post on Women," December 4, 2006, http://seattlepi.nwsource.com/local/294572_marshill04.html; People Against Fundamentalism, "People Against Fundamentalism Plans Protest against Mars Hill Seattle Pastor Mark Driscoll," accessed November 21, 2006, http://www.endfunamentalism.org.

85. Marsha King, "Pastor's Apology Diffuses Protest at Church," *Seattle Times*, December 4, 2006, http://www.seattletimes.com/seattle-news/pastors-apology-defuses-demonstration-at-church/. Driscoll posted an apology on his blog stating he was "sad and sorry to hear" that some people felt "personally attacked" by his remarks. Driscoll was dismissed from the *Seattle Times*, which reported that his status as a columnist had already been under review.

86. Worthen, "Smack Down?"
87. Mark Driscoll, "Where Is Jesus Today?," *Vintage Jesus* series, Mars Hill Church, November 5, 2006. Sermons used for analysis are noted in full at their first use, followed by shortened notes. For a chronological list of sermons analyzed, see Appendix.
88. Driscoll, "Above All."
89. Driscoll, *Confessions*, 131.
90. Worthen, "Smack Down?"
91. Worthen, "Smack Down?"
92. Mark Driscoll, "Under Authority Like Christ," *Christians Gone Wild* series, Mars Hill Church, July 23, 2006.
93. Driscoll, "Under Authority Like Christ."
94. Driscoll, "Under Authority Like Christ."
95. Worthen, "Smack Down."
96. Brandon O'Brien, "A Jesus for Real Men: What the New Masculinity Movement Gets Right and Wrong," *Christianity Today*, April 18, 2008, 50.
97. Mark Driscoll, "A Pastor's Love," *Christians Gone Wild* series, Mars Hill Church, September 24, 2006.
98. Worthen, "Smack Down?"
99. Worthen, "Smack Down?"
100. Barnett, "Cross Purposes." This sermon became infamous in the Seattle area and was referred to as the "women are saved through childbirth" sermon. The sermon was used to highlight Driscoll's directly attaching women's salvation to being mothers, whereas men's salvation was attached to their relationship with God.
101. Barnett, "Cross Purposes."
102. Mark Driscoll, *A Good Soldier: A Conversation with Mark Driscoll*, available at "A Good Soldier," YouTube video, posted by Resurgence, 9:07, April 28, 2007, http://www.youtube.com/watch?v=JIrIKbCz3n4.
103. Driscoll, "Above All."
104. Driscoll, "Good Soldier."
105. Mark Driscoll, "Church Planting in Corinth," *Christians Gone Wild* series, Mars Hill Church, January 8, 2006.
106. Portions of the timeline outlining the fall of Mars Hill Church have been adapted from Jennifer McKinney, "Mars Hill (Seattle)," *World Religions and Spirituality Project*, June 9, 2016, https://wrldrels.org/2016/10/08/mars-hill-seattle/.
107. Mars Hill Church, "The Story of Mars Hill Church," accessed December 2, 2014, http://marshill.com.
108. Campuses scheduled to open in January 2014 included Huntington Beach, CA; Phoenix, AZ; and Tacoma, WA. Additional campuses in Los Angeles, CA, and Spokane, WA, were being developed to open later in 2014.
109. Warren Throckmorton, "Former Mars Hill Pastor Dave Kraft Explains His Charges against Mark Driscoll," *Patheos*, May 21, 2014, http://www.patheos.com/blogs/warrenthrockmorton/2014/03/21/former-mars-hill-pastor-dave-kraft-explains-charges-against-mark-driscoll/.

110. Joel Connelly, "21 Former Mars Hill Pastors Lodge Formal Charges against Mark Driscoll," *Seattle Post-Intelligencer*, August 21, 2014, http://blog.seattlepi.com/seat tlepolitics/2014/08/21/21-former-mars-hill-pastors-lodge-formal-charges-against-driscoll/. Warren Throckmorton reported that several people provided evidence to support Kraft's charges to BOAA member Michael Van Skaik, who was assigned to chair the committee investigating the charges. Nothing, however, was done with the charges. Throckmorton writes that, "some of those who presented evidence received no response to the information submitted." See Throckmorton, "Former Mars Hill Pastor."

111. Alicia MacKenzie, "Mark Driscoll 'Crashes' John MacArthur's Strange Fire Conference?," *The Christian Post*, October 18, 2013, http://www.christianpost.com/ buzzvine/mark-driscoll-crashes-john-macarthurs-strange-fire-conference-photos-106976/. Over the years, Driscoll and MacArthur had theological disagreements over charismatic gifts of the spirit. Driscoll believes the gifts are available to modern Christians, whereas MacArthur is a "cessationist," meaning he does not believe the gifts of the Spirit are available to modern Christians.

112. MacKenzie, "Driscoll 'Crashes.'"

113. Wellman, Corcoran, and Stockly, *High*, 212.

114. Jonathan Merritt, "Mark Driscoll Accused of Plagiarism by Radio Host," *Religion News Service*, November 22, 201, https://religionnews.com/2013/11/22/mark-driscoll-accused-plagiarism-radio-host/; Warren Cole Smith, "More Publishers Investigate Mark Driscoll," *World Magazine*, January 2, 2014, http://www.worldmag.com/2014/01/more_publishers_investigate_driscoll.

115. Kate Tracy, "Publisher: Mark Driscoll Improperly Copied Paragraphs from Bible Commentary," *Christianity Today*, December 9, 2013, https://www.christianitytoday.com/news/2013/december/parsing-mark-driscoll-plagiarism-janet-mefferd-apologizes.html. While Tyndale, publisher of *Call to Resurgence*, stood by Driscoll, they later posted a letter on their website from Driscoll admitting that "mistakes were made" by a research assistant, who had inadvertently plagiarized the relevant passages. In January 2014, *World Magazine* reported that two more publishers, Crossway and NavPress, were investigating allegations of Driscoll's plagiarism. See Smith, "More Publishers."

116. Smith, "More Publishers."

117. The latter accusations eventually led to the filing of a civil racketeering lawsuit against Driscoll, accusing him and another elder of redirecting church funds for "a 'scam' designed to make Driscoll a best-selling author." See Nina Shapiro, "Racketeering Suit Claims Mark Driscoll Misused Mars Hill Donor Dollars," *Seattle Times*, February 29, 2016, http://www.seattletimes.com/seattle-news/mark-driscoll-accused-of-racketeering-at-mars-hill-church/.

118. Jeremy Weber, "Mark Driscoll Retracts Bestseller Book Status, Resets Life," *Christianity Today*, March 17, 2014, https://www.christianitytoday.com/news/2014/march/mark-driscoll-retracts-bestseller-status-resets-life.html. Driscoll also said he regretted how the church had handled the turnover for some key staff members who had "chosen to air their concerns online."

119. Shapiro, "Racketeering."

120. Warren Throckmorton, "Former Staffer Says That Mars Hill Church's Global Fund Was Restricted," *Patheos*, August 12, 2014, http://www.patheos.com/blogs/warrent hrockmorton/2014/08/12/former-staffer-says-that-mars-hill-churchs-global-fund-was-restricted/.

121. Elizabeth Drescher, "Mars Hill Defectors Refuse to Be Anonymous," *Medium: The Narthex*, July 27, 2014, https://medium.com/the-narthex/mars-hill-defectors-ref use-to-be-anonymous-dec1013eda7#:~:text=A%20group%20of%20former%20 members,experiences%20that%20they%20say%20drove. In the July video Driscoll intimated that his anonymous critics were former Mars Hill Church leaders who experienced "adverse personal implications" during two church organizational shifts in 2006–2007 and 2011–2012. Driscoll apologized for "not being as loving as I could or should have been to men, especially in some personal communications and conversations." The video transcription is available at https://gist.githubusercontent. com/anonymous/b1dd5d1b6b3a14b6e7f3/raw/6c9dfc093dda78bb1a6b7ae29a990 9045ad2a9e3/MHMW20140718.)

122. Connelly, "Dozens Protest."

123. Connelly, "Dozens Protest." Driscoll had transitioned from preaching primarily at the Seattle-Ballard campus to preaching primarily at the Bellevue campus.

124. Connelly, "Dozens Protest."

125. Joel Connelly, "A Big, Planned Mars Hill 'Jesus Festival' Disappears without a Trace," *Seattle Post-Intelligencer*, August 19, 2014, http://blog.seattlepi.com/seattlep olitics/2014/08/19/a-big-planned-mars-hill-jesus-festival-disappears-without-a-trace/.

126. Joel Connelly, "Mark Driscoll Returns Sunday; Churchgoers Told to Bring Bibles," *Seattle Post-Intelligencer*, August 20, 2014, http://blog.seattlepi.com/seattlepolit ics/2014/08/20/mark-driscoll-returns-sunday-mars-hill-churchgoers-told-bring-Bibles/.

127. Warren Throckmorton, "Twenty-One Former Mars Hill Church Pastors Bring Formal Charges against Mark Driscoll," *Patheos*, August 21, 2014, http://www.path eos.com/blogs/warrenthrockmorton/2014/08/21/former-mars-hill-church-past ors-bring-formal-charges-against-mark-driscoll/. The Acts 29 announcement was the last straw for the SBC's Lifeway Christian Resources, who pulled Driscoll's books from their website and all of their stores. See Sarah Pulliam Bailey, "Megapastor Mark Driscoll's Books Pulled from Major Christian Store in Wake of Scandal," *Huffington Post*, August 11, 2014, http://www.huffingtonpost.com/2014/08/11/ mark-driscoll-books-lifeway_n_5669700.html.

128. Throckmorton, "Twenty-One"; Joel Connelly, "21 Former Mars Hill Pastors Lodge Formal Charges against Mark Driscoll," *Seattle Post-Intelligencer*, August 21, 2014, http://blog.seattlepi.com/seattlepolitics/2014/08/21/21-former-mars-hill-pastors-lodge-formal-charges-against-driscoll/.

129. Connelly, "21 Former"; Throckmorton, "Twenty-One."

130. Connelly, "21 Former."

131. Sarah Pulliam Bailey, "Mark Driscoll to Step Down While Mars Hill Reviews Charges," *Religion News Service*, August 24, 2014, http://religionnews.com/2014/08/24/mark-driscoll-step-down-mars-hill-elders-review-charges/.

132. Bailey, "Step Down."

133. Bailey, "Step Down."

134. Bailey, "Step Down"; Michael Paulson, "Facing Ire, Mark Driscoll Says He Will Take a Leave," *New York Times*, August 24, 2014, http://www.nytimes.com/2014/08/25/us/facing-ire-mark-driscoll-says-he-will-take-a-leave.html?_r=0.

135. Warren Throckmorton, "Nine Current Mars Hill Church Elders Take Bold Stand," *Patheos*, August 28, 2014, http://www.patheos.com/blogs/warrenthrockmorton/2014/08/28/nine-current-mars-hill-church-elders-take-a-bold-stand/.

136. Bailey, "Step Down"; Throckmorton, "Nine Current."

137. Warren Throckmorton, "Mars Hill Church Leaders: Giving Is Down Due to 'Increase in Negative Media Attention,'" *Patheos*, August 30, 2014, http://www.patheos.com/blogs/warrenthrockmorton/2014/08/30/mars-hill-church-leaders-giving-is-down-due-to-increase-in-negative-media-attention/.

138. Warren Throckmorton, "Mars Hill Church to Close Three Locations; Another on Hold (Updated)," *Patheos*, September 7, 2014, http://www.patheos.com/blogs/warrenthrockmorton/2014/09/07/mars-hill-church-to-close-three-locations-another-on-hold/; Craig Welch, "More Trouble for Mars Hill: Cutting Jobs, Merging Churches," *Seattle Times*, September 7, 2014, http://www.seattletimes.com/seattle-news/more-trouble-for-mars-hill-cutting-jobs-merging-churches/.

139. Sarah Pulliam Bailey, "Exclusive: Mark Driscoll's Resignation Letter from Mars Hill Church," *Religion News Service*, October 15, 2014, http://religionnews.com/2014/10/15/exclusive-mark-driscolls-resignation-letter-to-mars-hill-church/.

140. Bailey, "Exclusive."

141. Sarah Pullium Bailey, "How the 'Cussin' Pastor' Got into Megatrouble," *Wall Street Journal*, November 13, 2014, http://www.wsj.com/articles/sarah-pulliam-bailey-how-the-cussin-pastor-got-into-megatrouble-1415924941. In 2020 blogger Warren Throckmorton obtained a copy of the original investigation report resulting from the charges filed against Driscoll by twenty-one former Mars Hill Church elders. While the BOAA corroborated Driscoll's guilt for many of the charges, they stated that he was not disqualified from ministry. According to Throckmorton, however, Mars Hill's Board of Elders disagreed with the BOAA ruling, believing that Driscoll should be removed from his teaching and administrative positions until he had completed a restoration process. See Throckmorton, "From the Past: The Mars Hill Church Board of Elders Wanted Mark Driscoll Out of Ministry," February 20, 2020, http://wthrockmorton.com/2020/02/20/from-the-past-the-mars-hill-church-board-of-elders-wanted-mark-driscoll-out-of-ministry.

142. Tim Barlass and Kate Aubusson, "Keep Out US Pastor Mark Driscoll, Hillsong Warned," *Sydney Morning Herald*, June 7, 2015, http://www.smh.com.au/action/printArticle? id = 996959510.

143. Nina Shapiro, "Evangelical Leaders Give Fallen Mars Hill Pastor Mark Driscoll a New Forum," *Seattle Times*, May 30, 2015, http://www.seattletimes.com/seattle-news/

evangelical-leaders-give-fallen-mars-hill-pastor-mark-driscoll-a-new-forum/. The thrust of the campaign to remove Driscoll from the Hillsong conference revolved around his antiwoman rhetoric. Yet many in the United States waging a battle against Driscoll noted their concerns were not about his misogyny, but his mismanagement and leadership style. Former Mars Hill deacon Brian Jacobsen stated, "While much of the pressure on Hillsong focused on Mark's comments about women, many of us are focusing on the issues of (alleged) fraud and abuse perpetrated by Mark and the other top leaders at Mars Hill Church." See Nina Shapiro, "Australian Megachurch Pulls Invitation to Ex-Mars Hill Leader," *Seattle Times*, June 8, 2015, https://www. seattletimes.com/seattle-news/australian-megachurch-pulls-invitation-to-ex-mars-hill-leader/.

144. In 2022, Brian Houston resigned from Hillsong after he was criminally charged with concealing knowledge of his father's past child sexual abuse and after he was accused of breaching the church's code of conduct by behaving inappropriately with two women. See Yan Zhuang, "Leader of Australian Megachurch Steps Down after Charge over Father's Sexual Abuse," *New York Times*, January 30, 2022, https://www. nytimes.com/2022/01/31/world/australia/brian-houston-hillsong.html;   Natasha Frost, "Founder of Australia's Hillsong Church Resigns amid Scandals," *New York Times*, March 23, 2022, https://www.nytimes.com/2022/03/23/world/australia/ brian-houston-hillsong-resign.html.

145. Laura Turner, "Mark Driscoll Rises from the Ashes in Phoenix," *Religion News Service*, February 5, 2016, http://religionnews.com/2016/02/05/mark-driscoll-rises-ashes-phoenix-commentary/.

146. Kevin Porter, "Protesters Cast a Shadow over Mark Driscoll's Trinity Church Open House," *The Christian Post*, March 31, 2016, http://www.christianpost.com/news/ mark-driscolls-trinity-church-open-house-overshadowed-by-protests-160602/.

147. James River Church, "Who May Ascend to the Mountain of the Lord?" Stronger Men's Conference 2020, accessed July 25, 2019, https://jamesriver.brushfire.com/ stronger-mens-conference-2020/453948.

148. James River Church, "2017 Stronger Men's Conference Sessions," accessed July 25, 2019, https://jamesriver.church/smcsessions.

149. Morgan Lee, "The Story of Mark Driscoll and Mars Hill Matter in 2021," *Christianity Today*, June 25, 2021, https://www.christianitytoday.com/ct/podcasts/quick-to-lis ten/rise-fall-mars-hill-mark-driscoll-podcast.html.

150. Jessica Johnson, "How Mega-Macho Pastor Mark Driscoll Helps Explain Trump's Evangelical Support," *Religion Dispatches*, March 8, 2016, http://religiondispatches. org/how-mega-macho-pastor-mark-driscoll-helps-explain-trumps-evangelical-support/.

151. Johnson, "Mega-Macho Pastor."

152. See Barney G. Glaser and Anselm L. Strauss, *The Discovery of Grounded Theory* (Chicago: Aldine de Gruyter, 1967); Anselm Strauss and Juliet Corbin, *Basics of Qualitative Research: Grounded Theory Procedures and Techniques* (Newbury Park: SAGE Publications, 1990).

Chapter 1

1. An earlier version of this chapter was presented as the 2015 Winifred Weter Memorial Lecture at Seattle Pacific University, and subsequently published in *The Priscilla Papers*.

2. Nancy Ammerman, *Baptist Battles: Social Change and Religious Conflict in the Southern Baptist Convention* (New Brunswick, NJ: Rutgers University Press, 1990), 24.

3. The Puritan ideal of hierarchy was itself a shift between medieval and early modern Christianity. The more removed medieval European women were from marriage, the closer to God they were assumed to be. Changing economic conditions and the rise of Reformation theology in early modern Christianity changed ideals of gender, placing women more firmly under the authority of husbands and limiting their economic and social opportunities outside of the household. Post-Reformation, Protestant women's perceived piety was tied to their marital status. See Beth Allison Barr, *The Making of Biblical Womanhood: How the Subjugation of Women Became Gospel Truth* (Grand Rapids, MI: Brazos Press, 2021).

4. Roger Finke and Rodney Stark, *The Churching of America, 1776–2005: Winners and Losers in Our Religious Economy* (New Brunswick, NJ: Rutgers University Press, 2005), 85–86.

5. Finke and Stark, *Churching*, 103, 107.

6. Susan Juster, *Disorderly Women: Sexual Politics and Evangelicalism in Revolutionary New England* (Ithaca, NY: Cornell University Press, 1994), 3; Finke and Stark, *Churching*, 105.

7. Ammerman, *Baptist Battles*, 24.

8. The mid-eighteenth-century evangelical movement in the United States was distinctive because it allowed women's preaching, teaching, pastoring, administering of the sacraments, and providing spiritual oversight to others. John Wesley, founder of Methodism, for example, "affirmed the ministries of . . . women in explicitly egalitarian language as of the exact same order as that of the men who had not received Anglican ordination whose public ministries he was also affirming." See Timothy Larsen, "Evangelicalism's Strong History of Women in Ministry," *Reformed Journal* 5, no. 32 (September/October 2017), https://reformedjournal.com/evangelicalisms-strong-history-women-ministry/.

9. Finke and Stark, *Churching*, 107.

10. Juster, *Disorderly Women*, 25, 44.

11. Julie Ingersoll, *Evangelical Christian Women: War Stories in the Gender Battles* (New York: New York University Press, 2003), 47; Ammerman, *Baptist Battles*, 89. Ammerman reports that more than 500 women had been ordained in the SBC by 1988.

12. Southern Baptist Convention (SBC), "The Baptist Faith & Message 2000," accessed April 7, 2015, http://www.sbc.net/bfm2000/bfm2000.asp. In 1979 the SBC's governing moderate faction was replaced by a fundamentalist faction. By 1984 the SBC had created a resolution emphasizing women's secondary creation. This was followed

in 1998 by a statement stipulating wives' submission to husbands, which culminated in the amendment to the Baptist Faith and Message in 2000. See Barr, *Biblical Womanhood*, 27.

13. Benton Johnson, "On Church and Sect," *American Sociological Review* 28, no. 4 (August 1963), 542. See also Finke and Stark, *Churching*; H. Richard Niebuhr, *The Social Sources of Denominationalism* (New York: Holt, 1987 [1929]); Rodney Stark and William Sims Bainbridge, *The Future of Religion: Secularization, Revival, and Cult Formation* (Berkeley: University of California Press, 1985); Rodney Stark and Roger Finke, *Acts of Faith: Explaining the Human Side of Religion* (Berkeley: University of California Press, 2000).

14. Catherine A. Brekus, "Female Preaching in Early Nineteenth-Century America," in *Women and the Church*, ed. Robert B. Kruschwitz (Waco, TX: The Center for Christian Ethics at Baylor University, 2009), 22.

15. Many Americans believe gender equality has been achieved. Unfortunately, US women continue to lag behind men in a variety of areas. In 2021 the United States ranked 30th out of 156 nations in gender equality (down from 23rd in 2006) and 87th (out of 156 nations) in the health and survival of women (down from 1st in 2006). See World Economic Forum, *Global Gender Gap Report, 2021*, March 30, 2021, https:// www.weforum.org/reports/global-gender-gap-report-2021.

16. Johnson, "On Church and Sect," 542. Laurence R. Iannaccone, "A Formal Model of Church and Sect," *American Journal of Sociology* 94 (Supplement 1988), S268. See also Finke and Stark, *Churching*; Laurence R. Iannaccone, "Why Strict Churches Are Strong," *American Journal of Sociology* 99, no. 5 (March 1994), 1180–1211; Benton Johnson, "A Critical Appraisal of the Church-Sect Typology," *American Sociological Review* 22, no. 1 (February 1957), 88–92; Benton Johnson, "Church and Sect Revisited," *Journal for the Scientific Study of Religion* 10, no. 2 (Summer 1971), 124–137; Dean D. Knudsen, John R. Earle, and Donald W. Shriver Jr., "The Conception of Sectarian Religion: An Effort at Clarification," *Review of Religious Research* 20, no. 1 (Autumn 1978), 44–60; Max Weber, *From Max Weber: Essays in Sociology*, ed. H. H. Gerth and C. Wright Mills (New York: Oxford University Press, 1958 [1913]); Ernst Troeltsch, *The Social Teachings of the Christian Churches, Vol. II*. Louisville, KY: Westminster John Knox Press, 1992 [1912]; Niebuhr, *Social Sources*. Sociologists Max Weber and Ernst Troeltsch similarly defined "church" as an organization accepting the social order, meaning the organization did not impose moral demands of its members that significantly differed from the wider culture. Sects required more commitment to rejecting the general sinfulness of the wider culture, demanding members overcome sin by living up to divine commandments. Theologian H. Richard Niebuhr emphasized the social nature of church and sect, writing that becoming a church or sect was "largely due to the social condition of those who form the sect or compose the church" (19). Once formed, Niebuhr noted, a religious group's theological doctrines and practices would then follow (not vice versa).

17. As organizational designations, sect and church operate as "ideal types," abstract descriptions of characteristics of a phenomenon. Rarely will a phenomenon perfectly correspond to an ideal type. For example, no religious body can completely

reject or completely assimilate to the social environment. See Max Weber, *Economy and Society, Volume I*, ed. Guenther Roth and Claus Wittich (Berkeley: University of California Press, 1978 [1922]).

18. Stark and Finke, *Acts of Faith*, 143.

19. Joseph O. Baker, "Social Sources of the Spirit: Connecting Rational Choice and Interactive Ritual Theories in the Study of Religion," *Sociology of Religion* 71, no. 4 (Winter 2010), 433.

20. Stark and Finke, *Acts of Faith*, 143–145. Whether real or otherwise, differences between the group and the outside world are at least perceived to be quite different.

21. Stark and Finke, *Acts of Faith*, 141–150.

22. Baker, "Social Sources," 450. See also Michael Hechter, *Principles of Group Solidarity* (Berkeley: University of California Press, 1987); Iannaccone, "Strict Churches"; Mancur Olson, *The Logic of Collective Action: Public Goods and the Theory of Groups* (Cambridge, MA: Harvard University Press, 1998 [1971]).

23. See Roger Finke, Matt Bahr, and Christopher P. Scheitle, "Toward Explaining Congregational Giving," *Social Science Research* 35, no. 3 (September 2006); Iannaccone, "Strict Churches"; Stark and Finke, *Acts of Faith*; Jeremy N. Thomas and Daniel V. A. Olson, "Testing the Strictness Thesis and Competing Theories of Congregational Growth," *Journal for the Scientific Study of Religion* 49, no. 4 (December 2010), 619–639.

24. Wellman, Corcoran, and Stockly, *High*, 22.

25. Baker, "Social Sources," 438–440; Iannaccone, "Strict Churches," 1200. Iannaccone writes that strictness does more to explain individual rates of religious participation than any other individual-level characteristic, including age, sex, race, region, income, education, marital status, or even personal beliefs.

26. Mark Chaves, "All Creatures Great and Small: Megachurches in Context," *Review of Religious Research* 47, no. 4 (June 2006), 336–337.

27. Wellman, Corcoran, and Stockly, *High*, 172.

28. See Dean M. Kelly, *Why Conservative Churches Are Growing* (Macon, GA: Mercer University Press, 1972); Wellman, Corcoran, and Stockly, *High*.

29. Hypermasculinity is an exaggerated masculinity emphasizing physical strength and aggression. Hypermasculinity is often used by men in dominant groups who perceive they are not masculine enough, or by men who are not members of dominant groups (e.g., men of color, poor or working class) in order to prove their masculinity. See Victor M. Rios, "The Consequences of the Criminal Justice Pipeline on Black and Latino Masculinity," *Annals of the American Academy of Political and Social Science* 623 (May 2009), 150–162.

30. "Gender" refers to the social, cultural, and psychological traits linked to females and males, whereas "sex" refers to the biological characteristics that distinguish females and males, emphasizing anatomy, physiology, hormones, and reproductive systems. See Jennifer McKinney and Kevin Neuhouser, "Divided by Gender: How Sociology Can Help," *Cultural Encounters* 9, no. 1 (Winter 2013), 38.

31. Sally K. Gallagher, "The Marginalization of Evangelical Feminism," *Sociology of Religion* 65, no. 3 (Autumn 2004), 218.

32. Gallagher, "Marginalization," 218.
33. Brekus, "Female Preaching," 21. In her work on medieval Christianity, historian Beth Allison Barr notes that these Scripture passages were part of the "household codes" of early Christianity and should be read as "resistance narratives to Roman patriarchy." Rather than subjugating women, Paul's letters invite everyone to participate: "Instead of justifying male authority . . . the Christian household codes affirm women as having equal worth to men. Instead of focusing on wifely submission . . . the Christian household codes demand that the husband do exactly the opposite of what Roman law allowed: sacrificing his life for his wife instead of exercising power over her life." See Barr, *Biblical Womanhood*, 46, 55.
34. Gallagher, "Marginalization," 219. See also, Rodney Stark, *The Rise of Christianity* (San Francisco: HarperSanFrancisco, 1997).
35. Brekus, "Female Preaching," 23.
36. In the twentieth century the translation of the Greek "Junia," a female name, began to be translated as the male name, "Junias," to align with the assumption that only men served as apostles. See Barr, *Biblical Womanhood*, 66–67.
37. Gallagher, "Marginalization," 219.
38. Gallagher, "Marginalization," 216.
39. Romans 12:2, emphasis added.
40. See Mayer N. Zald, "Theological Crucibles: Social Movements in and of Religion," *Review of Religious Research* 23, no. 4 (June 1982), 317–336.
41. Barr, *Biblical Womanhood*, 102. History and culture illustrate the fluidity of gender expectations across time, between and within cultures, as the "tale of two Baptists" shows.
42. The changes in gender ideologies within US culture spawned protest through the first wave of the feminist movement. Women and men gathered in 1848 for the Seneca Falls Women's Rights Convention and drafted a "Declaration of Sentiments" protesting the increasingly restrictive roles for women propagated by industrial culture. Three years later Sojourner Truth, who had been born into slavery, delivered her iconic "Ain't I a Woman?" speech at an Ohio women's rights convention. The speech became a rallying cry for First Wave feminism. See Suzanne Kelly, Gowri Parameswaran, and Nancy Schniedewind, *Women: Images and Realities* (New York: McGraw-Hill, 2012).
43. Brekus, "Female Preaching," 21.
44. Brekus, "Female Preaching," 22–23; Juster, *Disorderly Women*, 18. See also Nathan O. Hatch, *The Democratization of American Christianity* (New Haven, CT: Yale University Press, 1987).
45. Brekus, "Female Preaching," 23. Members of the sects drew from texts in Joel (2:28) and Acts (2:17) that "Your sons and daughters will prophesy," to support women's equality in the pulpit.
46. Brekus, "Female Preaching," 21.
47. Ammerman, *Baptist Battles*, 24; Brekus, "Female Preaching," 22; Finke and Stark, *Churching*, 73, 156. Finke and Stark report that between 1776 and 1850 the Methodists grew from less than 3 percent of the nation's church members to more than 34 percent. The Baptists also experienced significant growth. Whereas established state

churches coerced members by law and taxes to support their organizations, the dises-
tablishment of religion in the US Constitution gave religious groups equal footing in
pursuing adherents. A lack of religious regulation made persuasion the best tactic for
converting new members to religious organizations. See Finke and Stark, *Churching*.

48. Finke and Stark, *Churching*, 161.
49. Brekus, "Female Preaching," 27.
50. Ammerman, *Baptist Battles*, 30.
51. Finke and Stark, *Churching*, 188.
52. See Stephanie Coontz, *The Way We Never Were: American Families and the Nostalgia Trap* (New York: Basic Books, 1992); Stephanie Coontz, *The Way We Really Are: Coming to Terms with America's Changing Families* (New York: Basic Books 1997); Stephanie Coontz, *Marriage, a History: From Obedience to Intimacy or How Love Conquered Marriage* (New York: Viking, 2005); Michael Kimmel, *Manhood in America: A Cultural History* (New York: Oxford University Press, 2012); Bart Landry, *Black Working Wives: Pioneers of the American Family Revolution* (Berkeley: University of California Press, 2000).
53. Sara Moslener, *Virgin Nation: Sexual Purity and American Adolescence* (New York: Oxford University Press, 2015), 57; Gail Bederman, "'The Women Have Had Charge of the Church Work Long Enough': The Men and Religion Forward Movement of 1911–1912 and the Masculinization of Middle-Class Protestantism," *American Quarterly* 41, no. 3 (September 1989), 435. Prior to industrialization, Protestants saw religion as neither feminine nor masculine.
54. The Cult of True Womanhood was pervasive in American culture. White immigrant and working-class women masked their participation in paid labor by working from home (doing piece-work, taking in laundry, etc.). These families sent their children and husbands into the paid-labor force to make ends meet. Black families, on the other hand, expected wives and husbands to work outside of the home in paid labor and sent their children to school. Educating children was seen as the primary step toward better economic prospects for the next generation, as well as fomenting racial and gender equality. See Coontz, *Never Were*; Coontz, *Really Are*; Landry, *Black Working Wives*.
55. Finke and Stark, *Churching*, 175.
56. Phoebe Palmer, *The Promise of the Father* (New York: Garland, 1985 [1859]), 71.
57. See Coontz, *Never Were*; Landry, *Black Working Wives*.
58. Landry, *Black Working Wives*, 58.
59. Maggie Walker, quoted in Landry, *Black Working Wives*, 73.
60. Landry, *Black Working Wives*, 72.
61. Kimmel, *Manhood in America*, 158.
62. Historically the term "native-born" excluded Native Americans, referring instead to those born in the United States and/or one of its territories or born abroad of a US parent(s), as opposed to those who are "foreign-born." See United States Census Bureau, "Frequently Asked Questions," December 11, 2019, https://www.census.gov/topics/population/foreign-born/about/faq.html.
63. Bederman, "Women Have Had," 436.

64. Bederman, "Women Have Had," 435.

65. See Bederman, "Women Have Had"; Moslener, *Virgin Nation*; Margaret Lamberts Bendroth, *Fundamentalism and Gender 1875 to the Present* (New Haven, CT: Yale University Press, 1992); Kimmel, *Manhood in America*; Michael A. Messner, *Politics of Masculinities: Men in Movements* (Thousand Oaks, CA: Sage Publications, 1997); Clifford Putney, *Muscular Christianity: Manhood and Sports in Protestant America 1880–1920* (Cambridge, MA: Harvard University Press, 2001).

66. Kimmel, *Manhood in America*, 129.

67. Kimmel, *Manhood in America*, 129, 131. The exclusive nature of the movement, along with the aggressive masculine focus, made it popular with the Ku Klux Klan and other militaristic movements. These movements were organized around the practices of white, native-born Protestants, not immigrants, blacks, or Catholics. See Bederman, "Women Have Had."

68. Matthew Avery Sutton, *American Apocalypse: A History of Modern Evangelicalism* (Cambridge, MA: Belknap Press of Harvard University Press, 2014), 13, 16. See also Bederman, "Women Have Had"; Kimmel, *Manhood in America*; Messner, *Politics*; Moslener, *Virgin Nation*.

69. Sutton, *American Apocalypse*, 13.

70. Modernist interpretations of Scripture that gave more latitude to women reflected the larger culture. By the end of the nineteenth century, the Cult of True Womanhood and Cult of Self-Made Man had begun to wane. Women were also entering the paid-labor force, giving them more freedom and moving the culture toward a more egalitarian ideal of gender.

71. Moslener, *Virgin Nation*, 57.

72. Moslener, *Virgin Nation*, 58; Sutton, *American Apocalypse*, 3, 7.

73. Sutton, *American Apocalypse*, 139. The success of Muscular Christianity meant that women, previously considered the purveyors of religious faith for home, church, and society, lost much of their influence in Protestant denominational life. The vibrant women's missionary associations, which had been organized and run entirely by women, had been taken over by male denominational leaders by the end of the 1930s. See R. Pierce Beaver, *American Protestant Women in World Mission* (Grand Rapids, MI: Eerdmans Press, 1980); Patricia R. Hill, *The World Their Household: The American Women's Foreign Mission Movement and Cultural Transformation* (Ann Arbor: University of Michigan Press, 1985); Diane H. Lobody, "'That Language Might Be Given Me': Women's Experience in Early Methodism," in *Perspectives on American Methodism: Interpretive Essays*, ed. Russell E. Richey, Kenneth E. Rowe, and Jean Miller Schmidt (Nashville: Kingswood Books, 1993).

74. Sutton, *American Apocalypse*, 16.

75. Sutton, *American Apocalypse*, 139–140.

76. Moslener, *Virgin Nation*, 58. After the Scopes Monkey Trial in 1925, fundamentalism was caricatured as uneducated and provincial, and the movement began to turn against itself. In a quest for doctrinal purity, fundamentalism adopted separatism to distinguish themselves from less doctrinally pure Protestants and the culture-at-large. Increasingly practicing a "powerful legalism," fundamentalists maintained

strict practices to reinforce their separatism. Behavioral rules included no dancing, drinking, smoking, gambling, or playing cards. Additionally, women could not bob their hair or wear makeup, and were required to dress modestly. See Christian Smith, *American Evangelicalism: Embattled and Thriving* (Chicago: University of Chicago Press, 1998), 7–9.

77. Coontz, *Marriage*, 218.

78. Coontz, *Marriage*, 218. Coontz reports that between 1900 and the 1930s, two-and-a-half times the number of married women were working outside of the home than had previously.

79. Coontz, *Marriage*, 219.

80. Bendroth, *Fundamentalism*, 6.

81. Bendroth, *Fundamentalism*, 8. Bendroth notes that as dispensational premillennialists, fundamentalists believed that women were under a curse described in Genesis, which placed them in a subordinate position to men until Christ's Second Coming would lift their curse and the penalty of sin produced by the fall of humanity.

82. See Bendroth, *Fundamentalism*. Similar to the mid-nineteenth-century's Holiness movement, which defended women's primary roles in religion, the turn of the twentieth century birthed the Pentecostal movement, an interracial, mostly working-class movement, seeking to reinvigorate Christianity with a "holistic faith that approximated the experience of the first-century church" (see Sutton, *American Apocalypse*, 28). Pentecostals used Acts 2:17–20 to justify the inclusion of women as leaders and preachers in the movement (see Sutton, *American Apocalypse*).

83. Smith, *American Evangelicalism*, 10; Sally K. Gallagher and Christian Smith, "Symbolic Traditionalism and Pragmatic Egalitarianism: Contemporary Evangelicals, Families, and Gender," *Gender and Society* 13, no. 2 (April 1999), 212.

84. The historic, orthodox tradition of American Protestantism active in social outreach is known as "evangelical." The term "neo-evangelical" describes a post–World War II movement begun by fundamentalists to broaden its intellectual isolation and evangelistic appeal. See Bendroth, *Fundamentalism*, 5.

85. The United States experienced significant shifts in gender ideology between the Great Depression and World War II. Whereas women were often blamed for, and were treated poorly by employers during, the Depression, women enjoyed much more goodwill, better pay, and better working conditions during World War II, as industries quickly retooled to manufacture materials needed for the war effort. The Department of Defense commissioned campaigns to entice women into jobs, including the iconic Rosie the Riveters, and slogans like, "There's work to be done and a war to be won . . . NOW!" Women poured into the workforce during the war, increasing the female labor force by almost 60 percent in the United States between 1940 and 1945 and worked at jobs previously done by men as mechanics, pipe fitters, welders, and carpenters—jobs previously done exclusively by men. See Coontz, *Marriage*, 221, 226–227.

86. Coontz, *Marriage*, 226–227.

87. See Margaret Lamberts Bendroth, *Growing Up Protestant* (New Brunswick, NJ: Rutgers University Press, 2002); Andrew J. Cherlin, *The Marriage-Go-Round: The State of Marriage and the Family in America* (New York: Vintage Books, 2010); Coontz, *Never Were*; Coontz, *Really Are*; Coontz, *Marriage*; Gallagher, *Evangelical Identity*.

88. Coontz, *Marriage*, 229.

89. The iconic breadwinner/homemaker ideology never encompassed a majority of American families, even though an unprecedented number of white, middle-class families were able to live on the wages of one earner to fulfill them. See Coontz, *Never Were*; Coontz, *Really Are*; Landry, *Black Working Wives*.

90. Betty Friedan's classic work, *The Feminine Mystique*, was published in 1963 and describes how upper-middle-class white women suffered from "the problem with no name."

91. See Coontz, *Never Were*; Gallagher, *Evangelical Identity*; R. Marie Griffith, *God's Daughters: Evangelical Women and the Power of Submission* (Berkeley: University of California Press, 1997).

92. Sutton, *American Apocalypse*, 332.

93. Sutton, *American Apocalypse*, 333.

94. Seth Dowland, *Family Values and the Rise of the Christian Right* (Philadelphia: University of Pennsylvania Press, 2015), 17.

95. Dowland, *Family Values*, 17.

96. Dowland, *Family Values*, 8, 10.

97. Dowland, *Family Values*, 12. The "lines of authority" seemingly inherent to families and the nation were gendered and racialized, pushing conservative Christians to maintain (or take back) the status quo.

98. Anneke Stasson, "The Politicization of Family Life: How Headship Became Essential to Evangelical Identity in the Late Twentieth Century," *Religion and American Culture* 24, no. 1 (Winter 2014), 116. First proposed by Alice Paul in 1923, the Equal Rights Amendment (ERA) is a proposed amendment to the Constitution stating, "Equality of rights under the law shall not be denied or abridged by the United States or by any state on account of sex." The ERA was passed by the US Senate and House of Representatives on March 22, 1972, and was given a seven-year period to be ratified by at least thirty-eight states. Lacking the necessary number of states required for ratification, Congress extended the ratification deadline to 1982. Having failed to reach the necessary thirty-eight states for ratification again resulted in the ERA not being passed. In 2020, however, Virginia became the thirty-eighth state to ratify the ERA. In March of 2021, the House of Representatives voted to remove the time limit on ratifying the amendment. See Alice Paul Institute, "Equal Rights Amendment," accessed March 26, 2021, https://www.equalrightsamendment.org/.

99. Du Mez, "Donald Trump."

100. Du Mez, "Donald Trump."

101. Du Mez, "Donald Trump."

102. Gallagher, "Marginalization," 225.

103. Elisabeth Elliott, "The Essence of Femininity: A Personal Perspective," in *Recovering Biblical Manhood and Womanhood: A Response to Evangelical Feminism*, ed. John Piper and Wayne Grudem (Wheaton, IL: Crossway, 1991), 396; Beverley LaHaye quoted in Griffith, *God's Daughters*, 206; The Associated Press, "Robertson Letter Attacks Feminists," *New York Times*, August 26, 1992, https://www.nytimes.com/1992/08/26/us/robertson-letter-attacks-feminists.html.

104. Ingersoll, *Evangelical Christian Women*, 16.

105. Stasson, "Politicization," 116.

106. Ingersoll, *Evangelical Christian Women*, 45–46.

107. Du Mez, "Donald Trump."

108. Du Mez, "Donald Trump."

109. Gallagher, "Marginalization," 224.

110. Gallagher, "Marginalization," 224.

111. Gallagher, "Marginalization," 222–223.

112. Gallagher, "Marginalization," 226.

113. Gallagher, "Marginalization," 227.

114. Gallagher, "Marginalization," 227, 233.

115. Gallagher, "Marginalization," 226.

116. Gallagher, "Marginalization," 226; William Lockhart, "'We Are One Life,' But Not of One Gender Ideology: Unity, Ambiguity, and the Promise Keepers," *Sociology of Religion* 61, no. 1 (Spring 2000), 78.

117. Dowland, *Family Values*, 148. Dowland notes that the conservative evangelicals who opposed feminism did not acknowledge how white, middle-class mores shaped their opposition.

118. Dowland, *Family Values*, 141.

119. Dowland, *Family Values*, 131.

120. Dowland, *Family Values*, 134.

121. Dowland, *Family Values*, 134.

122. Dowland, *Family Values*, 131, 138.

123. See John P. Bartkowski, *Remaking the Godly Marriage: Gender Negotiation in Evangelical Families* (New Brunswick, NJ: Rutgers University Press, 2001); Gallagher, *Evangelical Identity*; Griffith, *God's Daughters*; W. Bradford Wilcox, *Soft Patriarchs, New Men: How Christianity Shapes Fathers and Husbands* (Chicago, IL: University of Chicago Press, 2004).

124. Gallagher, "Marginalization," 231. Gallagher writes, "What is the benefit, after all, of arguing that God calls men and women to share responsibility and authority within the household when the broader culture espouses the same ideal?" Gallagher suggested that practicing true egalitarianism could be a way for conservative Protestants to demonstrate their distinctiveness from the larger culture, for example, by having men and women share paid and unpaid family labor.

125. See Melinda L. Denton, "Gender and Marital Decision Making: Negotiating Religious Ideology and Practice," *Social Forces* 82, no. 3 (March 2004); Gallagher, *Evangelical Identity*; Sally K. Gallagher and Sabrina L. Wood, "Godly Manhood

Going Wild? Transformations in Conservative Protestant Masculinity," *Sociology of Religion* 66, no. 2 (Summer 2005); Griffith, *God's Daughters*; Wilcox, *Soft Patriarchs*.

126. Gallagher, *Evangelical Identity*, 230.

127. See John P. Bartkowski, *The Promise Keepers: Servants, Soldiers, and Godly Men* (New Brunswick, NJ: Rutgers University Press, 2004).

128. Bartkowski, *Promise Keepers*, 2. The Promise Keepers stadium events were a hallmark of the movement. Their 1997 "Stand in the Gap" event drew between 600,000 and 800,000 men. Bartkowski reports that just a few months after Stand in the Gap, Promise Keepers laid off their entire office staff due to their dwindling finances. The movement has never regained its prominence. In 2019, however, Promise Keepers announced their first stadium event in years. Promise Keepers continues to organize these stadium events, even though the 2021 event was canceled due to the COVID-19 pandemic. The website announcement for the January 2020 conference coupled hypermasculine rhetoric with the language of practical egalitarianism, stating that society had "pushed men to be passive and feminized" the event pointed to the Apostle Paul's saying, "Act like men," and "be strong." The conference was billed as inspiring men to "take up their responsibilities as servant kings." See https://promise keepers.org/.

129. Lockhart, "We Are One," 88.

130. Bartkowski, *Promise Keepers*, 41.

131. Wilcox, *Soft Patriarchs*.

132. The Associated Press, "Southern Baptist Convention Passes Resolution Opposing Women as Pastors," *New York Times*, June 15, 2000, http://www.nytimes.com/2000/06/15/us/southern-baptist-convention-passes-resolution-opposing-women-as-pastors.html.

133. SBC, "Baptist Faith."

134. Gallagher, "Marginalization," 228, emphasis added.

135. Kimmel, *Manhood in America*, 313.

136. Du Mez, "Donald Trump"; Stewart M. Hoover and Curtis D. Coats, *Does God Make the Man? Media, Religion, and the Crisis of Masculinity* (New York: New York University Press, 2015), 161. Hoover and Coats note that the movement is sometimes referred to as Mixed Martial Arts (MMA) Christianity because of its emphasis on a hypermasculine presentation of manhood.

137. Du Mez, "Donald Trump."

138. See John Eldredge, *Wild at Heart: Discovering the Secret of a Man's Soul* (Nashville, TN: Thomas Nelson Publishers, 2001).

139. See John Eldredge and Stasi Eldredge, *Captivating: Unveiling the Mystery of a Woman's Soul* (Nashville, TN: Thomas Nelson, 2005).

140. In her work on evangelicalism and masculinity, Du Mez writes that the dominant evangelical ideal of masculinity "is largely the creation of white evangelicals"—white men writing for white men: "With few exceptions, black men, Middle Eastern men, and Hispanic men are *not* called to a wild, militant masculinity. Their aggression, by contrast, is seen as dangerous, a threat to the stability of homes and nation" (*Jesus and John Wayne*, 301).

141. Not surprisingly, this divine design corresponded to, and validated, the norms of hegemonic masculinity. Hegemonic masculinities legitimate unequal relationships between men and women, masculinity and femininity, and within masculinities by materially embodying and/or discursively symbolizing "superior" gender qualities in relation to "inferior" gender qualities. See James W. Messerschmidt, *Hegemonic Masculinity: Formulation, Reformulation, and Amplification* (New York: Rowman & Littlefield, 2018).
142. Du Mez, "Donald Trump."
143. Jonathan Merrit, quoted in Fitzgerald, *Evangelicals*, 630.

Chapter 2

1. Du Mez, "Donald Trump."
2. Du Mez, "Donald Trump."
3. Du Mez, "Donald Trump."
4. Ed Kilgore, "Evangelicals Looking to Trump to Make America Manly Again," *New York Magazine*, December 2, 2016, http://nymag.com/daily/intelligencer/2016/12/ evangelicals-looking-to-trump-to-make-america-manly-again.html.
5. Mars Hill Church, "What We Believe," in *It's All about Jesus: 2013 Annual Report*, accessed October 1, 2014, http://www.marshillchurch.org/media/mars-hill-quarterly/mars-hill-church-annual-report-fy13.
6. Cecilia Ridgeway, "A Painful Lesson in Why We Have to Take Status Seriously," *Speak for Sociology*, December 22, 2016, http://speak4sociology.org/2016/12/22/a-painful-lesson-in-why-we-have-to-take-status-seriously/.
7. John P. Bartkowski, *The Promise Keepers: Servants, Soldiers, and Godly Men* (New Brunswick: Rutgers University Press, 2004), 42.
8. Mark Driscoll, "Jesus Died to Forgive Us," *Christ on the Cross* series, Mars Hill Church, November 6, 2005.
9. Mark Driscoll, "Men and Masculinity," *Proverbs* series, Mars Hill Church, October 28, 2001.
10. Driscoll, "Men and Masculinity."
11. Driscoll, "Evangelical Leader."
12. Mark Driscoll, "Episcopalians and Male Testosterone Show Corresponding Decline," *The Resurgence*, November 10, 2006, http://www.theresurgence.com/md_blog_2006-11-10_episcolpalians_and_male_testosterone_show_corresponding_decline.
13. Mark Driscoll, "Now the Mainline Churches Make Sense," *The Resurgence*, August 21, 2006, http://www.theresurgence.com/md_blog_2006-08-21_now_the_mainline_churches_make_sense.
14. Driscoll, "Episcopalians."
15. Driscoll, "Now the Mainline." Driscoll referred here to Gene Robinson, the Episcopal Church's first openly gay bishop, as well as the appointment of Katharine Jefferts-Schori's to Presiding Bishop in the worldwide Anglican Communion.

16. Mark Driscoll, "Pastor Jesus," *Christians Gone Wild* series, Mars Hill Church, January 15, 2006.

17. Mark Driscoll, "Above All Earthly Powers: The Supremacy of Christ in a Post-Modern World," *Desiring God: 2006 National Conference*, available at "Church Needs Dudes," YouTube video, posted by Josh Brage, 1:54, August 14, 2006, https://www.youtube.com/watch?v=lex6orNNzTs.

18. Driscoll, "Above All."

19. Driscoll, "Above All."

20. Mark Driscoll, "Church Planting in Corinth," *Christians Gone Wild* series, Mars Hill Church, January 8, 2006.

21. Driscoll, "Above All."

22. Driscoll, "Above All."

23. Driscoll, "Above All."

24. Driscoll, "Above All."

25. Driscoll, "Church Planting in Corinth."

26. Driscoll, "Church Planting in Corinth."

27. In the sermons analyzed, little is said about the Holy Spirit.

28. Christianity subscribes to a divine Trinity, described as God in three persons. The three persons of the Trinity are God the Father, Jesus the Son, and the Holy Spirit the Counselor. In the sermons used for this analysis, Driscoll preached very little on the Spirit.

29. Mark Driscoll, "Servants of Jesus," *Christians Gone Wild* series, Mars Hill Church, February 12, 2006.

30. Mark Driscoll, "Power from Jesus," *Christians Gone Wild* series, Mars Hill Church, March 10, 2006.

31. Driscoll, "Pastor Jesus."

32. Mark Driscoll, "Paying Your Pastors," *Christians Gone Wild* series, Mars Hill Church, June 4, 2006.

33. Driscoll, "Power from Jesus."

34. Mark Driscoll, "Spiritual Gifts, Part II," *Christians Gone Wild* series, Mars Hill Church, August 13, 2006.

35. Mark Driscoll, *A Good Soldier: A Conversation with Mark Driscoll*, available at "A Good Soldier," YouTube video, posted by Resurgence, 9:07, April 28, 2007, http://www.youtube.com/watch?v=JIrIKbCz3n4.

36. Driscoll, "Power from Jesus."

37. Driscoll, "Church Planting in Corinth."

38. See Cecilia L. Ridgeway, and Shelley J. Correll, "Unpacking the Gender System: A Theoretical Perspective in Gender Beliefs and Social Relations," *Gender and Society* 18, no. 4 (August 2004), 510–531; Douglas Shrock and Michael Schwalbe, "Man, Masculinity, and Manhood Acts," *Annual Review of Sociology* 35, no. 1 (August 2009), 277–295.

39. Mark Driscoll, "My Beloved Friend," *Peasant Princess* series, Mars Hill Church, October 19, 2008.

40. Mark Driscoll, "A Pastor's Love," *Christians Gone Wild* series, Mars Hill Church, September 24, 2006.

41. Driscoll, "A Pastor's Love."

42. See, for example, the 2009 *Trial* sermon "Men and Marriage."

43. Driscoll references the text of 1 Timothy 6:12, which says, "Fight the good fight of the faith; take hold of the eternal life, to which you were called and for which you made the good confession in the presence of many witnesses" (NRSV). Hebrews 12:1 is also referenced: "Therefore, since we are surrounded by so great a cloud of witnesses, let us also lay aside every weight and the sin that clings so closely, and let us run with perseverance the race that is set before us" (NRSV).

44. Driscoll, "Power from Jesus."

45. Driscoll, "Power from Jesus."

46. Driscoll, "Power from Jesus."

47. Driscoll, "Power from Jesus."

48. Driscoll, "Paying Your Pastors."

49. Driscoll, "Paying Your Pastors."

50. Driscoll, "Church Planting in Corinth."

51. Mark Driscoll, "Changed by Jesus," *Christians Gone Wild* series, Mars Hill Church, March 26, 2006.

52. See C. J. Pascoe, *Dude, You're a Fag: Masculinity and Sexuality in High School* (Berkeley: University of California Press, 2007).

53. Mark Driscoll, "Spiritual Gifts, Part IV," *Christians Gone Wild* series, Mars Hill Church, September 10, 2006.

54. Driscoll, "Servants of Jesus."

55. Driscoll, "Servants of Jesus."

56. Driscoll, "Changed by Jesus."

57. Driscoll, "Changed by Jesus."

58. Driscoll, "Changed by Jesus."

59. Driscoll, "Pastor Jesus."

60. Mark Driscoll, "Jesus Died to Forgive Us," *Christ on the Cross* series, Mars Hill Church, November 6, 2005.

61. Driscoll, "A Good Soldier."

62. Mark Driscoll, "Where Is Jesus Today?" *Vintage Jesus* series, Mars Hill Church, November 5, 2006.

63. Driscoll, "Where Is Jesus Today?"

64. Driscoll, "Where Is Jesus Today?" For alternative views of Jesus in the book of Revelation, see Brian Gamel, "The Victory of the Lamb: On Being Christians and Winners," *Christian Scholars Review*, Blog, February 16, 2022, https://christianschol ars.com/guest-post-the-victory-of-the-lamb-on-being-christians-and-winners/.

65. Driscoll, "Where Is Jesus Today?"

66. Driscoll, "Where Is Jesus Today?"

67. Driscoll, "Where Is Jesus Today?"

68. Mark Driscoll, "My Dove," *The Peasant Princess* series, Mars Hill Church, October 26, 2008.

69. Driscoll, "A Pastor's Love."

70. Driscoll, "Power from Jesus."

71. Driscoll, "A Pastor's Love."

72. Driscoll, "A Pastor's Love."

73. Driscoll, "A Pastor's Love."

74. Mark Driscoll, "Our Resurrection Bodies," *Christians Gone Wild* series, Mars Hill Church, April 9, 2006.

75. Driscoll, "Our Resurrection Bodies."

76. See Raewyn Connell, "A Very Straight Gay: Masculinity, Homosexual Experience, and the Dynamics of Gender," *American Sociological Review* 57, no. 6 (December 1992), 735–751; Michael A. Messner, *Politics of Masculinities: Men in Movements* (Thousand Oaks, CA: Sage Publications, 1997).

77. See Bartkowski, *The Promise Keepers.*

78. Mark Driscoll, "Friend with Benefits," *Real Marriage* series, Mars Hill Church, January 22, 2012.

79. Driscoll, "A Pastor's Love."

80. Church members signed a covenant that allowed the church to discipline members in accordance to church bylaws. Part of the discipline process was to "shun" (ex-communicate) members. So many reports of shunning had been published by the local press, that in 2012, Mars Hill Marketing Director Justin Dean released a statement acknowledging that the church employed the practice. See Jenkins, "How Evangelicals;" Solie, "Inside Mars Hill"; Tracy Vedder, "Ex-Members Say Mars Hill 'Shuns' to Punish Sinners," March 1, 2012, *Seattle Post-Intelligencer,* http://www.seattlepi.com/local/komo/article/Ex-members-say-mars-hill-shuns-to-punish-sinners.

81. Data are denoted using pseudonyms for forum contributors and interviewee's first names.

82. Driscoll, "Above All."

83. Andrew and his wife left Mars Hill a few months after being interviewed.

84. Mark Driscoll, "Sex: God, Gross, or Gift?" *Real Marriage* series, Mars Hill Church, February 19, 2012.

85. Mark Driscoll, "Women and Femininity," *Proverbs* series, Mars Hill Church, January 6, 2002.

86. See Tristan Bridges, and C. J. Pascoe, "Hybrid Masculinities: New Directions in the Sociology of Men and Masculinity," *Sociological Compass* 8, no. 3 (March 2014), 246–258; Tim Carrigan, Raewyn Connell, and John Lee, "Toward a New Sociology of Masculinity," *Theory and Society* 14, no. 5 (September 1985), 551–604; Kimmel, *Manhood in America.*

87. See Douglas Schrock and Michael Schwalbe, "Man, Masculinity, and Manhood Acts," *Annual Review of Sociology* 35, no. 1 (August 2009), 277–295."

88. See Schrock and Schwalbe, "Man, Masculinity."

Chapter 3

1. Mark Driscoll, "Women and Femininity," *Proverbs* series, Mars Hill Church, January 6, 2002.

2. The text of Titus 2:4–5 says, "So that they may encourage the young women to love their husbands, to love their children, to be self-controlled, chaste, good managers of the household, kind, being submissive to their husbands, so that the word of God may not be discredited." Driscoll also cited a verse from 1 Timothy 5:8 for men's call to the marketplace. The 1 Timothy text says, "And whoever does not provide for relatives, and especially for family members, has denied the faith and is worse than an unbeliever." Driscoll used these texts to justify a strict economic provider (men) and homemaker (women) gender theology. Historically, however, the home has been the site of family production, where men and women both worked.

3. Mark Driscoll, "Marriage and Men," *Trial* series, Mars Hill Church, March 22, 2009.

4. Driscoll, "Women and Femininity."

5. Driscoll, "Women and Femininity."

6. Driscoll, "Women and Femininity."

7. Mark Driscoll, "Women as Homebuilders," *Proverbs* series, Mars Hill Church, January 13, 2002.

8. Mark Driscoll, "Women as Wives," *Proverbs* series, Mars Hill Church, January 20, 2002.

9. Driscoll, "Women and Femininity."

10. Driscoll, "Women and Femininity."

11. Driscoll, "Women and Femininity."

12. Driscoll, "Women and Femininity."

13. Like other evangelicals, Driscoll's use of men and women being "the same," referred to egalitarian ideals of equality. Evangelicals largely see secular or mainline gender equality as erasing differences between men and women, in effect, making the two genders "the same."

14. Driscoll, "Women and Femininity."

15. Driscoll, "Women and Femininity."

16. Driscoll, "Women and Femininity."

17. See Genesis 3:14–19.

18. Driscoll, "Women and Femininity."

19. Driscoll, "Women and Femininity."

20. Driscoll, "Women and Femininity."

21. Mark Driscoll, "Under Authority Like Christ," *Christians Gone Wild* series, Mars Hill Church, July 23, 2006.

22. Driscoll, "Women and Femininity."

23. Driscoll, "Marriage and Men."

24. See Genesis 2:7–25 for the full text of this second biblical creation story. The precursor to the complementarian theology text is Genesis 1:26–31, which gives a different account of the creation story. In this first account of creation man and woman are created simultaneously: God says, "Let us make humankind in our image, according

to our likeness; and let them have dominion over the fish of the sea, and over the birds of the air, and over the cattle, and over all the wild animals of the earth, and over every creeping thing that creeps upon the earth. So, God created humankind in his image, in the image of God he created them; male and female he created them" (NRSV).

25. Driscoll, "Women and Femininity."

26. Driscoll, "Women and Femininity."

27. The text cited by Driscoll is 1 Corinthians 7:3–5, which reads, "The husband should give to his wife her conjugal rights, and likewise the wife to her husband. For the wife does not have authority over her own body, but the husband does; likewise the husband does not have authority over his own body, but the wife does. Do not deprive one another except perhaps by agreement for a set time, to devote yourselves to prayer, and then come together again, so that Satan may not tempt you because of your lack of self-control" (NRSV).

28. Driscoll, "Women as Wives."

29. Mark Driscoll, "Marriage and Women," *Trial* series, Mars Hill Church, March 15, 2009.

30. See Brenda E. Brasher, *Godly Women: Fundamentalism and Female Power* (New Brunswick, NJ: Rutgers University Press, 1998); Lynn Davidman, *Tradition in a Rootless World: Women Turn to Orthodox Judaism* (Berkeley: University of California Press, 1991); Betty A. DeBurg, *Ungodly Women: Gender and the First Wave of American Fundamentalism* (Minneapolis: Fortress Press, 1990); Griffith, *God's Daughters*; Judith Stacey, *Brave New Families: Stories of Domestic Upheaval in Late-Twentieth Century America* (Berkeley: University of California Press, 1990).

31. Gallagher and Smith, "Symbolic Traditionalism," 222.

32. See Gallagher, "Marginalization"; Gallagher and Smith, "Symbolic Traditionalism"; Wilcox, *Soft Patriarchs*.

33. Driscoll, "Women as Wives."

34. Driscoll, "Women as Wives."

35. Driscoll, "Women and Femininity."

36. Mark Driscoll, "One Body, Many Parts," *Christians Gone Wild* series, Mars Hill Church, July 30, 2006.

37. Driscoll, "Under Authority Like Christ."

38. Driscoll, "Under Authority Like Christ."

39. Driscoll, "Under Authority Like Christ."

40. Driscoll, "Women as Homebuilders."

41. Driscoll, "Women as Homebuilders."

42. Driscoll, "Women and Femininity."

43. Driscoll, "Women and Femininity."

44. Driscoll, "Women and Femininity."

45. Driscoll, "Women and Femininity."

46. Driscoll, "Women and Femininity."

47. Driscoll, "Women and Femininity."

48. Driscoll, "Women and Femininity."

49. See Coontz, *Never Were*; Coontz, *Really Are*; Landry, *Black Working Wives*.

50. See Bartkowski, *Remaking*; Cherlin *Marriage-Go-Round*; Coontz, *Never Were*; Coontz, *Really Are*; Landry, *Black Working Wives*; Stacey, *Brave New*.

51. See Cherlin *Marriage-Go-Round*; Coontz, *Never Were*; Coontz, *Really Are*; Landry, *Black Working Wives*; Stacey, *Brave New*.

52. Driscoll, "Women as Homebuilders."

53. Driscoll, "Women as Homebuilders."

54. Mark Driscoll, "Men and Masculinity," *Proverbs* series, Mars Hill Church, October 28, 2001.

55. Interestingly, the text describes the Proverbs 31 woman as providing for her family, the equivalent of the long decade's ideal of the breadwinner.

56. The New International Version (NIV) of the Bible was in use at Mars Hill in the early 2000s, when Driscoll preached on the Proverbs 31 woman.

57. Driscoll, "Women as Homebuilders."

58. Driscoll, "Men and Masculinity."

59. Driscoll, "Women as Homebuilders."

60. Driscoll, "Women as Homebuilders."

61. Driscoll, "Women as Homebuilders."

62. Driscoll, "Women and Femininity."

63. Driscoll, "Women as Homebuilders."

64. Driscoll, "Women as Wives."

65. Driscoll, "Women as Wives."

66. Driscoll, "Women as Wives."

67. Driscoll, "Women as Wives."

68. Driscoll, "Women as Wives."

69. Driscoll, "Women as Wives."

70. Driscoll, "Women as Wives."

71. Driscoll, "Servants of Jesus."

72. Driscoll, "Women as Wives."

73. Driscoll, "Women as Homebuilders."

74. Driscoll, "Women as Wives."

75. Mark Driscoll, "Men as Husbands," *Proverbs* series, November 4, 2001.

76. Driscoll, "Women as Wives."

77. Driscoll, "Women as Wives." The "riff" on disgraceful women appeared in an earlier *Proverbs* sermon, "Men as Husbands," and appeared again ten years later, almost verbatim, in the *Real Marriage* sermon series.

78. Driscoll, "Women as Wives."

79. Driscoll, "Women as Wives."

80. Driscoll, "Women as Wives."

81. Mark Driscoll, "Women as Mothers," *Proverbs* series, Mars Hill Church, January 27, 2002.

82. Driscoll, "Women as Mothers."

83. Driscoll, "Women as Mothers."

84. Driscoll, "Women as Mothers." Ironically, it would be difficult to find examples of the family that Driscoll calls "biblical" in the Bible. See Rodney Clapp, *Families*

at the Crossroads: Beyond Traditional and Modern Options (Downers Grove, IL: InterVarsity Press, 1993).

85. Driscoll, "Women and Femininity."
86. Driscoll, "Women as Mothers."
87. Driscoll, "Women as Mothers."
88. Driscoll, "Women and Femininity."
89. Driscoll, "Women and Femininity."
90. Driscoll, "Women as Mothers."
91. Driscoll, "Women as Mothers."
92. Driscoll, "Women as Mothers."
93. Driscoll, "Women as Mothers."
94. Driscoll, "Women as Mothers."
95. Driscoll, "Women as Mothers."
96. Driscoll, "Women as Mothers."
97. Driscoll, "Women as Mothers."
98. Mark Driscoll, "I Was a Wall," *Peasant Princess* series, Mars Hill Church, November 2, 2008.
99. Driscoll, "Women as Wives."
100. Driscoll, "Women as Wives."
101. Driscoll, "Women as Homebuilders."
102. Driscoll, "Women as Homebuilders."
103. Driscoll, "Women as Homebuilders."
104. Driscoll, "Women as Homebuilders."
105. Driscoll, "Women as Homebuilders."
106. Driscoll, "Women as Homebuilders."
107. Driscoll, "Women as Homebuilders."
108. Driscoll, "I Was a Wall."
109. In his sermon series, Driscoll refers to this biblical book as "Song of Solomon." It is also commonly known as "Song of Songs."
110. Mark Driscoll, "Sex: God, Gross, or Gift?" *Real Marriage* series, Mars Hill Church, February 19, 2012.
111. Mark Driscoll, "Dance of Mahanaim," *The Peasant Princess* series, Mars Hill Church, November 9, 2008.
112. Driscoll, "Dance of Mahanaim."
113. Driscoll, "Dance of Mahanaim."
114. Driscoll, "Dance of Mahanaim."
115. Mark Driscoll, "Good Sex, Bad Sex," *Christians God Wild* series, Mars Hill Church, April 23, 2006.
116. Driscoll, "Good Sex, Bad Sex."
117. Driscoll, "Good Sex, Bad Sex."
118. Driscoll, "Good Sex, Bad Sex."
119. Driscoll, "Good Sex, Bad Sex."
120. Mark Driscoll, "Selfish Lovers and Servant Lovers," *Real Marriage* series, Mars Hill Church, March 11, 2012. Circumstances allowing a spouse to not engage in sex

included having just had a baby, having a spouse deployed for the military, or if there is "a big sin" in the marriage that couples are "working through."

121. Driscoll, "Women as Wives."
122. Driscoll, "Women as Wives."
123. Driscoll, "Women as Wives."
124. Driscoll, "Women as Wives."
125. Driscoll, "Women as Wives."
126. Driscoll, "Good Sex, Bad Sex."
127. Driscoll, "Good Sex, Bad Sex."
128. Driscoll, "Dance of Mahanaim."
129. Driscoll, "Women and Femininity."
130. Driscoll, "Dance of Mahanaim."
131. Driscoll, "Dance of Mahanaim."
132. Driscoll, "Dance of Mahanaim."
133. Driscoll, "Sex: God, Gross, or Gift?"
134. Driscoll, "I Was a Wall."
135. Mark Driscoll, "Is Jesus the Only God?" *Vintage Jesus* series, Mars Hill Church, October 8, 2006.
136. Driscoll, "Is Jesus the Only God?"
137. Driscoll, "Good Sex, Bad Sex." This particular anecdote appeared in a number of sermons, as well as the book *Real Marriage*.
138. Driscoll, "Evangelical Leader."
139. Driscoll, "Women as Wives."
140. Driscoll, "Men as Husbands."
141. Driscoll, "Men as Husbands."
142. Driscoll, "Men as Husbands."
143. Elizabeth Pak, "A Desperate Housewife Comes Clean," June 29, 2007, Reforming the Feminine (blog), accessed April 18, 2008, http://voxpopnetwork.com/reforming thefeminine/category/professional/.
144. "Darla" is a pseudonym.
145. Lauren Sandler described similar dynamics at work for the women of Mars Hill. See Lauren Sandler, *Righteous: Dispatches from the Evangelical Youth Movement* (New York: Viking Press, 2006).
146. Driscoll, "Men as Husbands."
147. Driscoll, "Men as Husbands."
148. See Naomi Wolf, *The Beauty Myth: How Images of Beauty Are Used against Women* (New York: Anchor Books, 1991).
149. It is not uncommon for women in churches with complementarian theologies to deny or minimize abuse, believing the abuse is part of men exercising their authority. See Nancy Nason-Clark, "When Terror Strikes Home: The Interface between Religion and Domestic Violence," *Journal for the Scientific Study of Religion* 43, no. 3, 306.
150. It is common for abusers to blame women for their abuse, "claiming wives aren't submissive enough." See Nancy Nason-Clark et al., *Religion and Intimate Partner*

Violence: Understanding the Challenges and Proposing Solutions (New York: Oxford University, 2017), 66.

151. Patricia Homan and Amy Burdette, "When Religion Hurts: Structural Sexism and Health in Religious Congregations," *American Sociological Review* 86, no. 2 (April 2021), 238.

152. See Sandra L. Bem, *The Lenses of Gender: Transforming the Debate on Sexual Inequality* (New Haven, CT: Yale University Press, 1993).

153. Driscoll, "Women as Wives."

Chapter 4

1. See Nancy Ammerman, *Bible Believers: Fundamentalists in the Modern World* (New Brunswick, NJ: Rutgers University Press, 1993); Bartkowski, *Remaking*; Bendroth, *Fundamentalism*; Brasher, *Godly Women*; Gallagher, *Evangelical Identity*; Gallagher and Smith, "Symbolic Traditionalism."

2. See Denton, "Gender and Marital"; Gallagher, *Evangelical Identity*; Gallagher and Smith, "Symbolic Traditionalism"; Griffith, *God's Daughters*; Wilcox, *Soft Patriarchs*.

3. See Denton, "Gender and Marital"; Hoover and Coats, *Does God*. Hoover and Coats found nearly all of the evangelical men they interviewed used the language of headship to describe their roles, but their descriptions of how leadership worked "were conflicted and contradictory. Even those who seemed most confident in their ideas struggled for language to describe how headship played out in their everyday lives" (155). Though most of these men rejected the hypermasculine doctrine espoused by Driscoll, they were seeking relevant resources to help them navigate masculinity and manhood.

4. Driscoll, "Marriage and Women."

5. Driscoll, "Marriage and Men."

6. Driscoll, "Marriage and Men."

7. Driscoll, "Marriage and Men."

8. The aggressive marketing accompanying the campaign seemed successful. *Real Marriage* was listed on the New York Times bestseller list for the week of January 22, 2012. Two years later it was discovered that Mars Hill Church had spent $210,000 to hire public relations firm ResultSource to "game the system" by having the church purchase thousands of copies of the book. See Jessica Johnson, *Biblical Porn: Affect, Labor, and Pastor Mark Driscoll's Evangelical Empire* (Durham, NC: Duke University Press, 2018).

9. Rachel Held Evans wrote that she did not understand "why so many complementarians insist on hierarchal-based relationships in which wives submit to their husbands 'in everything,' while simultaneously acknowledging the importance of mutuality when it comes to sex." See Rachel Held Evans, "Driscoll, 'Real Marriage,' and Why Being a Pastor Doesn't Automatically Make You a Sex Therapist," Rachel Held Evans (blog), January 3, 2012, https://rachelheldevans.com/blog/mark-driscoll-real-marriage.

10. Mark Driscoll, "New Marriage, Same Spouse," *Real Marriage* series, Mars Hill Church, January 15, 2012.

11. See DeBurg, *Ungodly Women*; Dowland, *Family Values*.

12. Driscoll, "New Marriage, Same Spouse."

13. Driscoll, "New Marriage, Same Spouse."

14. Driscoll, "New Marriage, Same Spouse."

15. Mark Driscoll, "Divorce and Remarriage," *Christians Gone Wild* series, Mars Hill Church, May 14, 2006.

16. Driscoll, "New Marriage, Same Spouse."

17. Mark Driscoll, "Selfish Lovers and Servant Lovers," *Real Marriage* series, Mars Hill Church, March 11, 2012.

18. Driscoll, "Divorce and Remarriage."

19. Driscoll, "Divorce and Remarriage."

20. Driscoll, "Divorce and Remarriage."

21. Driscoll, "Friend with Benefits."

22. Mark Driscoll, "Do Not Awaken Love," *The Peasant Princess* series, Mars Hill Church, November 23, 2008.

23. Driscoll, "Do Not Awaken Love."

24. Driscoll, "Men as Husbands." Genesis 3 describes the encounter in the garden of Eden, when sin comes into the world and men and women are cursed because of it.

25. Mark Driscoll, "Men and Marriage," *Real Marriage* series, Mars Hill Church, January 29, 2012.

26. Driscoll, "Men and Marriage." Getting married "sooner, rather than later," allowed men to channel their sexual drives into marriage, rather than risk "sinful lust" and "inappropriate" sexual relationships.

27. Driscoll "New Marriage, Same Spouse."

28. Driscoll, "Women as Mothers."

29. Driscoll, "Divorce and Remarriage."

30. Driscoll, "Women and Femininity."

31. Driscoll, "Women and Femininity."

32. Driscoll, "Women as Mothers."

33. Driscoll, "Women as Mothers."

34. Driscoll, "Women as Mothers."

35. Driscoll, "Women as Mothers."

36. Driscoll, "Divorce and Remarriage."

37. Mark Driscoll, "Can We _____?" *Real Marriage* series, Mars Hill Church, March 18, 2012.

38. Mark Driscoll, "Sex: God, Gross, or Gift?" *Real Marriage* series, Mars Hill Church, February 19, 2012.

39. Driscoll, "Sex: God, Gross, or Gift?"

40. Driscoll, "Men and Marriage."

41. Driscoll, "Men and Marriage."

42. Driscoll, "Men and Marriage."

43. In another question from "Selfish Lovers and Servant Lovers," Grace Driscoll responded to a question asking if it's "unrealistic" to save sex for marriage by linking sex outside of marriage, for women, to abuse, saying there is "a high percentage of abuse with couples who are sexually active" (and not married). For women, sex in marriage is "the safe place" and to have sex outside of marriage, for women, "is dangerous."

44. See Mark Regnerus, *Forbidden Fruit: Sex and Religion in the Lives of American Teenagers* (New York: Oxford University Press, 2007); Moslener, *Virgin Nation*.

45. Driscoll, "Sex: God, Gross, or Gift?" When Driscoll reported he and Grace married young for "some reasons," the audience laughed, as he clearly attached "some reasons" to the couple's ability to resume their sexual relationship once married.

46. Driscoll, "Selfish Lovers and Servant Lovers."

47. Driscoll, "Selfish Lovers and Servant Lovers." This example was one of the few places Driscoll characterized Jesus's humanity, rather than his being warrior-god. Note that in this instance, Driscoll treated Jesus's status as a virgin as unusual for a man.

48. Driscoll, "Marriage and Men."

49. Driscoll, "New Marriage, Same Spouse."

50. Driscoll, "New Marriage, Same Spouse."

51. Driscoll, "Friend with Benefits."

52. Driscoll, "Friend with Benefits." Driscoll used Genesis 2:18 as a reference for his creation hierarchy/equality.

53. Driscoll, "New Marriage, Same Spouse."

54. Driscoll, "Friend with Benefits."

55. Driscoll refers to men and women being cursed, however in the Genesis 3 text, God cursed the serpent and the ground, not men or women. See Ellen F. Davis, *Opening Israel's Scriptures* (New York: Oxford University Press, 2019).

56. Driscoll, "Marriage and Men."

57. Driscoll, "Men as Husbands."

58. Driscoll, "Men and Marriage."

59. The assertion that hierarchy was embedded in creation, not just a result of "the fall," is a tenet of New Calvinism.

60. Driscoll, "Marriage and Men."

61. Driscoll imputes a hierarchy to the Trinity, where Jesus and the Spirit are subject to (secondary to) God. Christian theology is Trinitarian, meaning God in three persons: God, Jesus, and the Holy Spirit. As a statement of orthodox Christian faith, the Nicene Creed specifies that all three persons (facets) of God are coequal. See William G. Rusch, *The Trinitarian Controversy* (Minneapolis: Fortress Press, 1980).

62. Driscoll, "Men and Marriage."

63. Driscoll, "Men and Marriage." Similar to how other conservative Protestants hold to gender essentialist doctrines, Driscoll cited Ephesians 5, Colossians 3, 1 Peter 3, and 1 Corinthians 11 to justify his theology (see Chapter 1).

64. Driscoll, "Men and Marriage."

65. Driscoll, "Men and Marriage."

66. Driscoll, "Women as Wives."

67. Driscoll, "Women as Mothers."
68. Driscoll, "Women as Mothers."
69. Driscoll, "Men and Marriage."
70. Driscoll, "New Marriage, Same Spouse."
71. Driscoll, "New Marriage, Same Spouse."
72. Driscoll, "New Marriage, Same Spouse."
73. Driscoll, "Men and Marriage."
74. Driscoll, "Men and Marriage."
75. Driscoll, "Church Planting in Corinth."
76. Mark Driscoll, "The Respectful Wife," *Real Marriage* series, Mars Hill Church, February 5, 2012.
77. Driscoll, "Men and Marriage."
78. Driscoll, "The Respectful Wife."
79. Driscoll, "The Respectful Wife."
80. Driscoll, "Men as Husbands."
81. Driscoll, "The Respectful Wife." Driscoll's telling his audience they were "a joke" was not always gendered. He regularly denigrated men who did not meet his standard in the same way. In the 2009 "Marriage and Men" sermon, Driscoll berated the men in his audience similarly: "Some of you guys are such losers. You're a joke"; "You're a joke. You think you're cute. You're not. You're a joke. You're a freakin' joke. And deep down you know it."
82. Driscoll, "The Respectful Wife."
83. Driscoll, "The Respectful Wife."
84. Driscoll, "The Respectful Wife."
85. Driscoll, "The Respectful Wife."
86. Driscoll, "Can We _____?"
87. Driscoll, "Can We _____?"
88. Driscoll, "Sex: God, Gross, or Gift?"
89. Driscoll, "Can We _____?"
90. In the "Sex: God, Gross, or Gift?" sermon, Driscoll listed the reasons for sex, apart from pleasure, included procreation, knowledge (allowing deeper intimacy), protection (fulfilling their conjugal rights to not "fall into temptation" and sexual sin), comfort, and "oneness."
91. Driscoll, "Can We _____?"
92. Driscoll, "Can We _____?"
93. Driscoll, "Sex: God, Gross, or Gift?"
94. Driscoll, "Sex: God, Gross, or Gift?"
95. Driscoll, "Sex: God, Gross, or Gift?"
96. Mark Driscoll, "The Porn Path," *Real Marriage* series, Mars Hill Church, March 4, 2012.
97. Driscoll, "The Porn Path."
98. Driscoll, "Sex: God, Gross, or Gift?"
99. Driscoll, "Sex: God, Gross, or Gift?"
100. Driscoll, "Sex: God, Gross, or Gift?"

101. Driscoll, "Can We _____?"
102. Driscoll, "Sex: God, Gross, or Gift?"
103. Driscoll, "Sex: God, Gross, or Gift?"
104. In the beginning of his ministry at Mars Hill Church, Driscoll used the New International Version (NIV) as his core text. In the mid-2000s, he switched to the English Standard Version (ESV), written specifically from a New Calvinist perspective that translated (and added) words and phrases that emphasized traditional roles. See Samuel L. Perry, "The Bible as a Product of Cultural Power: The Case of Gender Ideology in the English Standard Version," *Sociology of Religion* 81, no. 1 (Spring 2020).
105. Driscoll, "Sex: God, Gross, or Gift?"
106. Driscoll, "Sex: God, Gross, or Gift?"
107. Driscoll, "The Porn Path."
108. Mark Driscoll, "The Little Foxes," *The Peasant Princess* series, Mars Hill Church, October 5, 2008.
109. Driscoll, "Good Sex, Bad Sex."
110. Driscoll, "Women as Wives."
111. Driscoll, "Good Sex, Bad Sex."
112. Driscoll, "Good Sex, Bad Sex."
113. Mark Driscoll, "Dance of Mahanaim," *The Peasant Princess* series, Mars Hill Church, November 9, 2008.
114. Driscoll, "Dance of Mahanaim."
115. Driscoll, "Dance of Mahanaim."
116. Driscoll, "Dance of Mahanaim."
117. Driscoll, "Can We _____?"
118. Mark Driscoll, "I Was a Wall," *The Peasant Princess* series, Mars Hill Church, November 2, 2008. In *Soft Patriarchs, New Men*, Wilcox found that fathers who attended church regularly were more likely to spend time with their children in youth-related activities, as well as in one-on-one interaction.
119. Driscoll, "I Was a Wall."
120. Driscoll, "Can We _____?"
121. Driscoll, "Can We _____?"
122. Driscoll, "Can We _____?"
123. Driscoll, "Can We _____?" Grace Driscoll's clarification that women were redeemed, rather than saved, through childbearing was significant, reflecting the controversy over Driscoll's "women are saved through childbearing" sermon from 2006.
124. Driscoll, "Can We _____?"
125. In the *Real Marriage* sermon, "Can We _____?," the Driscolls briefly addressed infertility, saying, "it's good to consider adoption. Jesus was adopted by his father, Joseph. . . . So, if there's an infertility issue, then perhaps adoption would be something meritorious of consideration." How women at Mars Hill interpreted the importance of being mothers, meant that experiencing infertility could be devastating, as described in Chapter 3.

126. Mark Driscoll. "Men as Fathers," *Proverbs* series, Mars Hill Church, November 11, 2001.

127. Driscoll, "Men as Husbands."

128. Driscoll, "Men as Husbands."

129. Driscoll, "Men and Masculinity."

130. Driscoll, "Men and Masculinity."

131. Driscoll, "Men and Masculinity."

132. Driscoll, "Men as Fathers."

133. Driscoll, "Men as Fathers."

134. Driscoll, "Men and Marriage."

135. Driscoll, "Men and Marriage."

136. Mark Driscoll, "My Dove," *The Peasant Princess* series, Mars Hill Church, October 26, 2008.

137. Driscoll, "My Dove."

138. Driscoll, "My Dove."

139. Driscoll, "My Dove." Driscoll did not mention how the abusive man's daughter felt about her father and his restitution.

140. Driscoll, "I Was a Wall."

141. Driscoll, "I Was a Wall."

142. Driscoll, "I Was a Wall."

143. Driscoll, "Men as Husbands."

144. Driscoll, "Selfish Lovers and Servant Lovers."

145. Driscoll, "Selfish Lovers and Servant Lovers."

146. Song of Solomon 8:8–9 says, "We have a little sister, and she has no breasts. What shall we do for our sister, on the day when she is spoken for? If she is a wall, we will build upon her a battlement of silver; but if she is a door, we will enclose her with boards of cedar."

147. Driscoll, "Women as Wives."

148. Driscoll, "Friend with Benefits."

149. Driscoll, "Friend with Benefits."

150. Driscoll, "Men and Marriage."

151. Driscoll, "Men and Marriage."

152. Driscoll, "Men and Marriage."

153. Driscoll, "My Dove."

154. Driscoll, "My Dove."

155. Driscoll, "The Little Foxes." Driscoll's complementarian theology relied on men working and women being at home. Yet he seemed to denigrate the arrangement here. In stating that wives could get "half of everything" a man owned, he implied that men earning the money in complementarian marriages meant household goods and assets belonged to them.

156. Driscoll, "The Little Foxes."

157. Driscoll, "New Marriage, Same Spouse."

158. Driscoll and Driscoll, *Real Marriage*, 11.

159. Driscoll and Driscoll, *Real Marriage*, 11–12.

160. Driscoll and Driscoll, *Real Marriage*, 13

161. Driscoll, "New Marriage, Same Spouse."

162. Driscoll, "New Marriage, Same Spouse."

163. "Clara" is a pseudonym.

164. The pastor mentoring Delilah's boyfriend cited Matthew 1:19 to let her boyfriend know he could "righteously" end their relationship. In Matthew 1:19 Joseph learns that Mary, his betrothed, is pregnant. Because Joseph was not the father of the child (Jesus), Joseph decided to end the betrothal, until an angel appeared explaining that the child's birth would fulfill a scriptural prophecy.

165. See Smith, *Evangelicalism*.

166. Mark Driscoll, "Humble Like Jesus," *Christians Gone Wild* series, Mars Hill Church, February 26, 2006.

167. After explaining the importance of adhering to Mars Hill Church's gender doctrine, where men were expected to be primary breadwinners, Kirsten told me that she was working part-time. She explained that her husband's job didn't pay enough to cover their household expenses, so she had taken a job. Kirsten further explained that they had not told their pastors and community group, expecting that her job would be a temporary arrangement. Kirsten had been working for more than two years at that point.

168. Studies examining gender norms and violence have found that "traditional gender ideologies increase the risk of violence." See Shelley D. Golden, Krista M. Perreira, and Piette Durrance, "Troubled Times, Troubled Relationships: How Economic Resources, Gender Beliefs, and Neighborhood Disadvantage Influence Intimate Partner Violence," *Journal of Interpersonal Violence* 28, no. 10 (2013), 2136.

Chapter 5

1. Mark Driscoll, "Power from Jesus," *Christians Gone Wild* series, Mars Hill Church, March 10, 2006. Driscoll referred to Judas, the disciple who betrayed Jesus to the religious authorities.

2. Mark Driscoll, "Changed by Jesus," *Christians Gone Wild* series, Mars Hill Church, March 26, 2006.

3. Driscoll, "Changed by Jesus."

4. Driscoll, "Changed by Jesus."

5. Driscoll, "Humble Like Jesus."

6. Joyful Exiles, "MH Church Website Forum—Jamie Munson 'Update on Paul Petry' Re 'Discipline' = Shunning," https://joyfulexiles.files.wordpress.com/2012/03/elders-mh-website-jamie-munson-update-on-paul-petry-forum-12-05-071.pdf. Paul and Jonna Petry have painstakingly documented these events.

7. Joyful Exiles, "MH Church."

8. Joyful Exiles, "MH Church."

9. Joyful Exiles, "MH Church."

10. Dear Driscoll, "Pastor Mark Driscoll Piling Dead Bodies behind His Bus," YouTube video, 2:29, May 31, 2021, https://www.youtube.com/watch?v=11Q5K26bup0.

11. Church members were incensed at the firing of the two popular pastors and made their displeasure known. As a result of the controversy, the church purged its membership rolls, requiring a new membership covenant be signed for those who wanted to continue participating fully in the church.

12. Stacey Solie, "Inside Mars Hill's Massive Meltdown," *Crosscut*, July 16, 2014, http://crosscut.com/2014/07/inside-mars-hills-big-meltdown/.

13. Solie, "Inside." In 2012, as the practice of shunning made local headlines, Mars Hill posted a statement reminding members that they had agreed to "submit" to church discipline "if the need should ever arise," when they signed the church's membership covenant. See Mars Hill Church, "A Response Regarding Church Discipline," February 13, 2012, http://marshill.com/2012/02/13/a-response-regarding-church-discipline.

14. Driscoll, *Leadership*, 26.

15. In her work on megachurches and the "evangelical industrial complex," Jessica Johnson states that leaders of nondenominational megachurches have a "sovereignty," affording them "a great deal of spiritual and administrative authority" to set the vision of the congregation. See "Megachurches, Celebrity Pastors, and the Evangelical Industrial Complex," in *Religion and Popular Culture in America, 3rd Edition*, ed. Bruce Forbes and Jeffrey Mahan (Berkeley: University of California Press, 2017), 162–163.

16. Iannaccone, "Strict Churches," 1202.

17. Iannaccone, "Strict Churches," 1203.

18. Several video clips of this portion of the 2009 "Marriage and Men" sermon have circulated online. For one example see JeremyMarriedGuy, "Mark Driscoll Screaming," YouTube, April 8, 2009, https://www.youtube.com/watch?v=Zkae AkJOOw8.

19. Raewyn Connell, *Masculinities* (Berkeley: University of California Press, 2005), 77.

20. Stacey, *Brave New*, 191.

21. Researchers have found a positive correlation between Calvinist beliefs and the acceptance of domestic violence myths. Both Calvinist beliefs and acceptance of domestic violence myths were defined by a nonacceptance of out-group members, hierarchical relationship, and complementarian gender ideologies/gender inequality. See Peter J. Jankowski et al., "Religious Beliefs and Domestic Violence Myths," *Psychology of Religion and Spirituality* 10, no. 4 (2018), 386–397.

22. Golden, Perreira, and Durrance, "Troubled Times," 2136; Nason-Clark et al., *Religion and Intimate Partner Violence*, 31.

23. Janet Jacobs, "The Economy of Love in Religious Commitment: The Deconversion of Women from Nontraditional Religious Movements," *Journal for the Scientific Study of Religion* 23, no. 2 (1984), 166; Nason-Clark, "Terror," 307.

24. Nason-Clark et al., *Religion and Intimate Partner Violence*, 1.

25. Nason-Clark et al., *Religion and Intimate Partner Violence*, 76.

26. Nason-Clark et al., *Religion and Intimate Partner Violence*, 1, 32.

27. Du Mez, *Jesus and John Wayne*, 280.

28. Tim Carrigan, Raewyn Connell, and John Lee, "Toward a New Sociology of Masculinity," *Theory and Society* 14, no. 5 (September 1985), 563.

29. Carrigan, Connell, and Lee, "Toward," 553; Carol Tavris, "Mismeasure of Woman," *Feminism and Psychology* 3, no. 2 (1993), 149.

30. Stacey, *Brave New*, 10.

31. Carrigan, Connell, and Lee, "Toward," 554.

32. See Coontz, *Never Were*.

33. Median household income in Seattle for 2014 was $70,975, whereas the national median household income was $53,657. See United States Census, "S1901: Income in the Past 12 Months (in 2014 Inflation-Adjusted Dollars)," *American Community Survey, 2014*, accessed April 6, 2020, https://data.census.gov/cedsci/table?q=househ old%20income%20seattle&tid=ACSST1Y2014 .S1901; United States Census, "Table H-8: Median Household Income by State," accessed April 6, 2020, https://www.cen sus.gov/data/tables/time-series/demo/income-poverty/historical-income-househo lds.html.

34. Kimmel, *Manhood in America*, 13.

35. Hoover and Coats, *Does God*, 19.

36. Hoover and Coats, *Does God*, 160.

37. Coontz, *Really Are*, 54.

38. Coontz, *Really Are*, 55.

39. See Bem, *The Lenses of Gender*.

40. Ridgeway and Correll, "Unpacking the Gender System," 510.

41. Ridgeway and Correll, "Unpacking the Gender System," 515.

42. Driscoll, "Women and Femininity."

43. Driscoll, "Women and Femininity."

44. Patricia Yancy Martin, "Gender as Social Institution," *Social Forces* 82, no. 4 (June 2004), 1258.

45. Martin, "Gender," 1257.

46. Barbara Risman, "Gender as a Social Structure: Theory Wrestling with Activism." *Gender and Society* 18, no. 4 (August 2004), 431.

47. Ridgeway and Correll, "Unpacking," 517.

48. See Gallagher and Smith, "Symbolic Traditionalism"; Griffith, *God's Daughters*.

49. See Mayer N. Zald and R. Ash Gardner, "Social Movement Organizations: Growth, Decay, and Change," in *Social Movements in an Organizational Society*, ed. Mayer N. Zald and John D. McCarthy (New Brunswick, NJ: Transaction, 1987).

50. Carrigan, Connell, and Lee, "Toward," 560.

51. Carrigan, Connell, and Lee, "Toward," 592.

52. See Joan Acker, "Women and Social Stratification: A Case of Intellectual Sexism," *American Journal of Sociology* 78, no. 4 (January 1973), 936–945.

53. Douglas Schrock and Michael Schwalbe, "Men, Masculinity, and Manhood Acts," *Annual Review of Sociology* 35, no. 1 (August 2009), 280.

54. Carrigan, Connell, and Lee, "Toward," 592. Hegemonic masculinity describes how some men inhabit positions of power and wealth, and how their positions

are legitimated and reproduced within the social relationships generating their dominance.

55. See Bridges and Pascoe, "Hybrid Masculinities"; Connell, *Masculinities*; Michael A. Messner, *Politics of Masculinities: Men in Movements* (Thousand Oaks, CA: Sage Publications, 1997).

56. Carrigan, Connell, and Lee, "Toward," 577.

57. See Julie Brines, "Economic Dependency, Gender, and the Division of Labor at Home," *American Journal of Sociology* 100, no. 3 (November 1994), 652–688; Connell, *Masculinities*; Kimmel, *Manhood in America*; Anthony E. Rotundo, *American Manhood: Transformations in Masculinity from the Revolution to the Modern Era* (New York: Basic Books, 1993).

58. Schrock and Schwalbe, "Manhood Acts," 278.

59. Bederman, "Women Have Had," 435.

60. See W. Bradford Wilcox, "Religion, Convention, and Paternal Involvement," *Journal of Marriage and the Family* 64, no. 3 (August 2002), 780–792; Wilcox, *Soft Patriarchs*.

61. Driscoll, "Men and Marriage."

62. Kimmel, *Manhood in America*, 39.

63. Stacey, *Brave New*, 69.

64. Lauren Schiller, "What White Supremacists and Incels Have in Common: Blaming Feminism," *Salon*, October 27, 2019, https://www.salon.com/2019/10/27/what-white-nationalists-and-incels-have-in-common-blaming-feminism/.

65. Michael Kimmel, *Healing from Hate: How Young Men Get into—and Out of—Violent Extremism* (Berkeley: University of California Press, 2018), 141.

66. Kimmel, *Healing*, 145.

67. Driscoll, "Women and Femininity."

68. Driscoll, "Under Authority Like Jesus."

69. Mark Driscoll, "More Salt in the Episcopal Wound," *The Resurgence*, June 22, 2006, http://theresurgence.com/md_blog_2006-06-22_more_salt_in_the_episcopalian_wounds. Driscoll's blog post referred to Presiding Bishop Katherine Jefferts-Schori's support for Bishop Gene Robinson's ordination as the first openly gay person to be ordained bishop in the Episcopal Church.

70. Mark Driscoll, "Those Bloody Presbyterians," *The Resurgence*, March 7, 2006, http://theresurgence.com/those_bloody_presbyterians.

71. Mark Driscoll, "Episcopalians and Male Testosterone Show Corresponding Decline." *The Resurgence*, November 10, 2006, http://www.theresurgence.com/md_blog_2006-11-10_episcolpalians_and_male_testosterone_show_corresponding_decline.

72. Mark Driscoll, "Now the Mainline Churches Make Sense," *The Resurgence*, August 21, 2006, http://www.theresurgence.com/md_blog_2006-08-21_now_the_mainline_churches_make_sense.

73. See Kevin Neuhouser, "Strict, But Not (Gender) Conservative: Revising the Strict Church Thesis in Light of Brazilian Pentecostalism," *Interdisciplinary Journal of Research on Religion* 13, no. 8 (2017), 1–28.

74. Kimmel, *Manhood in America*, 92.

75. Kimmel, *Manhood in America*, 92.

76. Driscoll, "Women and Femininity."

77. Driscoll, "Women and Femininity."

78. Stacey, *Brave New*, 259.

Conclusion

1. Worthen, "Match."

2. Worthen, "Match."

3. Ben Schreckenger, "Trump Attacks McCain: 'I Like People Who Weren't Captured,'" *Politico*, July 18, 2015, https://www.politico.com/story/2015/07/trump-attacks-mccain-i-like-people-who-werent-captured-120317.

4. PRRI, *Competing Visions of America: An Evolving Identity or a Culture under Attack? Findings from the 2021 American Values Survey* (Washington, DC: PRRI), 35.

5. Sarah Posner, "Amazing Disgrace," *New Republic*, March 20, 2017, https://newrepublic.com/article/140961/amazing-disgrace-donald-trump-hijacked-religious-right.

6. Theresa K. Vescio and Nathaniel E. C. Schermerhorn, "Hegemonic Masculinity Predicts 2016 and 2020 Voting and Candidate Evaluations," *PNAS* 118, no. 2, e2020589118, https://doi.org/10.1073/pnas.2020589118.

7. R. Marie Griffith, *Moral Combat: How Sex Divided American Christians and Fractured American Politics* (New York: Basic Books, 2017), 313.

8. Arlie Hochschild, *Strangers in Their Own Land: Anger and Mourning on the American Right* (New York: New Press, 2016), 229; Griffith, *Moral*, 316.

9. Trump's statement refers to former White House intern Monica Lewinsky, who had a relationship with Bill Clinton during his tenure as president.

10. Liza Featherstone, "Josh Hawley and the Republican Obsession with Manliness," *New York Times*, December 4, 2021, https://www.nytimes.com/2021/12/04/opinion/josh-hawley-republican-manliness.html.

11. Du Mez, *Jesus and John Wayne*, 304.

12. Cosper, "Who Killed Mars Hill."

13. Owen Strachan (@ostrachan), "Men today are often soft, weak, passive, unprotective. But physical discipline is key for men. Hear Paul: 'I batter my body and make it my slave' (1 Cor 9:27). Christic manhood is protective, sharp, watchful. The man who is willfully soft physically is often soft spiritually," Twitter, February 18, 2020, 6:22 a.m., https://twitter.com/ostrachan/status/1229773122049658882.

14. Owen Strachan (@ostrachan), "We men need to stop making excuses. We need to reject softness. We need to do hard things. We need to be first in battle and last in retreat. We need to be watchmen on the wall. We need to protect women & children. We need to fight evil. We need to bleed for the truth," Twitter, February 18, 2020, 6:23 a.m., https://twitter.com/ostrachan/status/1229773458462117888.

15. Owen Strachan (@ostrachan), "Biblical men take hits for the truth. Who today will suffer for the gospel? Who will be persecuted for righteousness' sake? Who will endure hatred for Christ? Who will suffer injury to overthrow evil? Who will be

unpopular to be faithful? Who will bleed for the truth?" Twitter, February 18, 2020, 6:31 a.m., https://twitter.com/ostrachan/status/1229775383257583622.

16. Sam Perry (@socofthesacred), "Let's clear this up. Unlikely John meant to convey Jesus beat humans w/a whip. The Greek is ambivalent. Some translations (e.g., NIV, GNB) clarify it's only animals. Contexts makes it clearer humans weren't whipped. But authoritarians like Walsh LOVE a Jesus who hurts people," Twitter, February 13, 2022, https://twitter.com/socofthesacred/status/1492993344011743235.

17. Perry, "Let's Clear."

18. Leah MariAnn Klett, "John MacArthur Clarifies Views on Beth Moore, Women Preachers:'EmpoweringWomenMakesWeakMen,'"*ChristianPost*,November13,2019, https://www.christianpost.com/news/john-macarthur-clarifies-views-on-beth-moore-women-preachers-empowering-women-makes-weak-men.html.

19. Azi Paybarah, "Missouri Pastor Who Sermonized That Women Must Look Good for Their Husbands Goes on Leave," *New York Times*, March 8, 2021, www.nytimes.com/2021/03/08/us/stewart-allen-clark-pastor-melania-trump.html. Clark's comments are so similar to Driscoll's, you can almost hear Driscoll shouting, "I've got a verse!"

20. Van Biema, "10 Ideas."

21. Hansen, "Young."

22. Mike Cosper, "The Brand," August 2, 2021, in *The Rise and Fall of Mars Hill*, produced by Mike Cosper, podcast, 60:00, https://www.christianitytoday.com/ct/podcasts/rise-and-fall-of-mars-hill/rise-fall-mars-hill-podcast-mark-driscoll-brand.html.

23. In another episode of *The Rise and Fall of Mars Hill*, former Mars Hill Executive Elder Sutton Turner, speaks to Driscoll's need to be accountable (submit) to other men. Turner reports that Driscoll's response to that suggestion was met with the statement that Driscoll couldn't be under the authority of a pastor/elder/man who was not as successful as he was. See Mike Cosper, "The Tempest," November 12, 2021, in *The Rise and Fall of Mars Hill*, produced by Mike Cosper, podcast, 2:35:00, https://www.christianitytoday.com/ct/podcasts/rise-and-fall-of-mars-hill/tempest-mars-hill-driscoll.html.

24. Samuel L. Perry, "The Bible as a Product of Cultural Power: The Case of Gender Ideology in the English Standard Version," *Sociology of Religion* 81, no. 1 (Spring 2020), 75. On the ESV website's homepage the Bible is marketed as an "essentially literal translation" (accessed February 24, 2022, https://www.esv.org/). Wayne Grudem, coauthor of *Recovering Biblical Manhood and Womanhood* and a central architect of the ESV, has also advanced a theology (with Bruce Ware) of the Trinity that makes Jesus subordinate to God. This theology would bolster a theology of masculine authority, by suggesting that as Jesus is subordinate to God, so women are subordinate to men. As Kristen Kobes Du Mez writes, this theology diverges from "roughly two millennia of Christian orthodoxy." See *Jesus and John Wayne*, 298.

25. Barr, "Biblical Womanhood," 132. In the early years of Mars Hill Church, Driscoll preached from the NIV, but switched to the ESV in the mid- to late-2000s.

26. Perry, "The Bible," 70.

27. Perry, "The Bible," 83.

28. Perry, "The Bible," 86.

29. In his work on marriage and evangelicalism, Bartkowski writes, "Evangelical purveyors of separate spheres theology draw on several carefully selected scriptural references to support their vision of dichotomized household roles and responsibilities." With the introduction of the ESV, text supporting these dichotomized household responsibilities now seem nonnegotiable. See Bartkowski, *Remaking*, 82.

30. Lydia Bean, *Politics of Evangelical Identity: Local Churches and Partisan Divides in the United States and Canada* (Princeton, NJ: Princeton University Press, 2014), 57.

31. Du Mez, *Jesus and John Wayne*, 272.

32. Warren Bird and Scott Thumma, *Megachurch 2020: The Changing Reality in America's Largest Church's*, Hartford Institute for Religion Research, https://faithcommunitiesto day.org/wp-content/uploads/2020/10/Megachurch-Survey-Report_HIRR_FACT-2020.pdf.

33. Mark Chaves, "All Creatures Great and Small: Megachurches in Context," *Review of Religious Research* 47, no. 4 (June 2006), 336–337. The same structural conditions that helped fuel the breadwinner/homemaker households of the "long decade"—suburbanization, new shopping centers, affordable automobiles, highways linking factories to residential communities—also gave rise to the American megachurch. See Eagle, "Historicizing."

34. Landon Schnable and Sean Block, "The Persistent and Exceptional History of American Religion: A Response to Recent Research," *Sociological Science* 4, (November 2017), 697.

35. Eagle, "Historicizing," 591; Wellman, Corcoran, and Stockly, *High*, 69. Eagle points out that Protestant megachurches date to the sixteenth-century, but in the United States they were not branded distinctively from other religious organizations until the 1980s. Ironically, the proliferation of megachurches post-1970s is tied to the social structural changes giving rise to dual-earning families. Eagle writes that the increase in women's labor force participation meant a decrease in a family's discretionary time, making "large, well-staffed congregations appealing," which aided in the popularity and growth of megachurches.

36. Wellman, Corcoran, and Stockly, *High*, 201, emphasis in the original.

37. Wellman, Corcoran, and Stockly, *High*, 201.

38. Wellman, Corcoran, and Stockly, *High*, 202.

39. Wellman, Corcoran, and Stockly, *High*, 202. See also Betty A. DeBurg, *Ungodly Women: Gender and the First Wave of American Fundamentalism* (Minneapolis: Fortress Press, 1990); Lynn Davidman, *Tradition in a Rootless World: Women Turn to Orthodox Judaism* (Berkeley: University of California Press, 1991); Brenda E. Brasher, *Godly Women: Fundamentalism and Female Power* (New Brunswick, NJ: Rutgers University Press, 1998); Griffith, *God's Daughters*; Gallagher and Smith, "Symbolic Traditionalism."

40. Wellman, Corcoran, and Stockly, *High*, 116. The typical megachurch pastor is male and white. The majority of megachurch participants are white and college-educated. See Bird and Thumma, *Megachurch*.

41. Wellman, Corcoran, and Stockly, *High*, 143.

42. Wellman, Corcoran, and Stockly, *High*, 212.

43. It is not uncommon to have outside critics and former members accuse authoritarian churches with abusive leadership. See Wellman, Corcoran, and Stockly, *High*, 193, 195.

44. Katie E. Corcoran, and James K. Wellman Jr., "'People Forget He's Human': Charismatic Leadership in Institutionalized Religion," *Sociology of Religion* 77, no. 4 (Winter 2016), 311.

45. Weber, *The Theory*, 358; Dawson, "Crises," 81.

46. Wellman, Corcoran, and Stockly, *High*, 142.

47. Erin C. Cassese, and Mirya R. Holman. "Religion, Gendered Authority, and Identity in American Politics." *Religion and Politics* 10, no. 1 (March 2017), 31.

48. Cassese and Holman, "Religion," 33.

49. Cassese and Holman, "Religion," 31.

50. Joseph O. Baker and Andrew L. Whitehead, "God's Penology: Belief in a Masculine God Predicts Support for Harsh Criminal Punishment and Militarism," *Punishment and Society* 22, no. 2 (April 2020), 135–142.

51. Andrew L. Whitehead, "Gender Ideology and Religion: Does a Masculine Image of God Matter?" *Review of Religious Research* 54, no. 2 (June 2012), 142.

52. Worthen, "Smack Down?"

53. Wellman, Corcoran, and Stockly, *High*, 144.

54. Whitehead and Perry, *Taking Back America*, 123.

55. Christian Smith, *American Evangelicalism: Embattled and Thriving* (Chicago: University of Chicago Press 1998), 136.

56. Smith, *Evangelicalism*, 137.

57. Emma Green, "Why White Evangelicals Are Feeling Hopeful about Trump." *The Atlantic*, December 1, 2016, https://www.theatlantic.com/politics/archive/2016/12/trump-white-evangelicals-communities/509084/.

58. Marti, *Blindspot*, 217.

59. Pierce Alexander Dignam and Deana A. Rohlinger, "Misogynistic Men Online: How the Red Pill Helped Elect Donald Trump," *Signs: Journal of Women in Culture and Society* 44, no. 3 (Spring 2019), 591.

60. Dignam and Rohlinger, "Misogynistic Men," 602.

61. Griffith, *Moral Combat*, 318.

62. Emily Crockett, "Why Misogyny Won," *Vox*, November 15, 2016, https://www.vox.com/identities/2016/11/15/13571478/trump-president-sexual-assault-sexism-misogyny-won.

63. Vescio and Schermerhorn, "Hegemonic Masculinity," 2.

64. Marti, *Blindspot*, 220.

65. Marti, *Blindspot*, 4, 6. Illustrating evangelical frustrations regarding religion and politics in America, Mark Driscoll marked Obama's second inauguration by tweeting, "Praying for our president, who today will place his hand on a Bible he does not believe to take an oath to a God he likely does not know." See Pastor Mark Driscoll (@ PastorMark), Twitter, January 21, 2013, https://twitter.com/pastormark/status/293391878949335043.

66. Du Mez, *Jesus and John Wayne*, 301.

67. Jack Jenkins, "For Insurrectionists, a Violent Faith Brewed from Nationalism, Conspiracies and Jesus," *Religion News Service*, January 12, 2021, https://religionn ews.com/2021/01/12/the-faith-of-the-insurrectionists/.

68. Whitehead and Perry, *Taking Back*, 105.

69. Du Mez, *Jesus and John Wayne*, 238; Marti, *Blindspot*, 6.

70. Du Mez, *Jesus and John Wayne*, 238; Marti, *Blindspot*, 23.

71. Michael O. Emmerson and Christian Smith, *Divided by Faith: Evangelical Religion and the Problem of Race in America* (New York: Oxford University Press, 2000), 9. In their work on evangelicalism and race, Emmerson and Smith found that evangelical beliefs in individual conversion, regeneration, and sin shape evangelical conscious-ness. This consciousness focuses on individuals, limiting evangelicals' ability to un-derstand how social structures, rather than individual sin or prejudice, perpetuate racialized social systems.

72. Robert P. Jones, *White Too Long* (New York: Simon & Schuster Paperbacks, 2020), 10. Trump signaled his adherence to these racialized and gendered values by taking a posture of white patriarchal authority when he referred to Haiti and African na-tions as "shithole" countries, or to Mexican men as "bad hombres," or generalizing to Mexican immigrants, saying, "They're bringing drugs. They're bringing crime. They're rapists." See Ali Vitali, Kasie Hunt, and Frank Thorp V, "Trump Referred to Haiti and African Nations as 'Shithole' Countries," *NBC News*, January 11, 2018, https://www.nbcnews.com/politics/white-house/trump-referred-haiti-african-countries-shithole-nations-n836946; Adam Kealoha Causey, "To Some, Trump's 'Bad Hombres' Is Much More Than a Botched Spanish Word," *PBS News Hour*, October 20, 2015, https://www.pbs.org/newshour/politics/trumps-bad-homb res-draws-jeers-spanish-lessons; Michelle Yee Hee Lee, "Donald Trump's False Comments Connecting Mexican Immigrants and Crime," *Washington Post*, July 8, 2015, https://www.washingtonpost.com/news/fact-checker/wp/2015/07/08/don ald-trumps-false-comments-connecting-mexican-immigrants-and-crime/.

73. Whitehead and Perry, *Taking Back*, 91.

74. Whitehead and Perry, *Taking Back*, 78.

75. Kristen Myers and Kirk Miller, "'Massive' Masculinity and the Mainstreaming of the Alt-Right in the West," *Gender and Society* (blog), March 16, 2017, https://gender society.wordpress.com/2017/03/16/massive-masculinity-and-the-mainstreaming-of-the-alt-right-in-the-west/.

76. Myers and Miller, "Massive."

77. Kimmel, *Healing*, 47.

78. Kimmel, *Healing*, 47–48.

79. Kimmel, *Healing*, 48.

80. In the month following Trump's election, bias-related intimidation and harassment increased and in his first year in office, hate crimes in America's largest ten cities increased. See C. J. Pascoe, "Homophobia Linked to Definition of Masculinity," *The Register-Guard*, May 24, 2017, https://www.registerguard.com/story/opinion/2017/05/24/homophobia-linked-to-definition-masculinity/11708172007/;   Richard

Fausset, Serge F. Kovaleski, and Alan Feuer, "A Year after Charlottesville, Disarray in the White Supremacist Movement," *New York Times*, August 13, 2018, https://www.nytimes.com/2018/08/13/us/charlottesville-unite-the-right-white-supremacists.html.

81. Brian Naylor, "Read Trump's January 6 Speech, a Key Part of Impeachment Trial," *NPR Politics*, February 10, 2021, https://www.npr.org/2021/02/10/966396848/read-trumps-jan-6-speech-a-key-part-of-impeachment-trial. During his impeachment trial, Trump's attorneys pointed to his saying that supporters should "peacefully and patriotically" make their voices heard as they would "soon be marching over to the Capitol building." Trump's attorneys argued Trump did not call for actual lawlessness and violence.

82. Jack Jenkins, "For Insurrectionists, a Violent Faith Brewed from Nationalism, Conspiracies and Jesus," *Religion News Service*, January 12, 2021, https://religionnews.com/2021/01/12/the-faith-of-the-insurrectionists/.

83. Jenkins, "For Insurrectionists."

84. Du Mez, *Jesus and John Wayne*, 253. After Trump's speech at the rally, thousands of his supporters followed his mandate, making their way to the Capitol building, where they breached the barricades, attacked Capitol police, and broke into the building. Five people were killed in the violence that ensued.

85. In a nationwide analysis, ABC News identified fifty-four criminal cases "where Trump was invoked in direct connection with violent acts, threats of violence, or allegations of assault." See Fabiola Cineas, "Donald Trump Is the Accelerant," *Vox*, January 9, 2021, https://www.vox.com/21506029/trump-violence-tweets-racist-hate-speech; Mike Levine, "'No Blame?' ABC News Finds 54 Cases Invoking 'Trump' in Connection with Violence, Threats, Alleged Assault," May 30, 2020, https://abcnews.go.com/Politics/blame-abc-news-finds-17-cases-invoking-trump/story?id=58912889. Trump's rhetoric could sound eerily like Driscoll's. At a February 23, 2016, rally, for example, Trump referred to a protestor and said, "I'd like to punch him in the face." Mocking the protestor, who was led away by security guards, Trump remarked, "There's a guy, totally disruptive, throwing punches. We're not allowed to punch back anymore. I love the old days. You know what they used to do to guys like that when they were in a place like this? They'd be carried out on a stretcher, folks." At a 2018 rally, referring to Montana's Republican Congressional Representative Greg Gianforte, who had body-slammed a reporter, Trump said, "Any guy who can body-slam . . . he's my guy."

86. *New York Times*, "Atlanta Shootings Live Updates: Suspect Had Visited Targeted Spas Before, Police Say," March 18, 2021, https://www.nytimes.com/live/2021/03/18/us/atlanta-shootings-massage-spa.

87. Greg Walters, "Atlanta Shooting Suspect's Church Bashed 'Radical Feminism' in Deleted Sermons," *Vice*, March 19, 2021, https://www.vice.com/en/article/n7vxpd/atlanta-shooting-suspects-church-bashed-radical-feminism-in-deleted-sermons. The church's statement on sexual immorality read, "We believe that any form of sexual immorality, such as adultery, fornication, homosexuality, bisexual conduct, bestiality, incest, polygamy, pedophilia, pornography, or any attempt to change one's

sex or disagreement with one's biological sex, is sinful and offensive to God." The congregation listed itself as part of the SBC's Founder's Ministries, which holds to New Calvinist doctrines including a hardline complementarianism. On the day of Long's attacks, Founder's Ministries posted a YouTube video as part of its *Wield the Sword* series, titled "Biblical Manhood and Womanhood." While the video discusses complementarian roles, the larger series was described as "a call to arms" aimed at (male) pastors to "take up the sword of the Spirit and wield it with courage." See Founders Ministries, "How Then Shall We Lead?" *Wield the Sword*, https://found ers.org/wieldthesword/.

88. Kimmel, *Healing*, 145.

89. The impetus for the August 2017 "Unite the Right" rally in Charlottesville, Virginia, is attributed to Dylan Roof's attack on the members of a historic Black church. After Roof's attack, momentum built across the country to remove Confederate monuments. The 2017 rally was orchestrated as a protest against having these monuments removed.

90. Roof had grown up in the Evangelical Lutheran Church of America, a mainline Protestant church that tends to be more socially and theologically liberal. The denomination has long ordained women, sanctions LGBTQ + marriages, and ordains LGBTQ + clergy. Roof's radicalization illustrates how Christian symbols and ideology can be adapted by white supremacy.

91. Jones, *White*, 140.

92. Julie Zauzmer, "The Alleged Synagogue Shooter Was a Churchgoer Who Talked Christian Theology, Raising Tough Questions for Evangelical Pastors," *Washington Post*, May 1, 2019, https://www.washingtonpost.com/religion/2019/05/01/alleged-synagogue-shooter-was-churchgoer-who-articulated-christian-theology-prompt ing-tough-questions-evangelical-pastors/. Earnest grew up in a conservative evangelical Orthodox Presbyterian Church (OPC), where his father was an elder. OPC congregations adhere to Reformed and complementarian doctrines. After reading Earnest's letter, one OPC pastor responded by saying, "We can't pretend as though we didn't have some responsibility for [Earnest]—he was radicalized into white nationalism from within the very midst of our church."

93. Driscoll and Driscoll, *Real Marriage*, 9–10.

94. Driscoll and Driscoll, *Real Marriage*, 9.

95. Driscoll and Driscoll, *Real Marriage*, 10.

96. Driscoll and Driscoll, *Real Marriage*, 14.

97. Driscoll and Driscoll, *Real Marriage*, 8–9.

98. Driscoll and Driscoll, *Real Marriage*, 9.

99. Wellman, Corcoran, and Stockly, *High*, 119.

100. Wellman, Corcoran, and Stockly, *High*, 190–191.

101. Driscoll's last publication had been *A Call to Resurgence* in 2013, the book that started the cascade of accusations regarding plagiarism and the misappropriation of funds for using a public relations firm to inflate the popularity of *Real Marriage*.

102. Matt Brown, "Real Conversations: Pastor Mark Driscoll, Part 2." *Debrief Show*, YouTube video, 1:07:25, June 4, 2019, https://www.youtube.com/watch?v=4OsQm6YU3OY.

103. Warren Throckmorton, "Mark Driscoll: The Five Points of Calvinism Are Garbage," *Patheos*, July 11, 2019, https://www.wthrockmorton.com/2019/07/11/mark-driscoll-five-points-of-calvinism-is-garbage/.

104. Driscoll's dispensing with Calvinism allowed him to build his new church apart from the Reformed structure of oversight that generally includes elders. Moving away from Calvinism also allowed him to dispense with organizations like Acts 29 or The Gospel Coalition interfering with his ministry.

105. Wellman, Corcoran, and Stockly, *High*, 116.

106. Julie Monea, "Postcards from Phoenix: When Family Ties Are Tested," Warren Throckmorton, blog, July 2, 2021, https://www.wthrockmorton.com/2021/07/02/postcards-from-phoenix-when-family-ties-are-tested/.

107. Kim Thompson, "Postcards from Phoenix: Friends May Not Be Friends Forever at The Trinity Church," Warren Throckmorton, blog, August 12, 2021, https://www.wthrockmorton.com/2021/08/12/postcards-from-phoenix-too-good-to-be-true/.

108. Wellman, Corcoran, and Stockly, *High*, 196.

109. Du Mez, *Jesus and John Wayne*, 274.

110. Stacey, *Brave New*, 260.

111. Stacey, *Brave New*, 260.

Appendix

1. Smith and Lee, "Changing Course?"; Woods, "Decline and Fall."

2. See Glaser and Strauss, *Discovery*; Strauss and Corbin, *Basics*.

Bibliography

Acker, Joan. "Women and Social Stratification: A Case of Intellectual Sexism." *American Journal of Sociology* 78, no. 4 (January 1973): 936–945.

Ammerman, Nancy. *Baptist Battles: Social Change and Religious Conflict in the Southern Baptist Convention.* New Brunswick, NJ: Rutgers University Press, 1990.

Ammerman, Nancy. *Bible Believers: Fundamentalists in the Modern World.* New Brunswick, NJ: Rutgers University Press, 1993.

Bailey, Sarah Pulliam. "Megapastor Mark Driscoll's Books Pulled from Major Christian Store in Wake of Scandal." *Huffington Post.* August 11, 2014. http://www.huffingtonpost.com/2014/08/11/mark-driscoll-books-lifeway_n_5669700.html.

Bailey, Sarah Pulliam. "Mark Driscoll to Step Down While Mars Hill Reviews Charges." *Religion News Service.* August 24, 2014. http://religionnews.com/2014/08/24/mark-driscoll-step-down-mars-hill-elders-review-charges/.

Bailey, Sarah Pulliam. "Exclusive: Mark Driscoll's Resignation Letter from Mars Hill Church." *Religion News Service.* October 15, 2014. http://religionnews.com/2014/10/15/ exclusive-mark-driscolls-resignation-letter-to-mars-hill-church/.

Bailey, Sarah Pulliam. "How the 'Cussin' Pastor' Got into Megatrouble." *Wall Street Journal.* November 13, 2014. http://www.wsj.com/articles/sarah-pulliam-bailey-how-the-cussin-pastor-got-into-megatrouble-1415924941.

Baker, Joseph O. "Social Sources of the Spirit: Connecting Rational Choice and Interactive Ritual Theories in the Study of Religion." *Sociology of Religion* 71, no. 4 (Winter 2010): 432–456.

Baker, Joseph O., and Andrew L. Whitehead. "God's Penology: Belief in a Masculine God Predicts Support for Harsh Criminal Punishment and Militarism." *Punishment and Society* 22, no. 2 (April 2020): 135–160.

Barlass, Tim, and Kate Aubusson. "Keep Out US Pastor Mark Driscoll, Hillsong Warned." *Sydney Morning Herald.* June 7, 2015. http://www.smh.com.au/action/printArticle?id=996959510.

Barnett, Erica C. "Cross Purposes." *Seattle Weekly.* May 4, 2006. http://www.thestranger.com/seattle/cross-purposes/Content?oid=32140.

Barr, Beth Allison. *The Making of Biblical Womanhood: How the Subjugation of Women Became Gospel Truth.* Grand Rapids, MI: Brazos Press, 2021.

Bartkowski, John P. *Remaking the Godly Marriage: Gender Negotiation in Evangelical Families.* New Brunswick, NJ: Rutgers University Press, 2001.

Bartkowski, John P. *The Promise Keepers: Servants, Soldiers, and Godly Men.* New Brunswick, NJ: Rutgers University Press, 2004.

Beaver, R. Pierce. *American Protestant Women in World Mission.* Grand Rapids, MI: Eerdmans Press, 1980.

Bederman, Gail. "'The Women Have Had Charge of the Church Work Long Enough': The Men and Religion Forward Movement of 1911–1912 and the Masculinization of Middle-Class Protestantism." *American Quarterly* 41, no. 3 (September 1989): 432–465.

Bem, Sandra L. *The Lenses of Gender: Transforming the Debate on Sexual Inequality.* New Haven, CT: Yale University Press, 1993.

Bendroth, Margaret Lambert. *Fundamentalism and Gender 1875 to the Present.* New Haven, CT: Yale University Press, 1992.

Bendroth, Margaret Lambert. *Growing Up Protestant.* New Brunswick, NJ: Rutgers University Press, 2002.

Bielo, James S. "Act Like Men: Social Engagement and Evangelical Masculinity." *Journal of Contemporary Religion* 29, no. 2 (2014): 233–248.

Bird, Warren, and Scott Thumma. *Megachurch 2020: The Changing Reality in America's Largest Churches.* Hartford, CT: Hartford Institute for Religion Research, 2020. https://faithcommunitiestoday.org/wp-content/uploads/2020/10/Megachurch-Survey-Report_HIRR_FACT-2020.pdf.

Brasher, Brenda E. *Godly Women: Fundamentalism and Female Power.* New Brunswick, NJ: Rutgers University Press, 1998.

Brekus, Catherine A. "Female Preaching in Early Nineteenth-Century America." In *Women and the Church*, edited by Robert B. Kruschwitz, 20–29. Waco, TX: The Center for Christian Ethics at Baylor University, 2009.

Bridges, Tristan, and C. J. Pascoe. "Hybrid Masculinities: New Directions in the Sociology of Men and Masculinity." *Sociological Compass* 8, no. 3 (March 2014): 246–258.

Brines, Julie. "Economic Dependency, Gender, and the Division of Labor at Home." *American Journal of Sociology* 100, no. 3 (November 1994): 652–688.

Carrigan, Tim, Raewyn Connell, and John Lee. "Toward a New Sociology of Masculinity." *Theory and Society* 14, no. 5 (September 1985): 551–604.

Cassese, Erin C., and Mirya R. Holman. "Religion, Gendered Authority, and Identity in American Politics." *Religion and Politics* 10, no. 1 (March 2017): 31–56.

Causey, Adam Kealoha. "To Some, Trump's 'Bad Hombres' Is Much More Than a Botched Spanish Word." *PBS News Hour.* October 20, 2015. https://www.pbs.org/newshour/politics/trumps-bad-hombres-draws-jeers-spanish-lessons.

Chaves, Mark. "All Creatures Great and Small: Megachurches in Context." *Review of Religious Research* 47, no. 4 (June 2006): 329–346.

Cherlin, Andrew J. *The Marriage-Go-Round: The State of Marriage and the Family in America.* New York: Vintage Books, 2010.

Christianity Today. "Avatar: 'The Most Satanic Film I've Ever Seen.'" February 26, 2020. https://www.christianitytoday.com/news/2010/february/avatar-most-satanic-film-ive-ever-seen.html.

Church Leaders. "John MacArthur: Mark Driscoll Paved the Way for Donald Trump." March 23, 2016. http://churchleaders.com/daily-buzz/276029-john-mcarthur-mark-driscoll-paved-way-donald-trump.html.

Clapp, Rodney. *Families at the Crossroads: Beyond Traditional and Modern Options.* Downers Grove, IL: InterVarsity Press, 1993.

Connell, Raewyn. "A Very Straight Gay: Masculinity, Homosexual Experience, and the Dynamics of Gender." *American Sociological Review* 57, no. 6 (December 1992): 735–751.

Connell, Raewyn. *Masculinities.* Berkeley: University of California Press, 2005.

Connelly, Joel. "A Big, Planned Mars Hill 'Jesus Festival' Disappears without a Trace." *Seattle Post-Intelligencer.* August 19, 2014. http://blog.seattlepi.com/seattlepolitics/2014/08/19/a-big-planned-mars-hill-jesus-festival-disappears-without-a-trace/.

Connelly, Joel. "Dozens Protest Mars Hill Church after Leader Resignations and Mark Driscoll Apology." *Seattle Post-Intelligencer.* August 3, 2014. http://blog.seattlepi.com/seattlepolitics/2014/08/03/mars-hill-church-protest-mars-hill-resignations-mark-driscoll-apology/.

Connelly, Joel. "Mark Driscoll Returns Sunday; Churchgoers Told to Bring Bibles." *Seattle Post-Intelligencer.* August 20, 2014. http://blog.seattlepi.com/seattlepolit ics/2014/08/20/mark-driscoll-returns-sunday-mars-hill-churchgoers-told-bring-Bibles/.

Connelly, Joel. "21 Former Mars Hill Pastors Lodge Formal Charges against Mark Driscoll." *Seattle Post-Intelligencer.* August 21, 2014. http://blog.seattlepi.com/seat tlepolitics/2014/08/21/21-former-mars-hill-pastors-lodge-formal-charges-against-driscoll/.

Constant, Paul. "Well, That Didn't Take Long: Mark Driscoll's Comeback Tour Began Last Night." *The Stranger.* October 21, 2014. http://slog.thestranger.com/slog/archives/2014/10/21/well-that-didn't-take-long-Mark-driscolls-comeback-tour-began-last-night.

Coontz, Stephanie. *The Way We Never Were: American Families and the Nostalgia Trap.* New York: Basic Books, 1992.

Coontz, Stephanie. *The Way We Really Are: Coming to Terms with America's Changing Families.* New York: Basic Books, 1997.

Coontz, Stephanie. *Marriage, a History: From Obedience to Intimacy; or, How Love Conquered Marriage.* New York: Viking, 2005.

Corcoran, Katie E., and James K. Wellman Jr. "'People Forget He's Human': Charismatic Leadership in Institutionalized Religion." *Sociology of Religion* 77, no. 4 (Winter 2016): 309–333.

Corprew, Charles S., III, Jamaal S. Matthews, and Avery DeVell Mitchell. "Men at the Crossroads: A Profile Analysis of Hypermasculinity in Emerging Adulthood." *Journal of Men's Studies* 22, no. 2 (Spring 2014): 105–121.

Crockett, Emily. "Why Misogyny Won." *Vox.* November 15, 2016. https://www.vox.com/identities/2016/11/15/13571478/trump-president-sexual-assault-sexism-misog yny-won.

Davidman, Lynn. *Tradition in a Rootless World: Women Turn to Orthodox Judaism.* Berkeley: University of California Press, 1991.

Dawson, Lorne. "Crises of Charismatic Legitimacy and Violent Behavior in New Religious Movements." In *Cults, Religion and Violence,* edited by David G. Bromley and J. Gordon Melton, 80–101. Cambridge: Cambridge University Press, 2002.

DeBurg, Betty A. *Ungodly Women: Gender and the First Wave of American Fundamentalism.* Minneapolis, MN: Fortress Press, 1990.

Denton, Melinda L. "Gender and Marital Decision Making: Negotiating Religious Ideology and Practice." *Social Forces* 82, no. 3 (March 2004): 1151–1180.

Diefendorf, Sarah. "Contemporary Evangelical Responses to Feminism and the Imagined Secular." *Signs: Journal of Women in Culture and Society* 44, no. 4 (Summer 2019): 1003–1026.

Dignam, Pierce Alexander, and Deana A. Rohlinger. "Misogynistic Men Online: How the Red Pill Helped Elect Donald Trump." *Signs: Journal of Women in Culture and Society* 44, no. 3 (Spring 2019): 589–612.

Dowland, Seth. *Family Values and the Rise of the Christian Right.* Philadelphia: University of Pennsylvania Press, 2015.

Drescher, Elizabeth. "Mars Hill Defectors Refuse to Be Anonymous." *Medium: The Narthex* July 27, 2014. https://medium.com/the-narthex/mars-hill-defectors-refuse-to-be-anonymous-dec1013eda7#:~:text=A%20group%20of%20former%20members,experiences%20that%20they%20say%20drove.

Driscoll, Mark. *Confessions of a Reformission Rev.: Hard Lessons from an Emerging Missional Church.* Grand Rapids, MI: Zondervan, 2006.

Driscoll, Mark. *On Church Leadership.* Wheaton, IL: Crossway Books, 2008.

Driscoll, Mark, and Grace Driscoll. *Real Marriage: The Truth about Sex, Friendship and Life Together.* Nashville, TN: Thomas Nelson, 2012.

Du Mez, Kristin Kobes. "Donald Trump and Militant Evangelical Masculinity." *Religion and Politics.* January 17, 2017. http://religionandpolitics.org/2017/01/17/donald-trump-and-militant-evangelical-masculinity/.

Du Mez, Kristin Kobes. *Jesus and John Wayne: How Evangelicals Corrupted a Faith and Fractured a Nation.* New York: Liveright, 2020.

Eagle, David E. "Historicizing the Megachurch." *Journal of Social History* 48, no. 3 (Spring 2015): 589–604.

Eldredge, John. *Wild at Heart: Discovering the Secret of a Man's Soul.* Nashville, TN: Thomas Nelson, 2001.

Eldredge, John, and Stasi Eldredge. *Captivating: Unveiling the Mystery of a Woman's Soul.* Nashville, TN: Thomas Nelson, 2005.

Elliott, Elisabeth. "The Essence of Femininity: A Personal Perspective." In *Recovering Biblical Manhood and Womanhood: A Response to Evangelical Feminism*, edited by John Piper and Wayne Grudem, 400–404. Wheaton, IL: Crossway, 1991.

Finke, Roger, Matt Bahr, and Christopher P. Scheitle. "Toward Explaining Congregational Giving." *Social Science Research* 35, no. 3 (September 2006): 620–641.

Finke, Roger, and Rodney Stark. *The Churching of America, 1776–2005: Winners and Losers in Our Religious Economy.* New Brunswick, NJ: Rutgers University Press, 2005.

Fitzgerald, Frances. *The Evangelicals: The Struggle to Shape America.* New York: Simon & Schuster, 2017.

Frost, Natasha. "Founder of Australia's Hillsong Church Resigns amid Scandals." *New York Times.* March 23, 2022. https://www.nytimes.com/2022/03/23/world/australia/brian-houston-hillsong-resign.html.

Gallagher, Sally K. *Evangelical Identity and Gendered Family Life.* New Brunswick, NJ: Rutgers University Press, 2003.

Gallagher, Sally K. "The Marginalization of Evangelical Feminism." *Sociology of Religion* 65, no. 3 (Autumn 2004): 215–237.

Gallagher, Sally K., and Christian Smith. "Symbolic Traditionalism and Pragmatic Egalitarianism: Contemporary Evangelicals, Families, and Gender." *Gender and Society* 13, no. 2 (April 1999): 211–233.

Gallagher, Sally K., and Sabrina L. Wood. "Godly Manhood Going Wild?: Transformations in Conservative Protestant Masculinity." *Sociology of Religion* 66, no. 2 (Summer 2005): 135–160.

Glaser, Barney G., and Anselm L. Strauss. *The Discovery of Grounded Theory.* Chicago: Aldine de Gruyter, 1967.

Golden, Shelley D., Krista M. Perreira, and Christine Piette Durrance. "Troubled Times, Troubled Relationships: How Economic Resources, Gender Beliefs, and Neighborhood Disadvantage Influence Intimate Partner Violence." *Journal of Interpersonal Violence* 28, no. 10 (July 2013): 2134–2155.

Gray, Rosie. "Trump Defends White Nationalist Protesters: 'Some Very Fine People on Both Sides.'" *The Atlantic*. August 15, 2017. https://www.theatlantic.com/politics/arch ive/2017/08/trump-defends-white-nationalist-protesters-some-very-fine-people-on-both-sides/537012/.

Green, Emma. "Why White Evangelicals Are Feeling Hopeful about Trump." *The Atlantic*. December 1, 2016. https://www.theatlantic.com/politics/archive/2016/12/trump-white-evangelicals-communities/509084/.

Green, Emma. "Franklin Graham Is the Evangelical Id." *The Atlantic*. May 21, 2017. https://www.theatlantic.com/politics/archive/2017/05/franklin-graham/527013/.

Griffith, R. Marie. *God's Daughters: Evangelical Women and the Power of Submission*. Berkeley: University of California Press, 1997.

Griffith, R. Marie. *Moral Combat: How Sex Divided American Christians and Fractured American Politics*. New York: Basic Books, 2017.

Hansen, Collin. "Pastor Provocateur." *Christianity Today*. June 3, 2007. http://www.christ ianitytoday.com/ct/channel/utilities/print.html?type=article&id=50001.

Hansen, Collin. *Young, Restless, and Reformed: A Journalist's Journey with the New Calvinism*. Wheaton, IL: Crossway Books, 2008.

Hartford Institute for Religion Research. "Megachurch Definition." Accessed February 13, 2022. http://hirr.hartsem.edu/megachurch/definition.html.

Hatch, Nathan O. *The Democratization of American Christianity*. New Haven, CT: Yale University Press, 1987.

Hechter, Michael. *Principles of Group Solidarity*. Berkeley: University of California Press, 1987.

Hill, Patricia R. *The World Their Household: The American Women's Foreign Mission Movement and Cultural Transformation*. Ann Arbor: University of Michigan Press, 1985.

Hinson, Keith. "Motions: GCR Task Force Endorsed." *Baptist Press*. June 25, 2009. http:// bpnews.net/bpnews.asp?id=30774.

Hochschild, Arlie. *Strangers in Their Own Land: Anger and Mourning on the American Right*. New York: New Press, 2016.

Homan, Patricia, and Amy Burdette. "When Religion Hurts: Structural Sexism and Health in Religious Congregations." *American Sociological Review* 86, no. 2 (April 2021): 234–255.

Hoover, Stewart M., and Curtis D. Coats. *Does God Make the Man? Media, Religion, and the Crisis of Masculinity*. New York: New York University Press, 2015.

Iannaccone, Laurence R. "A Formal Model of Church and Sect." *American Journal of Sociology* 94 (Supplement 1988): S241–S268.

Iannaccone, Laurence R. "Why Strict Churches Are Strong." *American Journal of Sociology* 99, no. 5 (March 1994): 1180–1211.

Ingersoll, Julie. *Evangelical Christian Women: War Stories in the Gender Battles*. New York: New York University Press, 2003.

Jacobs, Janet. "The Economy of Love in Religious Commitment: The Deconversion of Women from Nontraditional Religious Movements." *Journal for the Scientific Study of Religion* 23, no. 2 (1984): 155–171.

Jankowski, Peter J., Steven J. Sandage, Miriam Whitney Cornell, Cheryl Bissonette, Andy J. Johnson, Sarah A. Crabtree, and Mary L. Jensen. "Religious Beliefs and Domestic Violence Myths." *Psychology of Religion and Spirituality* 10, no. 4 (2018): 386–397.

Jenkins, Jack. "How Evangelicals Are Protesting the 'Rush Limbaugh of Christianity.'" *Think Progress.* August 5, 2014. http://thinkprogress.org/lgbt/2014/08/05/3467250/mark-driscoll-protest/.

Jenkins, Jack. "For Insurrectionists, a Violent Faith Brewed from Nationalism, Conspiracies and Jesus." *Religion News Service.* January 12, 2021. https://religionnews.com/2021/01/12/the-faith-of-the-insurrectionists/.

Johnson, Benton. "A Critical Appraisal of the Church-Sect Typology." *American Sociological Review* 22, no. 1 (February 1957): 88–92.

Johnson, Benton. "Church and Sect Revisited." *Journal for the Scientific Study of Religion* 10, no. 2 (Summer 1971): 124–137.

Johnson, Benton. "On Church and Sect." *American Sociological Review* 28, no. 4 (August 1963): 539–549.

Johnson, Jessica. "How Mega-Macho Pastor Mark Driscoll Helps Explain Trump's Evangelical Support." *Religion Dispatches.* March 8, 2016. http://religiondispatches.org/how-mega-macho-pastor-mark-driscoll-helps-explain-trumps-evangelical-support/.

Johnson, Jessica. "Megachurches, Celebrity Pastors, and the Evangelical Industrial Complex." In *Religion and Popular Culture in America*, 3rd ed., edited by Bruce Forbes and Jeffrey Mahan, 159–176. Berkeley: University of California Press, 2017.

Johnson, Jessica. *Biblical Porn: Affect, Labor, and Pastor Mark Driscoll's Evangelical Empire.* Durham, NC: Duke University Press, 2018.

Jones, Robert P. *White Too Long.* New York: Simon & Schuster Paperbacks, 2020.

Juster, Susan. *Disorderly Women: Sexual Politics and Evangelicalism in Revolutionary New England.* Ithaca, NY: Cornell University Press, 1994.

Kelley, Dean M. *Why Conservative Churches Are Growing.* Macon, GA: Mercer University Press, 1972.

Suzanne Kelly, Gowri Parameswaran, and Nancy Schniedewind. *Women: Images and Realities* New York: McGraw-Hill, 2012.

Kilgore, Ed. "Evangelicals Looking to Trump to Make America Manly Again." *New York Magazine.* December 2, 2016. http://nymag.com/daily/intelligencer/2016/12/evangelicals-looking-to-trump-to-make-america-manly-again.html.

Kimmel, Michael. *Manhood in America: A Cultural History.* New York: Oxford University Press, 2012.

Kimmel, Michael. *Healing from Hate: How Young Men Get into—and Out of—Violent Extremism.* Berkeley: University of California Press, 2018.

King, Marsha. "Pastor's Apology Diffuses Protest at Church." *Seattle Times.* December 4, 2006. http://www.seattletimes.com/seattle-news/pastors-apology-defuses-demonstration-at-church/.

Klett, Leah MariAnn. "John MacArthur Clarifies Views on Beth Moore, Women Preachers: 'Empowering Women Makes Weak Men.'" *The Christian Post.* November 13, 2019. https://www.christianpost.com/news/john-macarthur-clarifies-views-on-beth-moore-women-preachers-empowering-women-makes-weak-men.html.

Knudsen, Dean D., John R. Earle, and Donald W. Shriver Jr. "The Conception of Sectarian Religion: An Effort at Clarification." *Review of Religious Research* 20, no. 1 (Autumn 1978): 44–60.

Landry, Bart. *Black Working Wives: Pioneers of the American Family Revolution.* Berkeley: University of California Press, 2000.

Larsen, Timothy. "Evangelicalism's Strong History of Women in Ministry." *Reformed Journal* 5, no. 32 (September/October 2017). https://reformedjournal.com/evangelicalisms-strong-history-women-ministry/.

Lee, Michelle Yee Hee. "Donald Trump's False Comments Connecting Mexican Immigrants and Crime." *Washington Post.* July 8, 2015. https://www.washingtonpost.com/news/fact-checker/wp/2015/07/08/donald-trumps-false-comments-connecting-mexican-immigrants-and-crime/.

Lee, Morgan. "The Story of Mark Driscoll and Mars Hill Matter in 2021." Podcast, *Quick to Listen* Episode 270, 1 hour, https://www.christianitytoday.com/ct/podcasts/quick-to-listen/rise-fall-mars-hill-mark-driscoll-podcast.html.

Leibovitch, Lori. "Generation: A Look inside Fundamentalism's Answer to MTV; the Postmodern Church." *Mother Jones.* July 1, 1998. http://www.motherjones.com/politics/1998/07/generation.

Lobody, Diane H. "'That Language Might Be Given Me': Women's Experience in Early Methodism." In *Perspectives on American Methodism: Interpretive Essays*, edited by Russell E. Richey, Kenneth E. Rowe, and Jean Miller Schmidt, 127–144. Nashville, TN: Kingswood Books, 1993.

Lockhart, William. "'We Are One Life,' But Not of One Gender Ideology: Unity, Ambiguity, and the Promise Keepers." *Sociology of Religion* 61, no. 1 (Spring 2000): 73–92.

MacKenzie, Alicia. "Mark Driscoll 'Crashes' John MacArthur's Strange Fire Conference?" *The Christian Post.* October 18, 2013. http://www.christianpost.com/buzzvine/mark-driscoll-crashes-john-macarthurs-strange-fire-conference-photos-106976/.

Mars Hill Church. *This Is Mars Hill: 2010 Annual Church Report.* Accessed October 1, 2014. http://marshill.com/2011/02/20110130_mars-hill-church-annual-report-fy10_document.pdf.

Mars Hill Church. "A Response Regarding Church Discipline." February 13, 2012. http://marshill.com/2012/02/13/a-response-regarding-church-discipline.

Mars Hill Church. *It's All about Jesus: 2013 Annual Church Report.* Accessed October 1, 2014. http://www.marshillchurch.org/media/mars-hill-quarterly/mars-hill-church-annual-report-fy13.

Mars Hill Church. *The Story of Mars Hill Church.* Accessed December 2, 2014. http://marshill.com.

Marti, Gerardo. *American Blindspot: Race, Class, Religion, and the Trump Presidency.* New York: Rowman & Littlefield, 2020.

Martin, Patricia Yancy. "Gender as Social Institution." *Social Forces* 82, no. 4 (June 2004): 1249–1273.

McKinney, Jennifer. "Sects and Gender: Resistance and Reaction to Cultural Change." *Priscilla Papers* 29, no. 4 (Autumn 2015): 15–25.

McKinney, Jennifer, and Kevin Neuhouser. 2013. "Divided by Gender: How Sociology Can Help." *Cultural Encounters* 9, no. 1 (Winter 2013): 38–55.

Meeks, Gina. "Mark Driscoll Angers Twitterverse with Tweet about Hell." *Charisma News.* January 15, 2014. https://www.charismanews.com/us/42428-mark-driscoll-angers-twitterverse-with-tweet-about-hell.

Merritt, Jonathan. "Mark Driscoll Accused of Plagiarism by Radio Host." *Religion News Service.* November 22, 2013. https://religionnews.com/2013/11/22/mark-driscoll-accused-plagiarism-radio-host/.

Messerschmidt, James W. *Hegemonic Masculinity: Formulation, Reformulation, and Amplification.* New York: Rowman & Littlefield, 2018.

Messner, Michael A. *Politics of Masculinities: Men in Movements*. Thousand Oaks, CA: Sage Publications, 1997.

Miller, Donald. *Blue Like Jazz: Non-religious Thoughts on Christian Spirituality*. Nashville, TN: Thomas Nelson, 2003.

Miller, Sharon Hodde. "Much Ado about Mark Driscoll." *Christianity Today*, Her. Meneutics. July 15, 2011. https://www.christianitytoday.com/ct/2011/julyweb-only/much-ado-about-mark-driscoll.html.

Molinet, Jason. "Church Reeling after Founding Pastor Calls Women 'Penis Homes.'" *New York Daily News*. September 10, 2014. http://www.nydailynews.com/news/natio nal/ church-reeling-pastor-calls-women-penis-homes-article-1.1934308.

Moslener, Sara. *Virgin Nation: Sexual Purity and American Adolescence*. New York: Oxford University Press, 2015.

Nason-Clark, Nancy. "When Terror Strikes Home: The Interface between Religion and Domestic Violence." *Journal for the Scientific Study of Religion* 43, no. 3 (2004): 303–310.

Nason-Clark, Nancy, Barbara Fisher-Townsend, Catherine Holtmann, and Stephen McMullin. *Religion and Intimate Partner Violence: Understanding the Challenges and Proposing Solutions*. New York: Oxford University Press, 2017.

Niebuhr, H. Richard. *The Social Sources of Denominationalism*. New York: Holt, 1987 [1929].

Neuhouser, Kevin. "Strict, but Not (Gender) Conservative: Revising the Strict Church Thesis in Light of Brazilian Pentecostalism." *Interdisciplinary Journal of Research on Religion* 13, no. 8 (2017): 1–28.

O'Brien, Brandon. "A Jesus for Real Men: What the New Masculinity Movement Gets Right and Wrong." *Christianity Today*. April 18, 2008. https://www.christianitytoday.com/ct/2008/april/27.48.html.

Oliphint, Jared. "John Piper's Twelve Features for the New Calvinism." *Reformed Forum*. March 17, 2014. https://reformedforum.org/john-pipers-twelve-features-new-calvinism/.

Olson, Mancur. *The Logic of Collective Action: Public Goods and the Theory of Groups*. Cambridge, MA: Harvard University Press, 1998 [1971].

Oppenheimer, Mark. "Evangelicals Find Themselves in the Midst of a Calvinist Revival." *New York Times*. January 3, 2014. http://www.nytimes.com/2014/01/04/us/a-calvinist-revival-for-evangelicals.html.

Palmer, Phoebe. *The Promise of the Father*. New York: Garland, 1985 [1859].

Paulson, Michael. "Facing Ire, Mark Driscoll Says He Will Take a Leave." *New York Times*. August 24, 2014. http://www.nytimes.com/2014/08/25/us/facing-ire-mark-driscoll-says-he-will-take-a-leave.html?_r=0.

Paybarah, Azi. "Missouri Pastor Who Sermonized That Women Must Look Good for Their Husbands Goes on Leave." *New York Times*. March 8, 2021. www.nytimes.com/2021/03/08/us/stewart-allen-clark-pastor-melania-trump.html.

Perry, Samuel L. "The Bible as a Product of Cultural Power: That Case of Gender Ideology in the English Standard Version." *Sociology of Religion* 81, no. 1 (Spring 2020): 68–92.

Pasco, C. J. *Dude, You're a Fag: Masculinity and Sexuality in High School*. Berkeley: University of California Press, 2007.

Porter, Kevin. "Protesters Cast a Shadow over Mark Driscoll's Trinity Church Open House." *Christian Post*. March 31, 2016. http://www.christianpost.com/news/mark-driscolls-trinity-church-open-house-overshadowed-by-protests-160602/.

Posner, Sarah. "Amazing Disgrace." *New Republic*. March 20, 2017. https://newrepublic. com/article/140961/amazing-disgrace-donald-trump-hijacked-religious-right.

PRRI. *Dueling Realities amid Multiple Crises, Trump and Biden Supporters See Different Priorities and Futures for the Nation: Findings from the 2020 American Values Survey* Washington, DC: PRRI, 2020.

PRRI. *Competing Visions of America: An Evolving Identity or a Culture under Attack? Findings from the 2021 American Values Survey.* Washington, DC: PRRI, 2021.

Putney, Clifford. *Muscular Christianity: Manhood and Sports in Protestant America 1880–1920.* Cambridge, MA: Harvard University Press, 2001.

Regnerus, Mark. *Forbidden Fruit: Sex and Religion in the Lives of American Teenagers.* New York: Oxford University Press, 2007.

Ridgeway, Cecilia. "A Painful Lesson in Why We Have to Take Status Seriously." *Speak for Sociology.* December 22, 2016. http://speak4sociology.org/2016/12/22/a-painful-les son-in-why-we-have-to-take-status-seriously/.

Ridgeway, Cecilia L., and Shelley J. Correll. "Unpacking the Gender System: A Theoretical Perspective in Gender Beliefs and Social Relations." *Gender and Society* 18, no. 4 (August 2004): 510–531.

Rios, Victor M. "The Consequences of the Criminal Justice Pipeline on Black and Latino Masculinity." *Annals of the American Academy of Political and Social Science* 623, (May 2009): 150–162.

Risman, Barbara. "Gender as a Social Structure: Theory Wrestling with Activism." *Gender and Society* 18, no. 4 (August 2004): 429–450.

Rotundo, E. Anthony. *American Manhood: Transformations in Masculinity from the Revolution to the Modern Era.* New York: Basic Books, 1993.

Rucker, Philip. "Trump Says Megyn Kelly Had 'Blood Coming Out of Her Whatever.'" *Washington Post.* April 8, 2015. https://www.washingtonpost.com/news/post-polit ics/wp/2015/08/07/trump-says-foxs-megyn-kelly-had-blood-coming-out-of-her-wherever/.

Rusch, William G. *The Trinitarian Controversy.* Minneapolis: Fortress Press, 1980.

Sandler, Lauren. *Righteous: Dispatches from the Evangelical Youth Movement.* New York: Viking Press, 2006.

Schiller Lauren. "What White Supremacists and Incels Have in Common: Blaming Feminism." *Salon.* October 27, 2019. https://www.salon.com/2019/10/27/what-white-nationalists-and-incels-have-in-common-blaming-feminism/.

Schnable, Landon, and Sean Block. "The Persistent and Exceptional History of American Religion: A Response to Recent Research." *Sociological Science* 4 (November 2017): 686–700.

Schreckenger, Ben. "Trump Attacks McCain: 'I Like People Who Weren't Captured.'" *Politico.* July 18, 2015. https://www.politico.com/story/2015/07/trump-attacks-mcc ain-i-like-people-who-werent-captured-120317.

Schrock, Douglas, and Michael Schwalbe. "Man, Masculinity and Manhood Acts." *Annual Review of Sociology* 35, no. 1 (August 2009): 277–295.

Seattle Post-Intelligencer. "Mars Hill Pastor Responds to Uproar over Blog Post on Women." December 4, 2006. http://seattlepi.nwsource.com/local/294572_marshil l04.html.

Shapiro, Nina. "Evangelical Leaders Give Fallen Mars Hill Pastor Mark Driscoll a New Forum." *Seattle Times.* May 30, 2015. http://www.seattletimes.com/seattle-news/evan gelical-leaders-give-fallen-mars-hill-pastor-mark-driscoll-a-new-forum/.

Shapiro, Nina. "Australian Megachurch Pulls Invitation to Ex–Mars Hill Leader." *Seattle Times.* June 8, 2015. https://www.seattletimes.com/seattle-news/australian-megachurch-pulls-invitation-to-ex-mars-hill-leader/.

Shapiro, Nina. "Racketeering Suit Claims Mark Driscoll Misused Mars Hill Donor Dollars." *Seattle Times.* February 29, 2016. http://www.seattletimes.com/seattle-news/mark-driscoll-accused-of-racketeering-at-mars-hill-church/.

Smidt, Jen. "Complementarian Relationships in Marriage." In Mars Hill Church, *This Is Mars Hill: 2010 Annual Church Report.* Accessed October 1, 2014. http://marshill.com/2011/02/20110130_mars-hill-church-annual-report-fy10_document.pdf.

Smith, Christian. *American Evangelicalism: Embattled and Thriving.* Chicago: University of Chicago Press, 1998.

Smith, Warren Cole. "More Publishers Investigate Mark Driscoll." *World Magazine.* January 2, 2014. http://www.worldmag.com/2014/01/more_publishers_investigate_driscoll.

Smith, Warren Cole, and Sophia Lee. "Changing Course?" *World Magazine.* July 25, 2014. http://www.worldmag.com/2014/07/changing_course.

Solie Stacey. "Inside Mars Hill's Massive Meltdown." *Crosscut.* July 16, 2014. http://crosscut.com/2014/07/inside-mars-hills-big-meltdown/.

Stacey, Judith. *Brave New Families: Stories of Domestic Upheaval in Late-Twentieth Century America.* Berkeley: University of California Press, 1990.

Stark, Rodney. *The Rise of Christianity.* San Francisco: HarperSanFrancisco, 1997.

Stark, Rodney, and William Sims Bainbridge. *The Future of Religion: Secularization, Revival, and Cult Formation.* Berkeley: University of California Press, 1985.

Stark, Rodney, and Roger Finke. *Acts of Faith: Explaining the Human Side of Religion.* Berkeley: University of California Press, 2000.

Stasson, Anneke. "The Politization of Family Life: How Headship Became Essential to Evangelical Identity in the Late Twentieth Century." *Religion and American Culture: A Journal of Interpretation* 24, no. 1 (Winter 2014): 100–138.

Strauss, Anselm, and Juliet Corbin. *Basics of Qualitative Research: Grounded Theory Procedures and Techniques.* Newbury Park: SAGE Publications, 1990.

Sutton, Matthew Avery. *American Apocalypse: A History of Modern Evangelicalism.* Cambridge, MA: Belknap Press of Harvard University Press, 2014.

Tavris, Carol. "The Mismeasure of Woman." *Feminism and Psychology* 3, no. 2 (1993): 149–168.

The Associated Press. "Robertson Letter Attacks Feminists." *New York Times.* August 26, 1992. https://www.nytimes.com/1992/08/26/us/robertson-letter-attacks-feminists.html.

The Associated Press. "Southern Baptist Convention Passes Resolution Opposing Women as Pastors." *New York Times.* June 15, 2000. http://www.nytimes.com/2000/06/15/us/southern-baptist-convention-passes-resolution-opposing-women-as-pastors.html.

Church Report. 2006. "The Church Report's 50 Most Influential Churches for 2006." *The Church Report Magazine.* July 11, 2006. http://churchrelevance.com/2006/07/11/the-church-reports-50-most-influential-churches-for-2006/The 50 Most Influential Churches for 2006.

New York Times. "Transcript: Donald Trump's Taped Comments about Women." October 8, 2016. https://www.nytimes.com/2016/10/08/us/donald-trump-tape-transcript.html.

New York Times. "Atlanta Shootings Live Updates: Suspect Had Visited Targeted Spas Before, Police Say." March 18, 2021. https://www.nytimes.com/live/2021/03/18/us/atla nta-shootings-massage-spa.

Thomas, Jeremy N., and Daniel V. A. Olson. "Testing the Strictness Thesis and Competing Theories of Congregational Growth." *Journal for the Scientific Study of Religion* 49, no. 4 (December 2010): 619–639.

Tracy, Kate. "Publisher: Mark Driscoll Improperly Copied Paragraphs from Bible Commentary." *Christianity Today.* December 9, 2013. https://www.christianitytoday. com/news/2013/december/parsing-mark-driscoll-plagiarism-janet-mefferd-apologi zes.html.

Troeltsch, Ernst. *The Social Teachings of the Christian Churches, Vol. II.* Louisville, KY: Westminster John Knox Press, 1992 [1912].

Tu, Janet I. "Pastor Mark Packs 'Em In." *Pacific Northwest Magazine.* November 28, 2003. http://community.seattletimes.nwsource.com/archive/?date=20031128&slug = pacific-preacher30.

Tu, Janet I. "Yoga 'Demonic'? Critics Call Ministers' Warning a Stretch." October 8, 2010. https://www.seattletimes.com/seattle-news/yoga-demonic-critics-call-minist ers-warning-a-stretch/#:~:text=%E2%80%9CShould%20Christians%20stay%20a way%20from,for%20a%20little%20demon%20class.%E2%80%9D.

Turner, Laura. "Mark Driscoll Rises from the Ashes in Phoenix." *Religion News Service.* February 5, 2016. http://religionnews.com/2016/02/05/mark-driscoll-rises-ashes-phoenix-commentary/.

Van Biema, David. "Ten Ideas Changing the World Right Now: The New Calvinism." *Time Magazine.* March 12, 2009. http://content.time.com/time/specials/packages/ article/ 0,28804,1884779_1884782_1884760,00.html.

Vedder, Tracy. "Ex-Members Say Mars Hill 'Shuns' to Punish Sinners." March 1, 2012. *Seattle Post-Intelligencer.* http://www.seattlepi.com/local/komo/article/Ex-members-say-mars-hill-shuns-to-punish-sinners.

Vescio, Theresa K., and Nathaniel E. C. Schermerhorn. "Hegemonic Masculinity Predicts 2016 and 2020 Voting and Candidate Evaluations." *PNAS* 118, no. 2 (January 2021), e2020589118 https://doi.org/10.1073/pnas.2020589118.

Vitali, Ali, Kasie Hunt, and Frank Thorp, V. "Trump Referred to Haiti and African Nations as 'Shithole' Countries." *NBC News.* January 11, 2018. https://www.nbcnews.com/polit ics/white-house/trump-referred-haiti-african-countries-shithole-nations-n836946.

Walters, Greg. "Atlanta Shooting Suspect's Church Bashed 'Radical Feminism' in Deleted Sermons." *Vice.* March 19, 2021. https://www.vice.com/en/article/n7vxpd/atlanta-shooting-suspects-church-bashed-radical-feminism-in-deleted-sermons.

Watkins, Eli. "Trump: Taking Down Confederate Memorials Is 'Changing History.'" *CNN Politics.* August 17, 2017. https://edition.cnn.com/2017/08/15/politics/donald-trump-robert-e-lee/index.html.

Weber, Jeremy. "Mark Driscoll Retracts Bestseller Book Status, Resets Life." *Christianity Today.* March 17, 2014. https://www.christianitytoday.com/news/2014/march/mark-driscoll-retracts-bestseller-status-resets-life.html.

Weber, Max. *From Max Weber: Essays in Sociology.* Edited by H. H. Gerth and C. Wright Mills. New York: Oxford University Press, 1958 [1913].

Weber, Max. *Economy and Society, Volume I.* Edited by Guenther Roth and Claus Wittich. Berkeley: University of California Press, [1922] 1978.

Weber, Max. *The Theory of Social and Economic Organization*, translated by A. M. Henderson and Talcott Parsons. New York: Free Press, 1964.

Wehner, Peter. "The Deepening Crisis in Evangelical Christianity." *The Atlantic.* July 5, 2019. https://www.theatlantic.com/ideas/archive/2019/07/evangelical-christians-face-deepening-crisis/593353/.

Welch, Craig. "More Trouble for Mars Hill: Cutting Jobs, Merging Churches." *Seattle Times* September 7, 2014. http://www.seattletimes.com/seattle-news/more-trouble-for-mars-hill-cutting-jobs-merging-churches/.

Wellman, James K., Jr. *Evangelical vs. Liberal: The Clash of Christian Cultures in the Pacific Northwest.* New York: Oxford University Press, 2008.

Wellman, James K., Jr., and Katie E. Corcoran. "Religion and Regional Culture: Embedding Religious Commitment within Place." *Sociology of Religion* 74, no. 4 (Winter 2013): 496–520.

Wellman, James K., Jr., Katie E. Corcoran, and Kate J. Stockly. *High on God: How Megachurches Won the Heart of America.* New York: Oxford University Press, 2020.

Whitehead, Andrew L. "Gender Ideology and Religion: Does a Masculine Image of God Matter?" *Review of Religious Research* 54, no. 2 (June 2012): 139–156.

Whitehead, Andrew L., and Samuel L. Perry. *Taking Back America for God: Christian Nationalism in the United States.* New York: Oxford University Press, 2020.

Wilcox, W. Bradford. "Religion, Convention, and Paternal Involvement." *Journal of Marriage and the Family* 64, no. 3 (August 2002): 780–792.

Wilcox, W. Bradford. *Soft Patriarchs, New Men: How Christianity Shapes Fathers and Husbands.* Chicago, IL: University of Chicago Press, 2004.

Wolf, Naomi. *The Beauty Myth: How Images of Beauty Are Used against Women.* New York: Anchor Books, 1991.

Woods, Mark. "Decline and Fall: The Slow Erosion of Mars Hill." *Christianity Today.* November 4, 2014. http://christianitytoday.com/decline.and.fall.the.slow.erosion.of.Mars.hill/42568.htm?print=1.

World Economic Forum, *Global Gender Gap Report, 2021,* March 30, 2021, https://www.weforum.org/reports/global-gender-gap-report-2021

Worthen, Molly. "Who Would Jesus Smack Down?" *New York Times Magazine.* January 11, 2009. http://www.nytimes.com/2009/01/11/magazine/11punk-t.html.

Worthen, Molly. "A Match Made in Heaven: Why Conservative Evangelicals Have Lined Up behind Trump." *The Atlantic.* May 2017. https://www.theatlantic.com/magazine/archive/2017/a-match-made-in-heaven/521409/.

Zald, Mayer N. "Theological Crucibles: Social Movements in and of Religion." *Review of Religious Research* 23, no. 4 (June 1982): 317–336.

Zald, Mayer N., and R. Ash Gardner. "Social Movement Organizations: Growth, Decay, and Change." In *Social Movements in an Organizational Society,* edited by Mayer N. Zald and John D. McCarthy, 121–141. New Brunswick, NJ: Transaction, 1987.

Zauzmer, Julie. "The Alleged Synagogue Shooter Was a Churchgoer Who Talked Christian Theology, Raising Tough Questions for Evangelical Pastors." *Washington Post.* May 1, 2019. https://www.washingtonpost.com/religion/2019/05/01/alleged-synagogue-shooter-was-churchgoer-who-articulated-christian-theology-prompting-tough-questions-evangelical-pastors/.

Zhuang, Yan. "Leader of Australian Megachurch Steps Down after Charge over Father's Sexual Abuse." *New York Times.* January 31, 2022. https://www.nytimes.com/2022/01/31/world/australia/brian-houston-hillsong.html.

Index

For the benefit of digital users, indexed terms that span two pages (e.g., 52–53) may, on occasion, appear on only one of those pages.